THE RECORD OF A

FALLEN VAMPIRE

I read a lot of things to help me draw and often find my interest captured by something I never expected to care about. The submarines in this volume, for example—which is not to say I want to go aboard one.
–*Yuri Kimura*

Artist Yuri Kimura debuted two short stories in Japan's *Gangan Powered* after winning the Enix Manga Award. Shortly thereafter, she began *The Record of a Fallen Vampire*, which was serialized in Japan's *Monthly Shonen Gangan* through March 2007.

Author Kyo Shirodaira is from Nara prefecture. In addition to *The Record of a Fallen Vampire*, Shirodaira has scripted the manga *Spiral: The Bonds of Reasoning*. Shirodaira's novel *Meitantei ni Hana wo* was nominated for the 8th Annual Ayukawa Tetsuya Award in 1997.

THE RECORD OF A

FALLEN VAMPIRE

STORY BY: KYO SHIRODAIRA   ART BY: YURI KIMURA

6

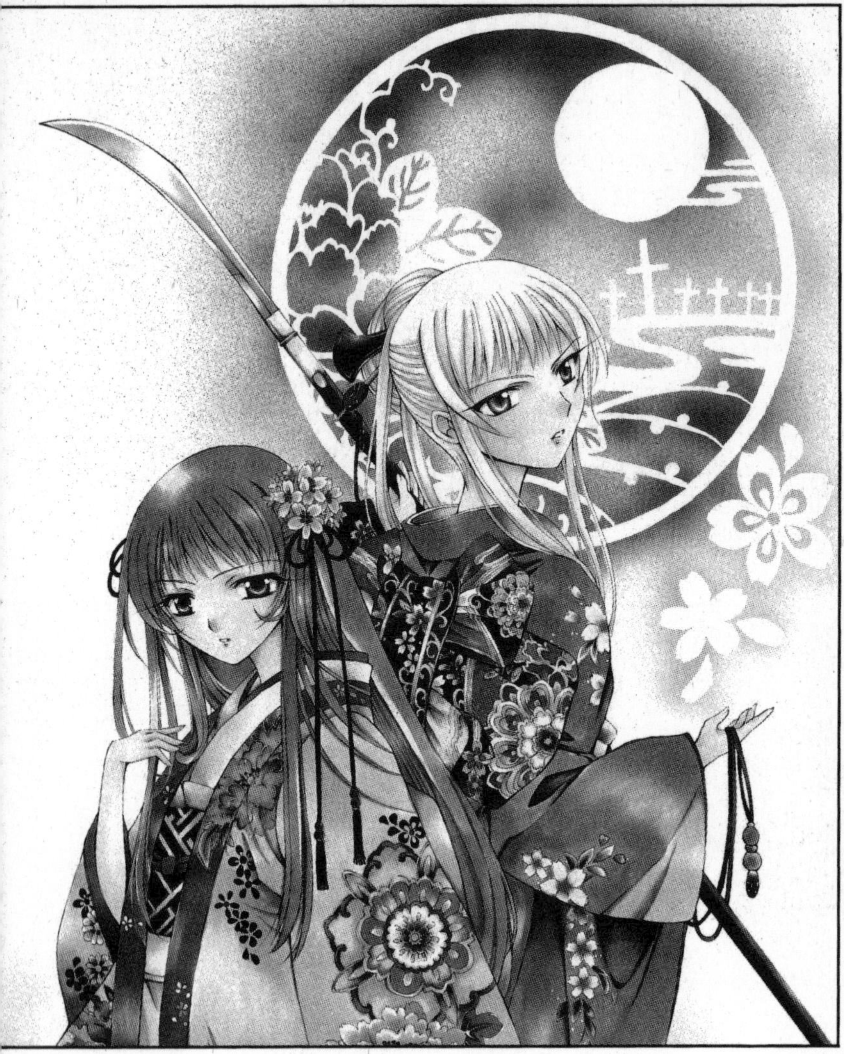

CONTENTS

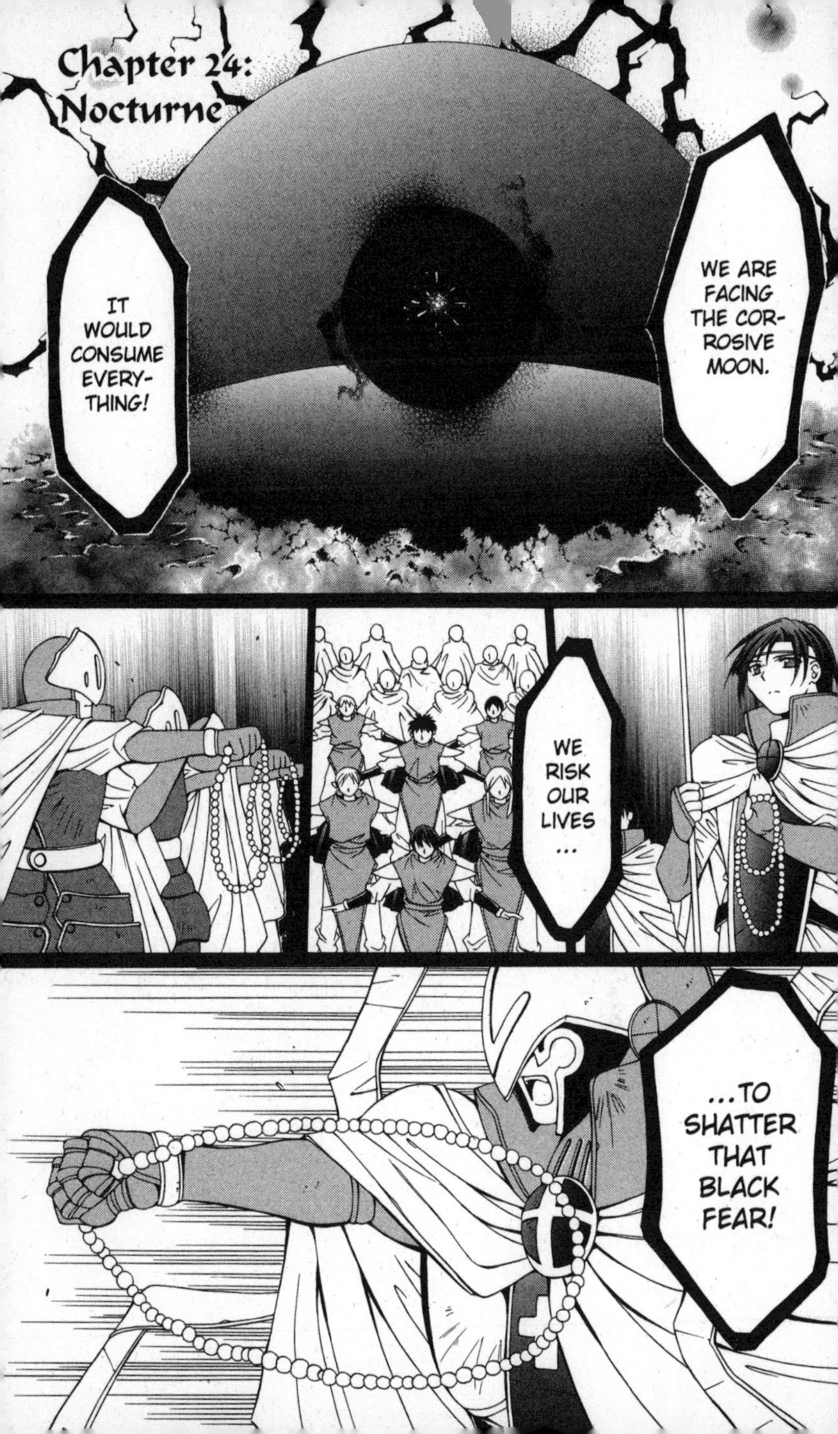
Chapter 24: Nocturne
WE ARE FACING THE COR-ROSIVE MOON.
IT WOULD CONSUME EVERY-THING!
WE RISK OUR LIVES ...
...TO SHATTER THAT BLACK FEAR!

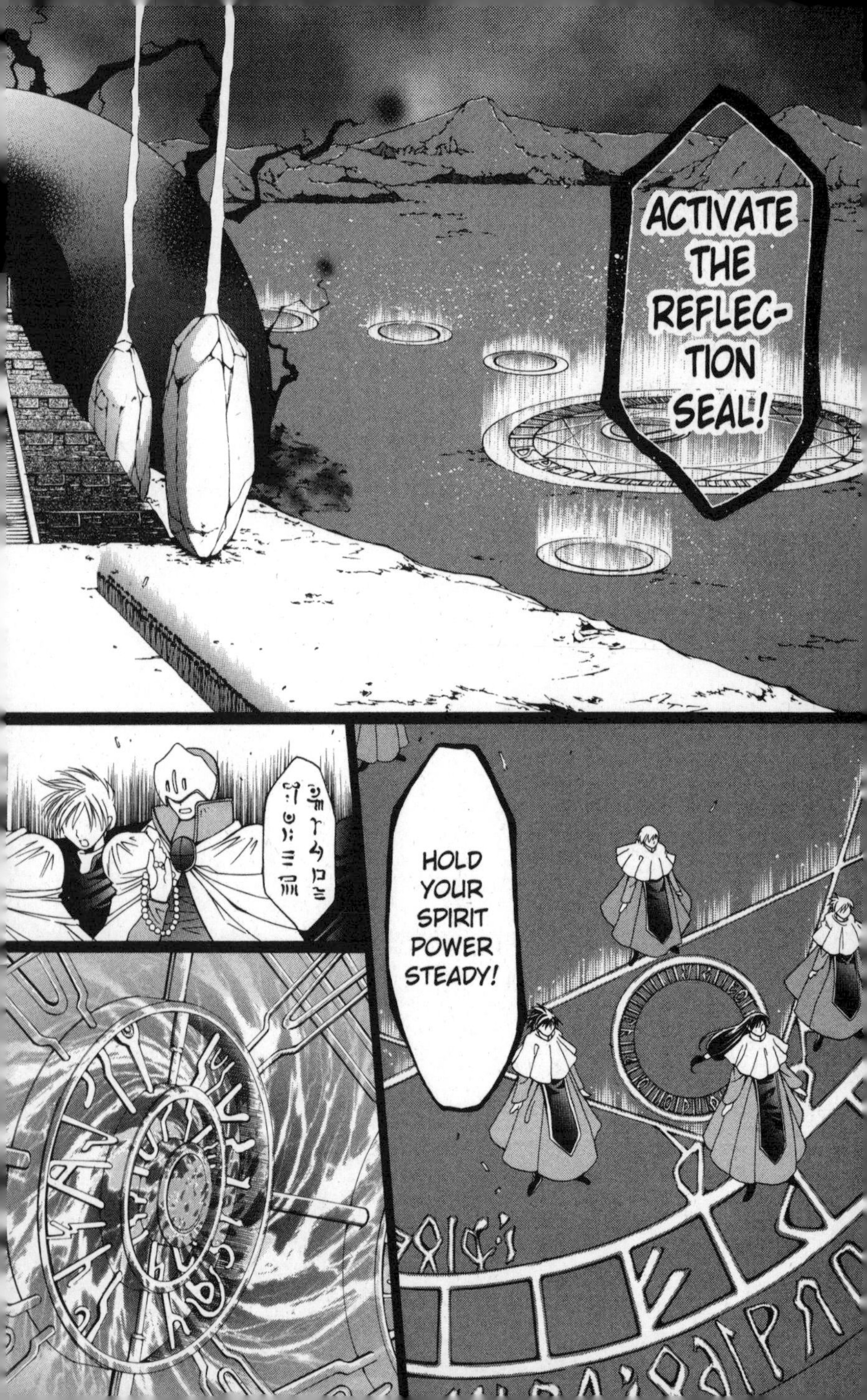
ACTIVATE THE REFLECTION SEAL!
HOLD YOUR SPIRIT POWER STEADY!

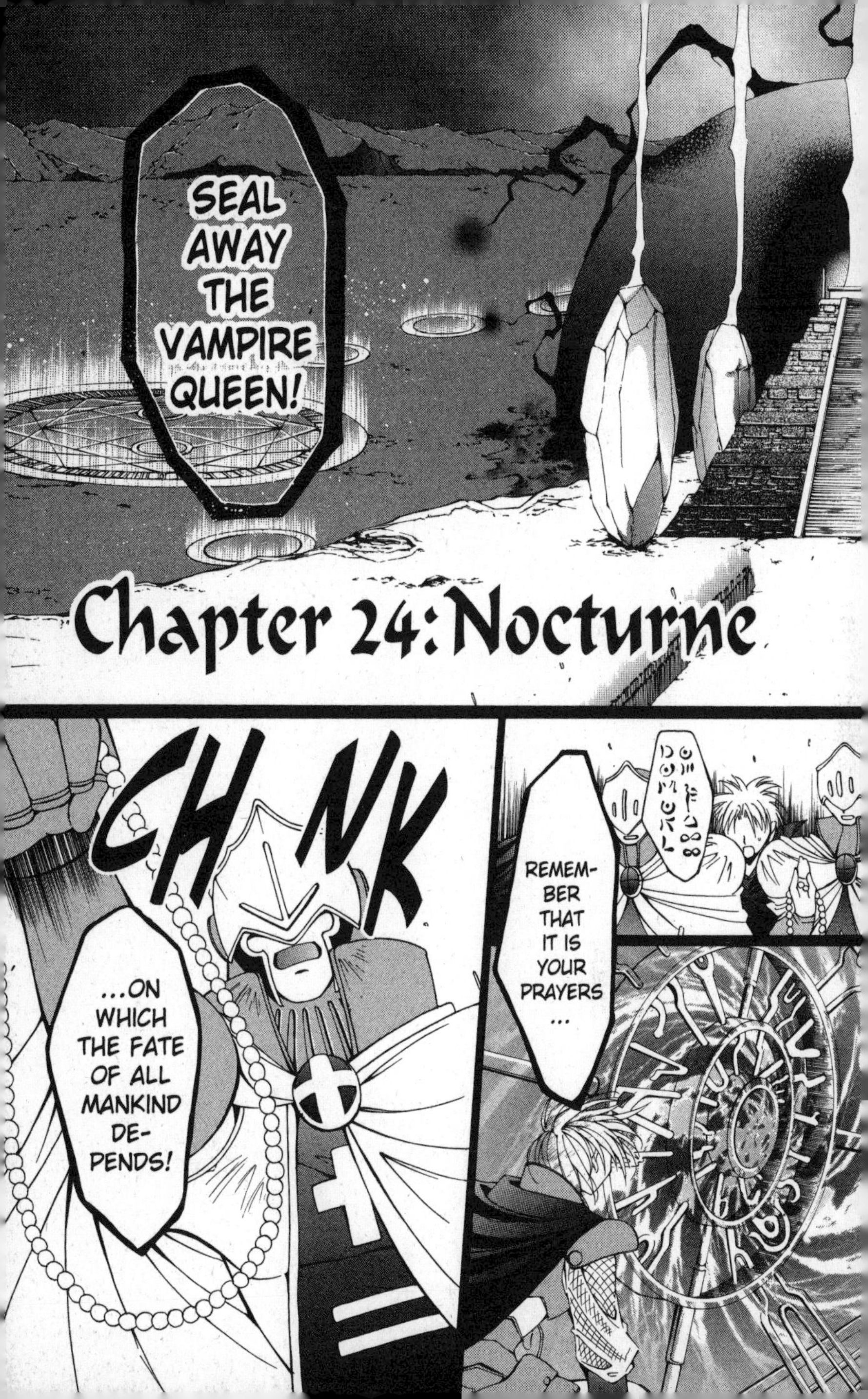
SEAL AWAY THE VAMPIRE QUEEN!
Chapter 24: Nocturne
REMEM-BER THAT IT IS YOUR PRAYERS...
CH NK
...ON WHICH THE FATE OF ALL MANKIND DE-PENDS!

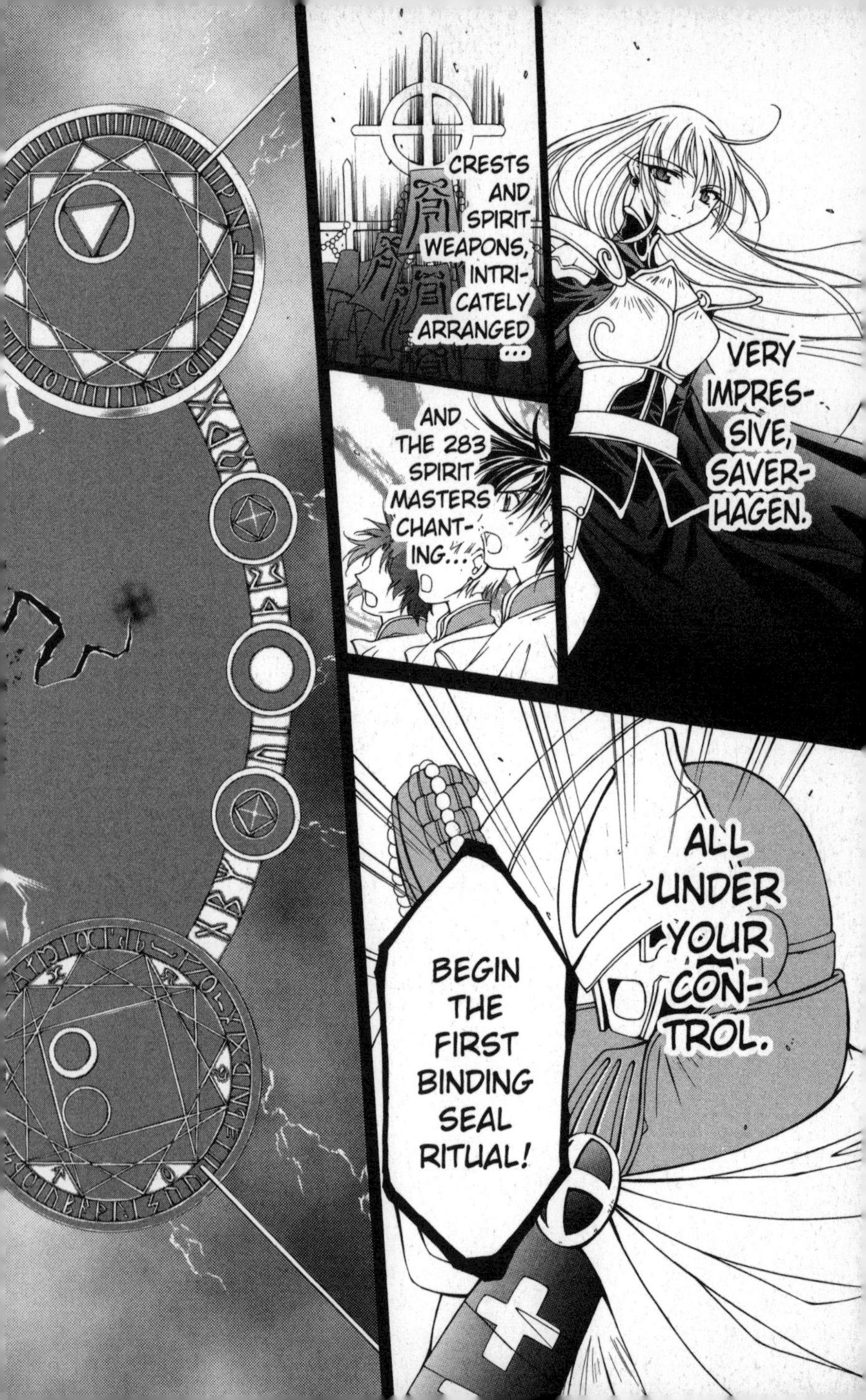
VERY IMPRES-SIVE, SAVER-HAGEN.
CRESTS AND SPIRIT WEAPONS, INTRI-CATELY ARRANGED...
AND THE 283 SPIRIT MASTERS CHANT-ING...
ALL UNDER YOUR CON-TROL.
BEGIN THE FIRST BINDING SEAL RITUAL!

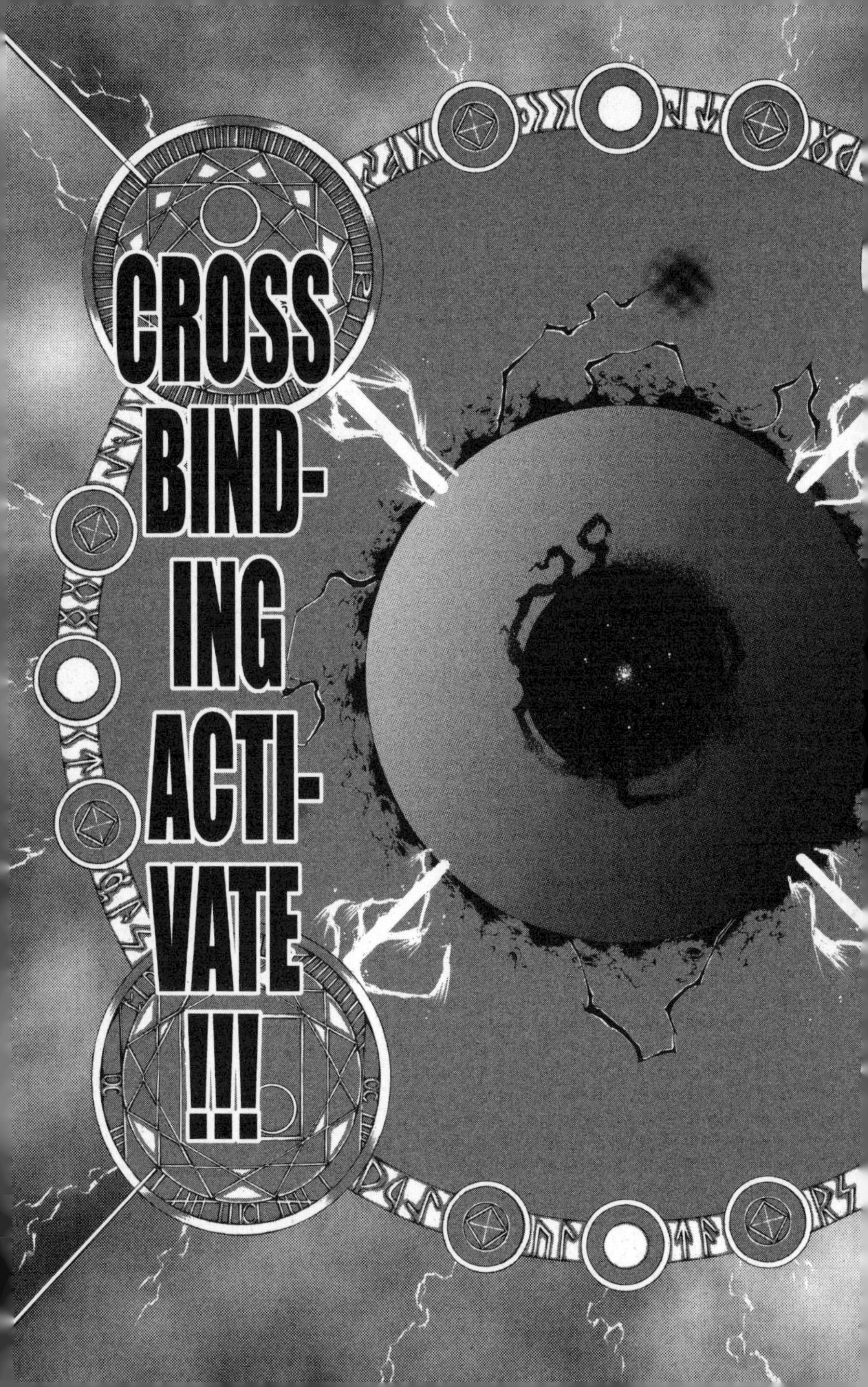
CROSS BIND-ING ACTI-VATE!!!

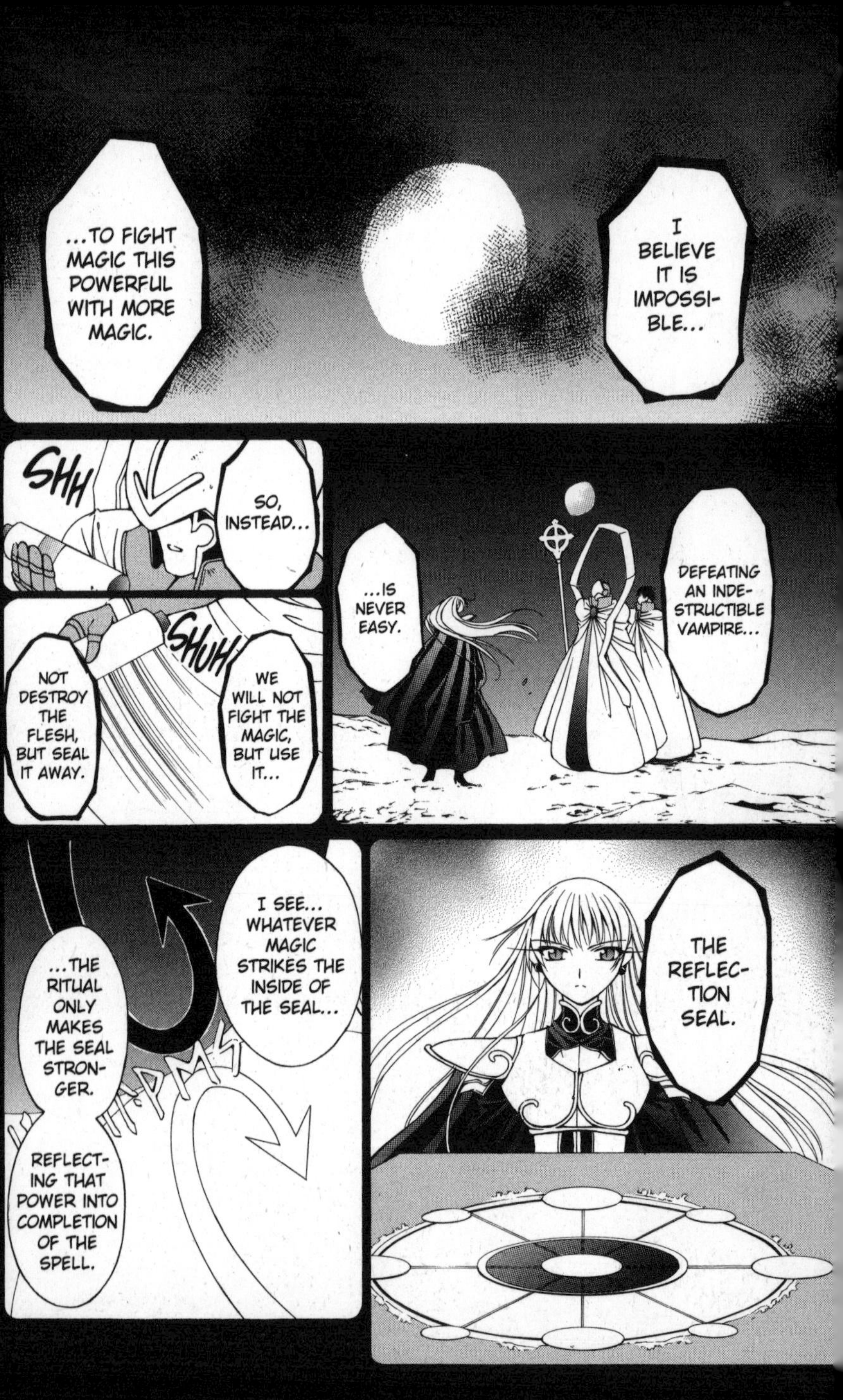
I BELIEVE IT IS IMPOSSIBLE...
...TO FIGHT MAGIC THIS POWERFUL WITH MORE MAGIC.
DEFEATING AN INDESTRUCTIBLE VAMPIRE...
...IS NEVER EASY.
SHH
SO, INSTEAD...
SHUH
WE WILL NOT FIGHT THE MAGIC, BUT USE IT...
NOT DESTROY THE FLESH, BUT SEAL IT AWAY.
THE REFLECTION SEAL.
I SEE... WHATEVER MAGIC STRIKES THE INSIDE OF THE SEAL...
...THE RITUAL ONLY MAKES THE SEAL STRONGER.
REFLECTING THAT POWER INTO COMPLETION OF THE SPELL.

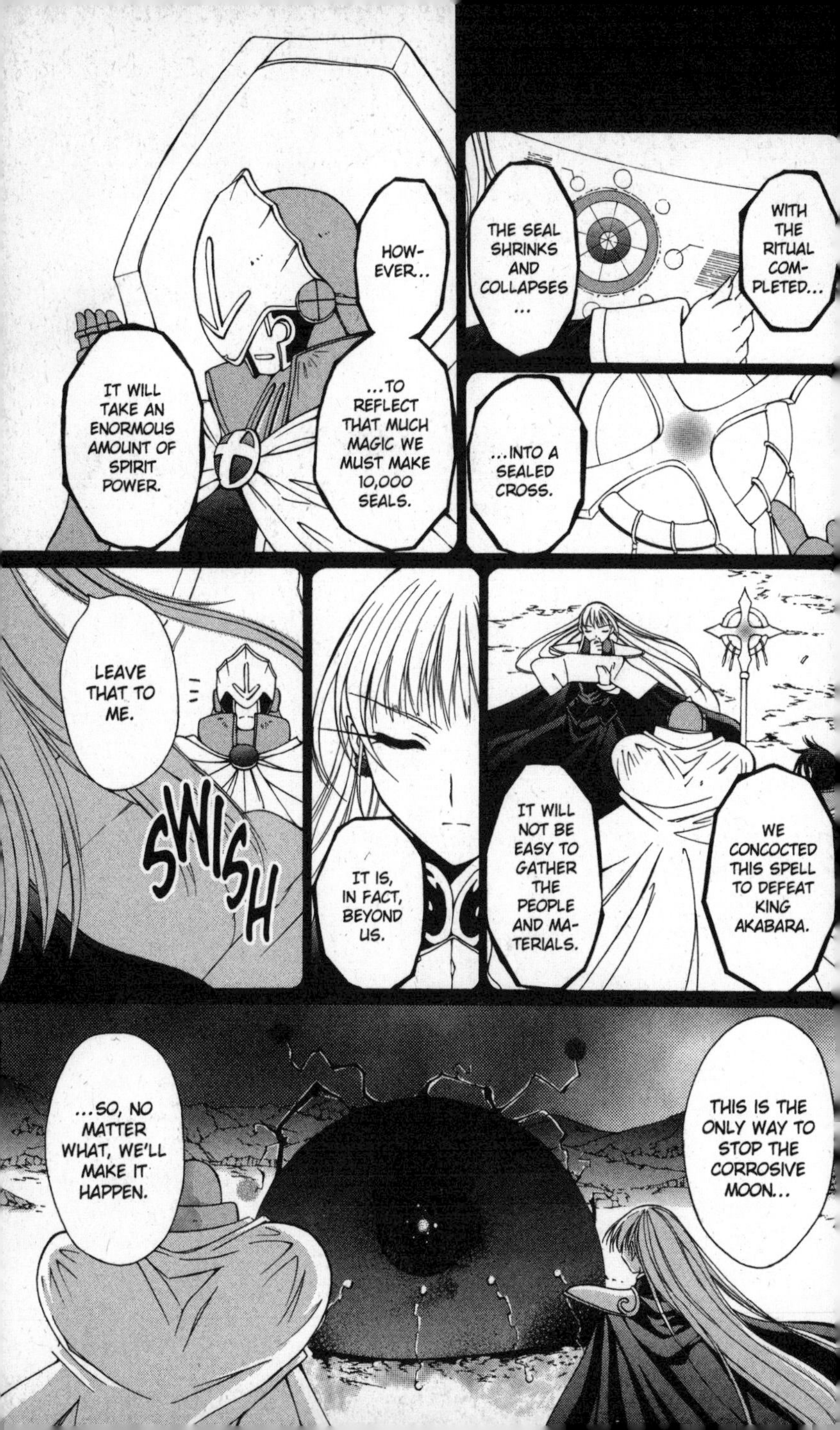
WITH THE RITUAL COM-PLETED...
THE SEAL SHRINKS AND COLLAPSES ...
...INTO A SEALED CROSS.
HOW-EVER...
...TO REFLECT THAT MUCH MAGIC WE MUST MAKE 10,000 SEALS.
IT WILL TAKE AN ENORMOUS AMOUNT OF SPIRIT POWER.
WE CONCOCTED THIS SPELL TO DEFEAT KING AKABARA.
IT WILL NOT BE EASY TO GATHER THE PEOPLE AND MA-TERIALS.
IT IS, IN FACT, BEYOND US.
LEAVE THAT TO ME.
SWISH
THIS IS THE ONLY WAY TO STOP THE CORROSIVE MOON...
...SO, NO MATTER WHAT, WE'LL MAKE IT HAPPEN.

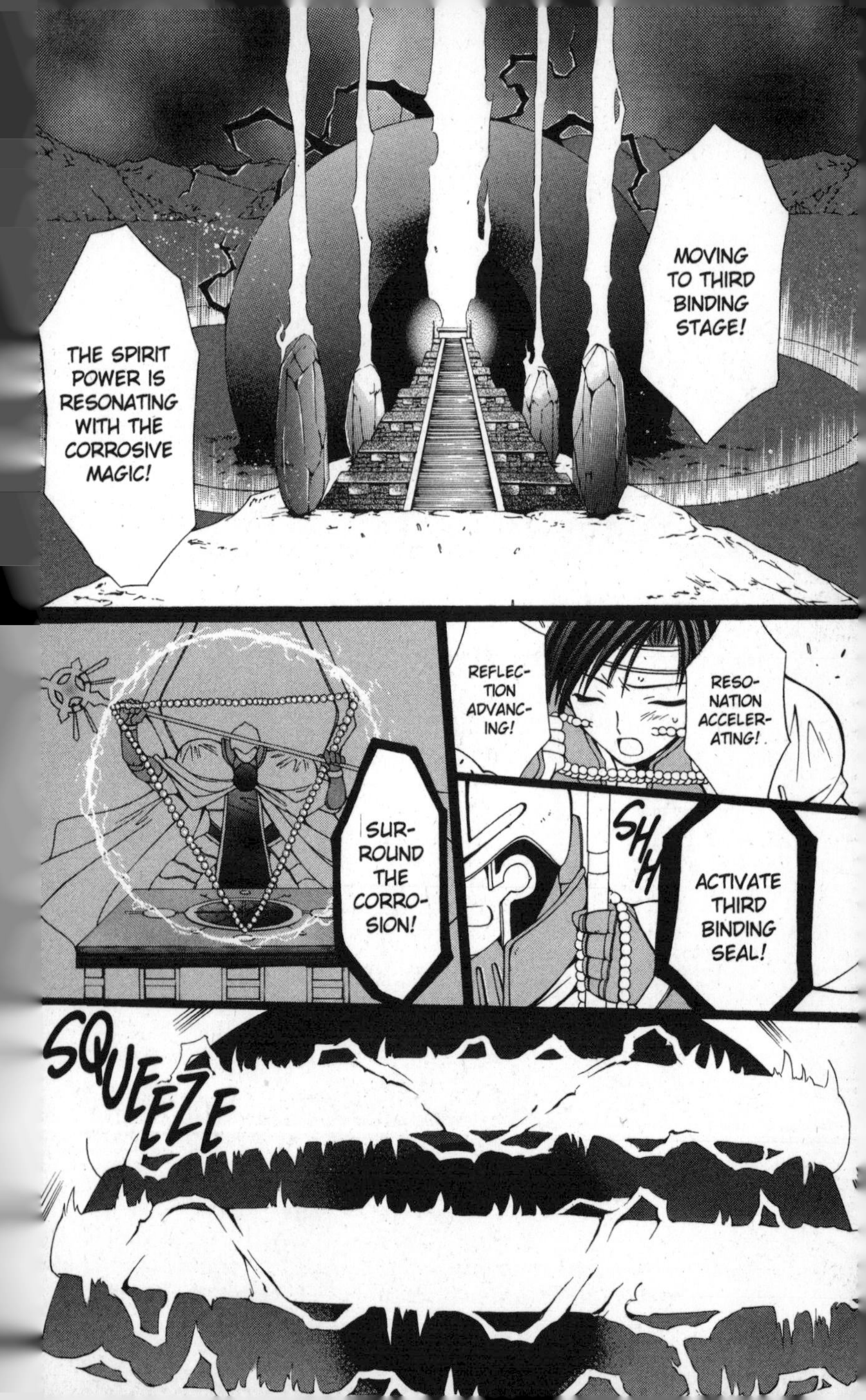
MOVING TO THIRD BINDING STAGE!
THE SPIRIT POWER IS RESONATING WITH THE CORROSIVE MAGIC!
RESO-NATION ACCELER-ATING!
REFLEC-TION ADVANC-ING!
SHH
ACTIVATE THIRD BINDING SEAL!
SUR-ROUND THE CORRO-SION!
SQUEEZE

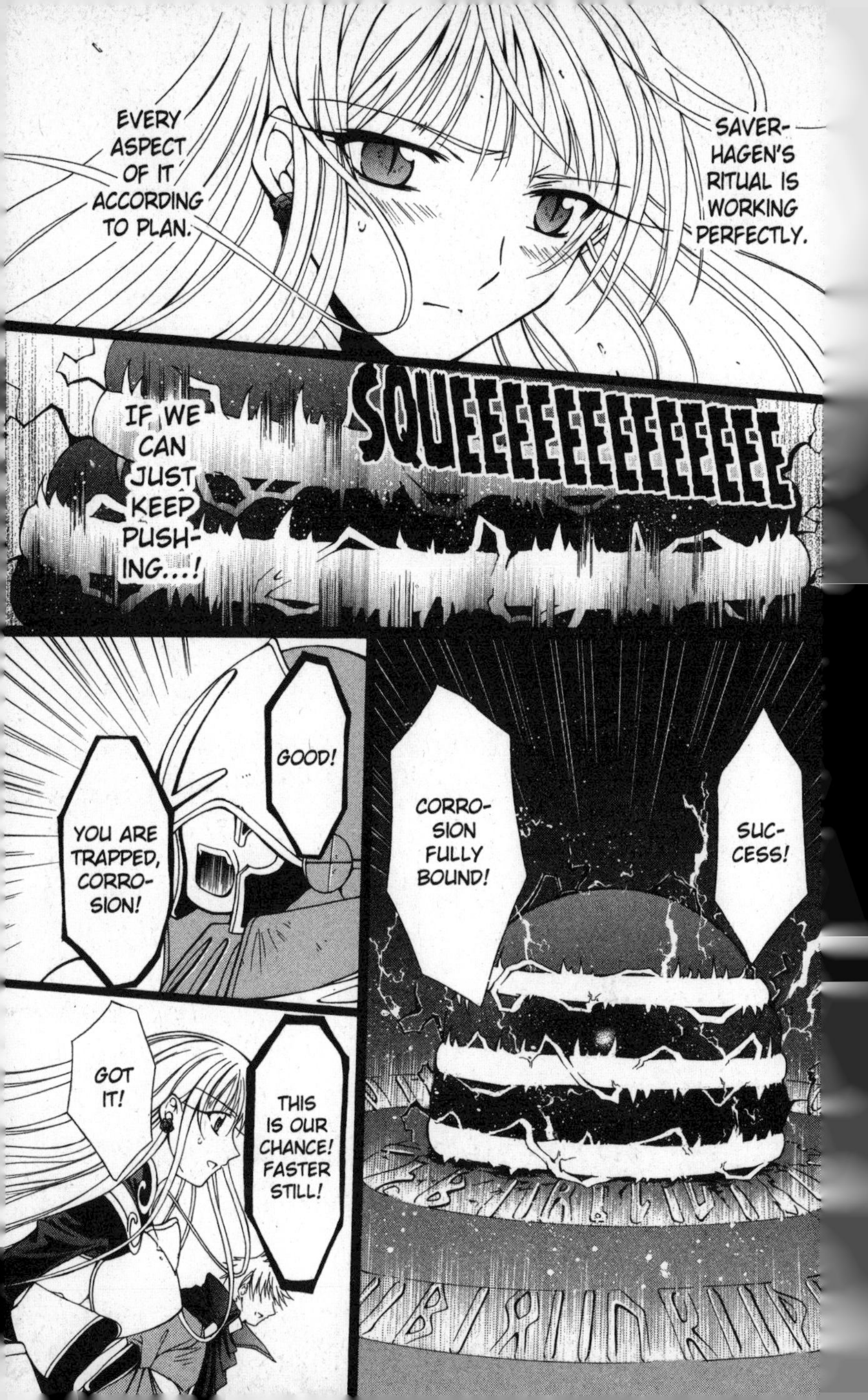
SAVER-HAGEN'S RITUAL IS WORKING PERFECTLY.
EVERY ASPECT OF IT ACCORDING TO PLAN.
SQUEEEEEEEEEEEEEE
IF WE CAN JUST KEEP PUSHING...!
SUC-CESS!
CORRO-SION FULLY BOUND!
GOOD!
YOU ARE TRAPPED, CORRO-SION!
THIS IS OUR CHANCE! FASTER STILL!
GOT IT!

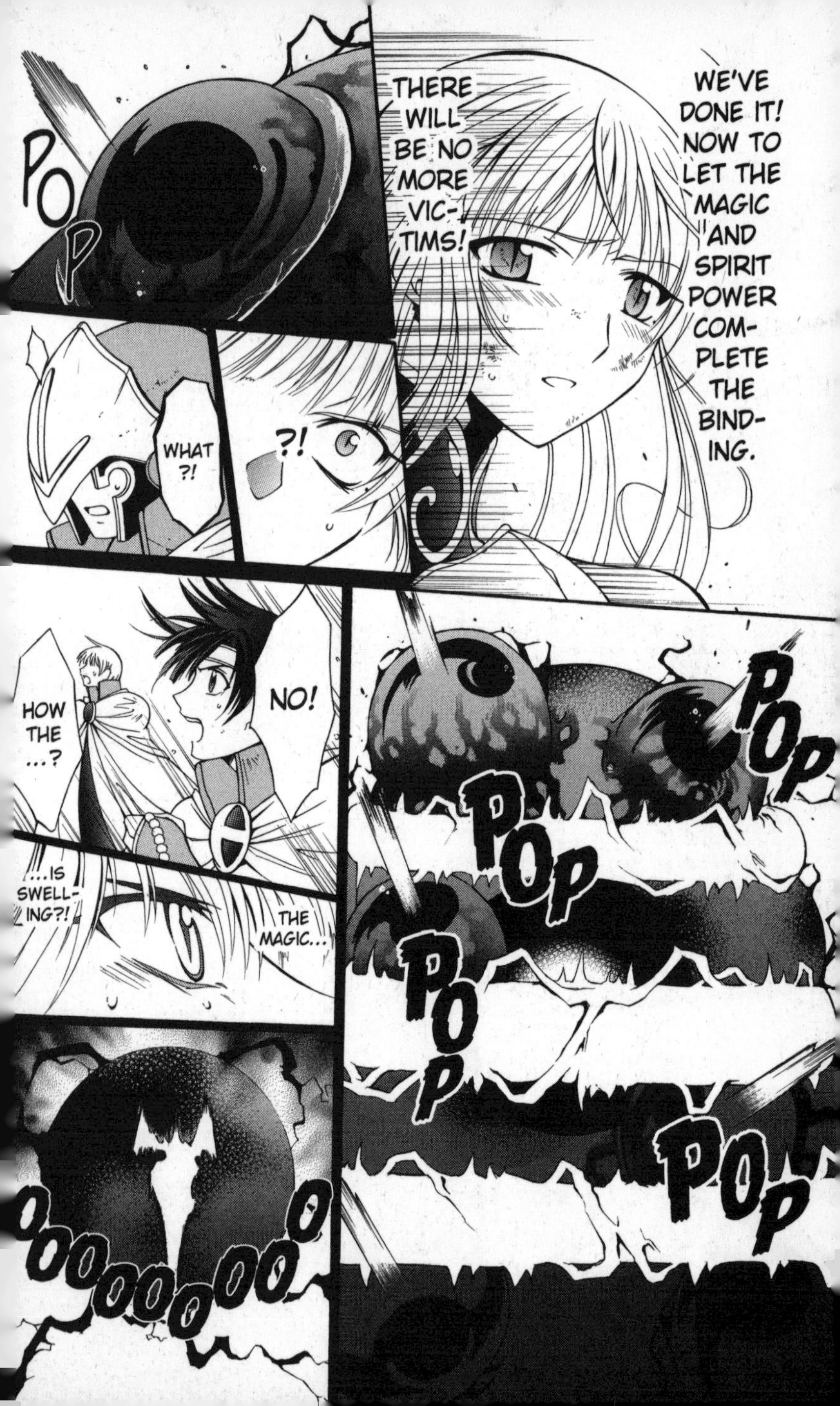
WE'VE DONE IT! NOW TO LET THE MAGIC AND SPIRIT POWER COMPLETE THE BIND-ING.
THERE WILL BE NO MORE VIC-TIMS!
POP
?!
WHAT ?!
POP POP POP POP
NO!
HOW THE ...?
THE MAGIC...
...IS SWELL-ING?!
OOOOOOOOOOO

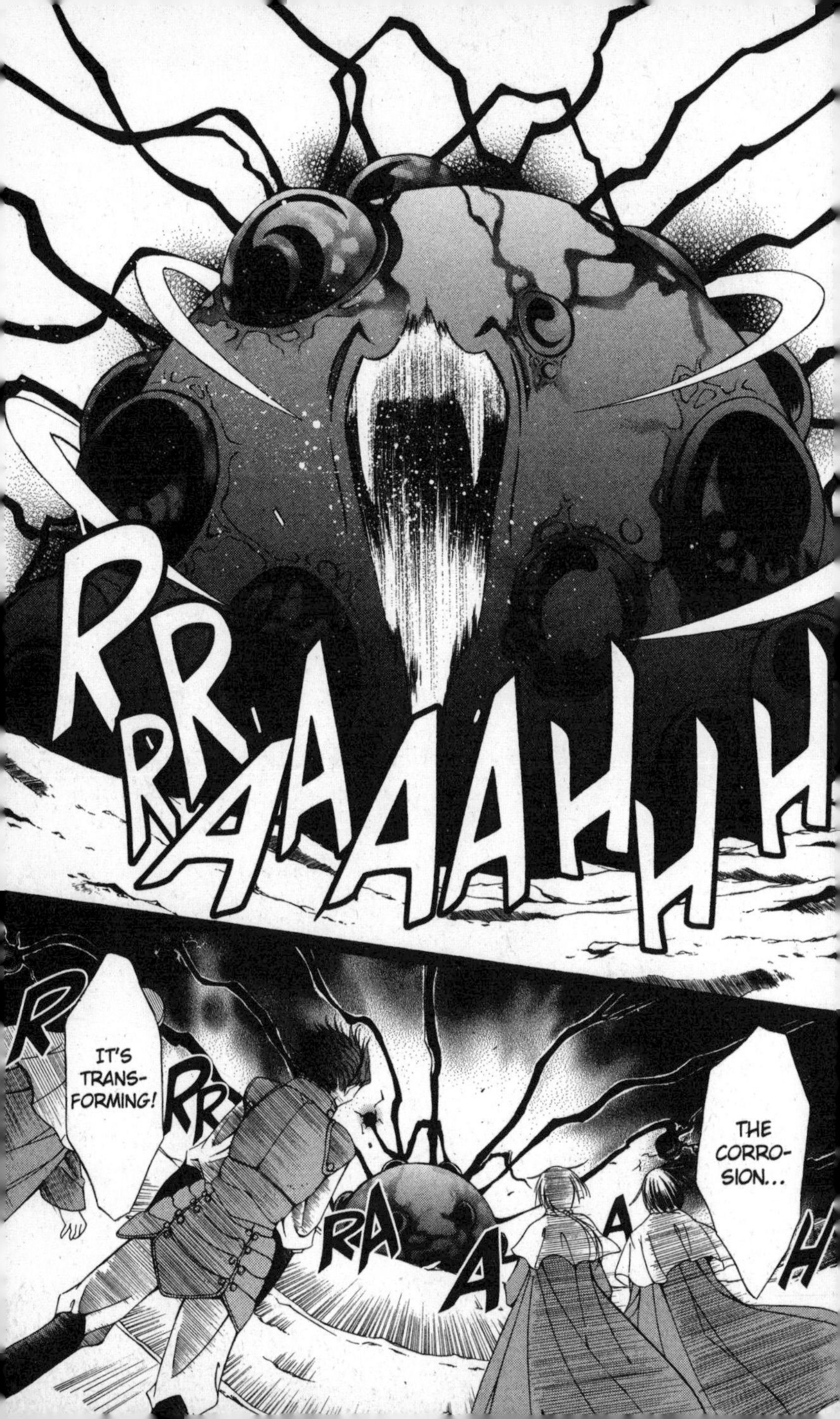
RRRAAAAAHHH
THE CORRO-SION...
IT'S TRANS-FORMING!

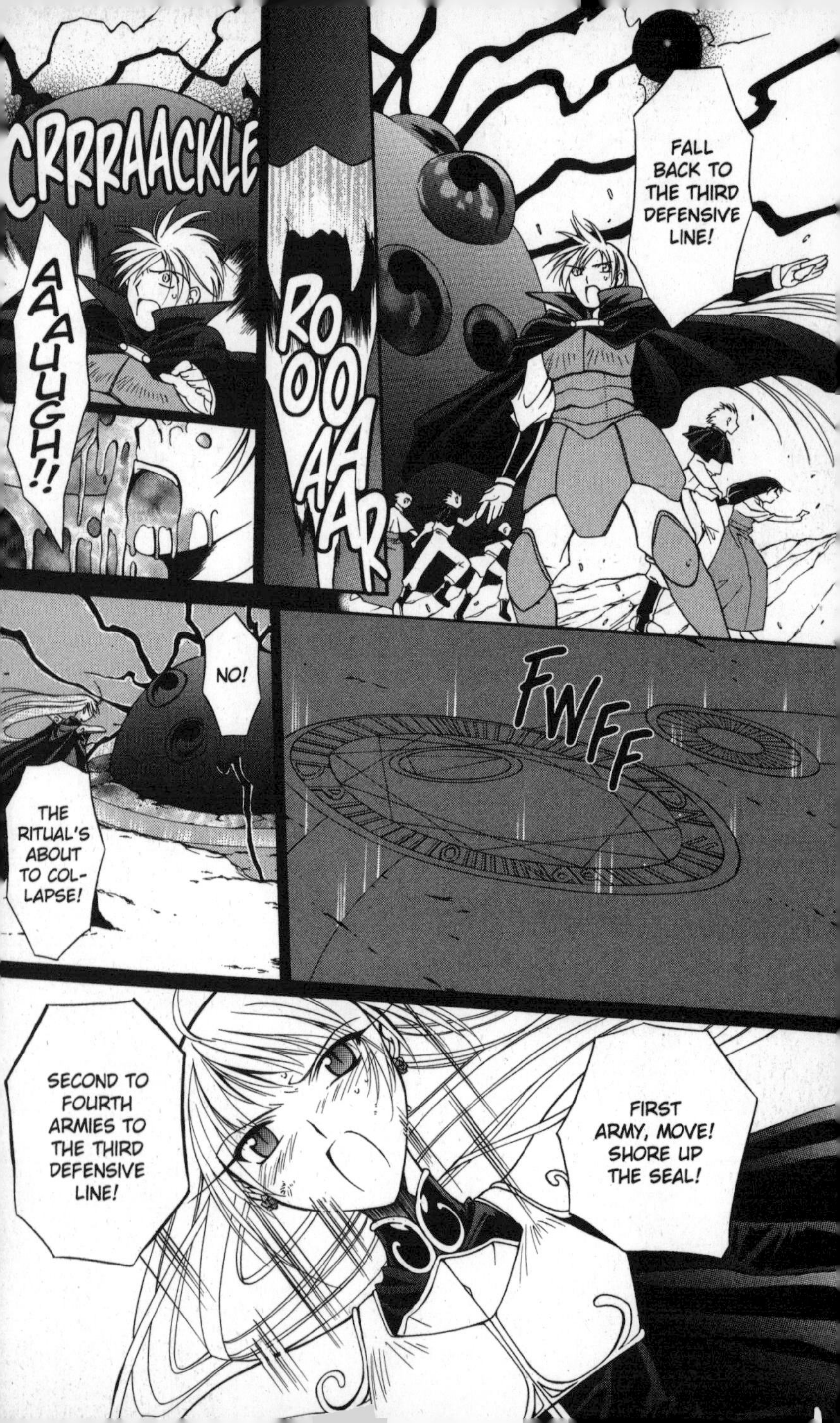
FALL BACK TO THE THIRD DEFENSIVE LINE!
ROOOAAAR
CRRRAACKLE
AAAUUGH!!
FWFF
NO!
THE RITUAL'S ABOUT TO COL-LAPSE!
FIRST ARMY, MOVE! SHORE UP THE SEAL!
SECOND TO FOURTH ARMIES TO THE THIRD DEFENSIVE LINE!

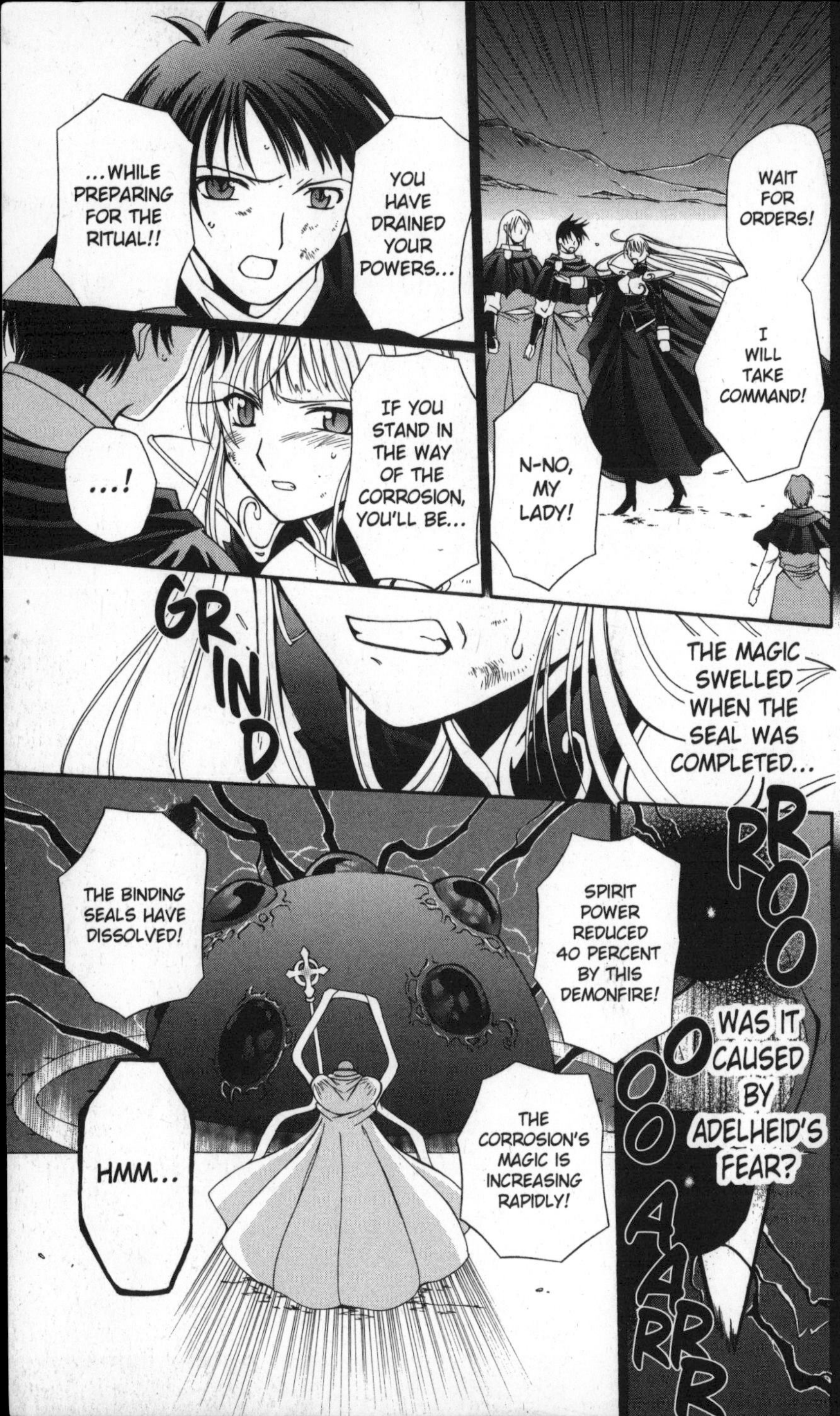
WAIT FOR ORDERS!
I WILL TAKE COMMAND!
N-NO, MY LADY!
YOU HAVE DRAINED YOUR POWERS...
...WHILE PREPARING FOR THE RITUAL!!
IF YOU STAND IN THE WAY OF THE CORROSION, YOU'LL BE...
...!
THE MAGIC SWELLED WHEN THE SEAL WAS COMPLETED...
GRIND
RROOOOOOAARR
WAS IT CAUSED BY ADELHEID'S FEAR?
SPIRIT POWER REDUCED 40 PERCENT BY THIS DEMONFIRE!
THE BINDING SEALS HAVE DISSOLVED!
THE CORROSION'S MAGIC IS INCREASING RAPIDLY!
HMM...

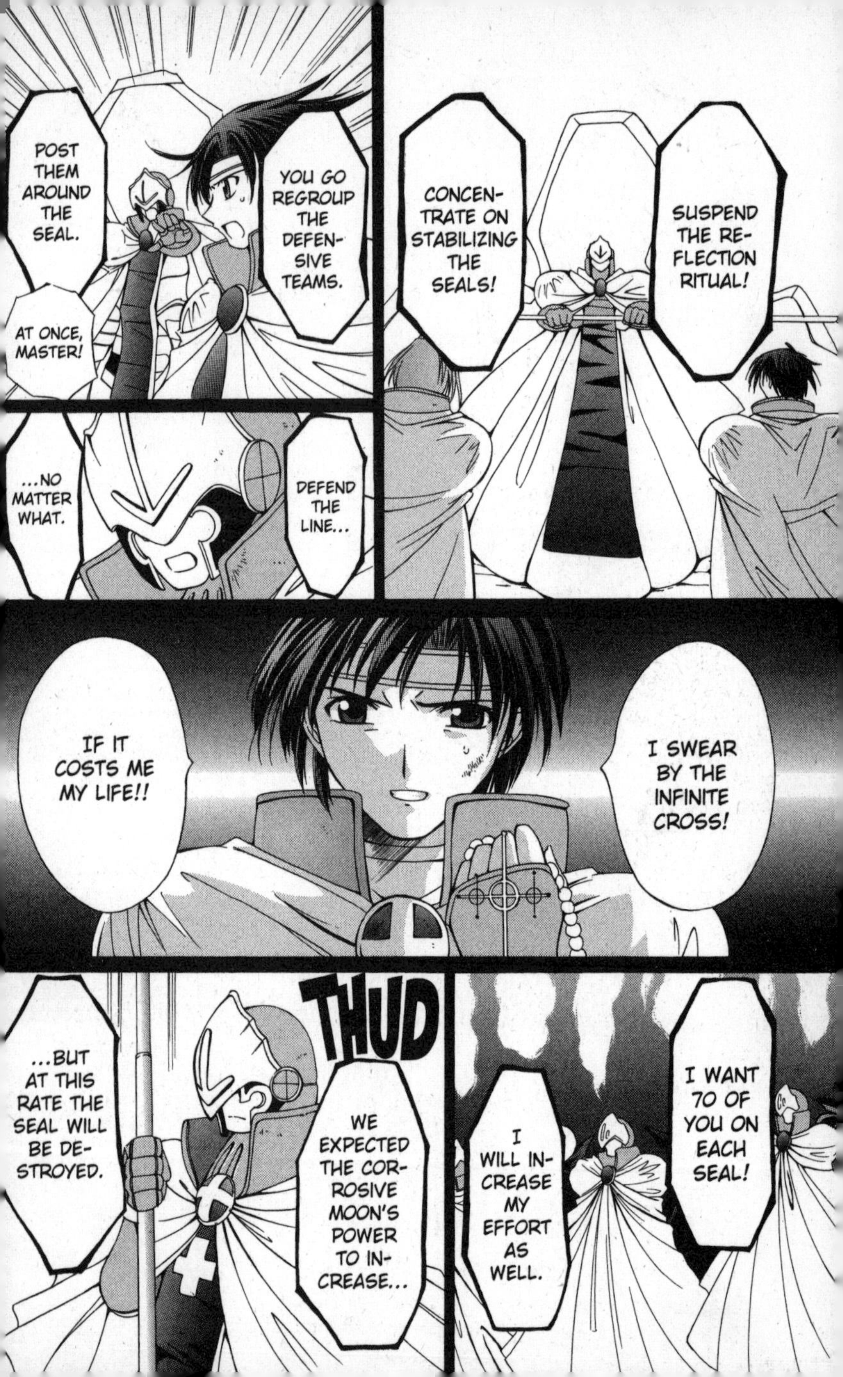
SUSPEND THE REFLECTION RITUAL!
CONCENTRATE ON STABILIZING THE SEALS!
YOU GO REGROUP THE DEFENSIVE TEAMS.
POST THEM AROUND THE SEAL.
AT ONCE, MASTER!
DEFEND THE LINE...
...NO MATTER WHAT.
I SWEAR BY THE INFINITE CROSS!
IF IT COSTS ME MY LIFE!!
I WANT 70 OF YOU ON EACH SEAL!
I WILL INCREASE MY EFFORT AS WELL.
THUD
WE EXPECTED THE CORROSIVE MOON'S POWER TO INCREASE...
...BUT AT THIS RATE THE SEAL WILL BE DESTROYED.

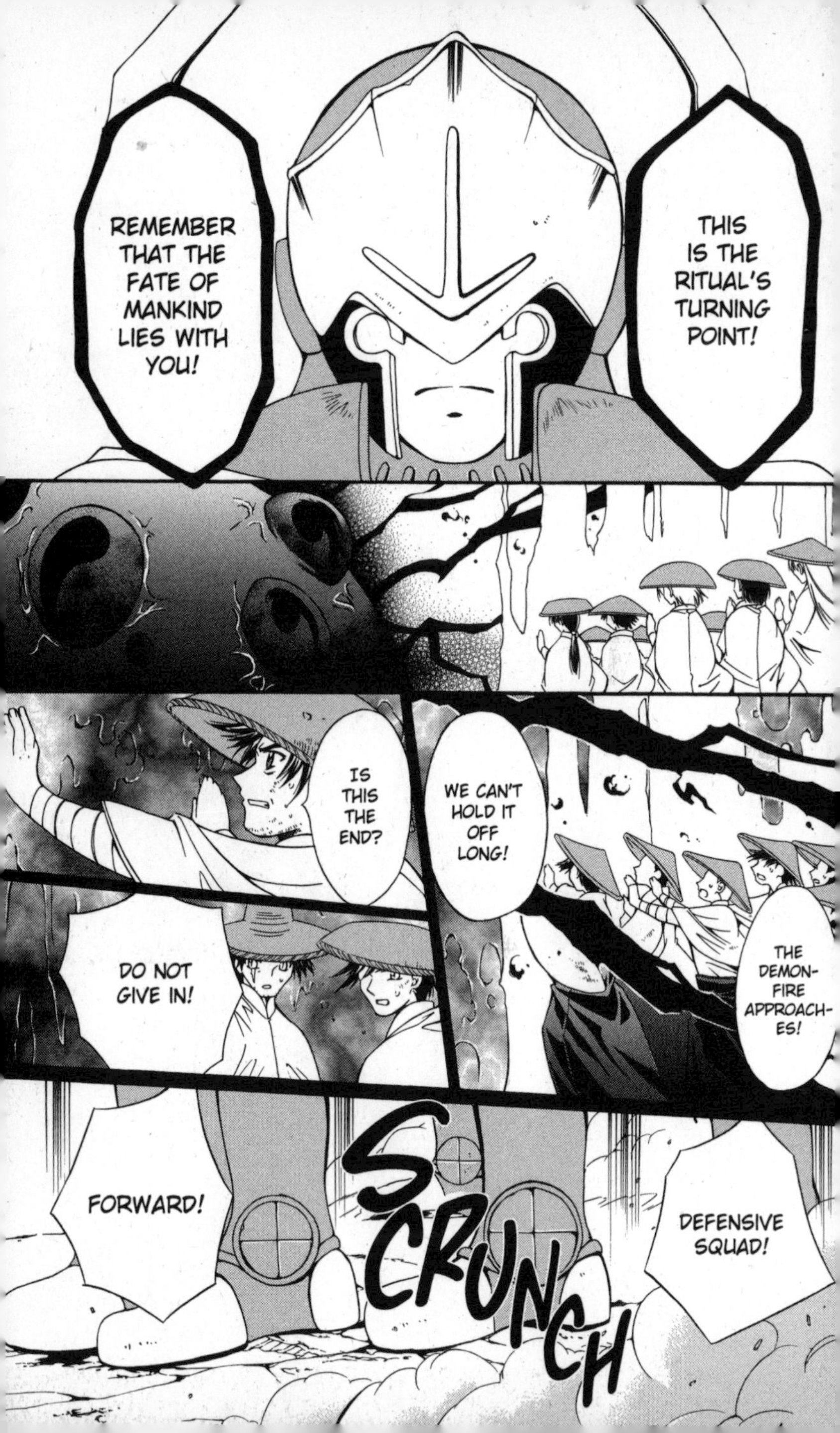
THIS IS THE RITUAL'S TURNING POINT!
REMEMBER THAT THE FATE OF MANKIND LIES WITH YOU!
WE CAN'T HOLD IT OFF LONG!
THE DEMON-FIRE APPROACHES!
IS THIS THE END?
DO NOT GIVE IN!
DEFENSIVE SQUAD!
SCRUNCH
FORWARD!

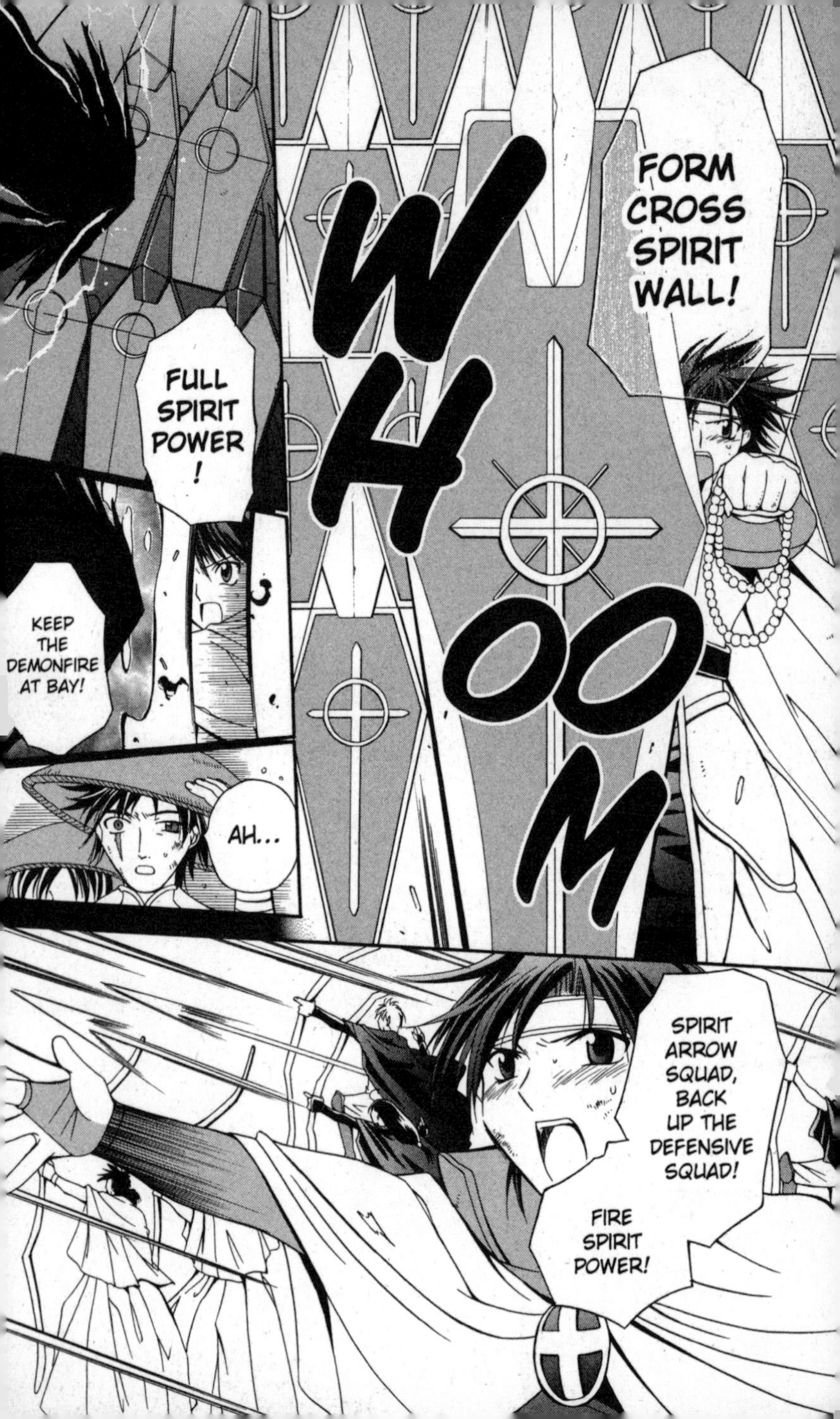
FORM CROSS SPIRIT WALL!
WHOOM
FULL SPIRIT POWER!
KEEP THE DEMONFIRE AT BAY!
AH...
SPIRIT ARROW SQUAD, BACK UP THE DEFENSIVE SQUAD!
FIRE SPIRIT POWER!

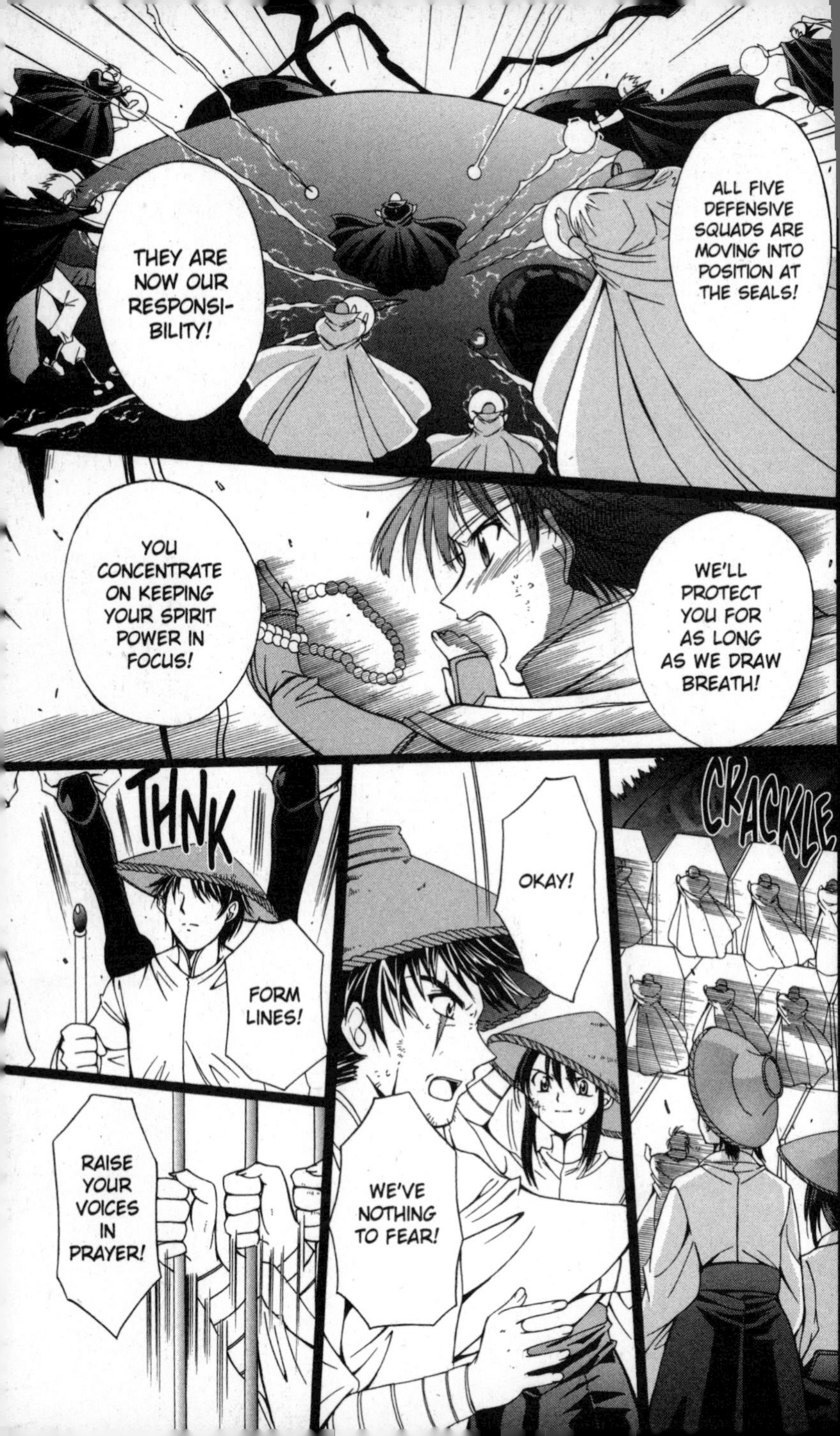
ALL FIVE DEFENSIVE SQUADS ARE MOVING INTO POSITION AT THE SEALS!
THEY ARE NOW OUR RESPONSI-BILITY!
WE'LL PROTECT YOU FOR AS LONG AS WE DRAW BREATH!
YOU CONCENTRATE ON KEEPING YOUR SPIRIT POWER IN FOCUS!
CRACKLE
OKAY!
WE'VE NOTHING TO FEAR!
THNK
FORM LINES!
RAISE YOUR VOICES IN PRAYER!

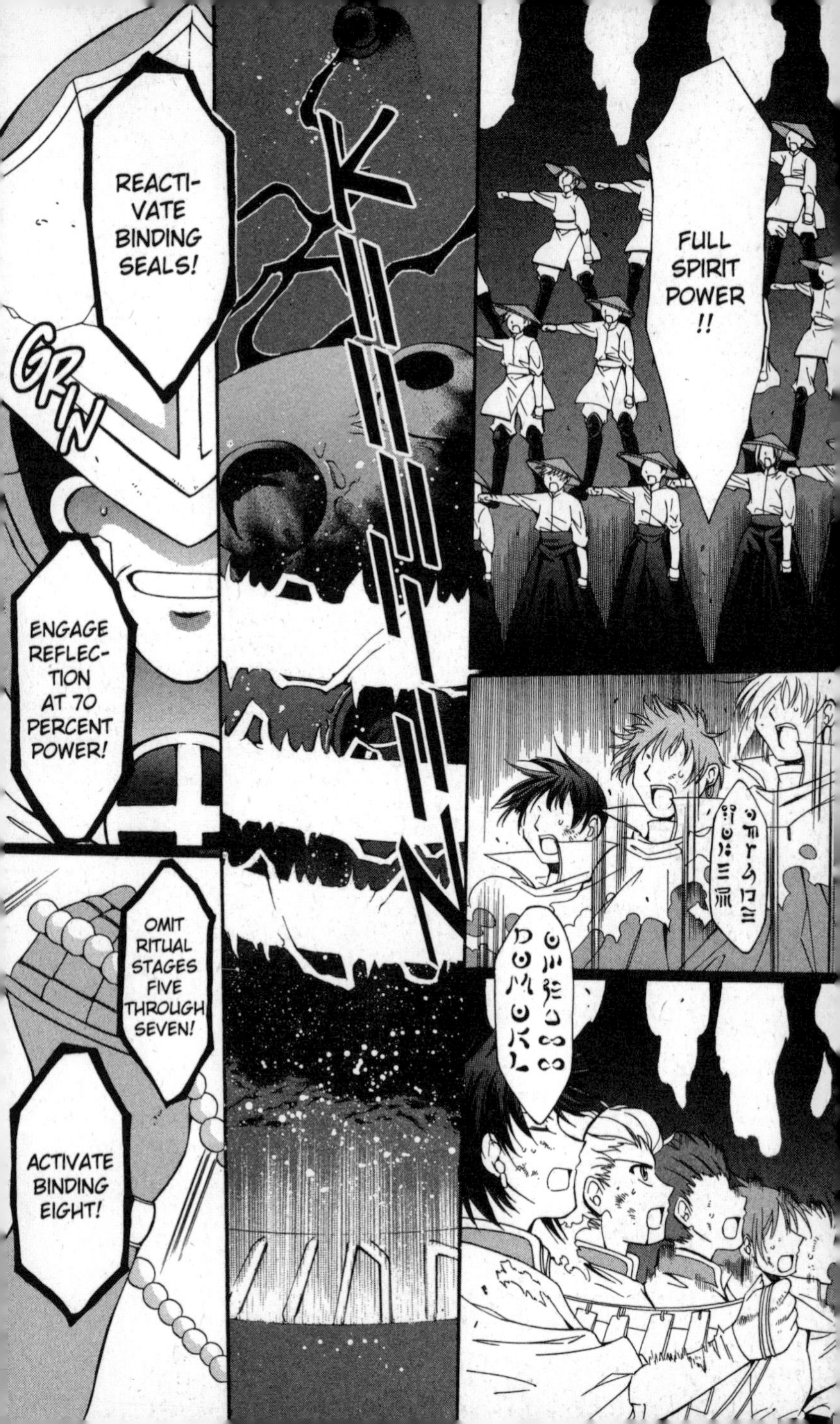
FULL SPIRIT POWER!!
KIIIIIIN
REACTI-VATE BINDING SEALS!
GRIN
ENGAGE REFLEC-TION AT 70 PERCENT POWER!
OMIT RITUAL STAGES FIVE THROUGH SEVEN!
ACTIVATE BINDING EIGHT!

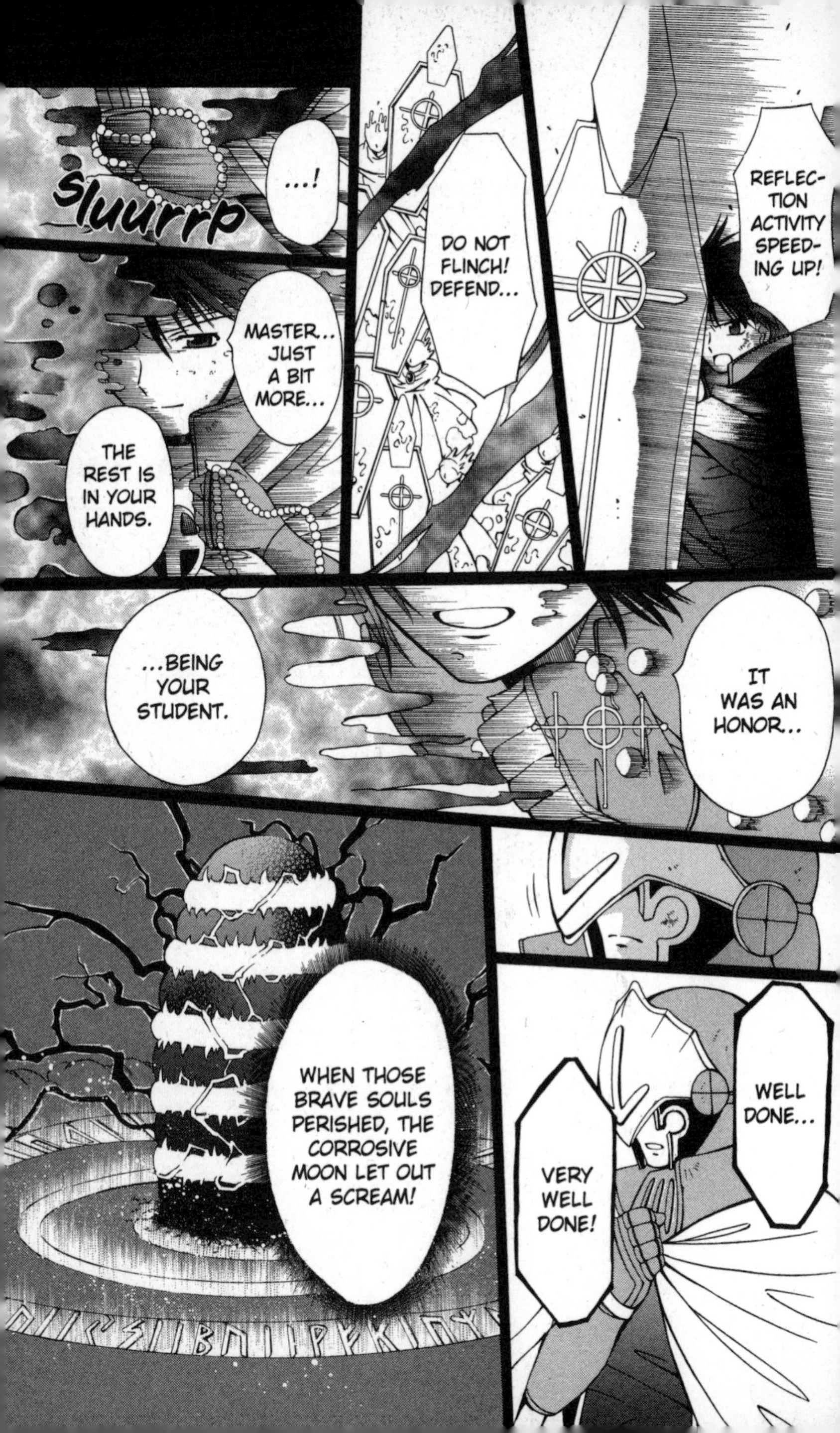
REFLECTION ACTIVITY SPEEDING UP!
DO NOT FLINCH! DEFEND...
...!
Sluurrp
MASTER... JUST A BIT MORE...
THE REST IS IN YOUR HANDS.
IT WAS AN HONOR...
...BEING YOUR STUDENT.
WELL DONE...
VERY WELL DONE!
WHEN THOSE BRAVE SOULS PERISHED, THE CORROSIVE MOON LET OUT A SCREAM!

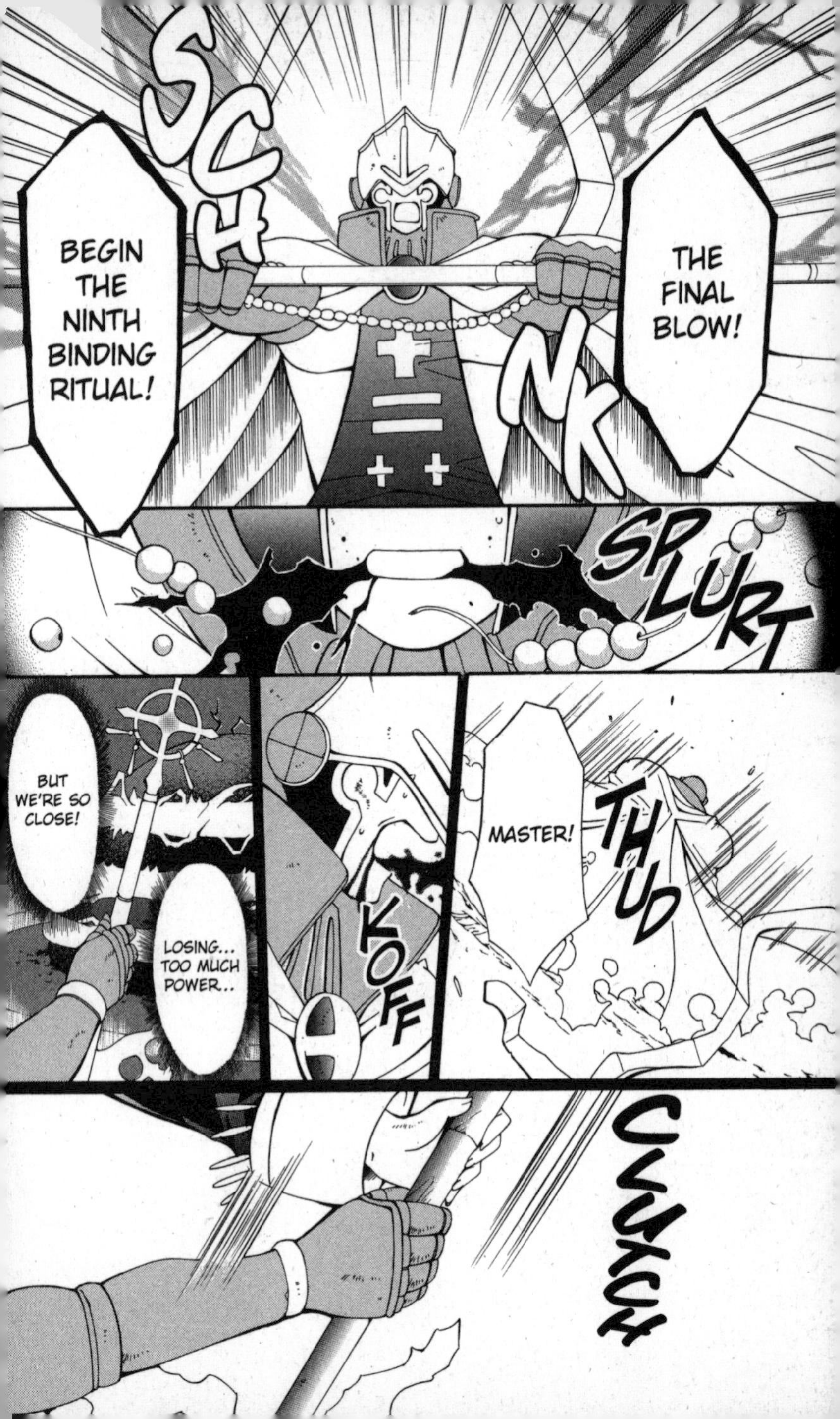
SCH
NK
THE FINAL BLOW!
BEGIN THE NINTH BINDING RITUAL!
SPLURT
MASTER!
THUD
KOFF
BUT WE'RE SO CLOSE!
LOSING... TOO MUCH POWER...
CLUTCH

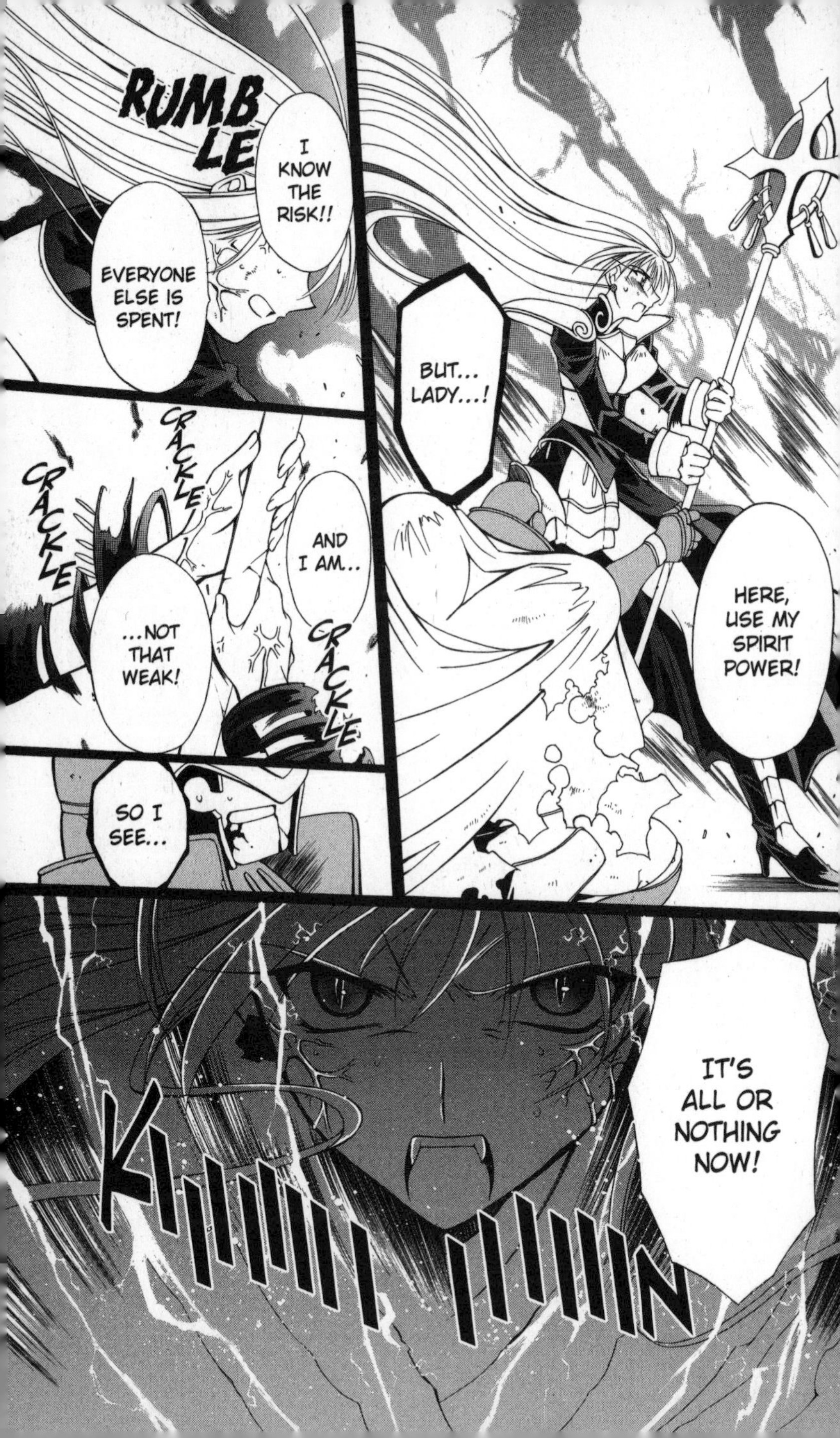
BUT... LADY...!
HERE, USE MY SPIRIT POWER!
RUMBLE
I KNOW THE RISK!!
EVERYONE ELSE IS SPENT!
CRACKLE
CRACKLE
AND I AM...
...NOT THAT WEAK!
CRACKLE
SO I SEE...
IT'S ALL OR NOTHING NOW!
KIIIIIIIIIIIN

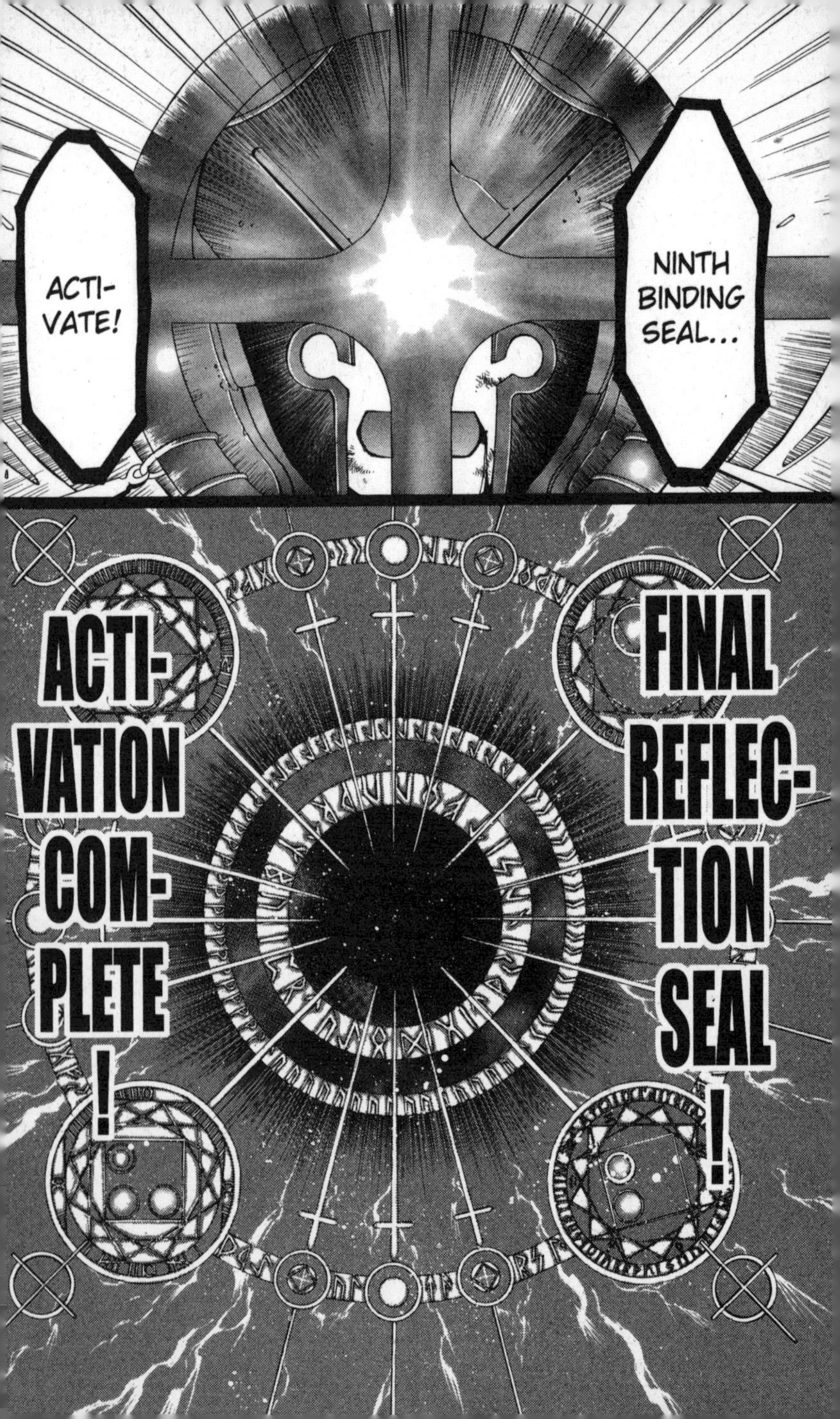
NINTH BINDING SEAL...
ACTI-VATE!
FINAL REFLEC-TION SEAL!
ACTI-VATION COM-PLETE!

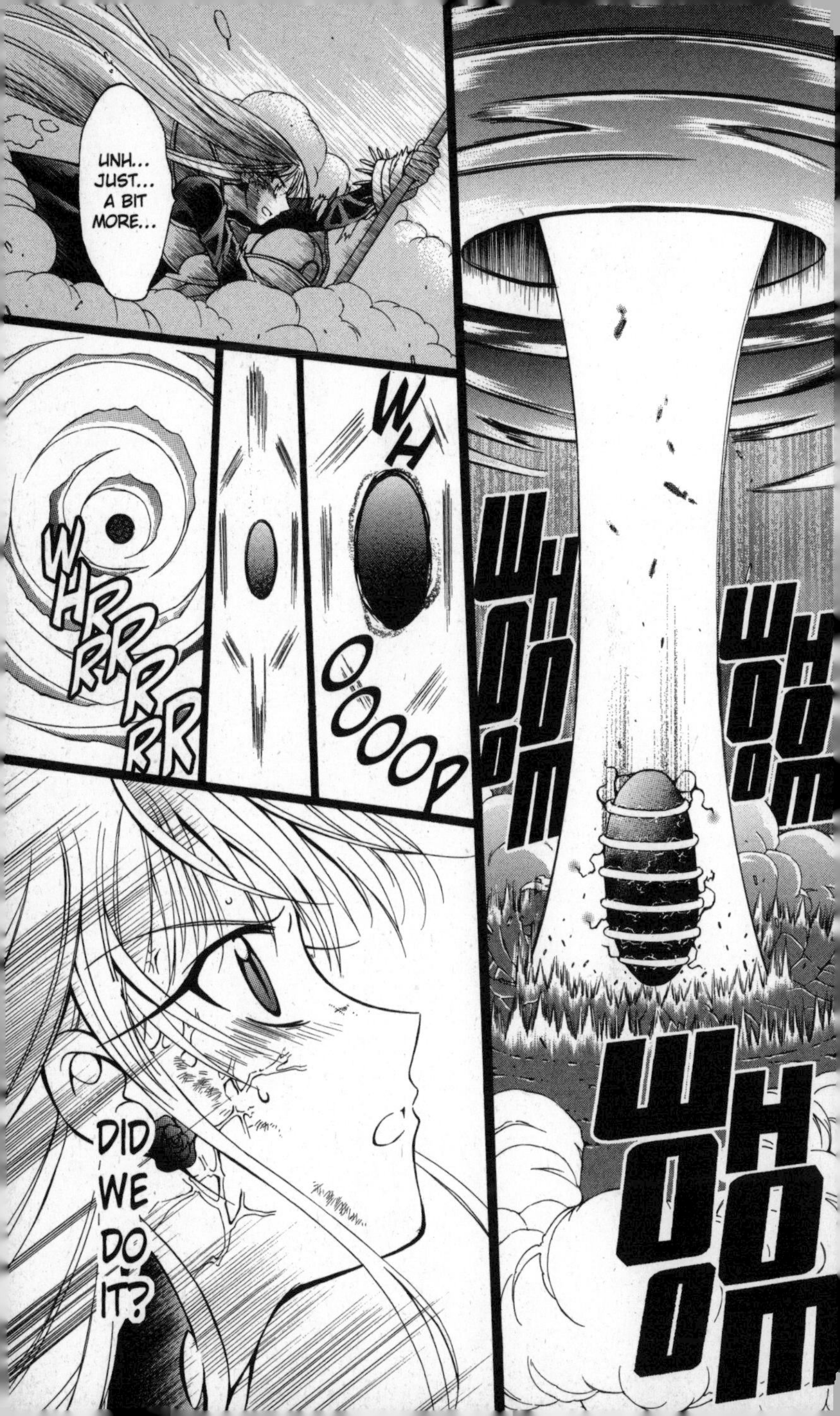
WHOOOM
WHOOM
WHOOOM
UNH... JUST... A BIT MORE...
WHOOOOOP
WHRRRRRR
DID WE DO IT?

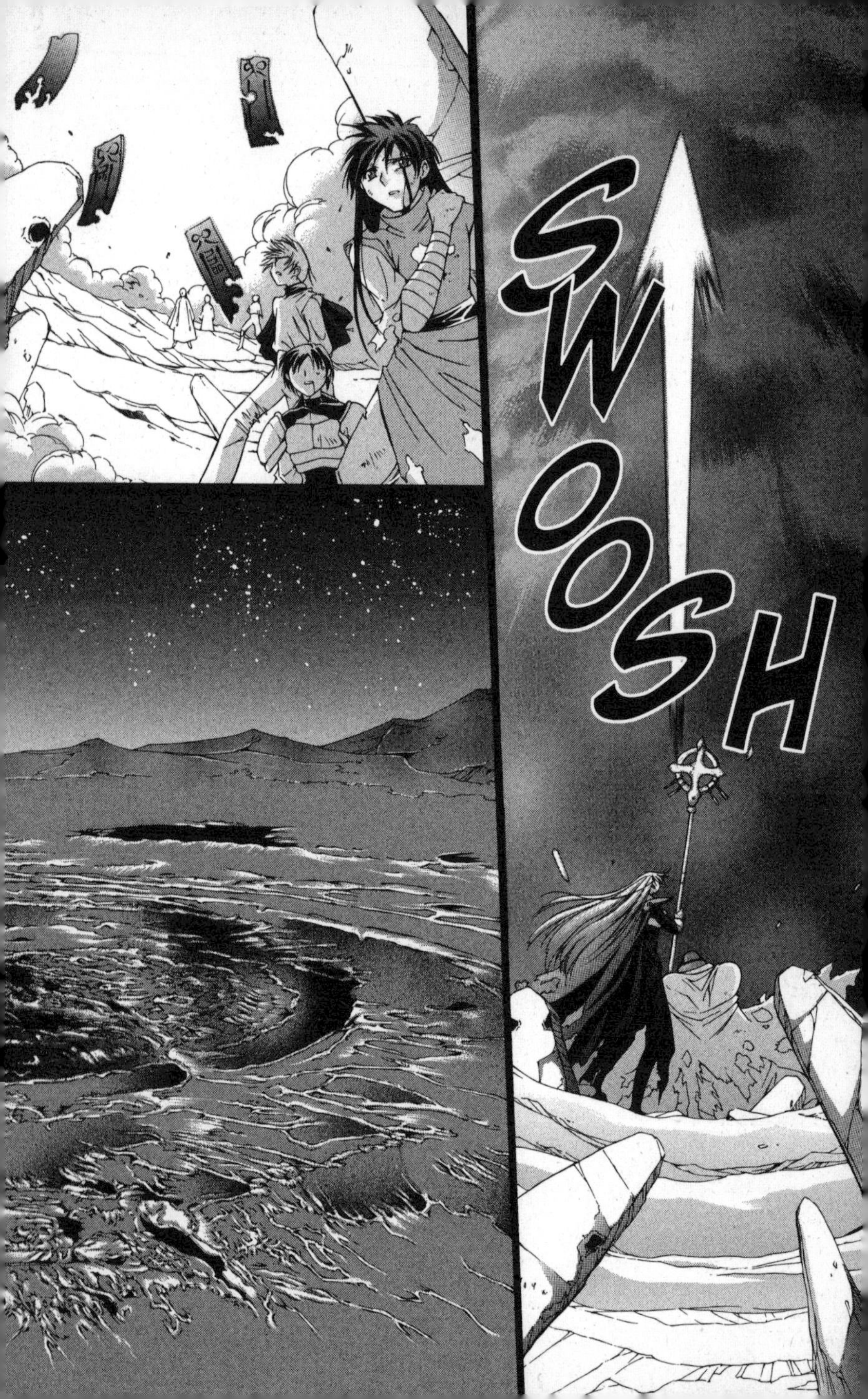
SWOOOSH

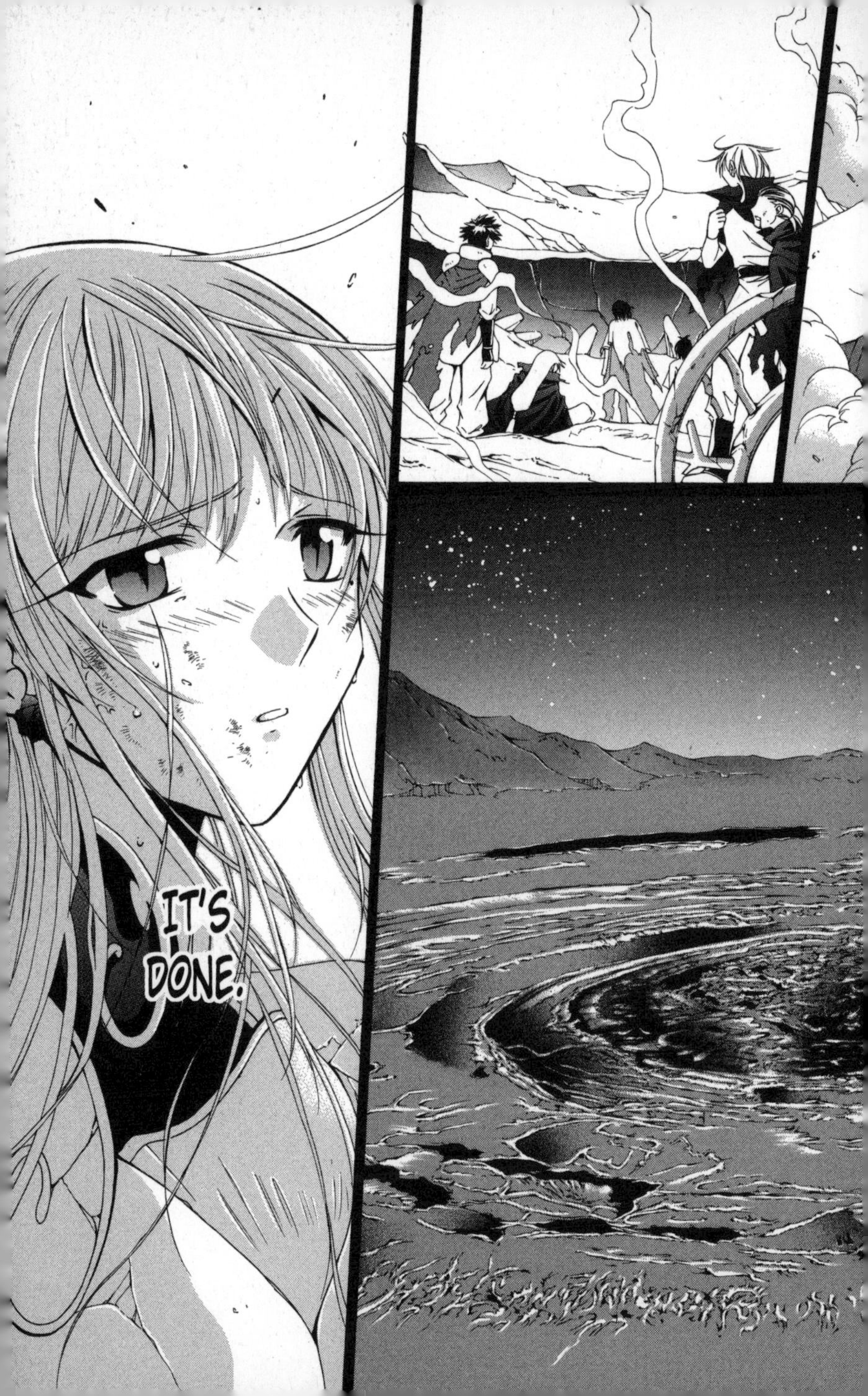
IT'S DONE.

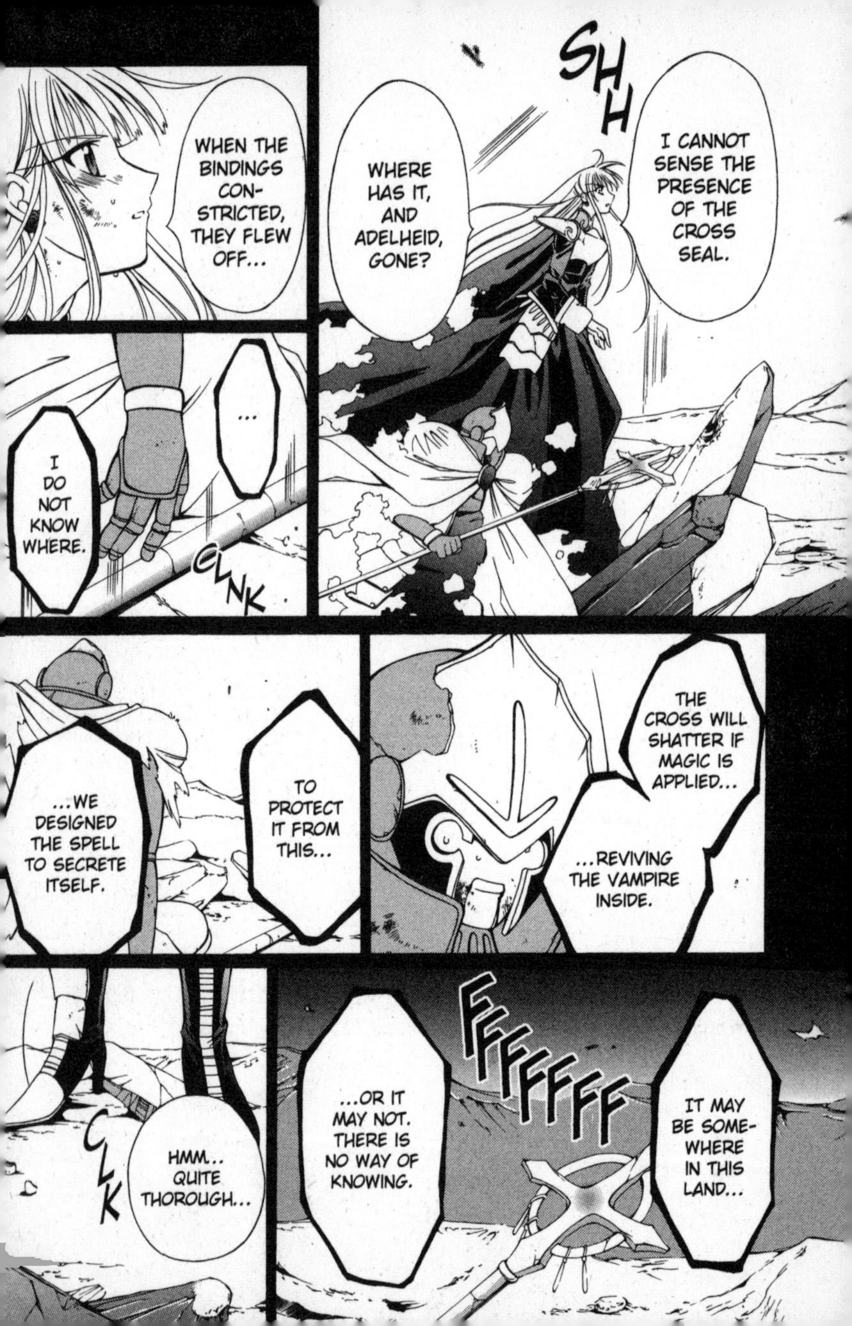
SHH
I CANNOT SENSE THE PRESENCE OF THE CROSS SEAL.
WHERE HAS IT, AND ADELHEID, GONE?
WHEN THE BINDINGS CON-STRICTED, THEY FLEW OFF...
...
I DO NOT KNOW WHERE.
CLNK
THE CROSS WILL SHATTER IF MAGIC IS APPLIED...
...REVIVING THE VAMPIRE INSIDE.
TO PROTECT IT FROM THIS...
...WE DESIGNED THE SPELL TO SECRETE ITSELF.
FFFFFFF
IT MAY BE SOME-WHERE IN THIS LAND...
...OR IT MAY NOT. THERE IS NO WAY OF KNOWING.
CLK
HMM.. QUITE THOROUGH...

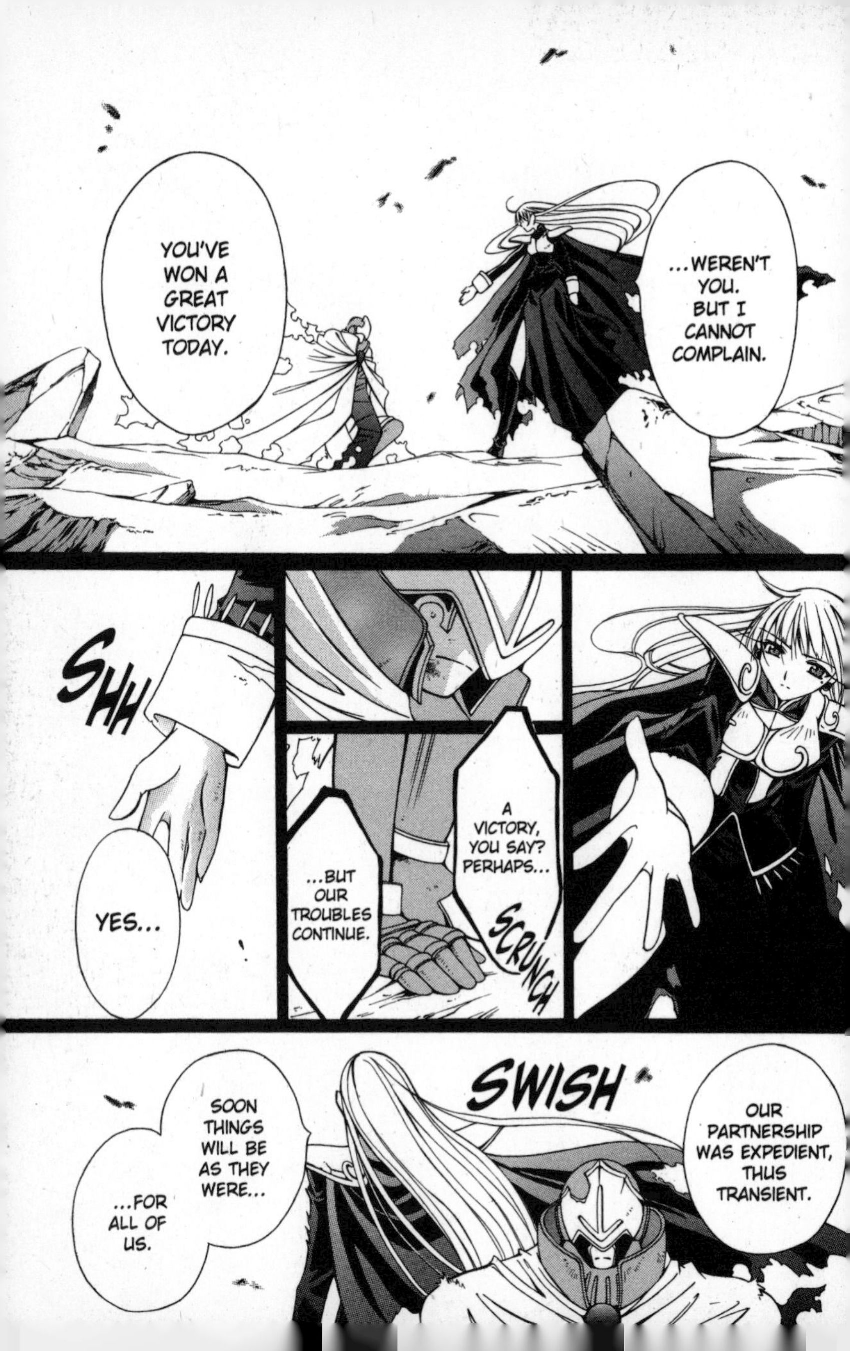
...WEREN'T YOU. BUT I CANNOT COMPLAIN.
YOU'VE WON A GREAT VICTORY TODAY.
A VICTORY, YOU SAY? PERHAPS...
SCRUNCH
...BUT OUR TROUBLES CONTINUE.
SHH
YES...
OUR PARTNERSHIP WAS EXPEDIENT, THUS TRANSIENT.
SWISH
SOON THINGS WILL BE AS THEY WERE...
...FOR ALL OF US.

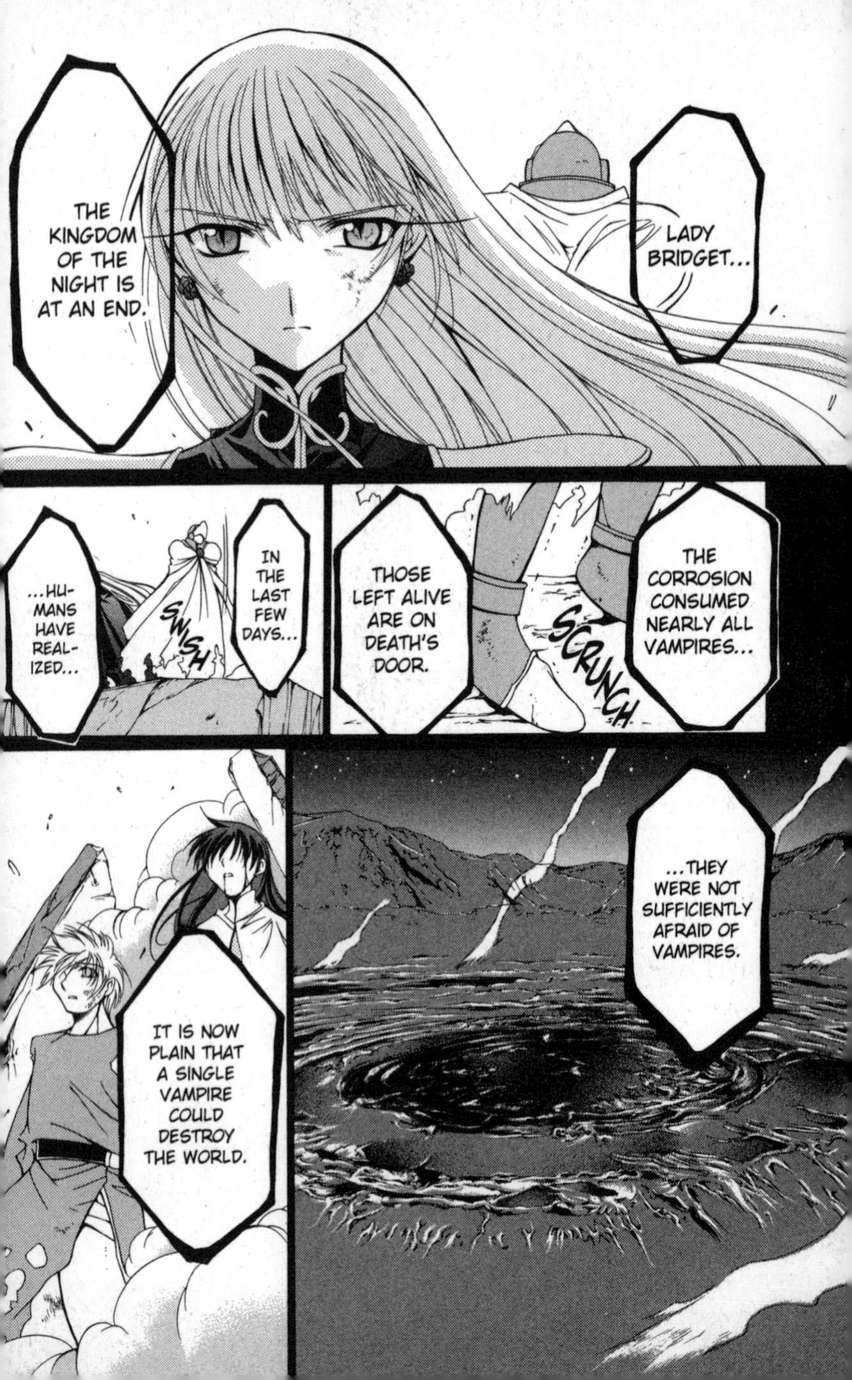
LADY BRIDGET...
THE KINGDOM OF THE NIGHT IS AT AN END.
THE CORROSION CONSUMED NEARLY ALL VAMPIRES...
SCRUNCH
THOSE LEFT ALIVE ARE ON DEATH'S DOOR.
IN THE LAST FEW DAYS...
SWISH
...HU-MANS HAVE REAL-IZED...
...THEY WERE NOT SUFFICIENTLY AFRAID OF VAMPIRES.
IT IS NOW PLAIN THAT A SINGLE VAMPIRE COULD DESTROY THE WORLD.

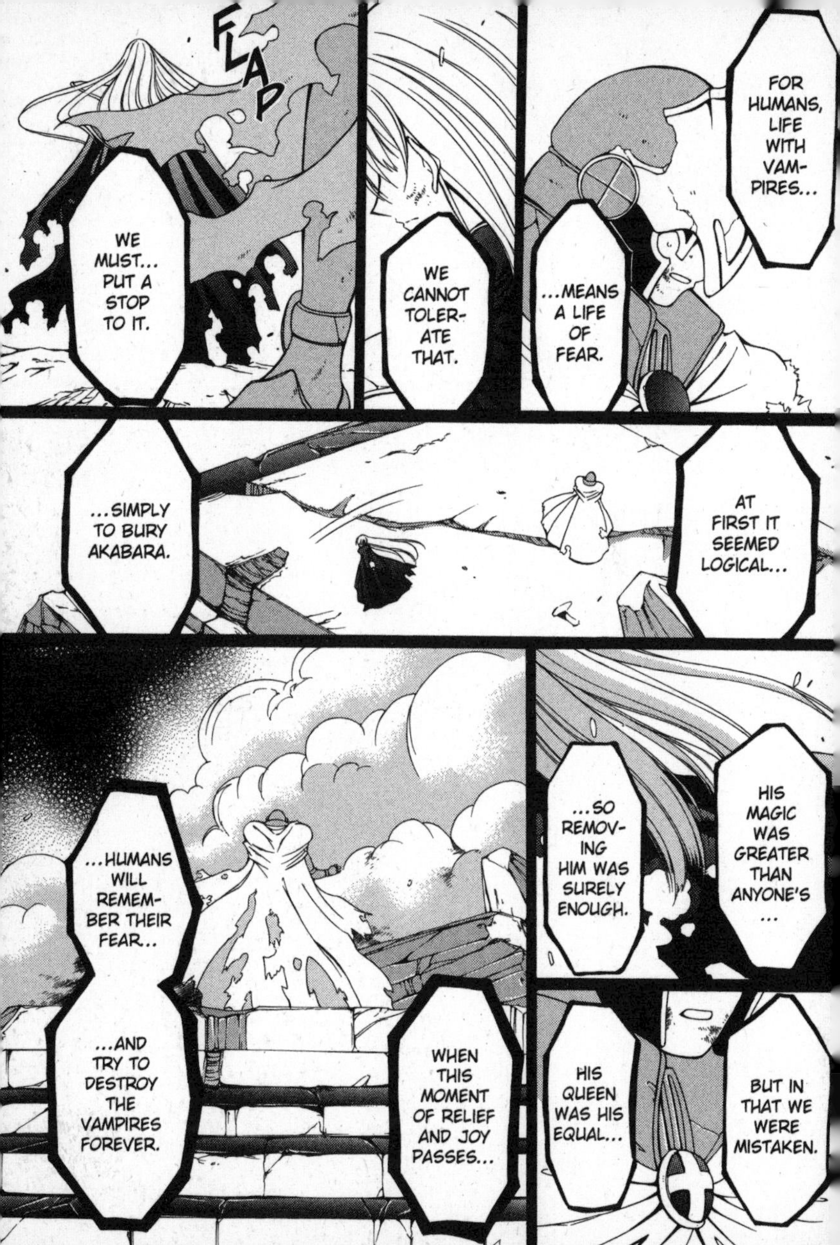
FOR HUMANS, LIFE WITH VAMPIRES...
...MEANS A LIFE OF FEAR.
WE CANNOT TOLERATE THAT.
FLAP
WE MUST... PUT A STOP TO IT.
AT FIRST IT SEEMED LOGICAL...
...SIMPLY TO BURY AKABARA.
HIS MAGIC WAS GREATER THAN ANYONE'S...
...SO REMOVING HIM WAS SURELY ENOUGH.
BUT IN THAT WE WERE MISTAKEN.
HIS QUEEN WAS HIS EQUAL...
WHEN THIS MOMENT OF RELIEF AND JOY PASSES...
...HUMANS WILL REMEMBER THEIR FEAR...
...AND TRY TO DESTROY THE VAMPIRES FOREVER.

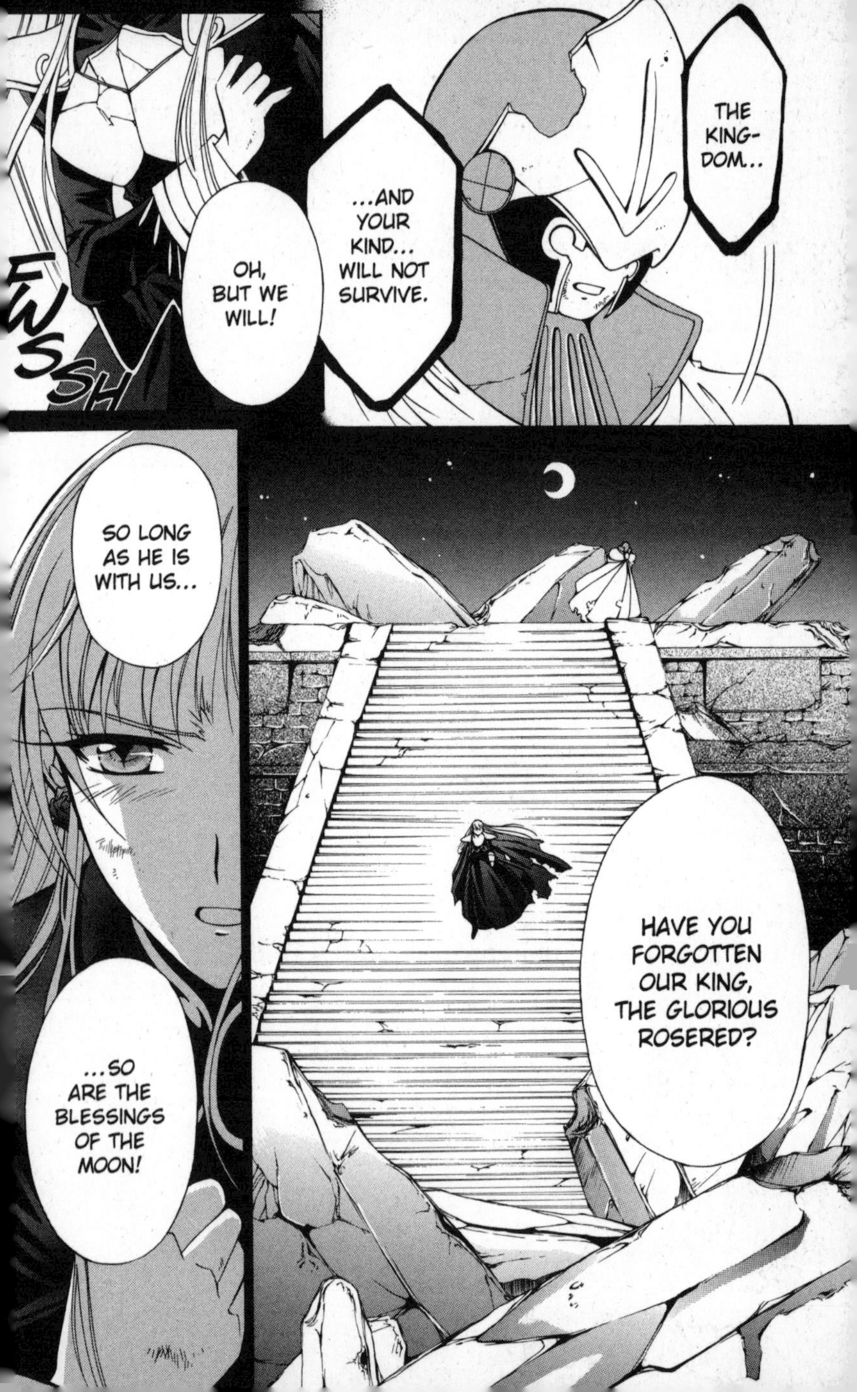
THE KING-DOM...
...AND YOUR KIND... WILL NOT SURVIVE.
OH, BUT WE WILL!
FWSSH
HAVE YOU FORGOTTEN OUR KING, THE GLORIOUS ROSERED?
SO LONG AS HE IS WITH US...
...SO ARE THE BLESSINGS OF THE MOON!

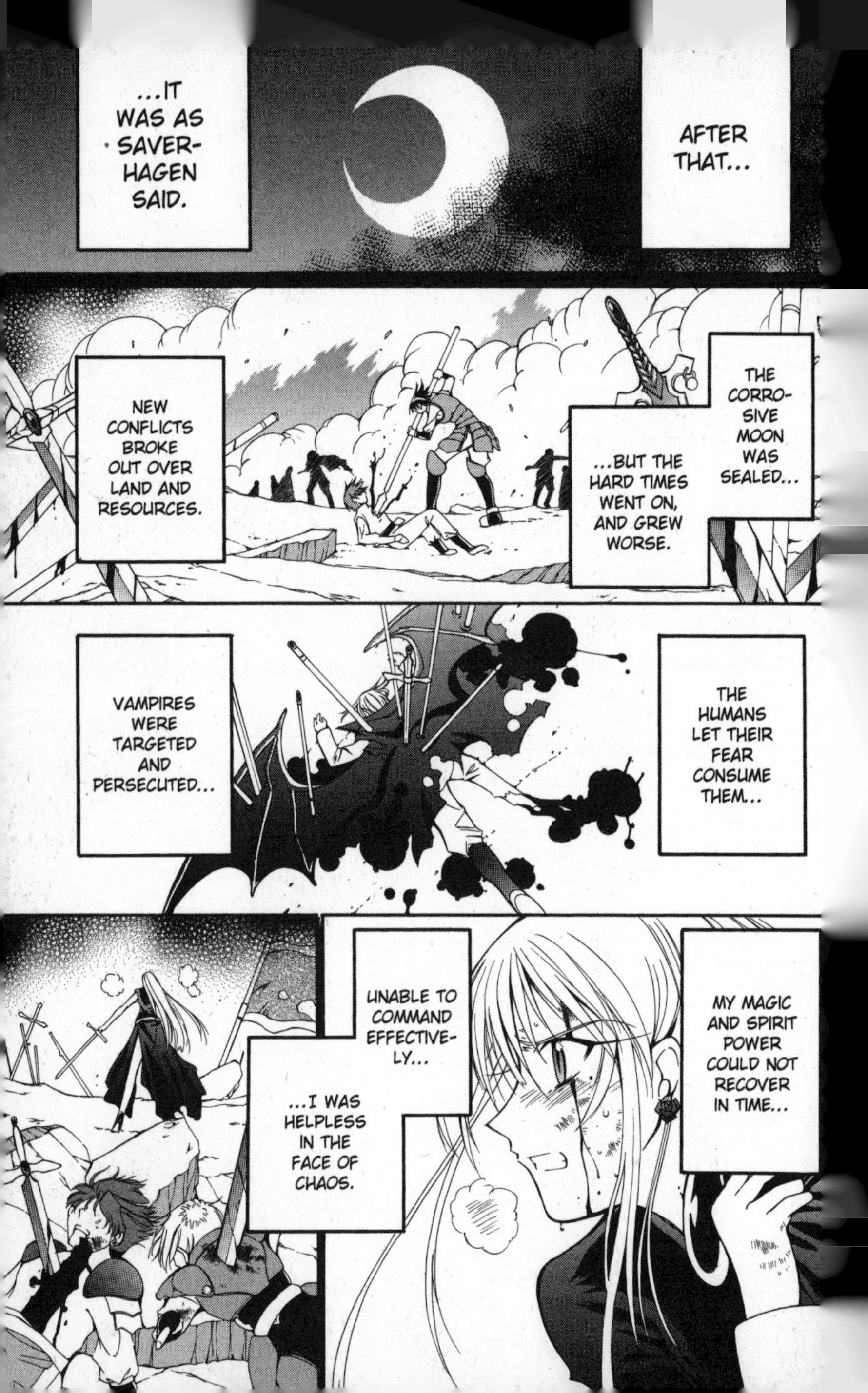
AFTER THAT...
...IT WAS AS SAVER-HAGEN SAID.
THE CORRO-SIVE MOON WAS SEALED...
...BUT THE HARD TIMES WENT ON, AND GREW WORSE.
NEW CONFLICTS BROKE OUT OVER LAND AND RESOURCES.
THE HUMANS LET THEIR FEAR CONSUME THEM...
VAMPIRES WERE TARGETED AND PERSECUTED...
MY MAGIC AND SPIRIT POWER COULD NOT RECOVER IN TIME...
UNABLE TO COMMAND EFFECTIVE-LY...
...I WAS HELPLESS IN THE FACE OF CHAOS.

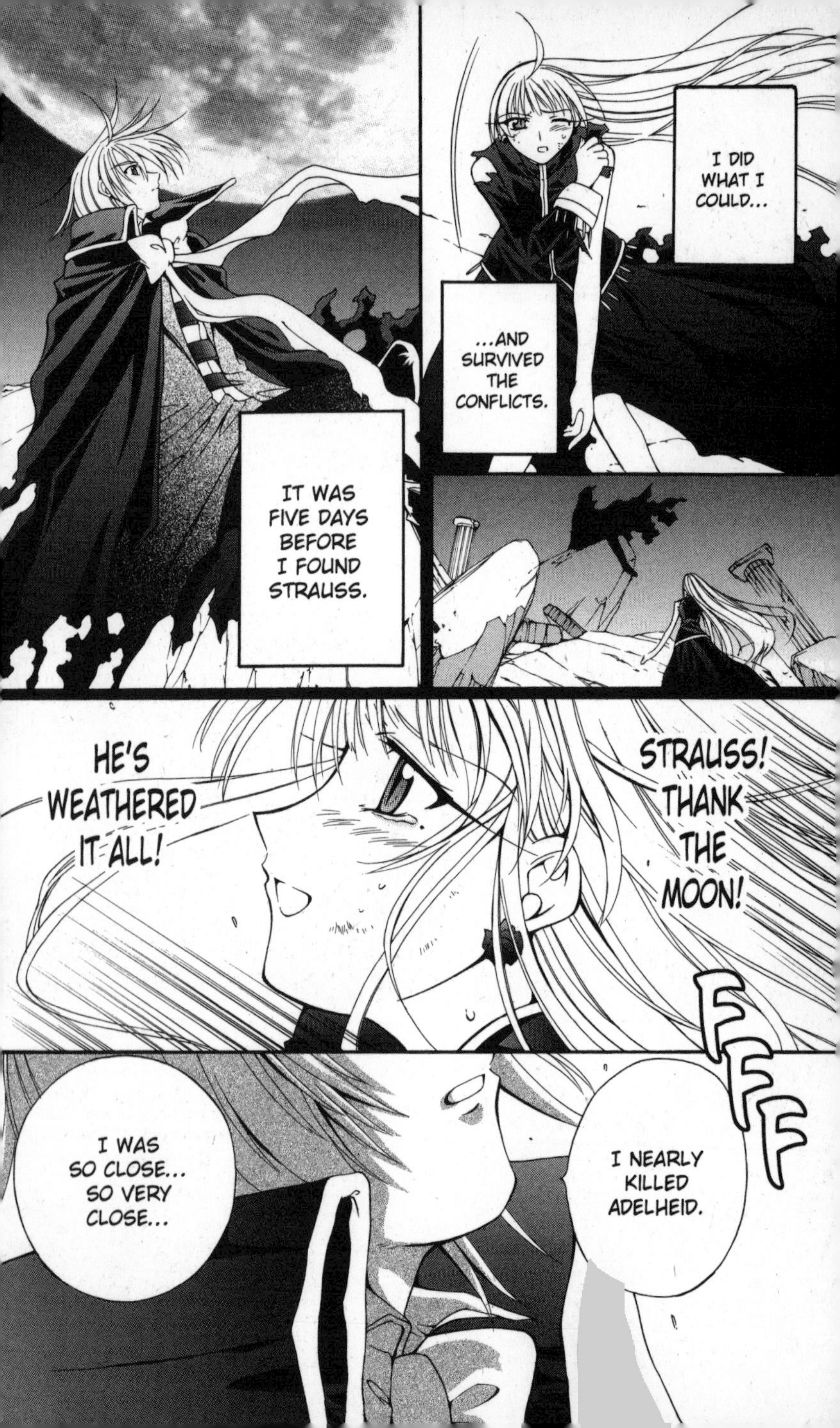
I DID WHAT I COULD...
...AND SURVIVED THE CONFLICTS.
IT WAS FIVE DAYS BEFORE I FOUND STRAUSS.
STRAUSS! THANK THE MOON!
HE'S WEATHERED IT ALL!
FFF
I NEARLY KILLED ADELHEID.
I WAS SO CLOSE... SO VERY CLOSE...

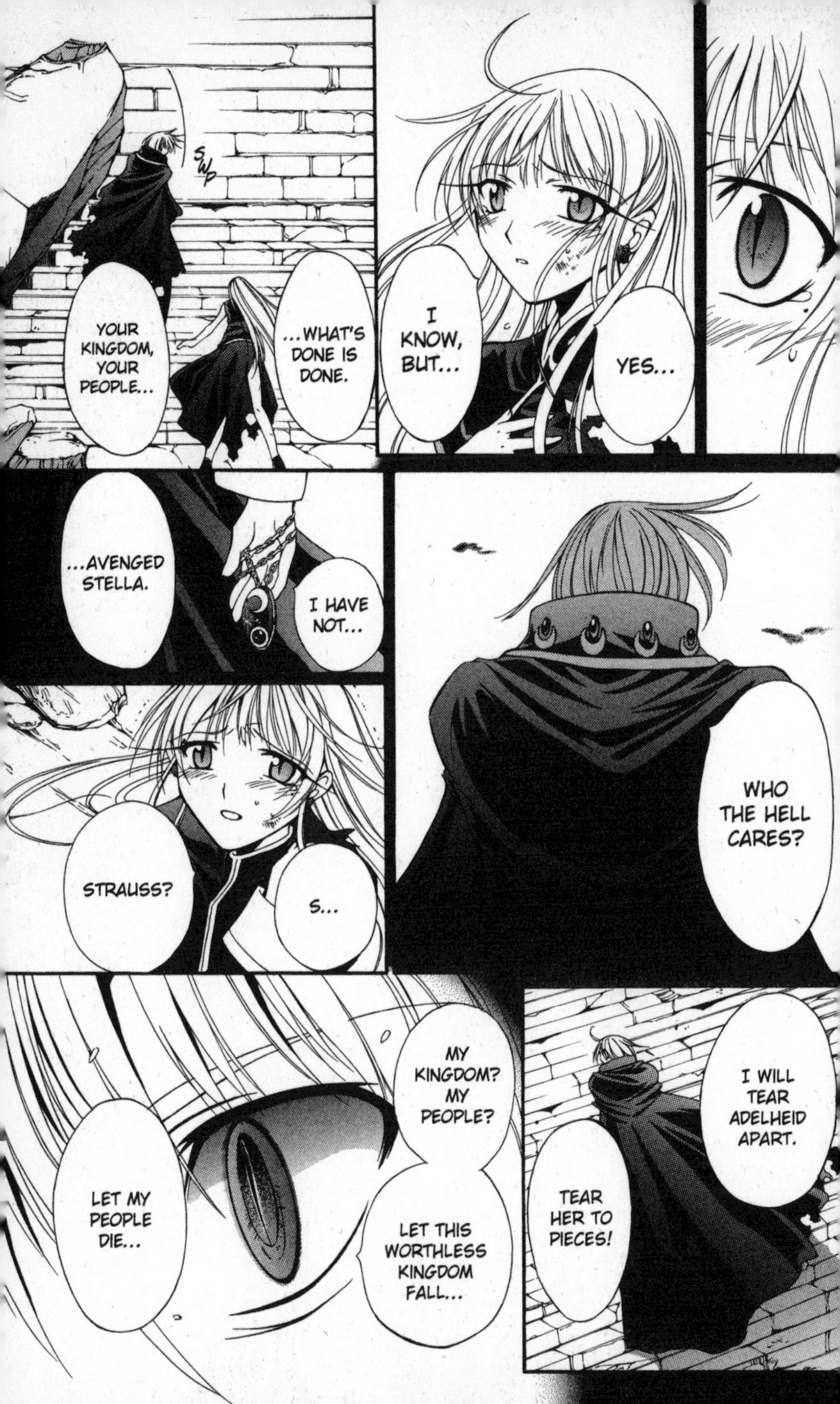
YES...
I KNOW, BUT...
SWP
...WHAT'S DONE IS DONE.
YOUR KINGDOM, YOUR PEOPLE...
WHO THE HELL CARES?
I HAVE NOT...
...AVENGED STELLA.
S...
STRAUSS?
I WILL TEAR ADELHEID APART.
TEAR HER TO PIECES!
MY KINGDOM? MY PEOPLE?
LET THIS WORTHLESS KINGDOM FALL...
LET MY PEOPLE DIE...

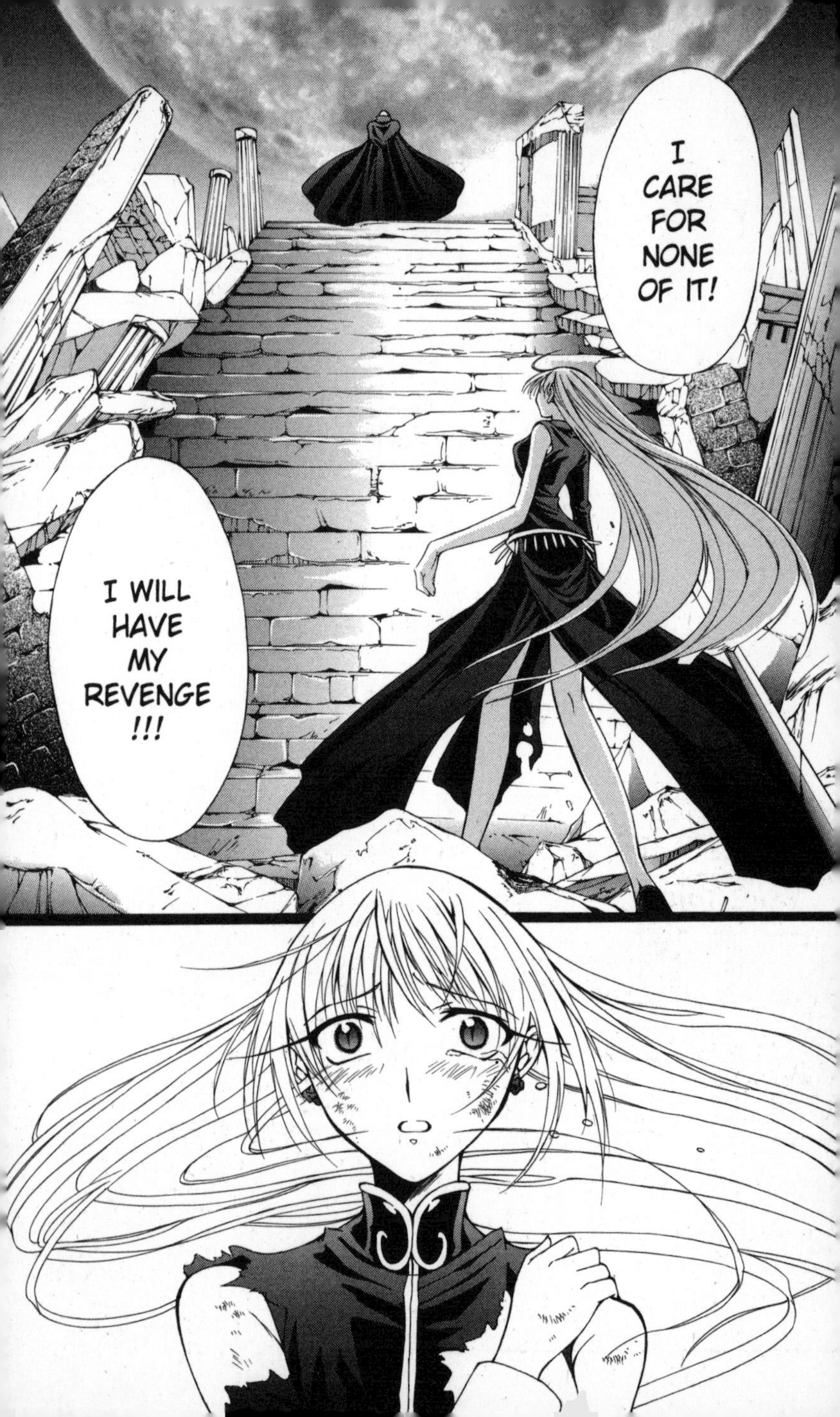
I CARE FOR NONE OF IT!
I WILL HAVE MY REVENGE!!!

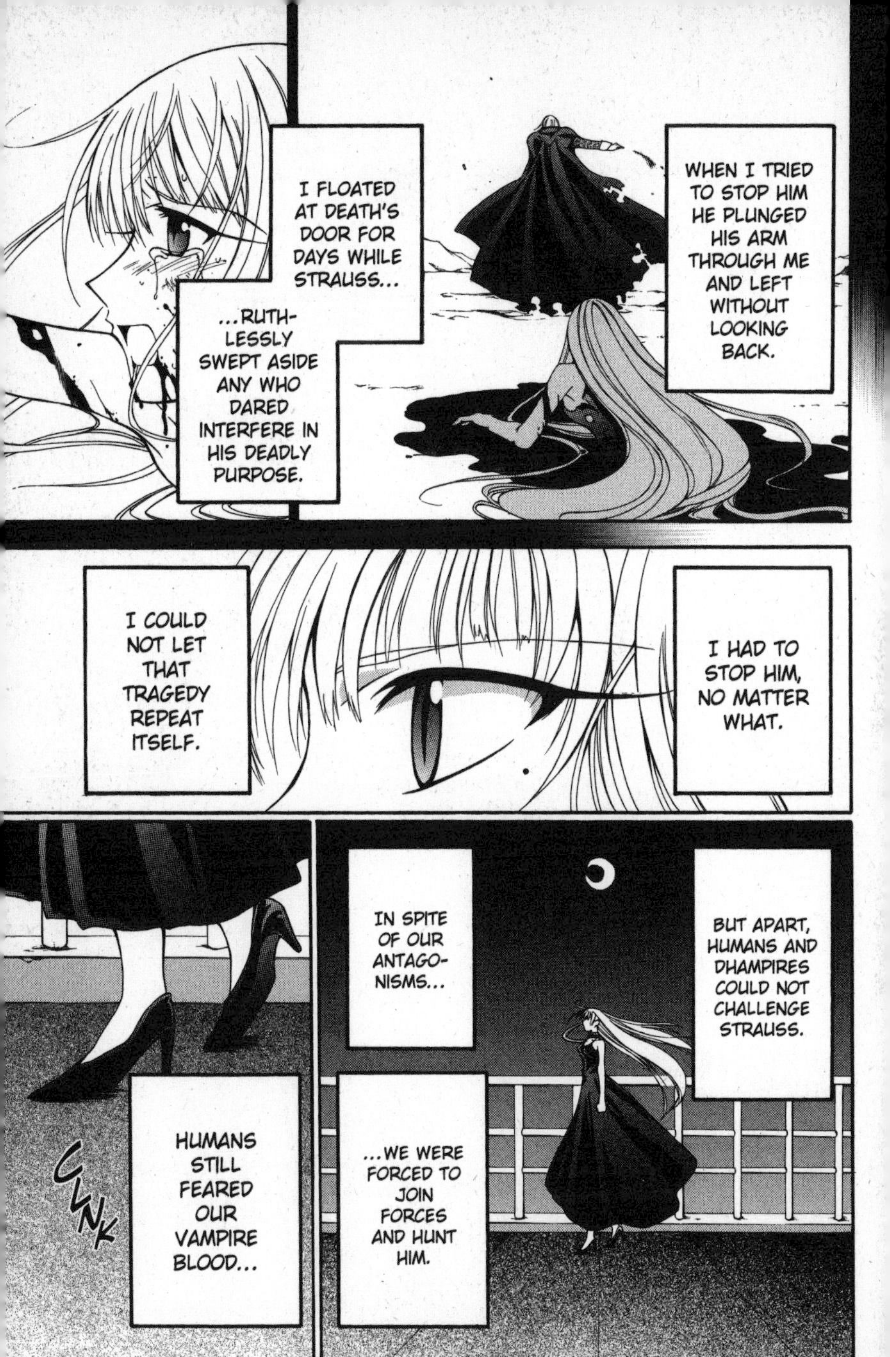

WHEN I TRIED TO STOP HIM HE PLUNGED HIS ARM THROUGH ME AND LEFT WITHOUT LOOKING BACK.
I FLOATED AT DEATH'S DOOR FOR DAYS WHILE STRAUSS...
...RUTH-LESSLY SWEPT ASIDE ANY WHO DARED INTERFERE IN HIS DEADLY PURPOSE.
I HAD TO STOP HIM, NO MATTER WHAT.
I COULD NOT LET THAT TRAGEDY REPEAT ITSELF.
BUT APART, HUMANS AND DHAMPIRES COULD NOT CHALLENGE STRAUSS.
IN SPITE OF OUR ANTAGO-NISMS...
...WE WERE FORCED TO JOIN FORCES AND HUNT HIM.
HUMANS STILL FEARED OUR VAMPIRE BLOOD...
CLUNK

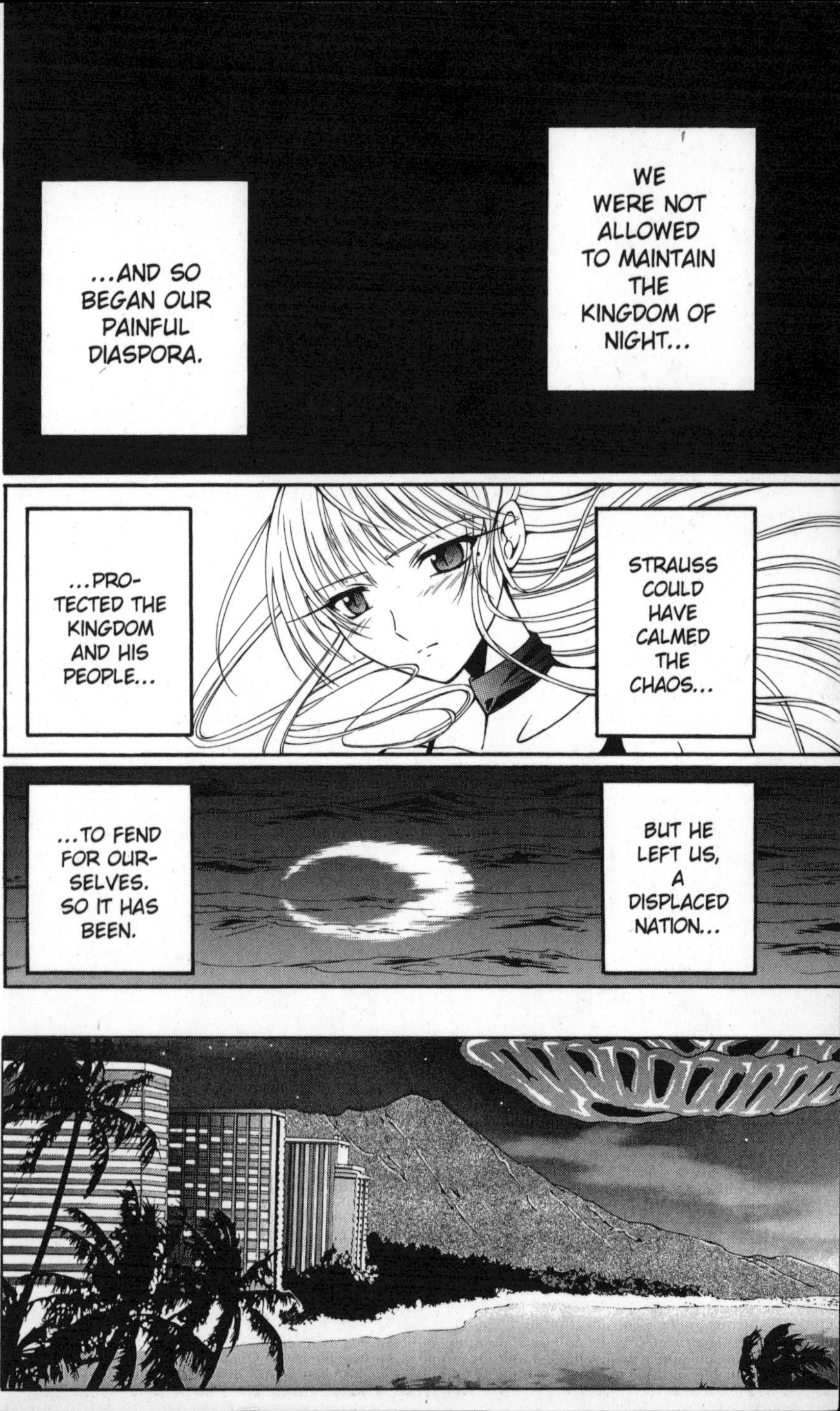
WE WERE NOT ALLOWED TO MAINTAIN THE KINGDOM OF NIGHT...
...AND SO BEGAN OUR PAINFUL DIASPORA.
STRAUSS COULD HAVE CALMED THE CHAOS...
...PROTECTED THE KINGDOM AND HIS PEOPLE...
BUT HE LEFT US, A DISPLACED NATION...
...TO FEND FOR OURSELVES. SO IT HAS BEEN.

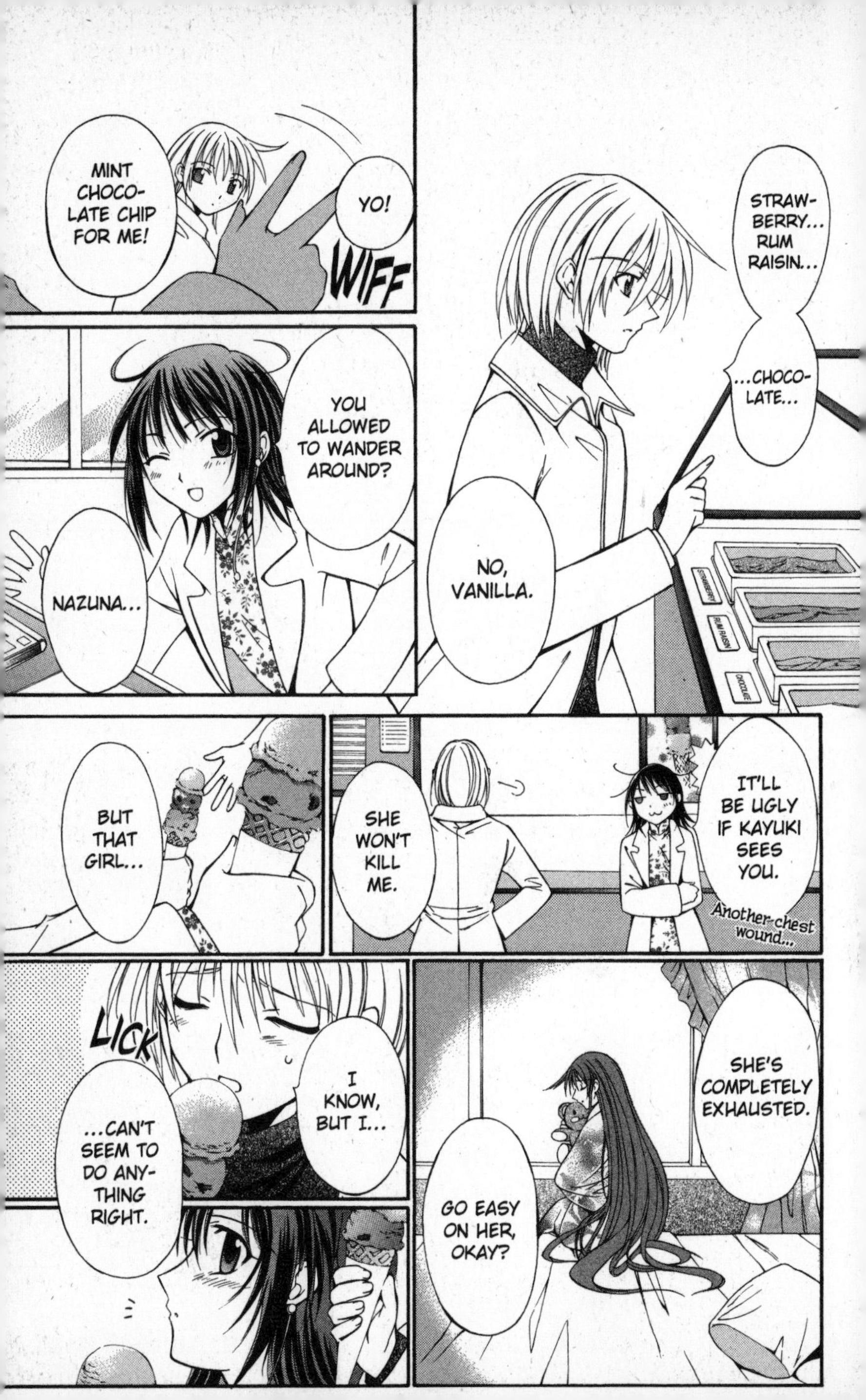
STRAW-BERRY... RUM RAISIN...
...CHOCO-LATE...
NO, VANILLA.
STRAWBERRY
RUM RAISIN
CHOCOLATE
YO!
WIFF
MINT CHOCO-LATE CHIP FOR ME!
YOU ALLOWED TO WANDER AROUND?
NAZUNA...
IT'LL BE UGLY IF KAYUKI SEES YOU.
Another-chest wound...
SHE WON'T KILL ME.
BUT THAT GIRL...
SHE'S COMPLETELY EXHAUSTED.
GO EASY ON HER, OKAY?
I KNOW, BUT I...
LICK
...CAN'T SEEM TO DO ANY-THING RIGHT.

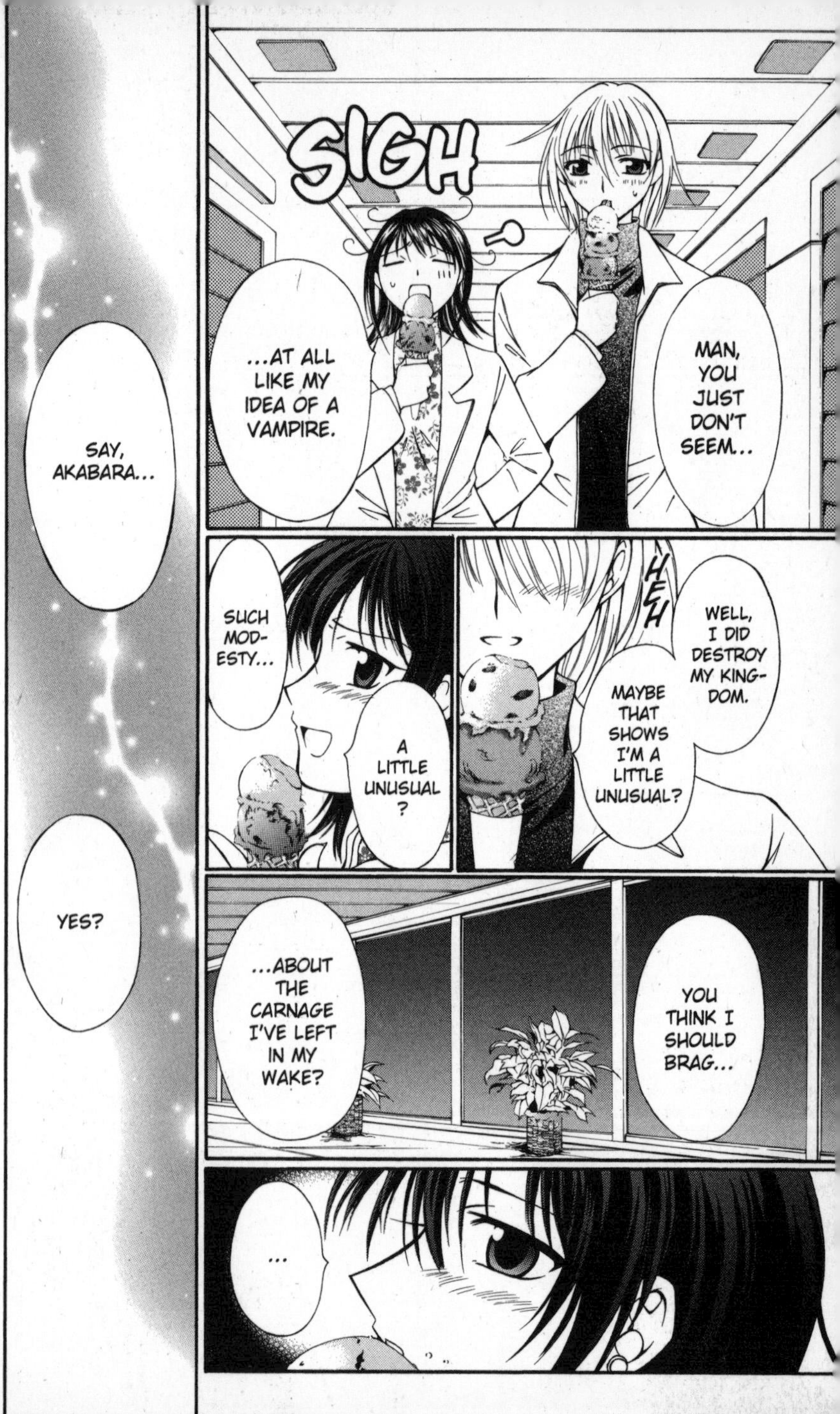
MAN, YOU JUST DON'T SEEM...
...AT ALL LIKE MY IDEA OF A VAMPIRE.
SIGH
HEH
WELL, I DID DESTROY MY KING-DOM.
MAYBE THAT SHOWS I'M A LITTLE UNUSUAL?
A LITTLE UNUSUAL?
SUCH MOD-ESTY...
YOU THINK I SHOULD BRAG...
...ABOUT THE CARNAGE I'VE LEFT IN MY WAKE?
...
SAY, AKABARA...
YES?

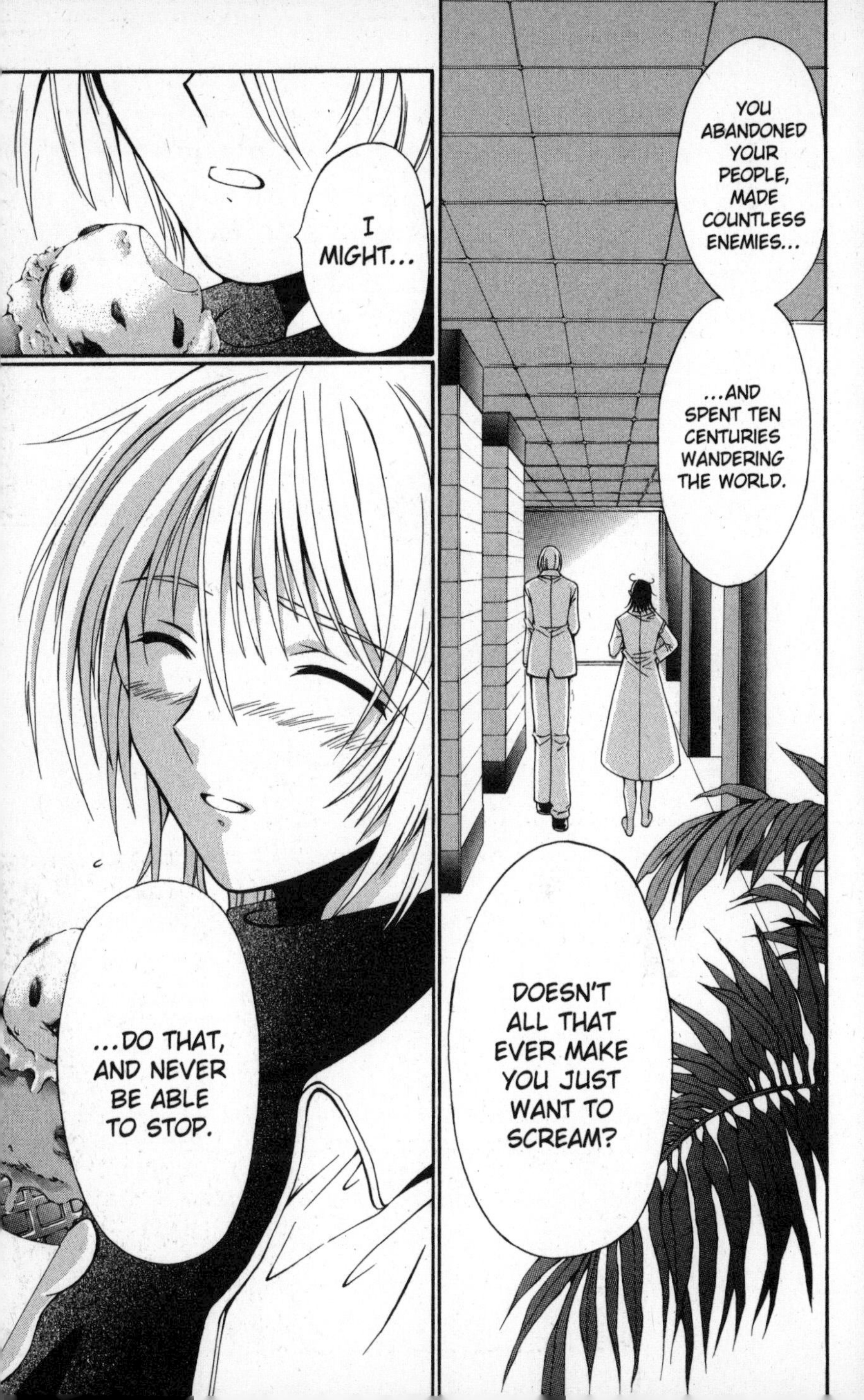
YOU ABANDONED YOUR PEOPLE, MADE COUNTLESS ENEMIES...
...AND SPENT TEN CENTURIES WANDERING THE WORLD.
DOESN'T ALL THAT EVER MAKE YOU JUST WANT TO SCREAM?
I MIGHT...
...DO THAT, AND NEVER BE ABLE TO STOP.

THE RECORD OF A
FALLEN VAMPIRE

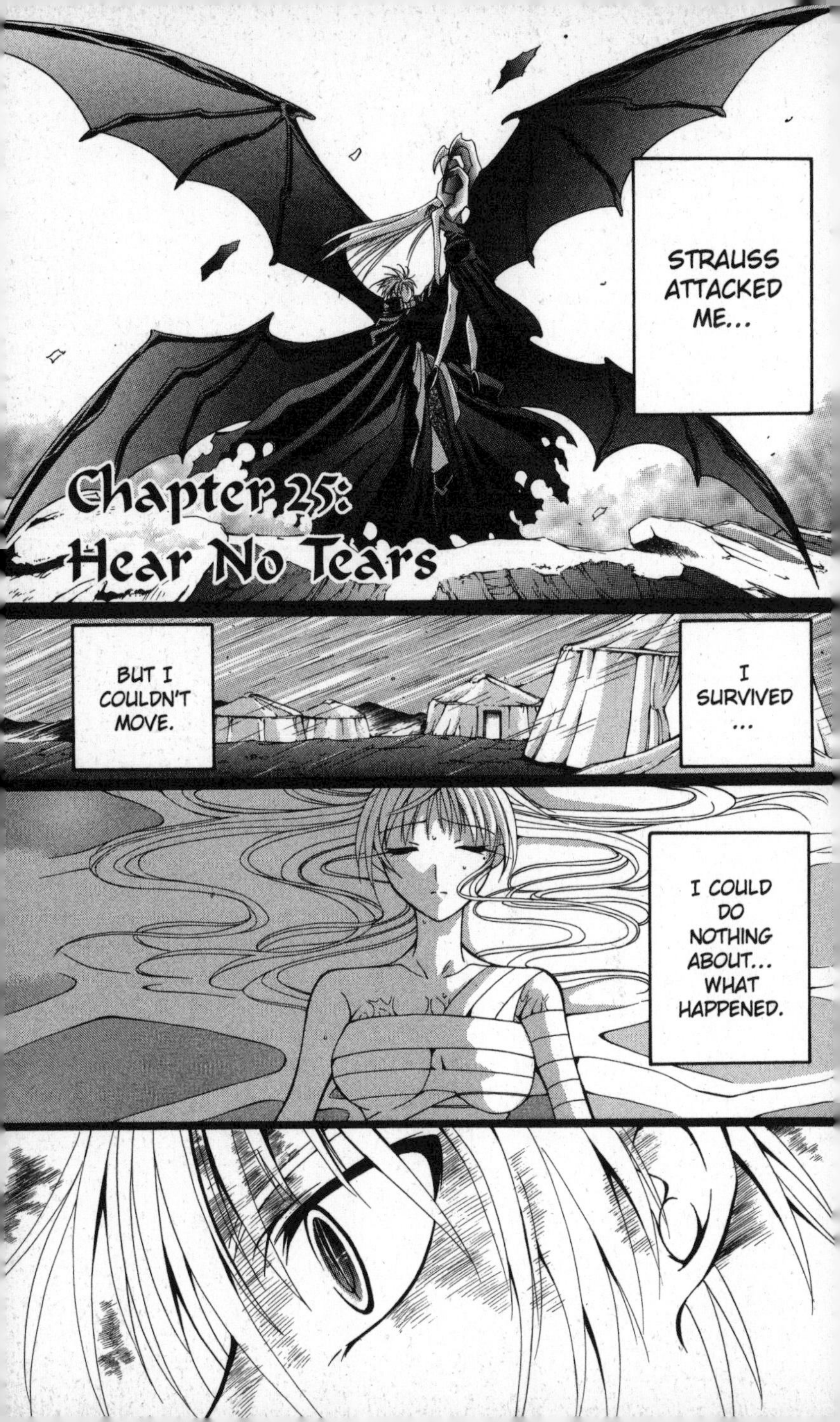
STRAUSS ATTACKED ME...
Chapter 25: Hear No Tears
I SURVIVED ...
BUT I COULDN'T MOVE.
I COULD DO NOTHING ABOUT... WHAT HAPPENED.

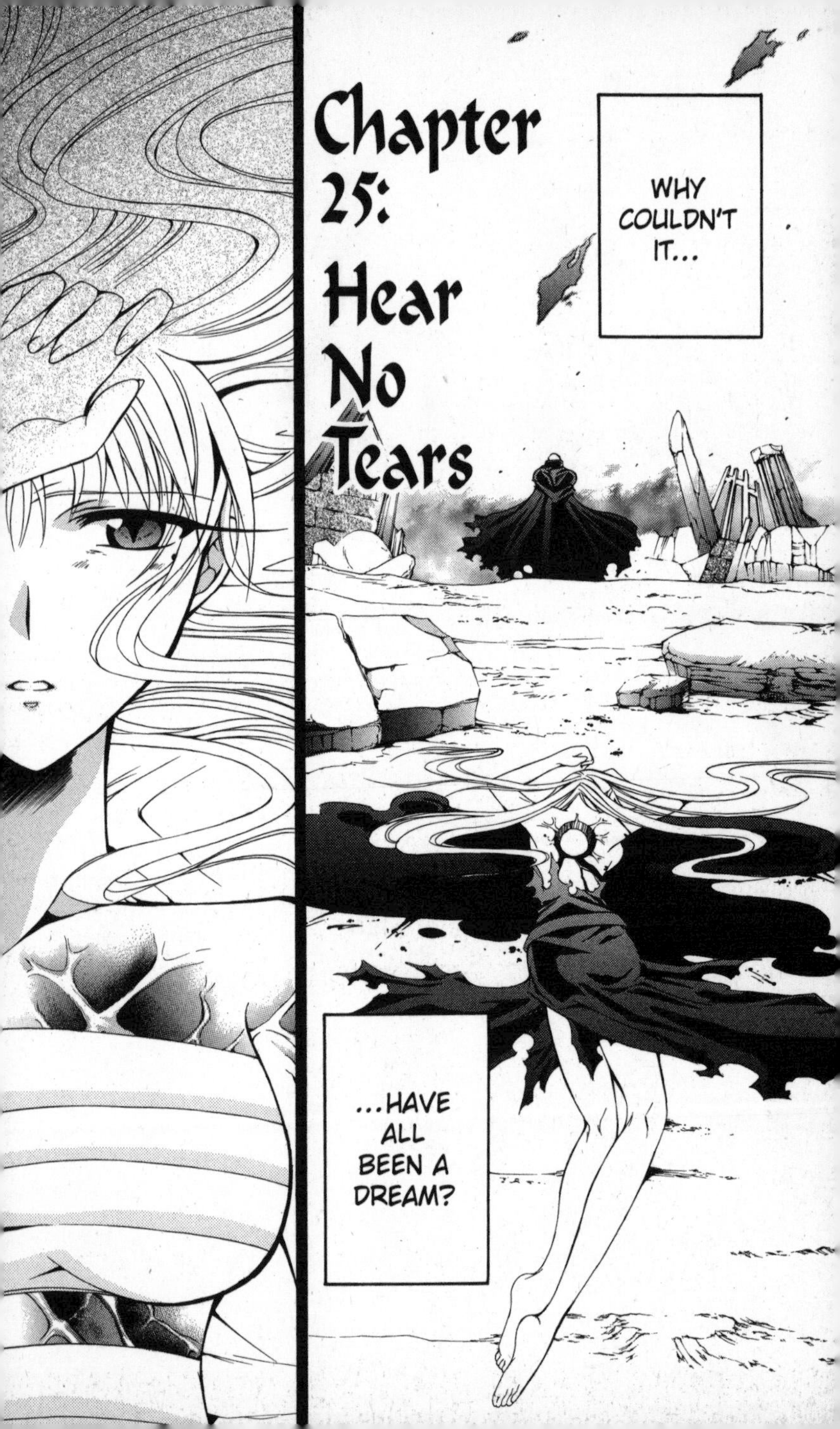
Chapter 25: Hear No Tears
WHY COULDN'T IT...
...HAVE ALL BEEN A DREAM?

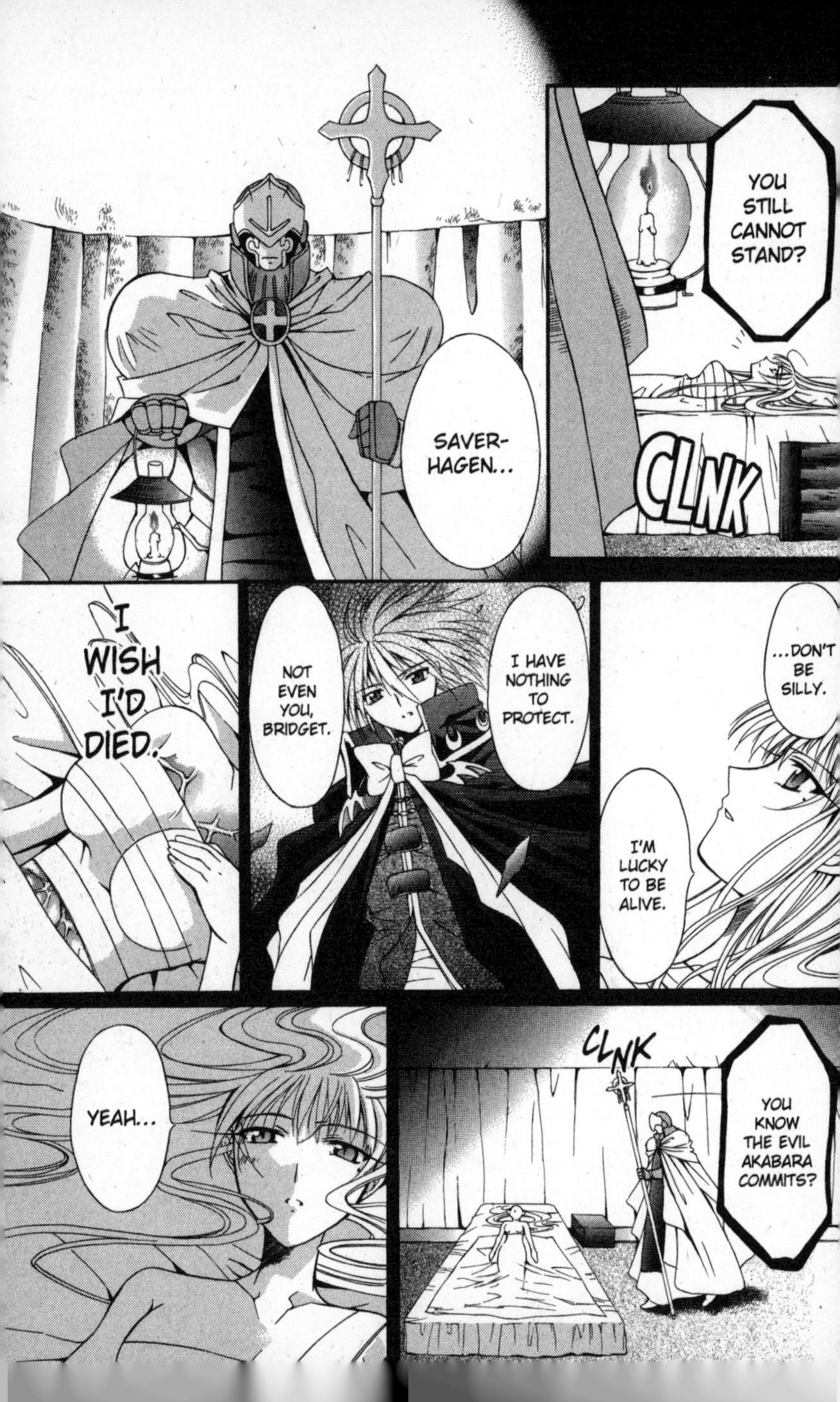
YOU STILL CANNOT STAND?
CLNK
SAVER-HAGEN...
...DON'T BE SILLY.
I'M LUCKY TO BE ALIVE.
I HAVE NOTHING TO PROTECT.
NOT EVEN YOU, BRIDGET.
I WISH I'D DIED.
CLNK
YOU KNOW THE EVIL AKABARA COMMITS?
YEAH...

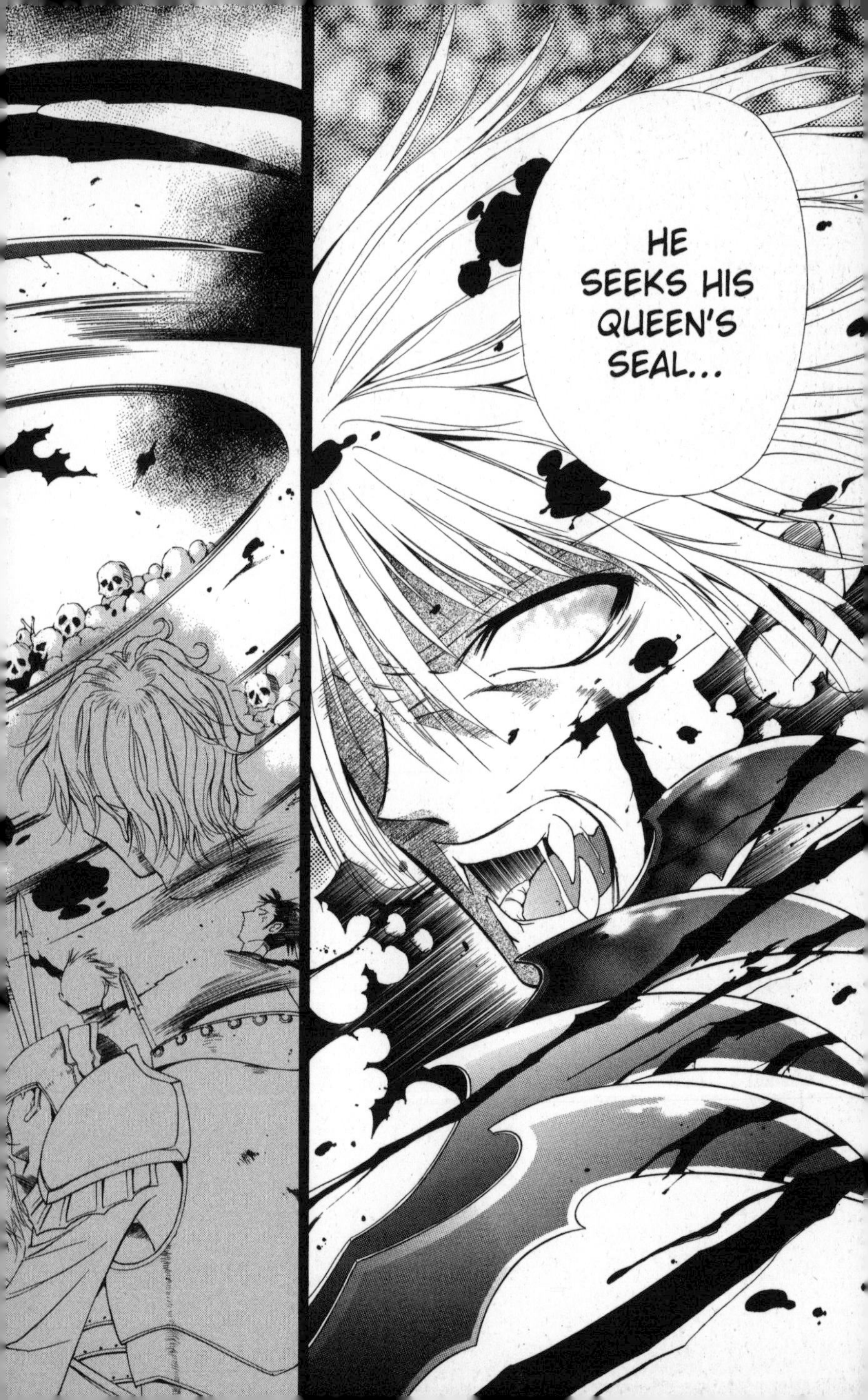
HE SEEKS HIS QUEEN'S SEAL...

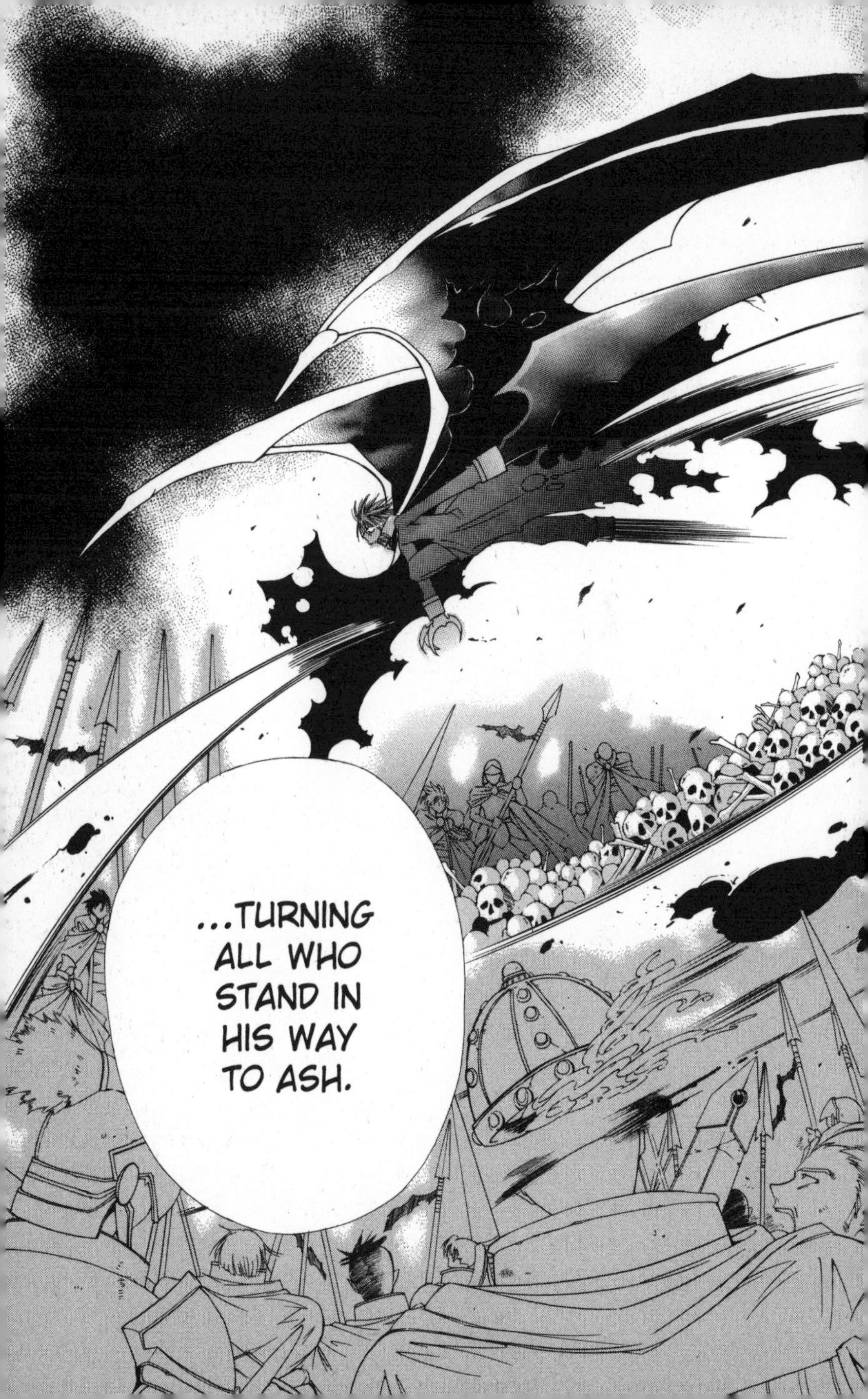
...TURNING ALL WHO STAND IN HIS WAY TO ASH.

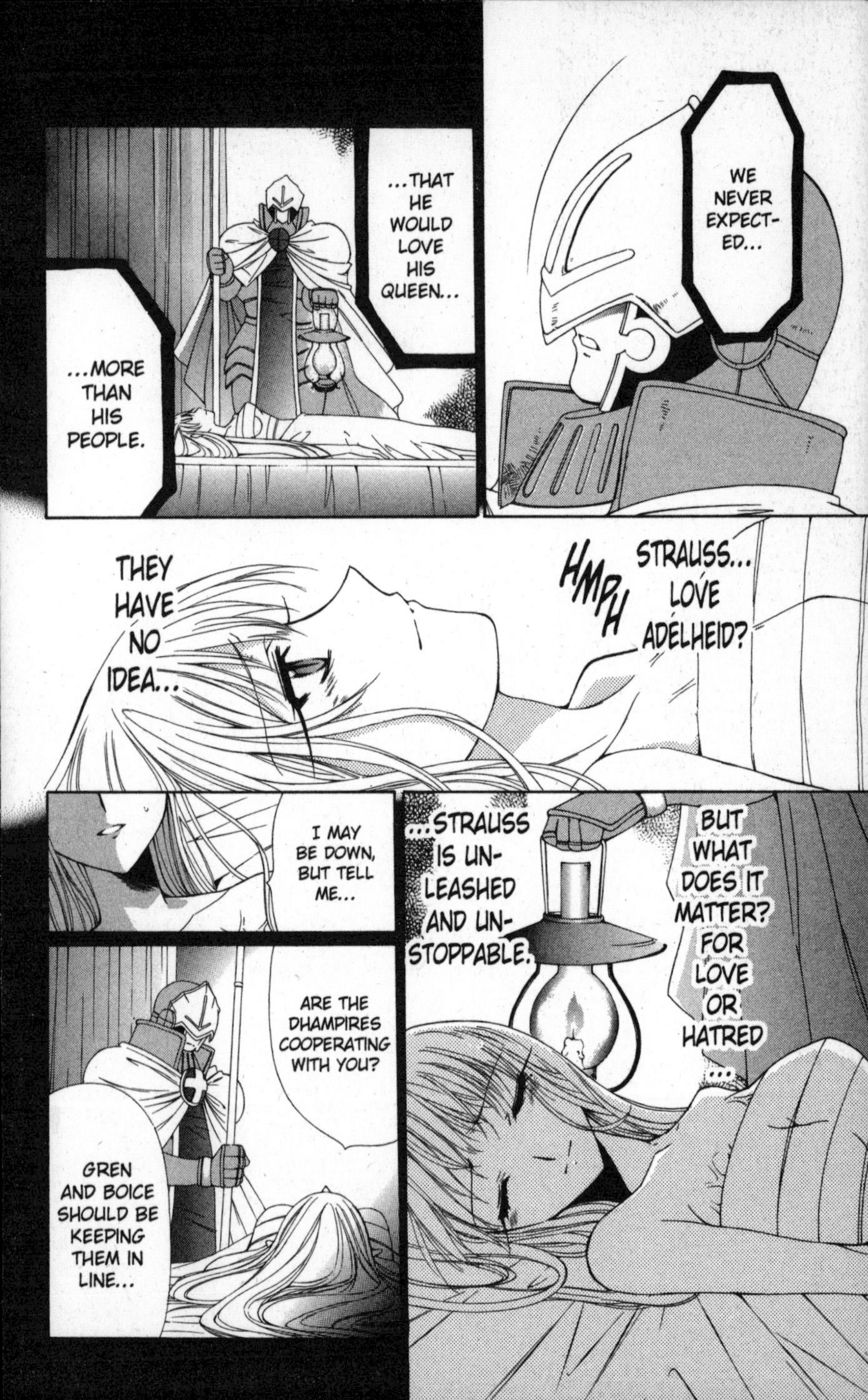
WE NEVER EXPECTED...
...THAT HE WOULD LOVE HIS QUEEN...
...MORE THAN HIS PEOPLE.
STRAUSS... LOVE ADELHEID?
HMPH
THEY HAVE NO IDEA...
BUT WHAT DOES IT MATTER? FOR LOVE OR HATRED...
...STRAUSS IS UNLEASHED AND UNSTOPPABLE.
I MAY BE DOWN, BUT TELL ME...
ARE THE DHAMPIRES COOPERATING WITH YOU?
GREN AND BOICE SHOULD BE KEEPING THEM IN LINE...

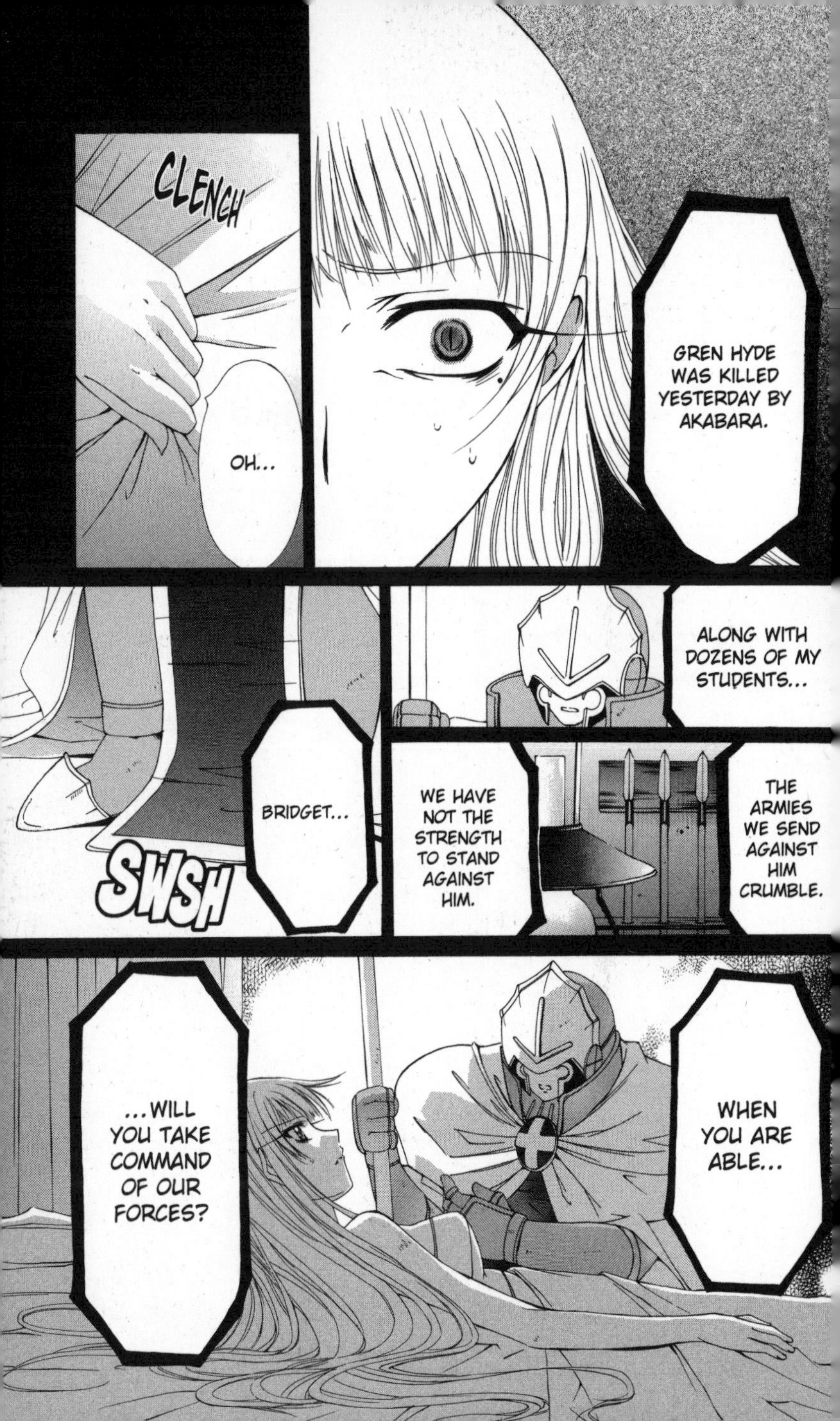
GREN HYDE WAS KILLED YESTERDAY BY AKABARA.
CLENCH
OH...
ALONG WITH DOZENS OF MY STUDENTS...
THE ARMIES WE SEND AGAINST HIM CRUMBLE.
WE HAVE NOT THE STRENGTH TO STAND AGAINST HIM.
SWSH
BRIDGET...
WHEN YOU ARE ABLE...
...WILL YOU TAKE COMMAND OF OUR FORCES?

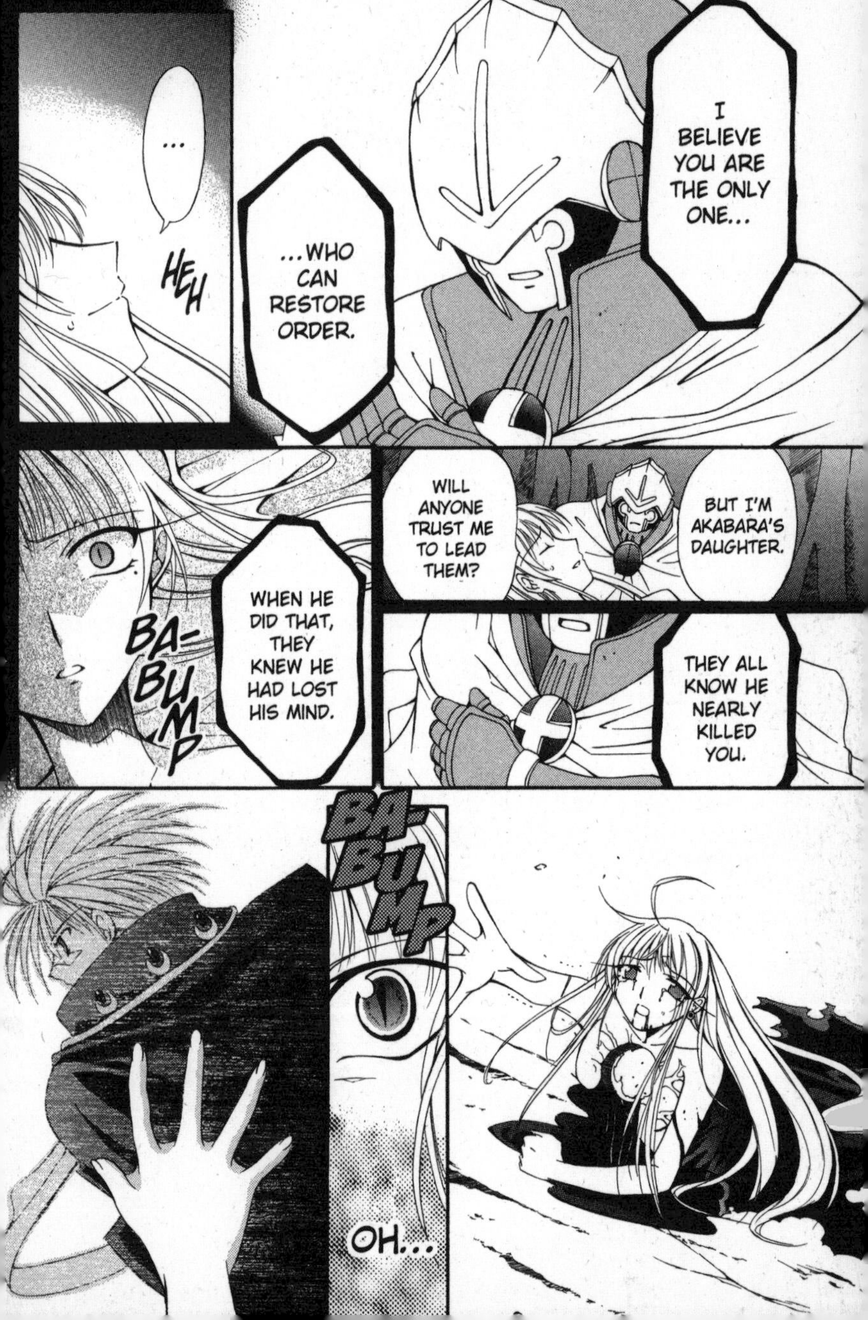
I BELIEVE YOU ARE THE ONLY ONE...
...WHO CAN RESTORE ORDER.
...
HEH
BUT I'M AKABARA'S DAUGHTER.
WILL ANYONE TRUST ME TO LEAD THEM?
THEY ALL KNOW HE NEARLY KILLED YOU.
WHEN HE DID THAT, THEY KNEW HE HAD LOST HIS MIND.
BA-BUMP
BA-BUMP
OH...

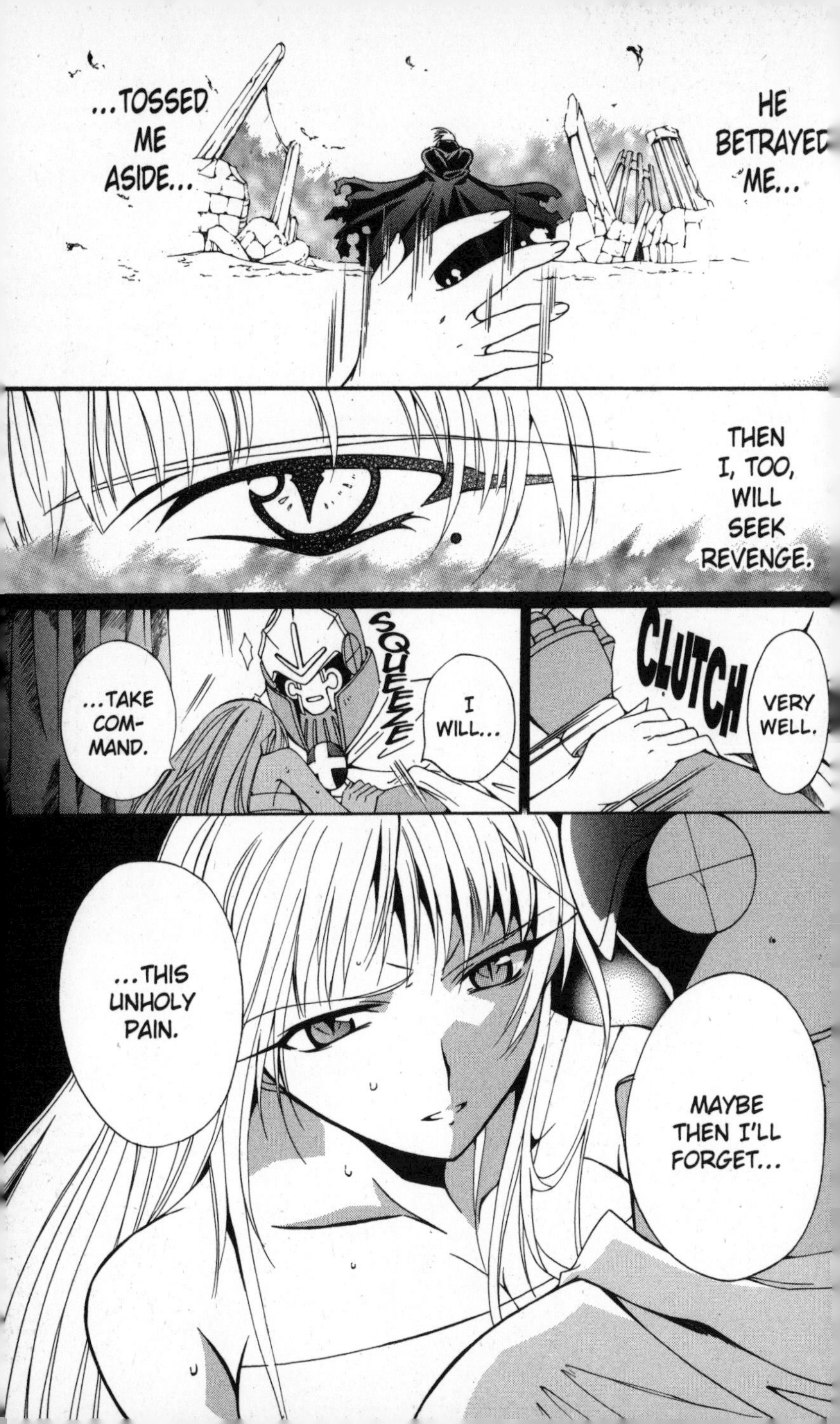
HE BETRAYED ME...
...TOSSED ME ASIDE...
THEN I, TOO, WILL SEEK REVENGE.
CLUTCH
VERY WELL.
I WILL...
SQUEEZE
...TAKE COM-MAND.
MAYBE THEN I'LL FORGET...
...THIS UNHOLY PAIN.

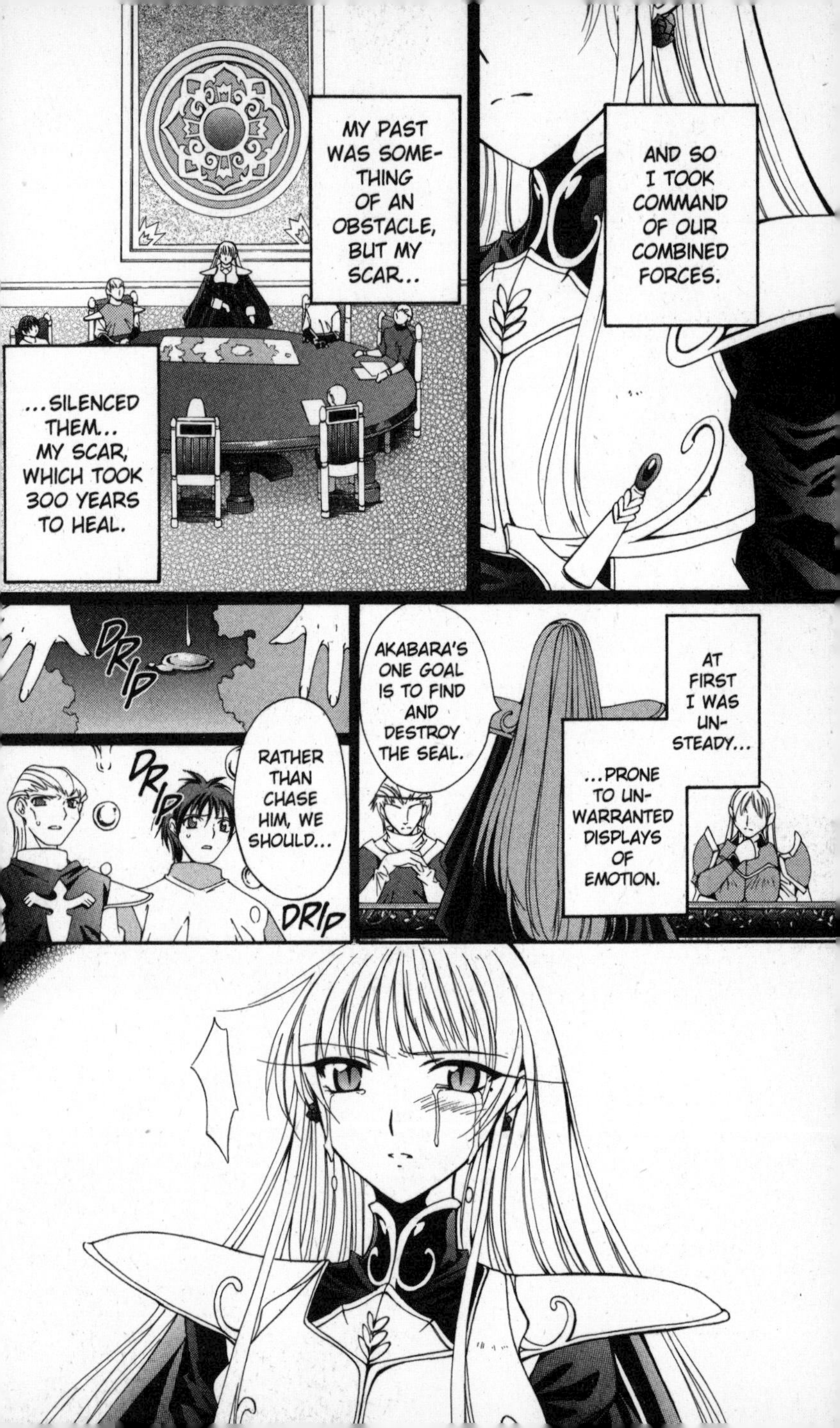
AND SO I TOOK COMMAND OF OUR COMBINED FORCES.
MY PAST WAS SOME-THING OF AN OBSTACLE, BUT MY SCAR...
...SILENCED THEM... MY SCAR, WHICH TOOK 300 YEARS TO HEAL.
AT FIRST I WAS UN-STEADY...
...PRONE TO UN-WARRANTED DISPLAYS OF EMOTION.
AKABARA'S ONE GOAL IS TO FIND AND DESTROY THE SEAL.
DRIP
DRIP
RATHER THAN CHASE HIM, WE SHOULD...
DRIP

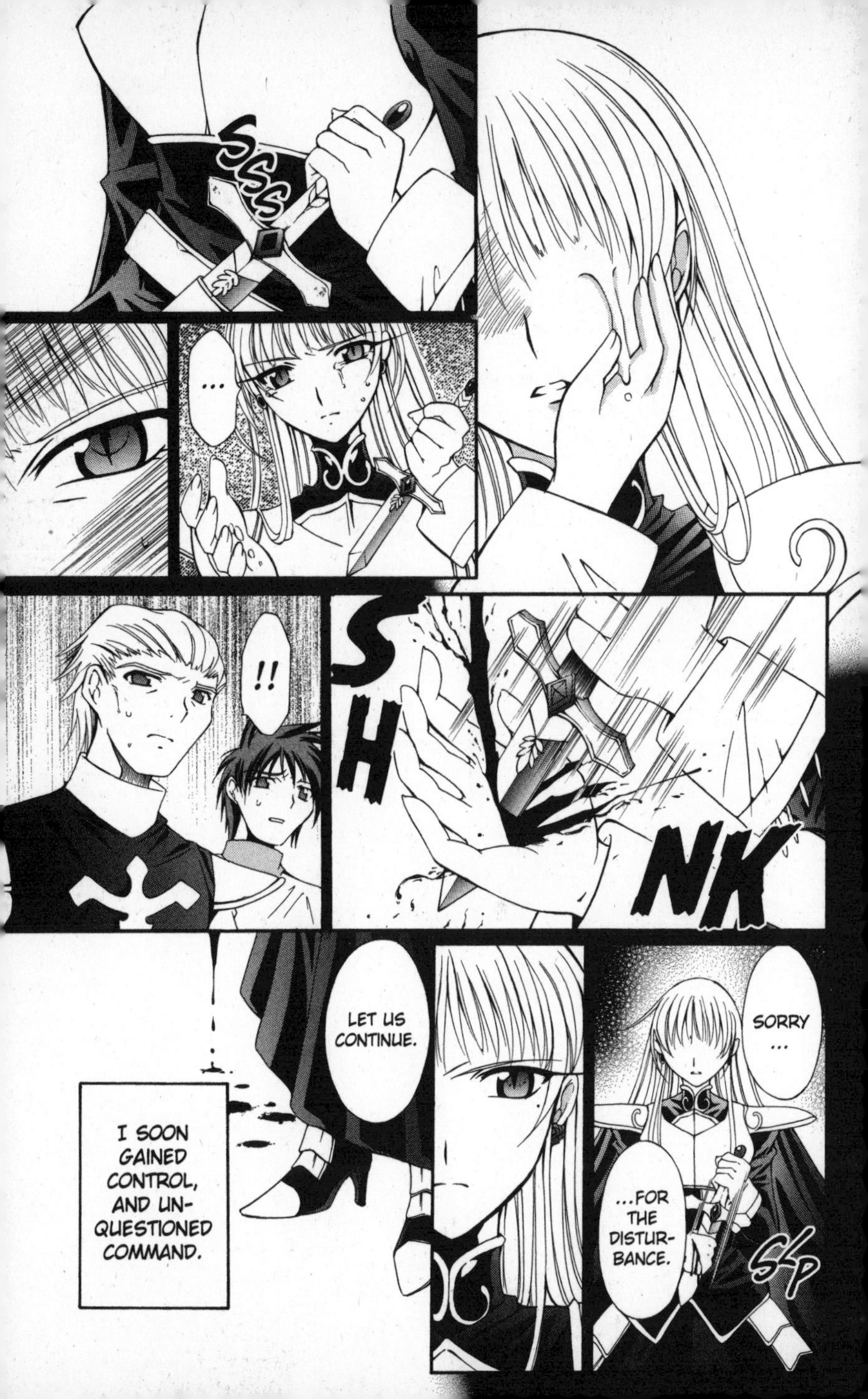
SSS
...
!!
SHNK
SORRY...
...FOR THE DISTURBANCE.
SLP
LET US CONTINUE.
I SOON GAINED CONTROL, AND UNQUESTIONED COMMAND.

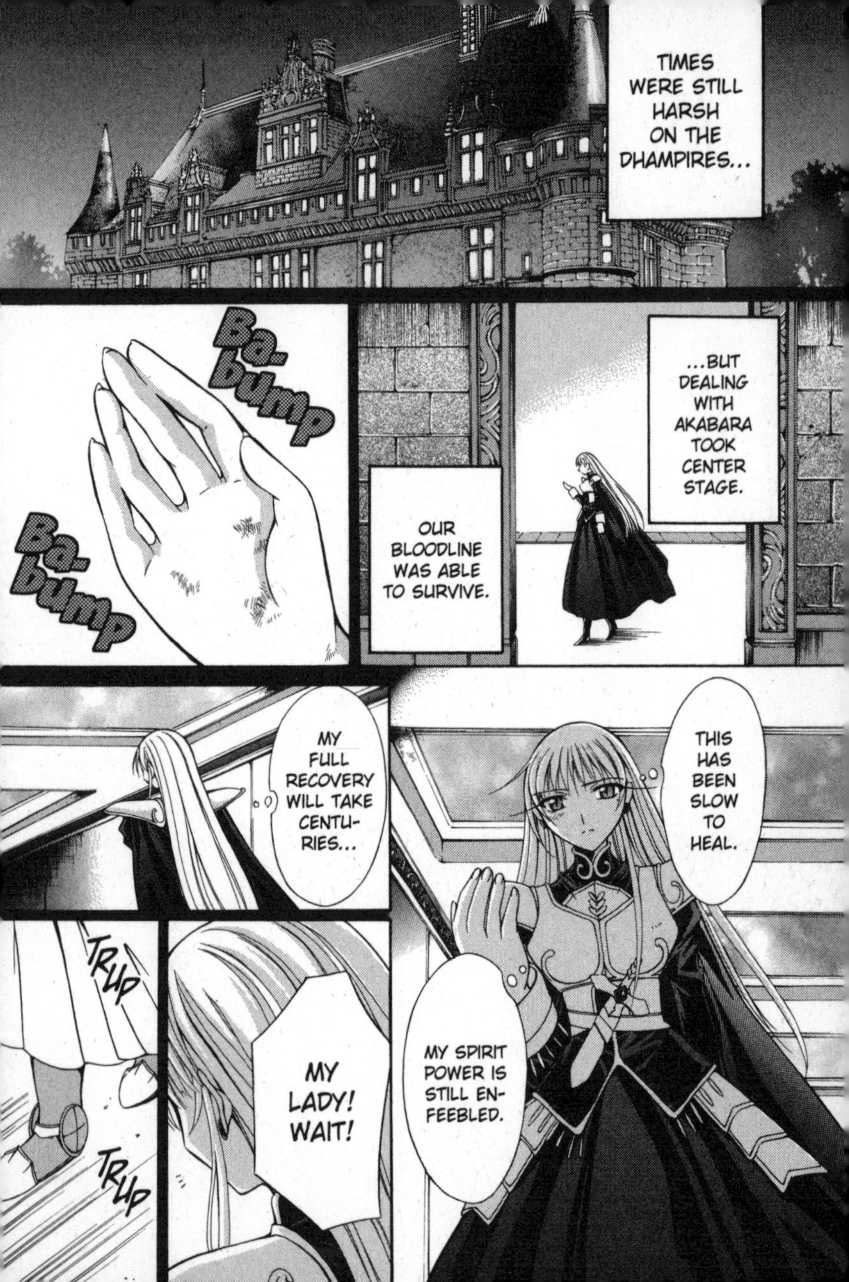
TIMES WERE STILL HARSH ON THE DHAMPIRES...
...BUT DEALING WITH AKABARA TOOK CENTER STAGE.
OUR BLOODLINE WAS ABLE TO SURVIVE.
Ba-bump
Ba-bump
THIS HAS BEEN SLOW TO HEAL.
MY SPIRIT POWER IS STILL EN-FEEBLED.
MY FULL RECOVERY WILL TAKE CENTU-RIES...
MY LADY! WAIT!
TRUP
TRUP

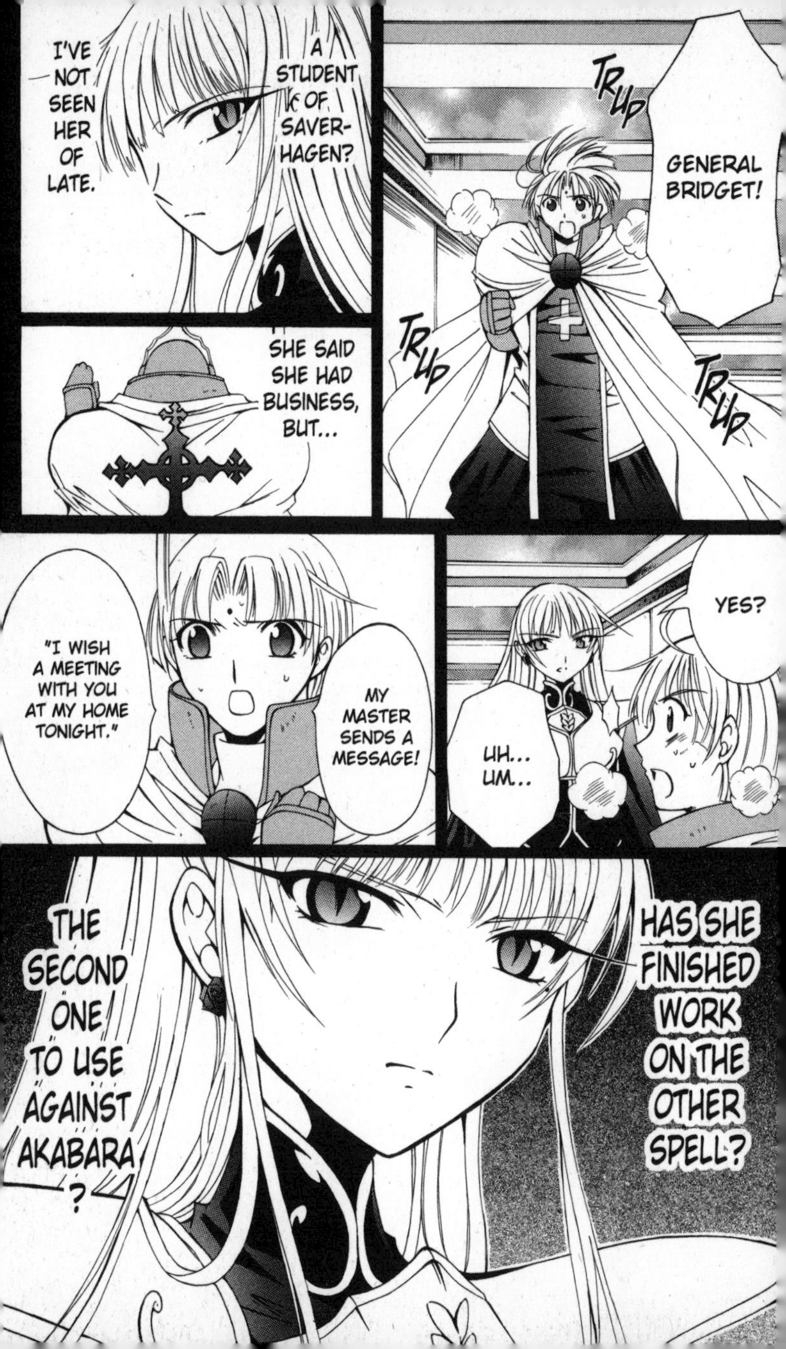
TRUP
GENERAL BRIDGET!
TRUP
TRUP
A STUDENT OF SAVER-HAGEN?
I'VE NOT SEEN HER OF LATE.
SHE SAID SHE HAD BUSINESS, BUT...
YES?
UH... UM...
MY MASTER SENDS A MESSAGE!
"I WISH A MEETING WITH YOU AT MY HOME TONIGHT."
HAS SHE FINISHED WORK ON THE OTHER SPELL?
THE SECOND ONE TO USE AGAINST AKABARA?

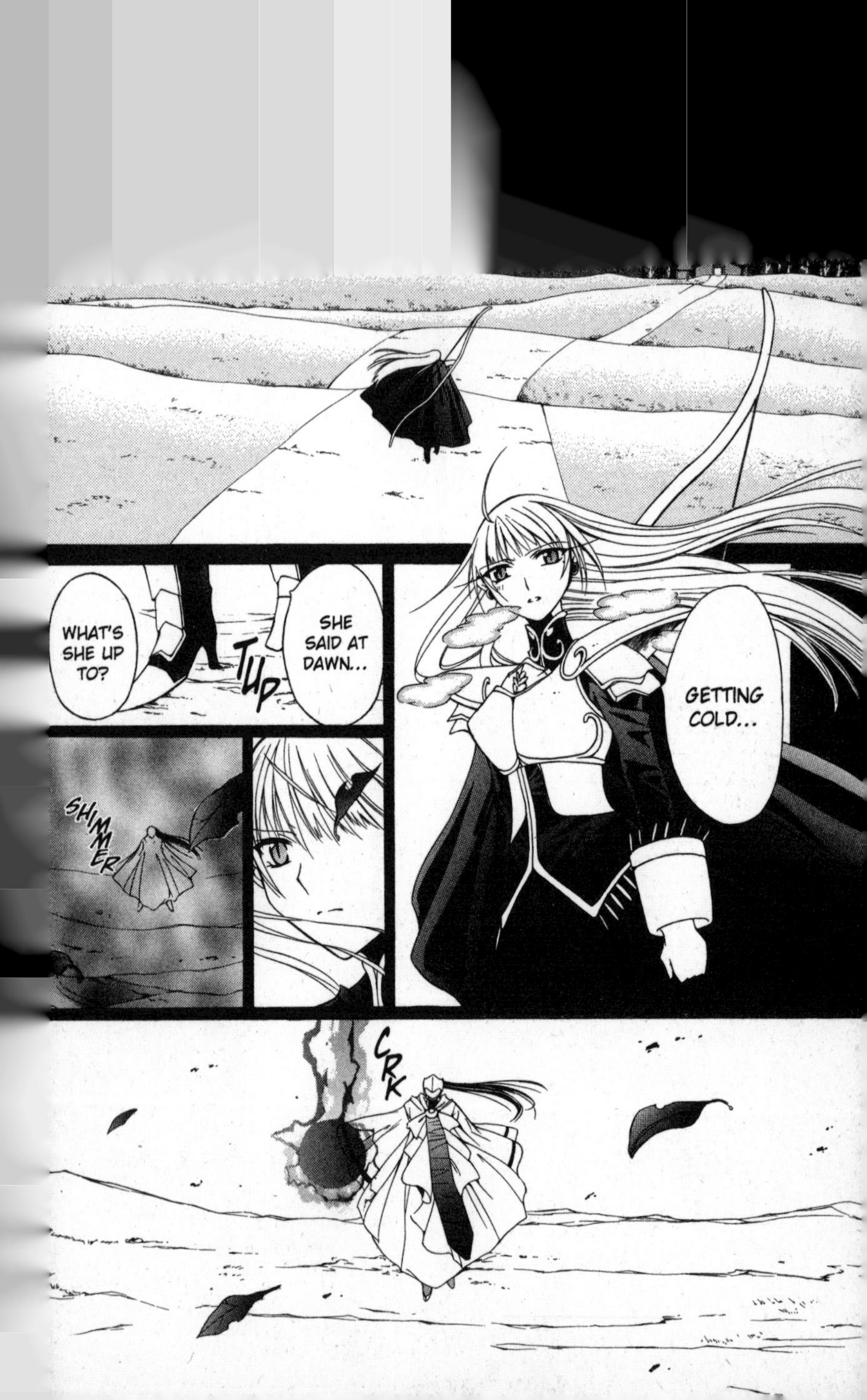
GETTING COLD...
SHE SAID AT DAWN...
TUP
WHAT'S SHE UP TO?
SHIMMER
CRK

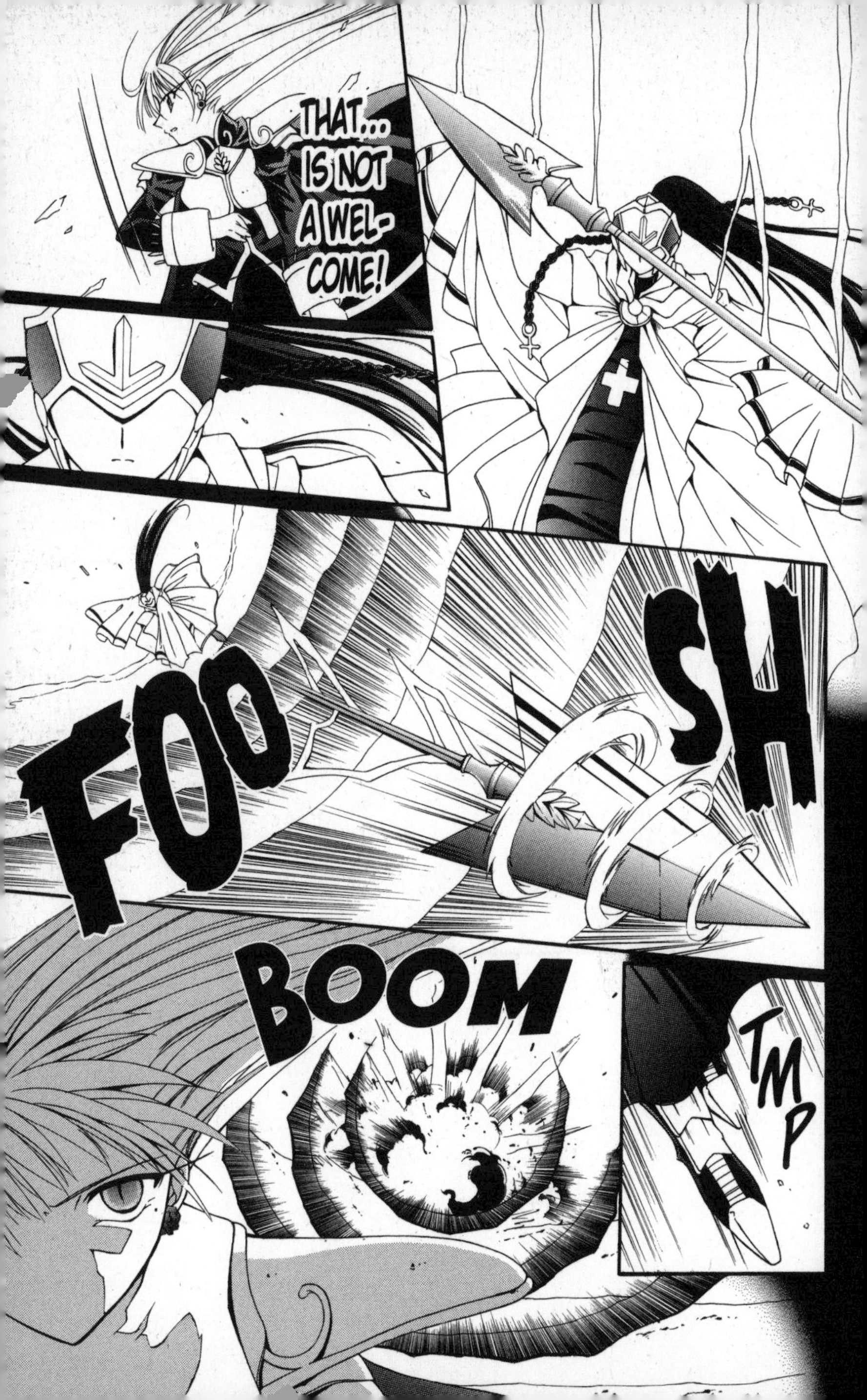
THAT... IS NOT A WEL-COME!
FOOSH
BOOM
TMP

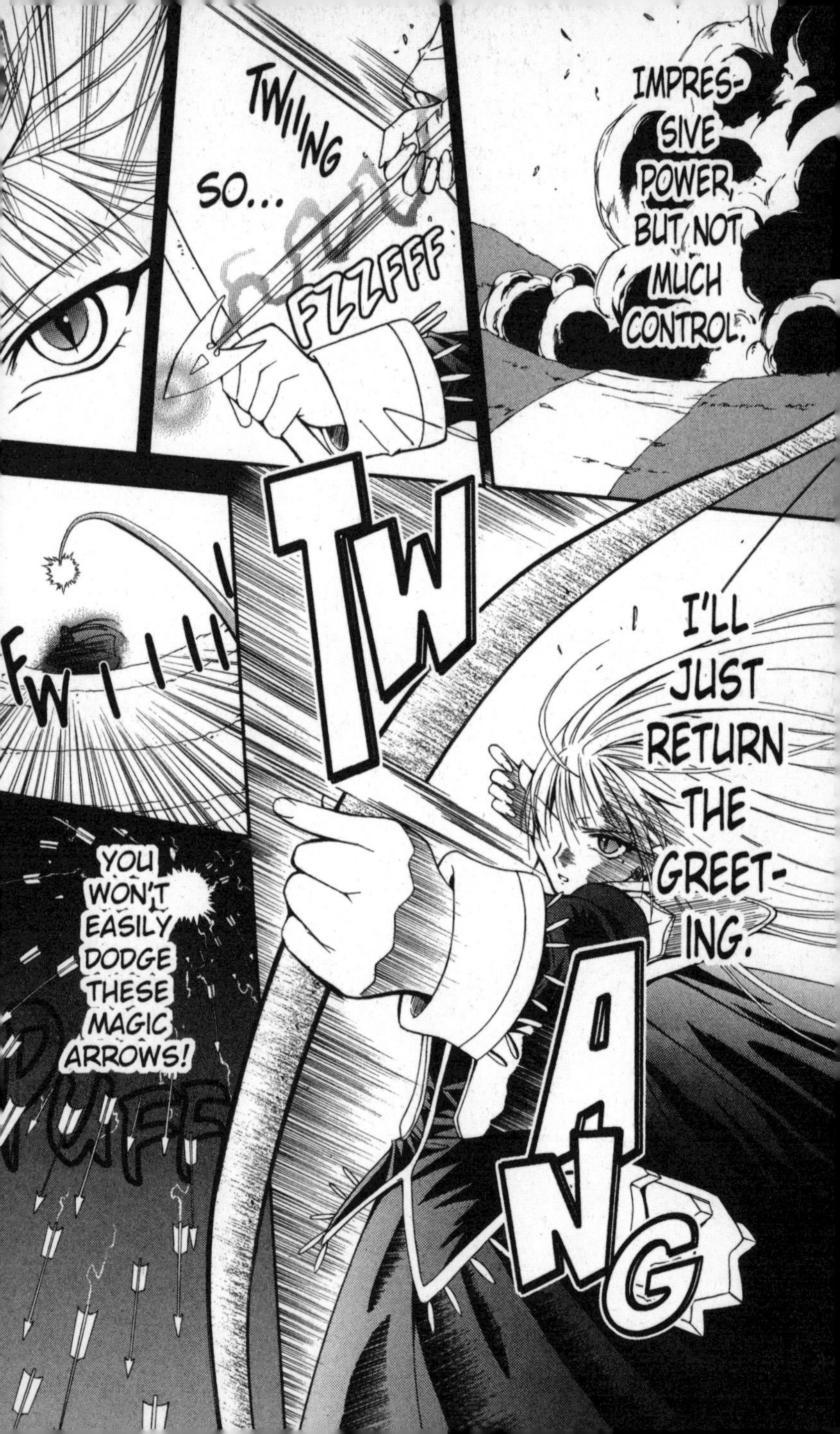
IMPRES-SIVE POWER, BUT NOT MUCH CONTROL.
TWIIING
SO...
FZZFFF
I'LL JUST RETURN THE GREET-ING.
TWANG
FWIIII
YOU WON'T EASILY DODGE THESE MAGIC ARROWS!
PUFF

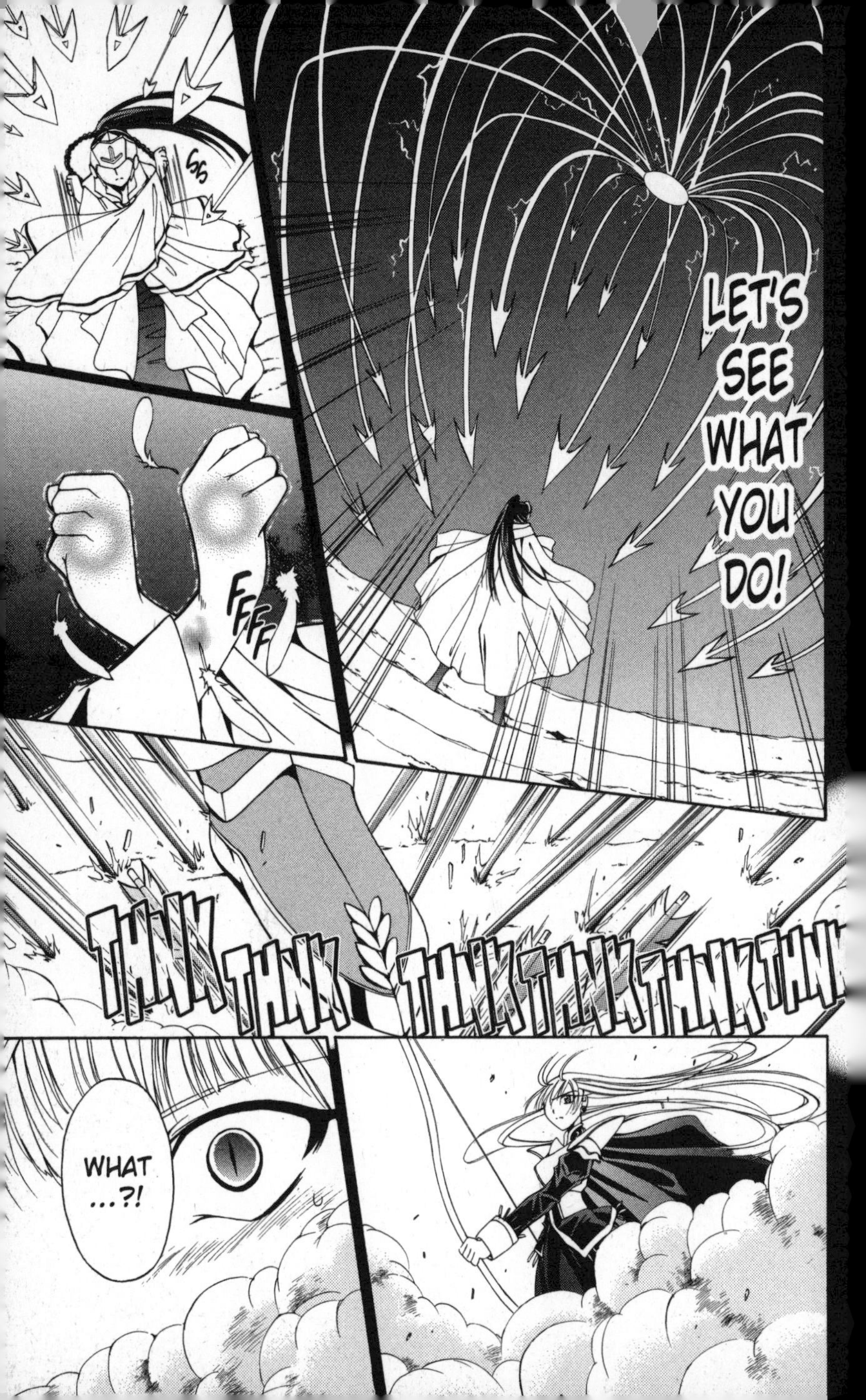
LET'S SEE WHAT YOU DO!
SS
FFFF
THNK
THNK
THNK
THNK
THNK
THNK
WHAT ...?!

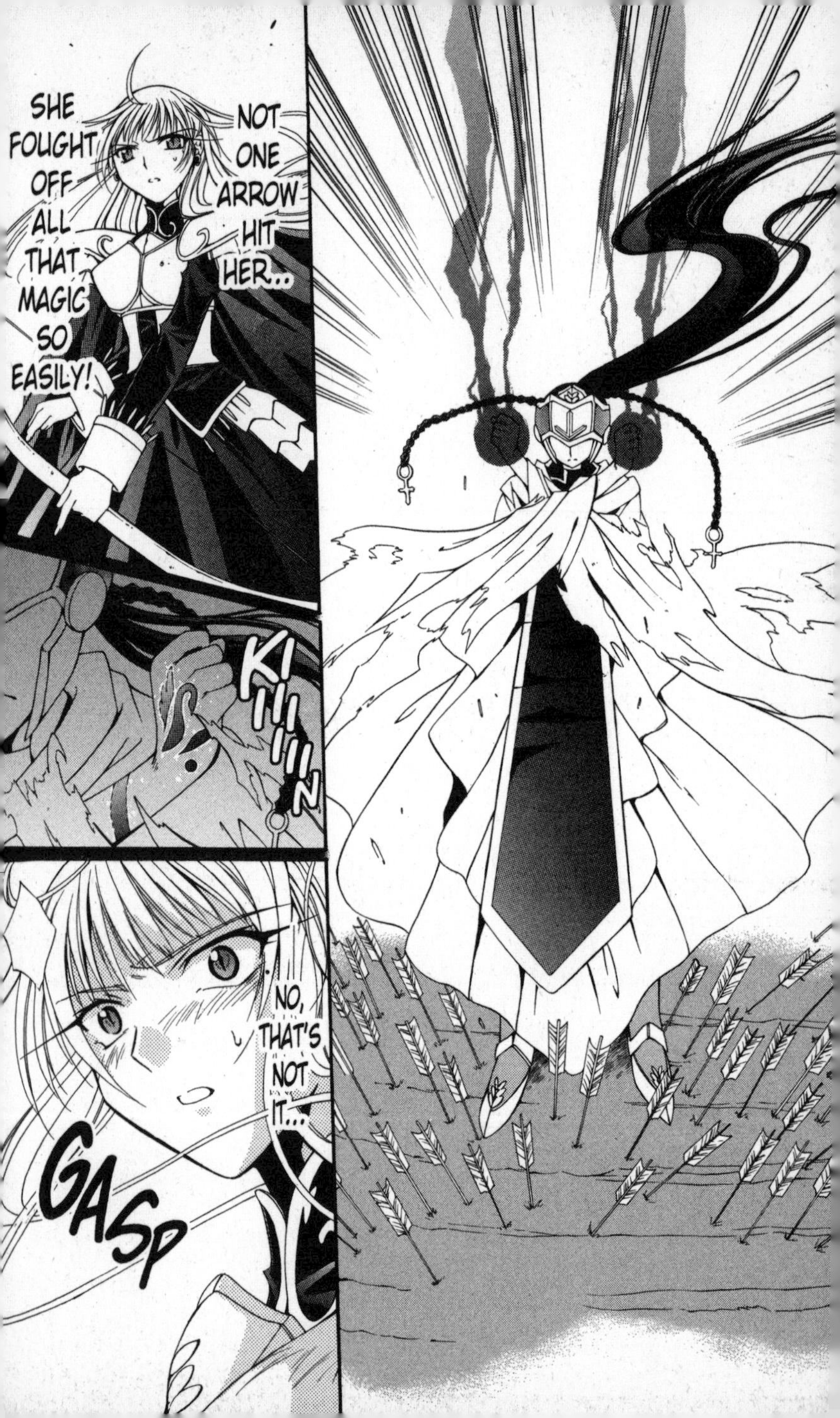
NOT ONE ARROW HIT HER...
SHE FOUGHT OFF ALL THAT MAGIC SO EASILY!
KIIIIIIIN
NO, THAT'S NOT IT...
GASP

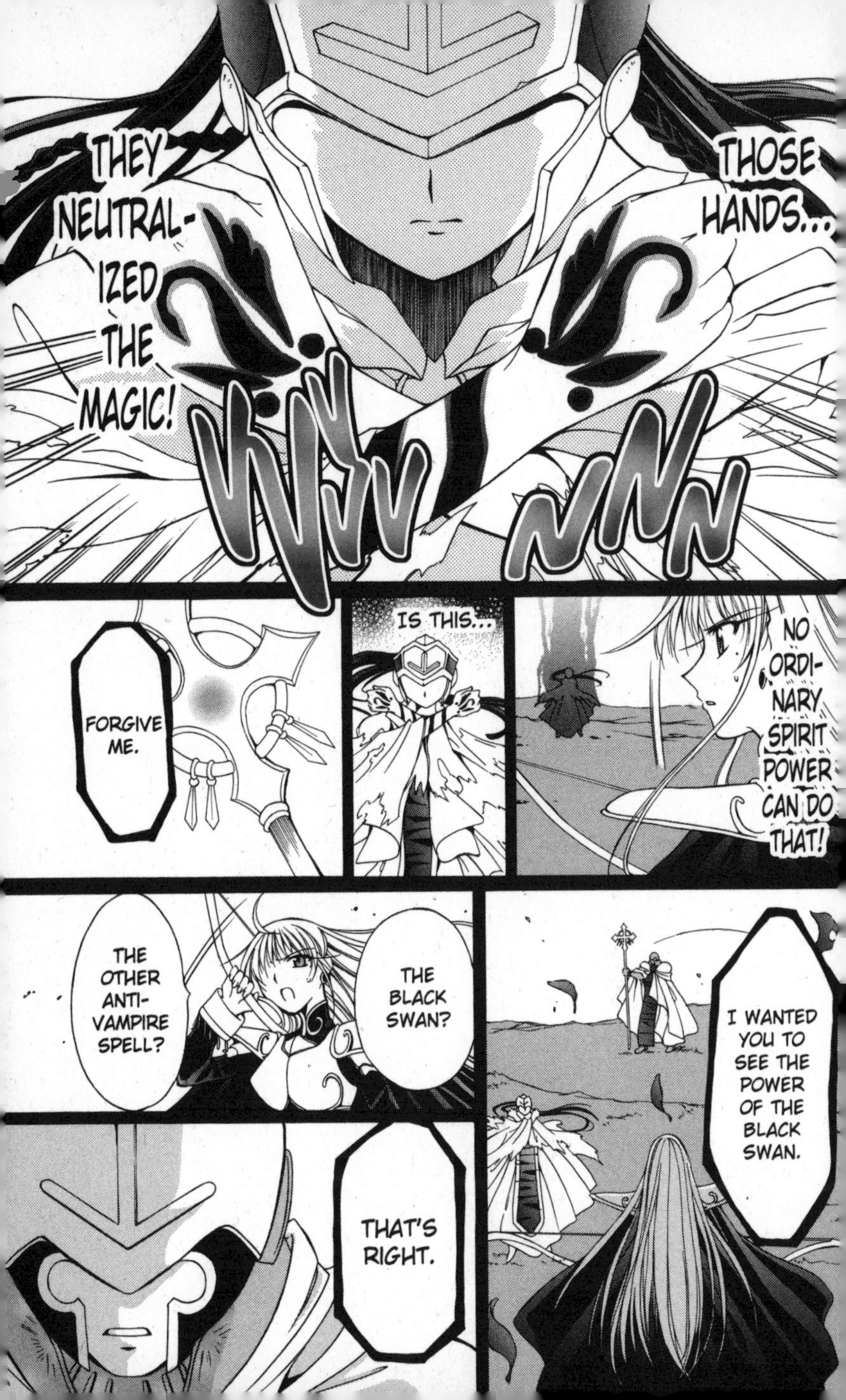

THOSE HANDS...
THEY NEUTRAL-IZED THE MAGIC!
NO ORDINARY SPIRIT POWER CAN DO THAT!
IS THIS...
FORGIVE ME.
I WANTED YOU TO SEE THE POWER OF THE BLACK SWAN.
THE BLACK SWAN?
THE OTHER ANTI-VAMPIRE SPELL?
THAT'S RIGHT.

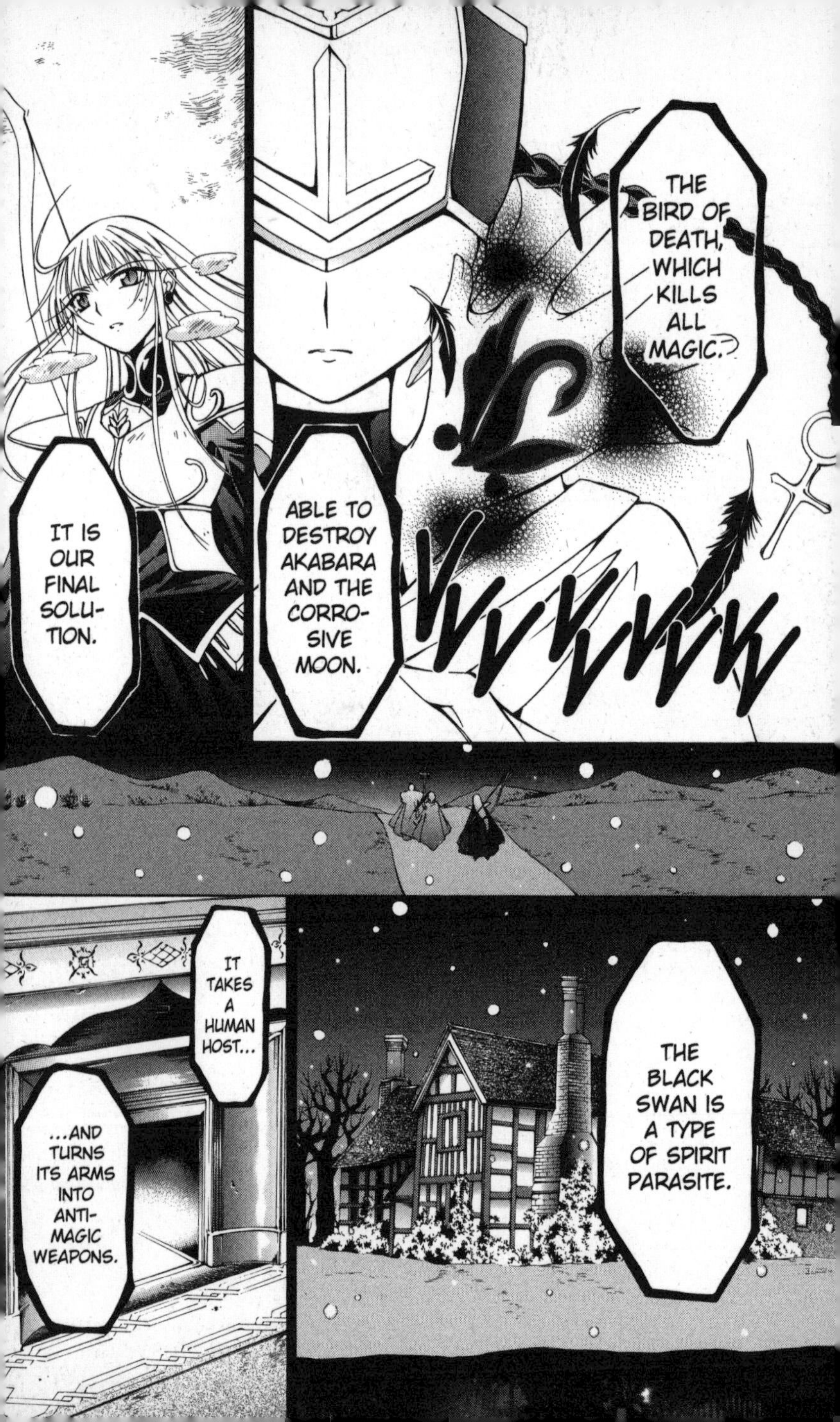
THE BIRD OF DEATH, WHICH KILLS ALL MAGIC.
ABLE TO DESTROY AKABARA AND THE CORROSIVE MOON.
IT IS OUR FINAL SOLUTION.
THE BLACK SWAN IS A TYPE OF SPIRIT PARASITE.
IT TAKES A HUMAN HOST...
...AND TURNS ITS ARMS INTO ANTI-MAGIC WEAPONS.

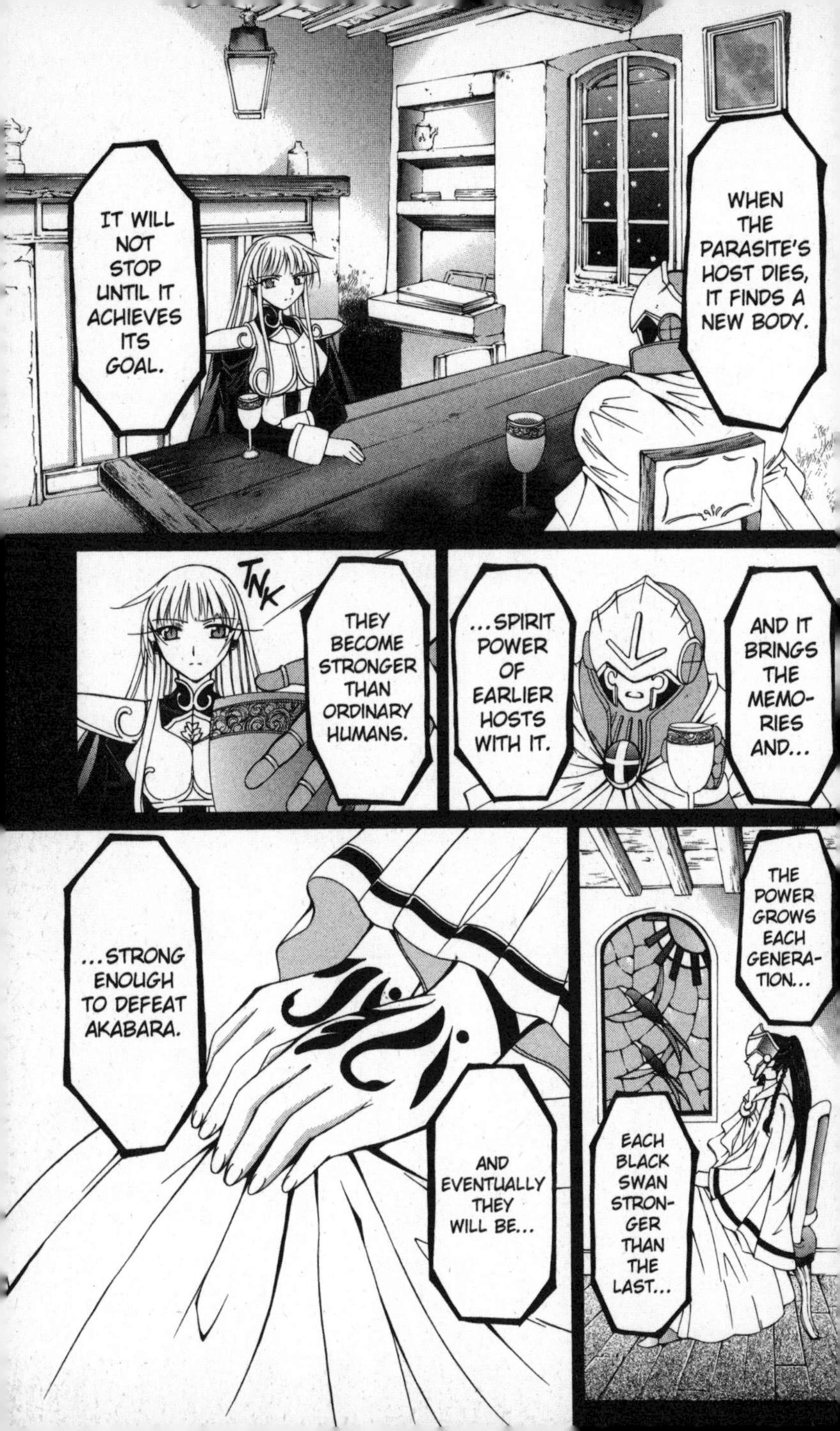
WHEN THE PARASITE'S HOST DIES, IT FINDS A NEW BODY.
IT WILL NOT STOP UNTIL IT ACHIEVES ITS GOAL.
AND IT BRINGS THE MEMO-RIES AND...
...SPIRIT POWER OF EARLIER HOSTS WITH IT.
THEY BECOME STRONGER THAN ORDINARY HUMANS.
TNK
THE POWER GROWS EACH GENERA-TION...
EACH BLACK SWAN STRON-GER THAN THE LAST...
AND EVENTUALLY THEY WILL BE...
...STRONG ENOUGH TO DEFEAT AKABARA.

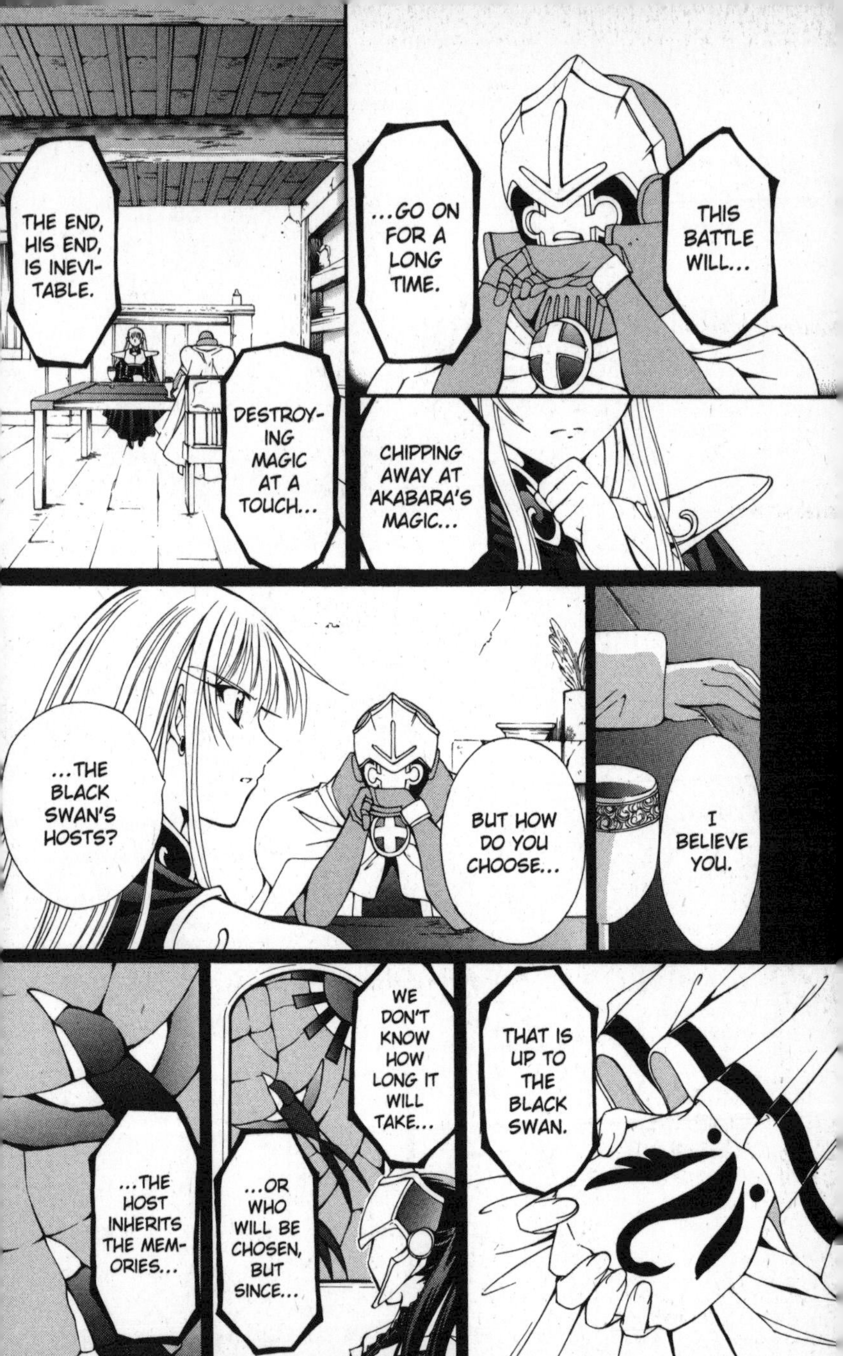
THIS BATTLE WILL...
...GO ON FOR A LONG TIME.
CHIPPING AWAY AT AKABARA'S MAGIC...
DESTROYING MAGIC AT A TOUCH...
THE END, HIS END, IS INEVITABLE.
I BELIEVE YOU.
BUT HOW DO YOU CHOOSE...
...THE BLACK SWAN'S HOSTS?
THAT IS UP TO THE BLACK SWAN.
WE DON'T KNOW HOW LONG IT WILL TAKE...
...OR WHO WILL BE CHOSEN, BUT SINCE...
...THE HOST INHERITS THE MEMORIES...

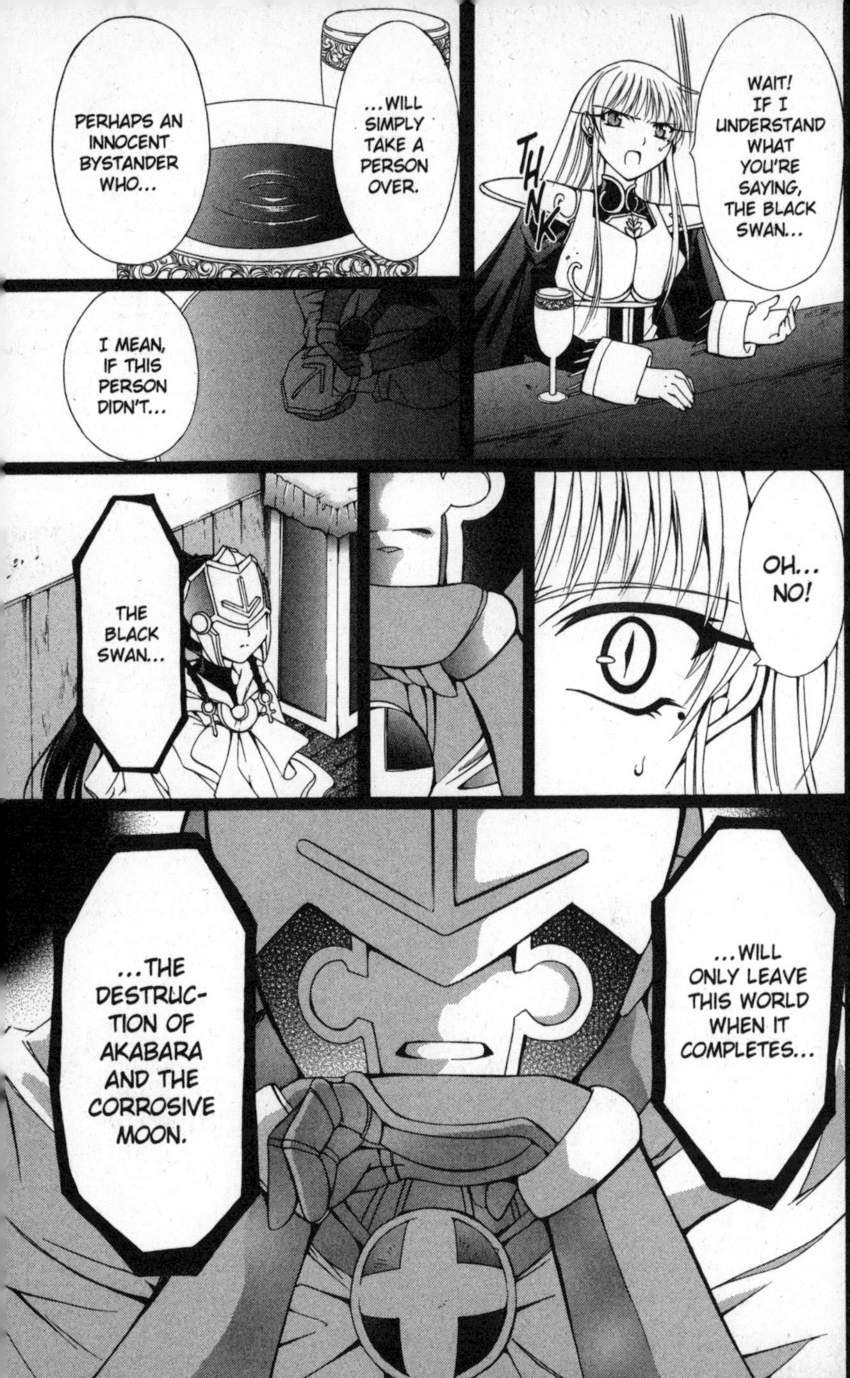
WAIT! IF I UNDERSTAND WHAT YOU'RE SAYING, THE BLACK SWAN...
THNK
...WILL SIMPLY TAKE A PERSON OVER.
PERHAPS AN INNOCENT BYSTANDER WHO...
I MEAN, IF THIS PERSON DIDN'T...
OH... NO!
THE BLACK SWAN...
...WILL ONLY LEAVE THIS WORLD WHEN IT COMPLETES...
...THE DESTRUC-TION OF AKABARA AND THE CORROSIVE MOON.

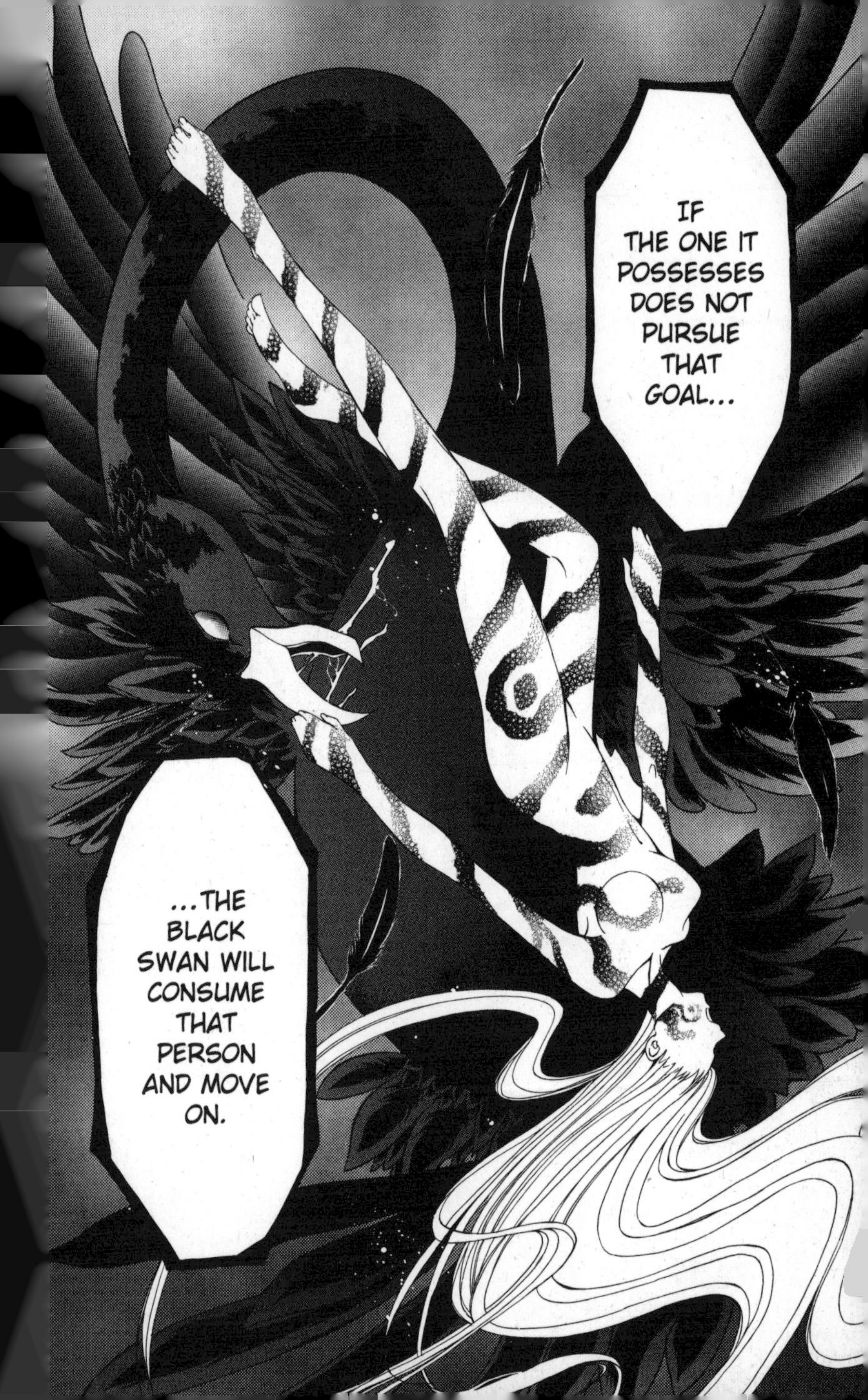
IF THE ONE IT POSSESSES DOES NOT PURSUE THAT GOAL...
...THE BLACK SWAN WILL CONSUME THAT PERSON AND MOVE ON.

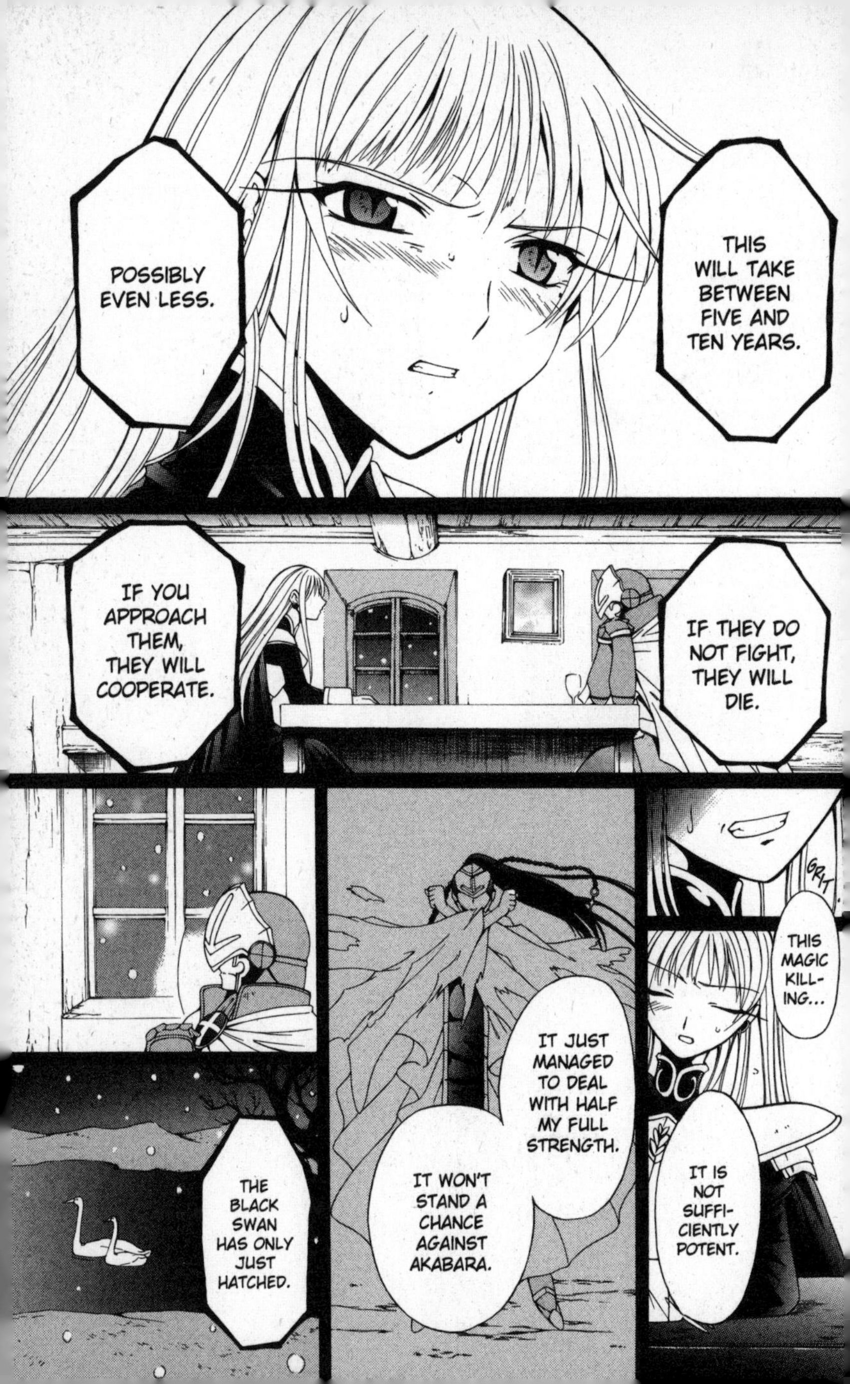
THIS WILL TAKE BETWEEN FIVE AND TEN YEARS.
POSSIBLY EVEN LESS.
IF THEY DO NOT FIGHT, THEY WILL DIE.
IF YOU APPROACH THEM, THEY WILL COOPERATE.
GRIT
THIS MAGIC KILLING...
IT IS NOT SUFFICIENTLY POTENT.
IT JUST MANAGED TO DEAL WITH HALF MY FULL STRENGTH.
IT WON'T STAND A CHANCE AGAINST AKABARA.
THE BLACK SWAN HAS ONLY JUST HATCHED.

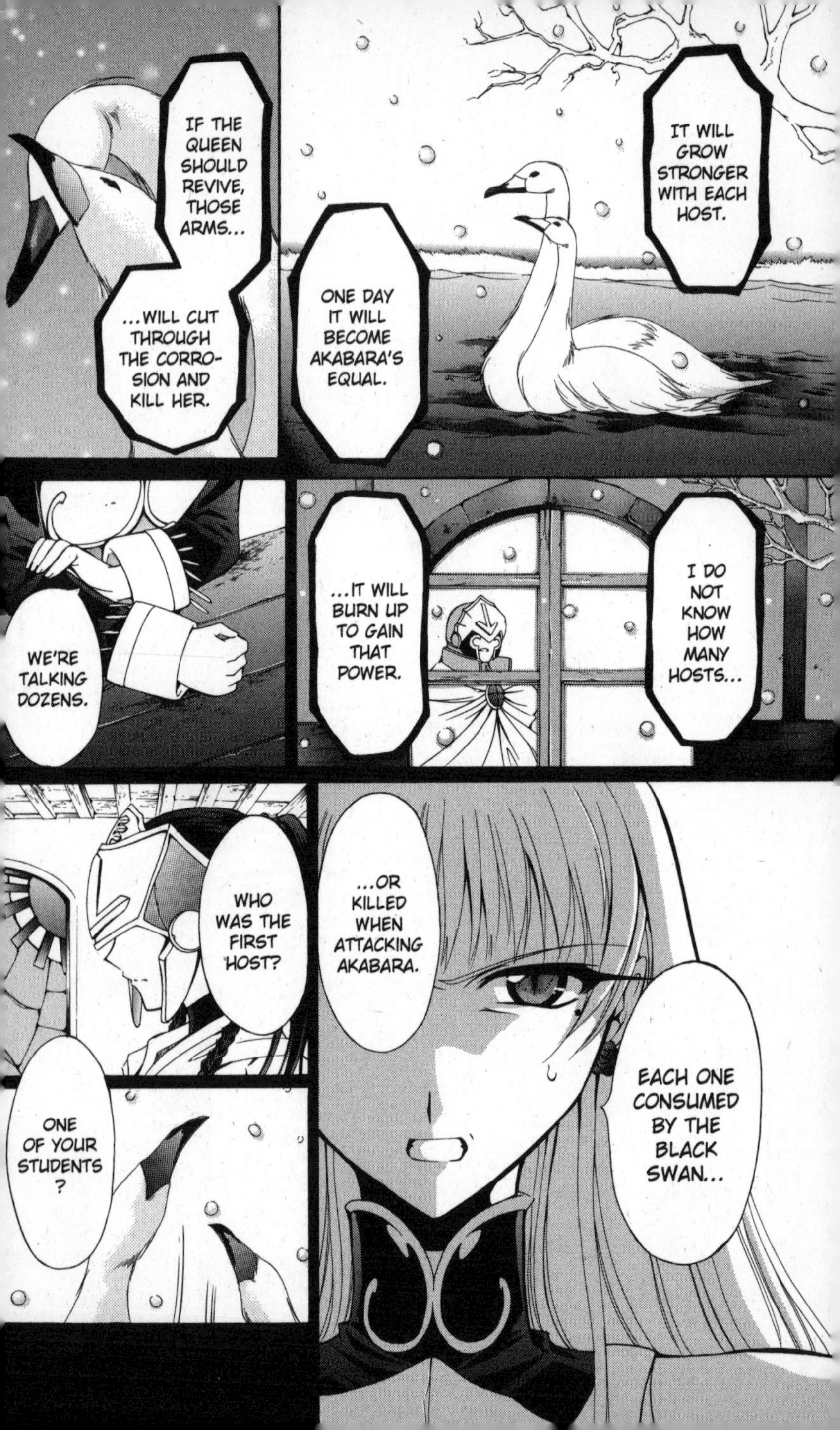
IT WILL GROW STRONGER WITH EACH HOST.
ONE DAY IT WILL BECOME AKABARA'S EQUAL.
IF THE QUEEN SHOULD REVIVE, THOSE ARMS...
...WILL CUT THROUGH THE CORRO-SION AND KILL HER.
I DO NOT KNOW HOW MANY HOSTS...
...IT WILL BURN UP TO GAIN THAT POWER.
WE'RE TALKING DOZENS.
EACH ONE CONSUMED BY THE BLACK SWAN...
...OR KILLED WHEN ATTACKING AKABARA.
WHO WAS THE FIRST HOST?
ONE OF YOUR STUDENTS?

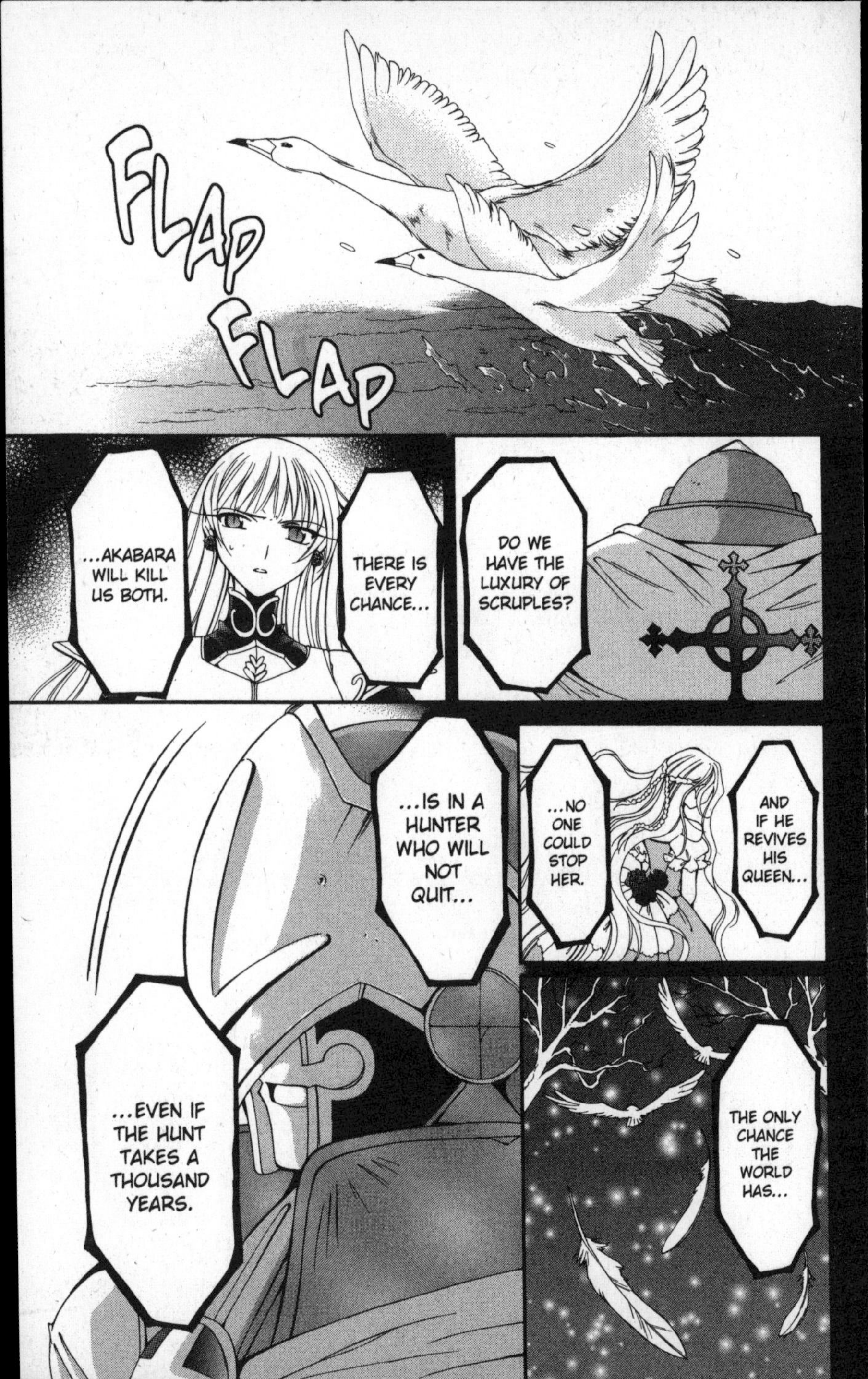
FLAP FLAP
DO WE HAVE THE LUXURY OF SCRUPLES?
THERE IS EVERY CHANCE...
...AKABARA WILL KILL US BOTH.
AND IF HE REVIVES HIS QUEEN...
...NO ONE COULD STOP HER.
THE ONLY CHANCE THE WORLD HAS...
...IS IN A HUNTER WHO WILL NOT QUIT...
...EVEN IF THE HUNT TAKES A THOUSAND YEARS.

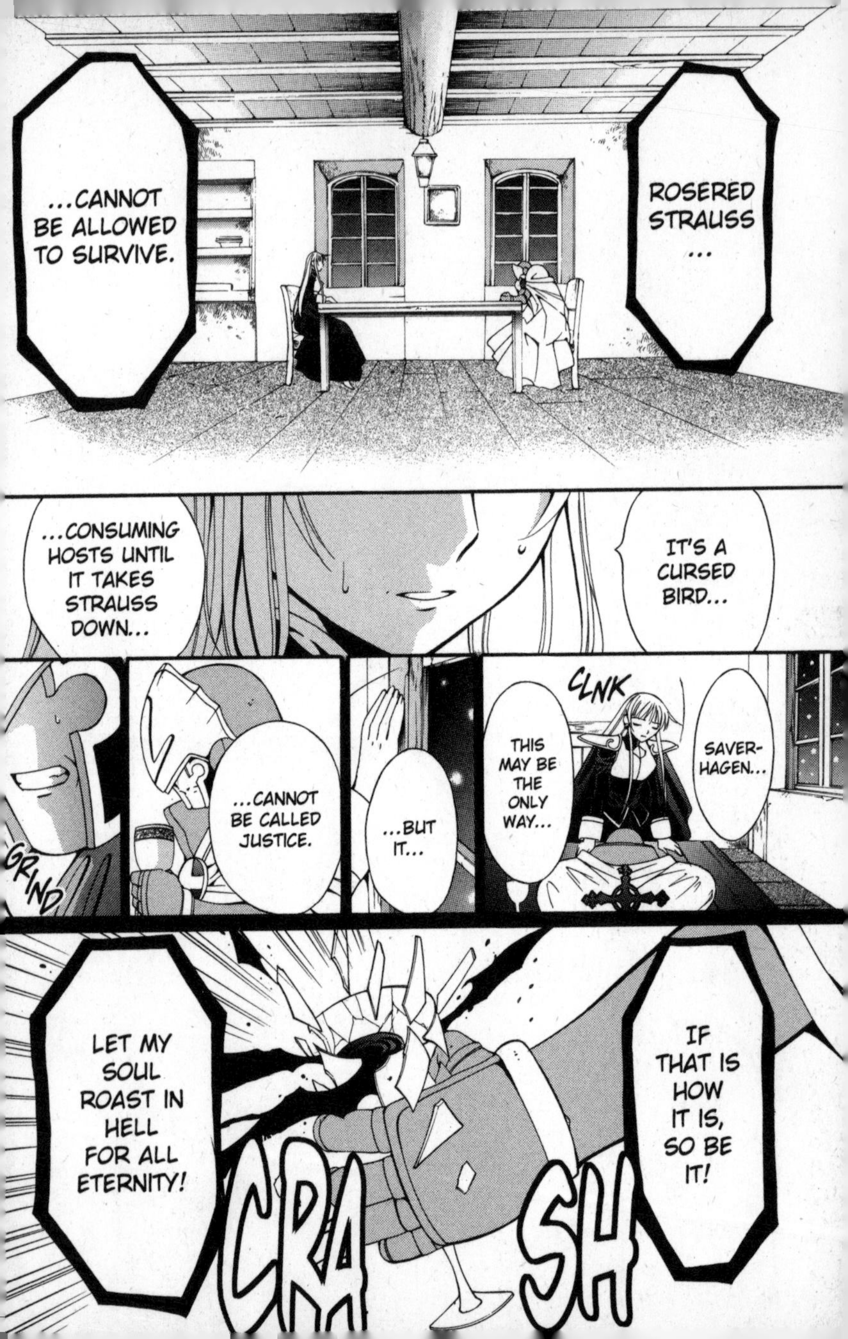
ROSERED STRAUSS...
...CANNOT BE ALLOWED TO SURVIVE.
IT'S A CURSED BIRD...
...CONSUMING HOSTS UNTIL IT TAKES STRAUSS DOWN...
SAVER-HAGEN...
CLNK
THIS MAY BE THE ONLY WAY...
...BUT IT...
...CANNOT BE CALLED JUSTICE.
GRIND
IF THAT IS HOW IT IS, SO BE IT!
LET MY SOUL ROAST IN HELL FOR ALL ETERNITY!
CRASH

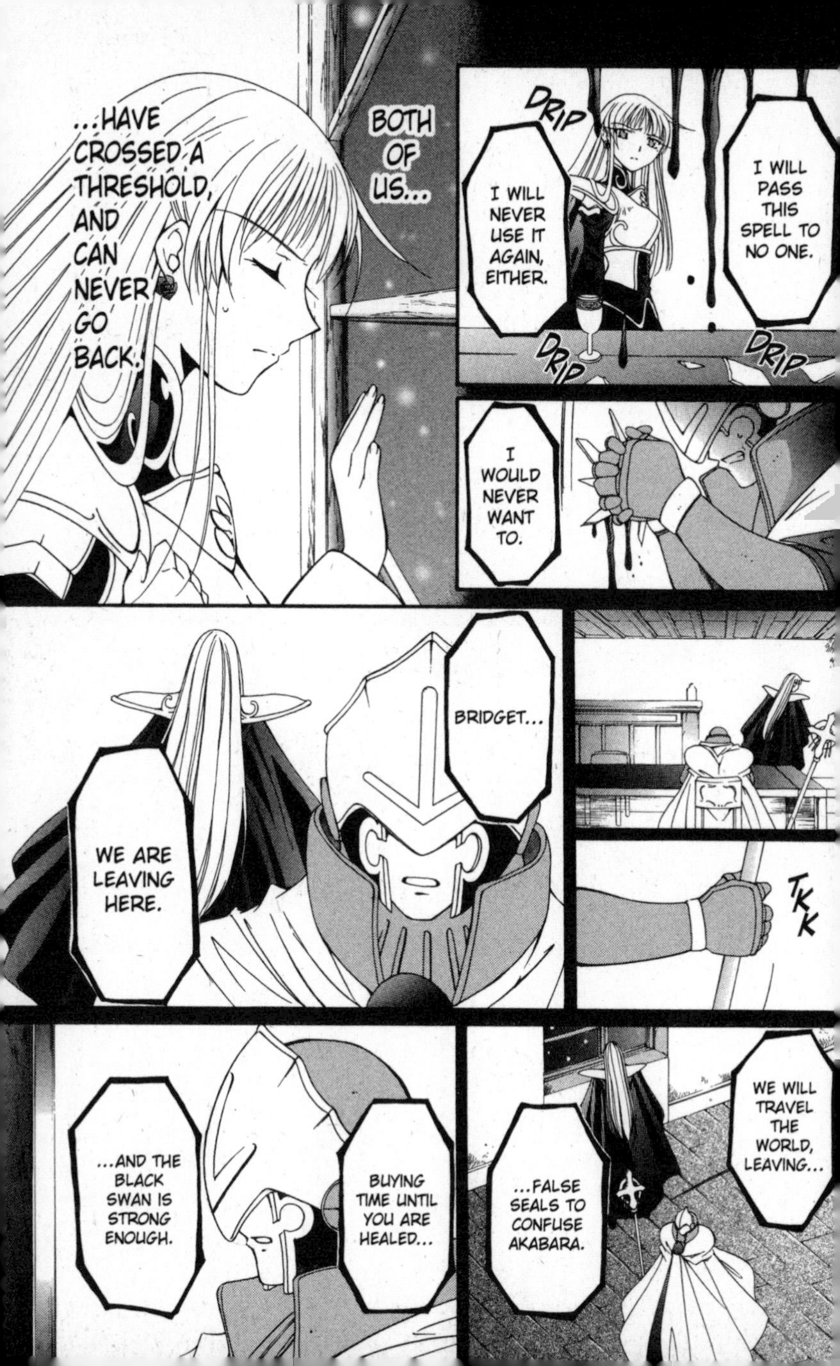
DRIP
I WILL PASS THIS SPELL TO NO ONE.
I WILL NEVER USE IT AGAIN, EITHER.
DRIP
DRIP
I WOULD NEVER WANT TO.
BOTH OF US...
...HAVE CROSSED A THRESHOLD, AND CAN NEVER GO BACK.
TKK
BRIDGET...
WE ARE LEAVING HERE.
WE WILL TRAVEL THE WORLD, LEAVING...
...FALSE SEALS TO CONFUSE AKABARA.
BUYING TIME UNTIL YOU ARE HEALED...
...AND THE BLACK SWAN IS STRONG ENOUGH.

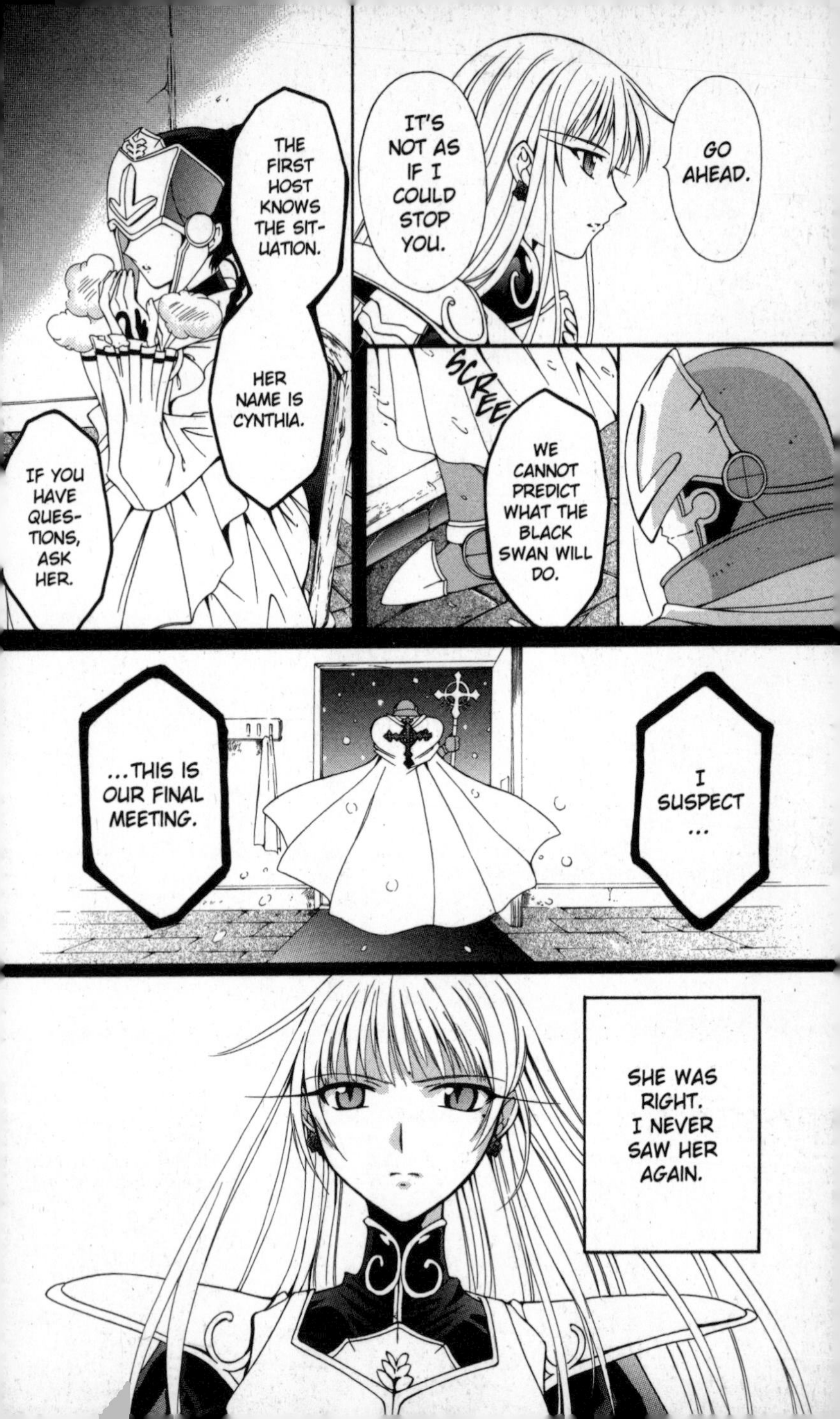
GO AHEAD.
IT'S NOT AS IF I COULD STOP YOU.
SCREE
WE CANNOT PREDICT WHAT THE BLACK SWAN WILL DO.
THE FIRST HOST KNOWS THE SIT-UATION.
HER NAME IS CYNTHIA.
IF YOU HAVE QUES-TIONS, ASK HER.
I SUSPECT...
...THIS IS OUR FINAL MEETING.
SHE WAS RIGHT. I NEVER SAW HER AGAIN.

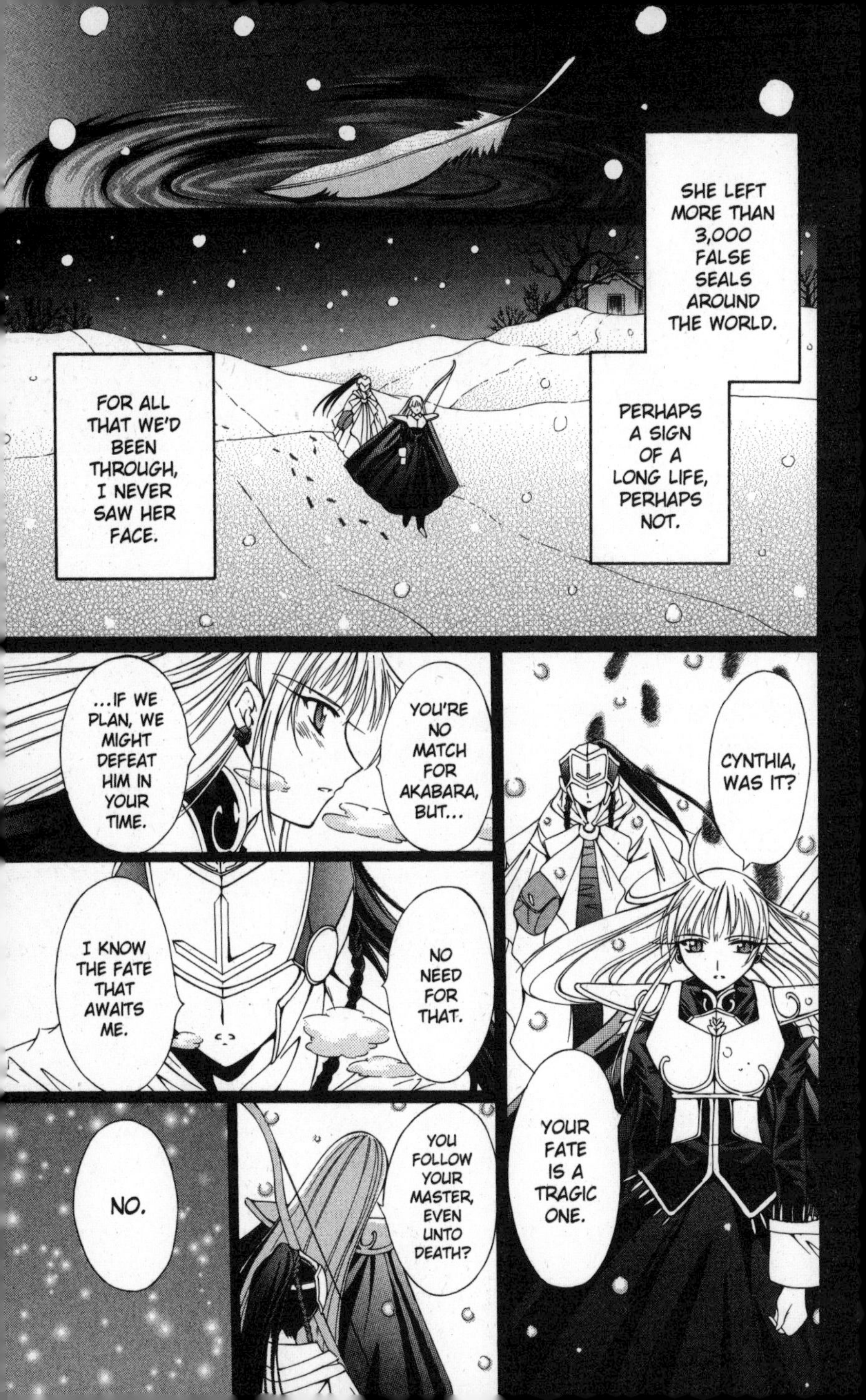
SHE LEFT MORE THAN 3,000 FALSE SEALS AROUND THE WORLD.
PERHAPS A SIGN OF A LONG LIFE, PERHAPS NOT.
FOR ALL THAT WE'D BEEN THROUGH, I NEVER SAW HER FACE.
CYNTHIA, WAS IT?
YOUR FATE IS A TRAGIC ONE.
YOU'RE NO MATCH FOR AKABARA, BUT...
...IF WE PLAN, WE MIGHT DEFEAT HIM IN YOUR TIME.
NO NEED FOR THAT.
I KNOW THE FATE THAT AWAITS ME.
YOU FOLLOW YOUR MASTER, EVEN UNTO DEATH?
NO.

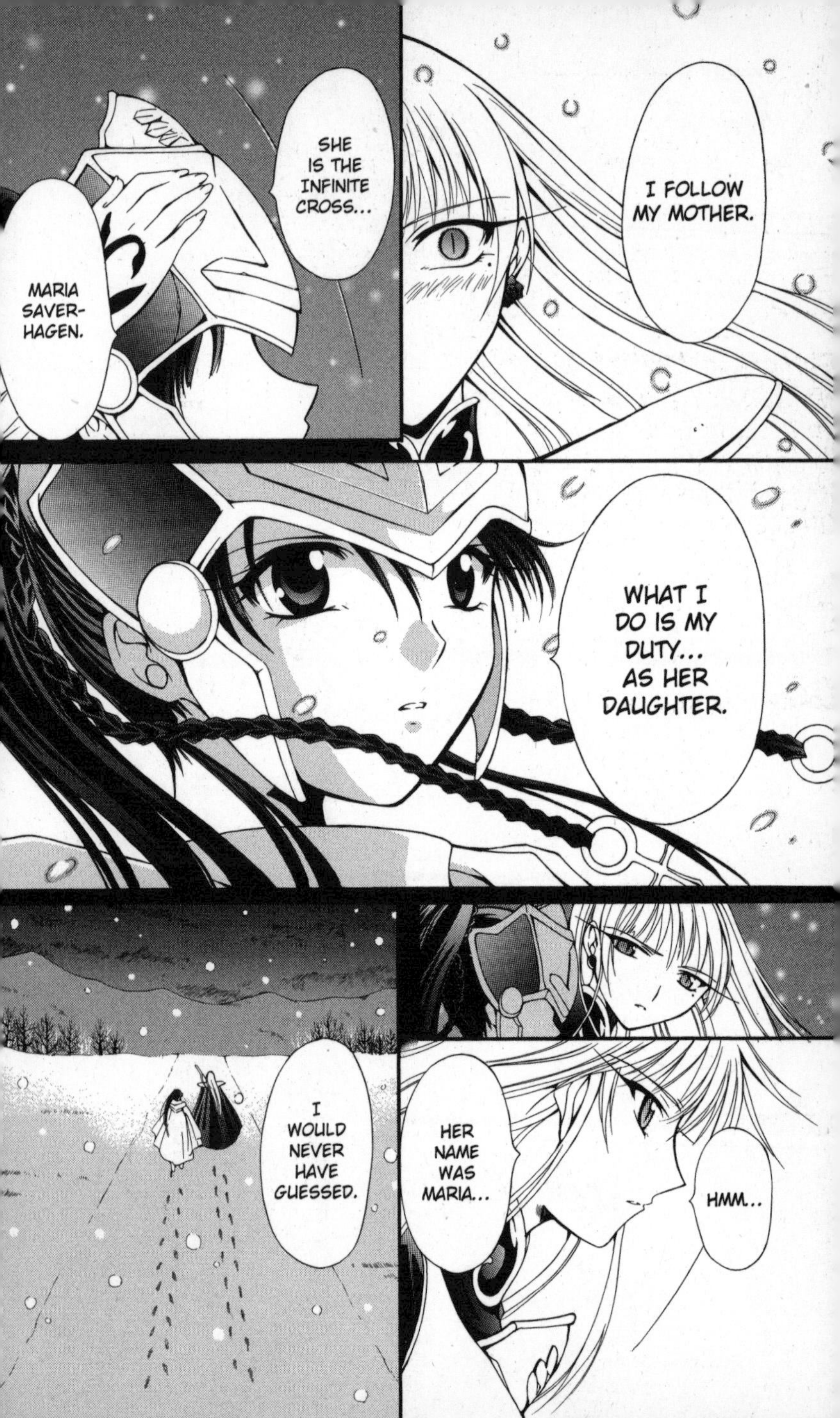
I FOLLOW MY MOTHER.
SHE IS THE INFINITE CROSS...
MARIA SAVER-HAGEN.
WHAT I DO IS MY DUTY... AS HER DAUGHTER.
HMM..
HER NAME WAS MARIA...
I WOULD NEVER HAVE GUESSED.

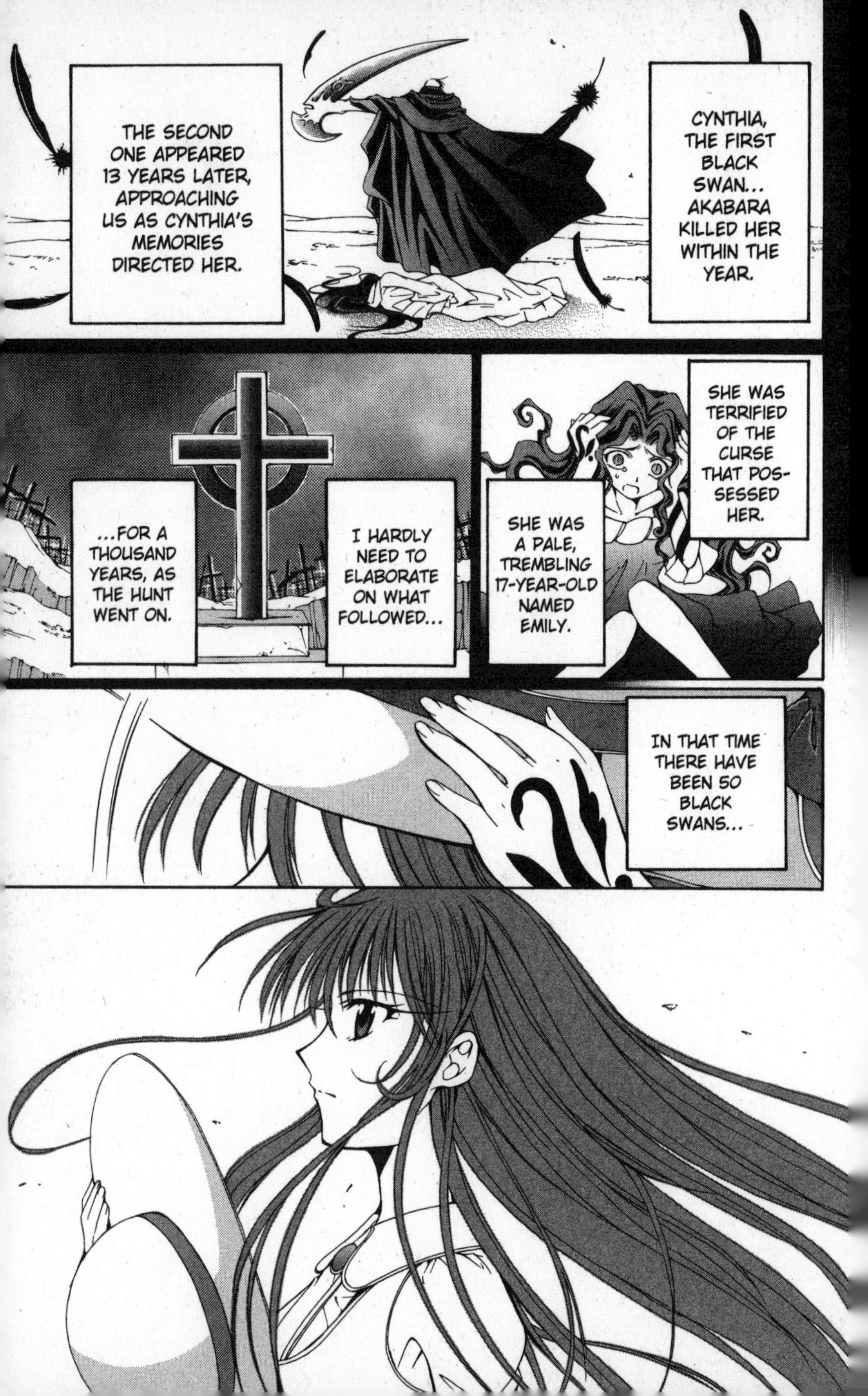
CYNTHIA, THE FIRST BLACK SWAN... AKABARA KILLED HER WITHIN THE YEAR.
THE SECOND ONE APPEARED 13 YEARS LATER, APPROACHING US AS CYNTHIA'S MEMORIES DIRECTED HER.
SHE WAS TERRIFIED OF THE CURSE THAT POS-SESSED HER.
SHE WAS A PALE, TREMBLING 17-YEAR-OLD NAMED EMILY.
I HARDLY NEED TO ELABORATE ON WHAT FOLLOWED...
...FOR A THOUSAND YEARS, AS THE HUNT WENT ON.
IN THAT TIME THERE HAVE BEEN 50 BLACK SWANS...

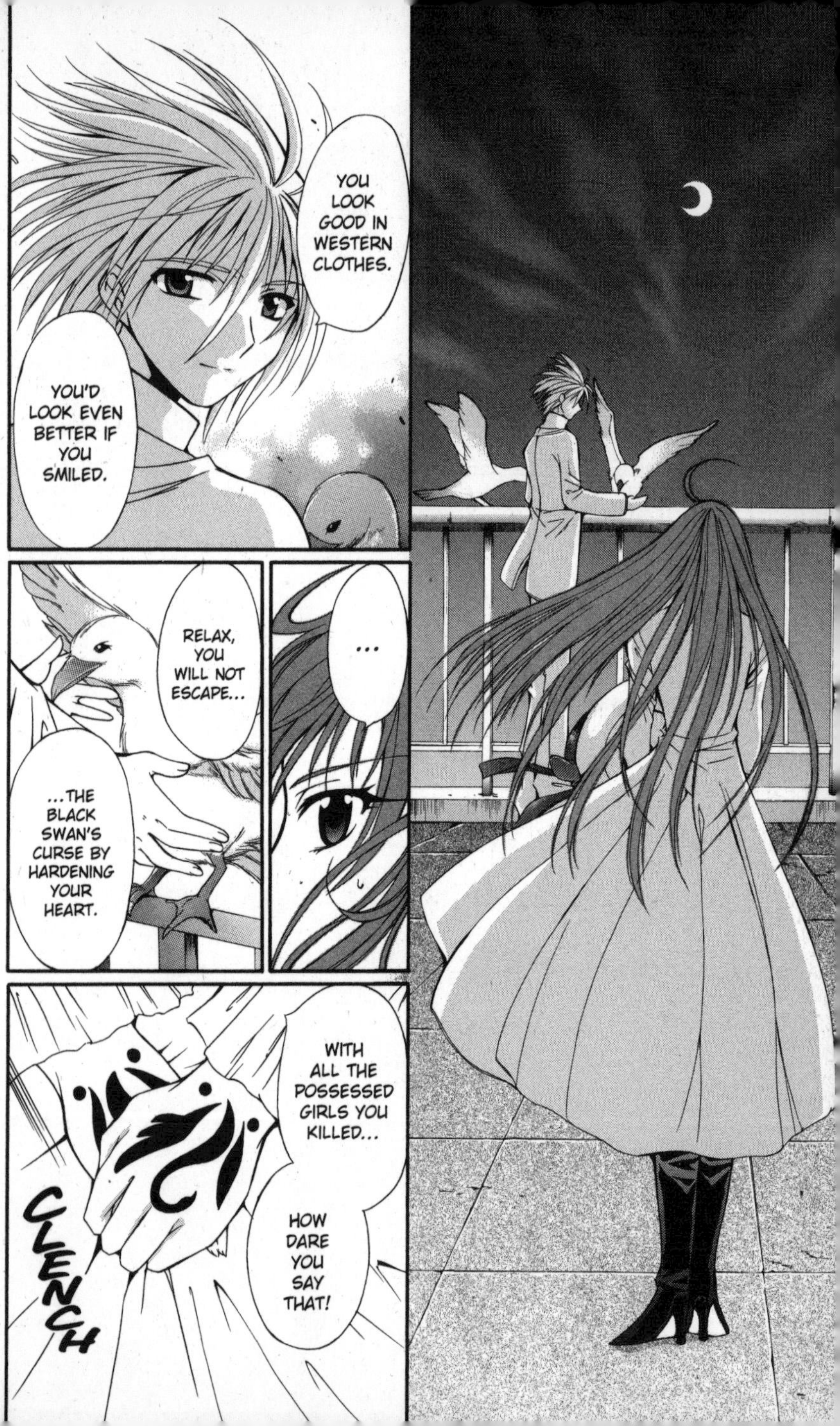
YOU LOOK GOOD IN WESTERN CLOTHES.
YOU'D LOOK EVEN BETTER IF YOU SMILED.
...
RELAX, YOU WILL NOT ESCAPE...
...THE BLACK SWAN'S CURSE BY HARDENING YOUR HEART.
WITH ALL THE POSSESSED GIRLS YOU KILLED...
HOW DARE YOU SAY THAT!
CLENCH

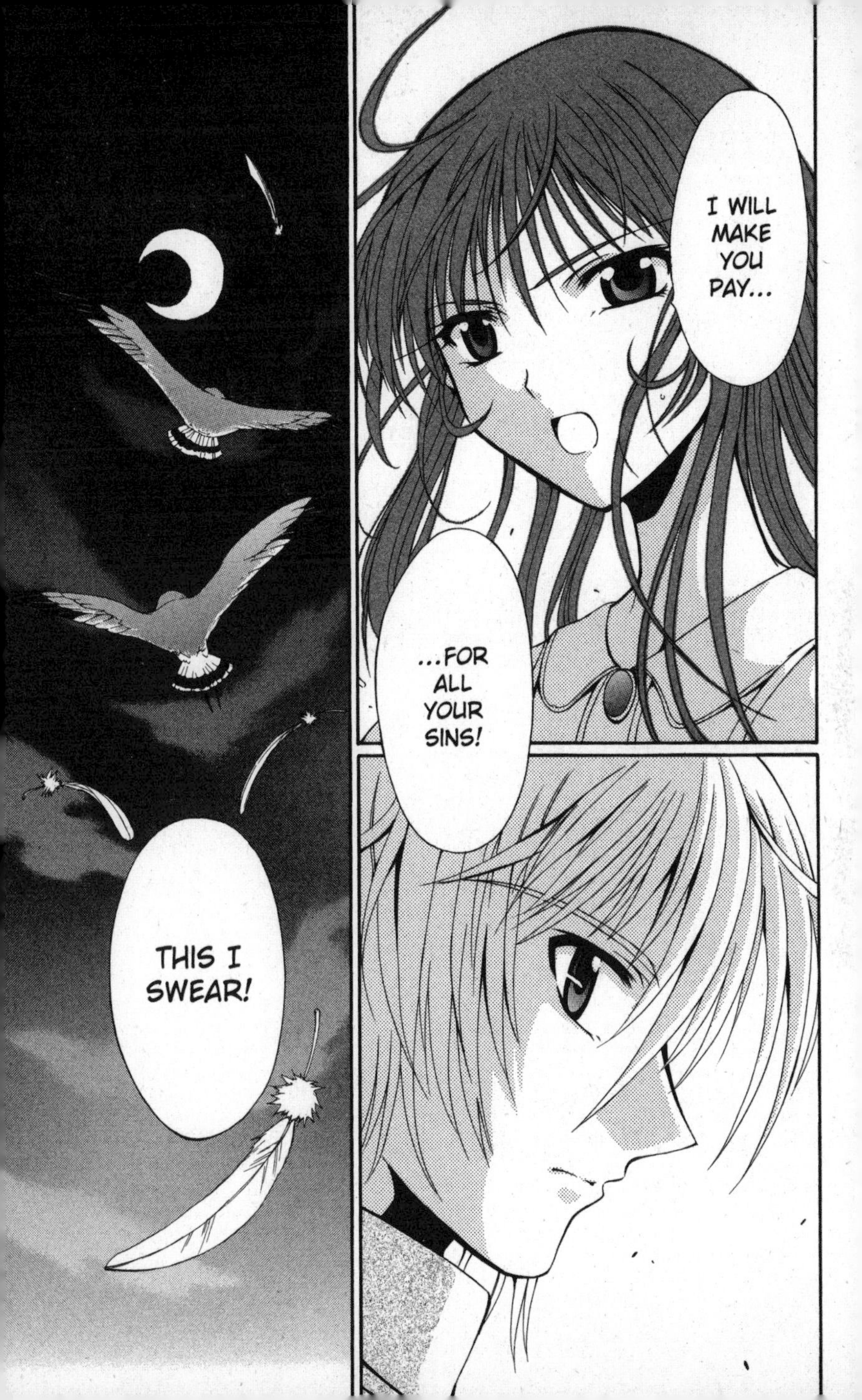
I WILL MAKE YOU PAY...
...FOR ALL YOUR SINS!
THIS I SWEAR!

THE RECORD OF A

FALLEN VAMPIRE

Chapter 26: Out of the Maze

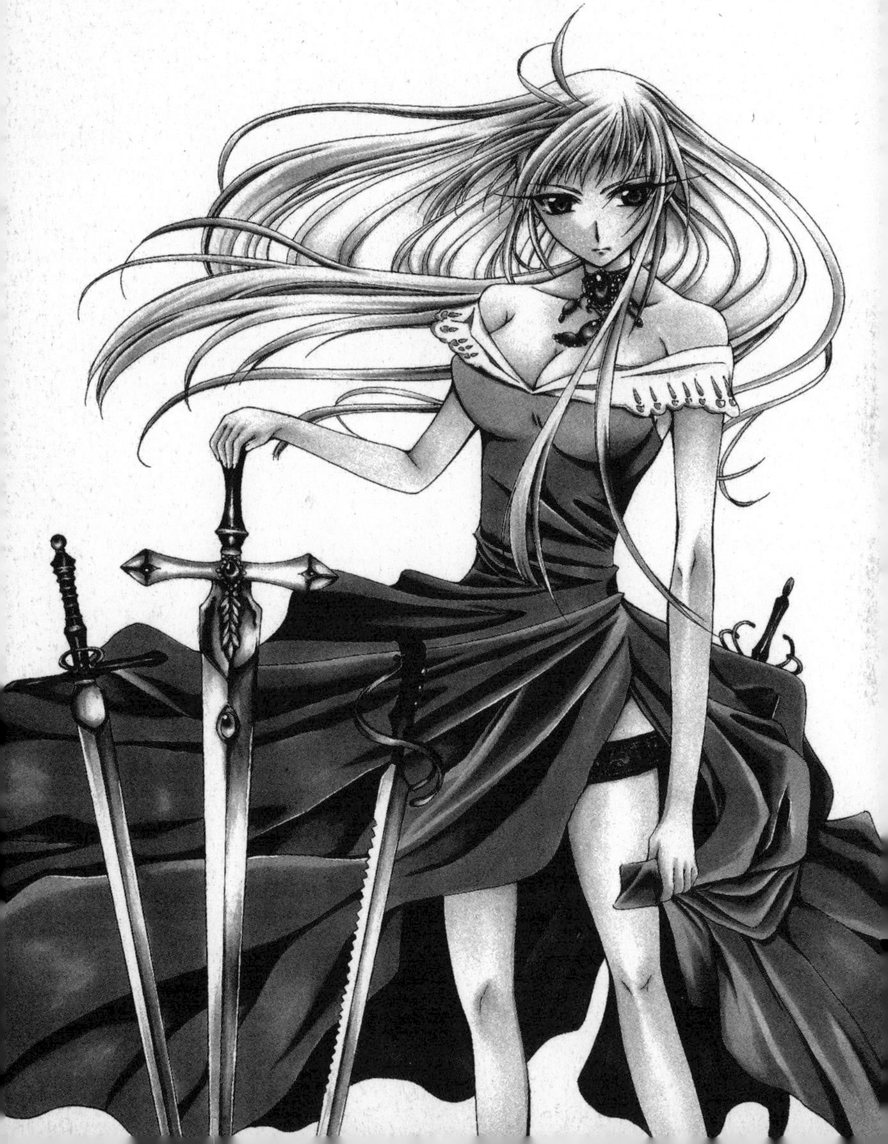

THE RECORD OF A

FALLEN VAMPIRE

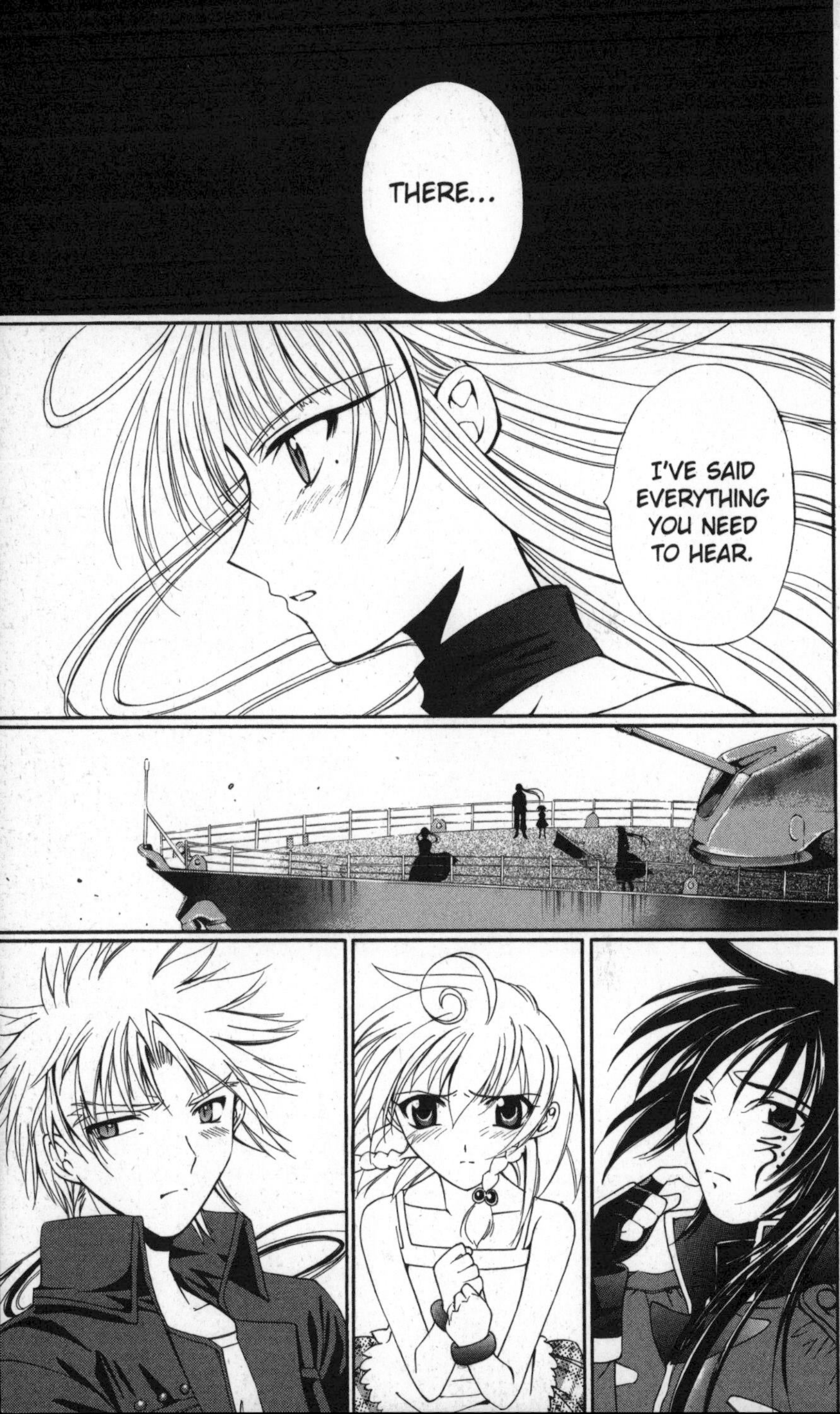
THERE...
I'VE SAID EVERYTHING YOU NEED TO HEAR.

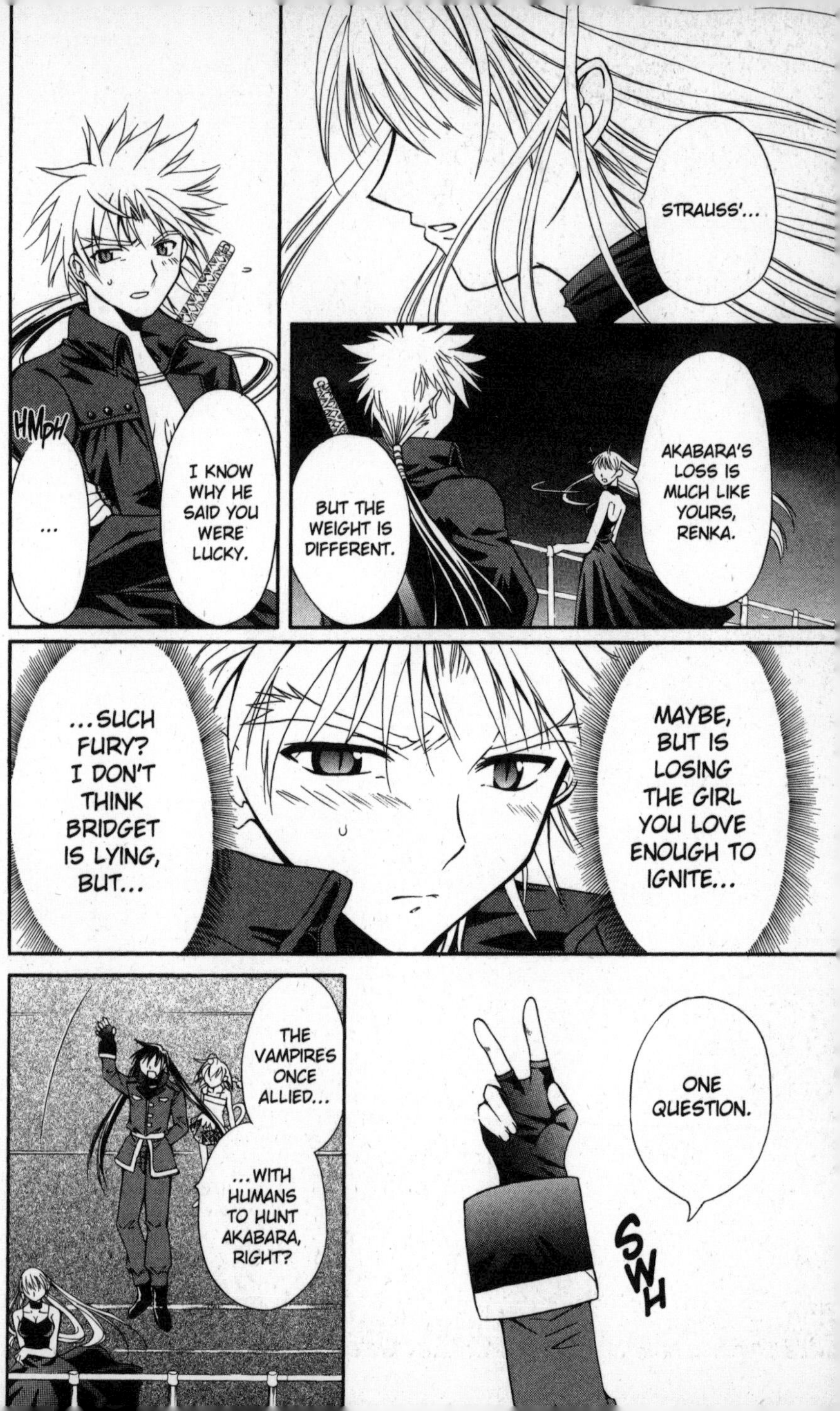
STRAUSS'...
AKABARA'S LOSS IS MUCH LIKE YOURS, RENKA.
BUT THE WEIGHT IS DIFFERENT.
I KNOW WHY HE SAID YOU WERE LUCKY.
HMPH
...
MAYBE, BUT IS LOSING THE GIRL YOU LOVE ENOUGH TO IGNITE...
...SUCH FURY? I DON'T THINK BRIDGET IS LYING, BUT...
ONE QUESTION.
SWH
THE VAMPIRES ONCE ALLIED...
...WITH HUMANS TO HUNT AKABARA, RIGHT?

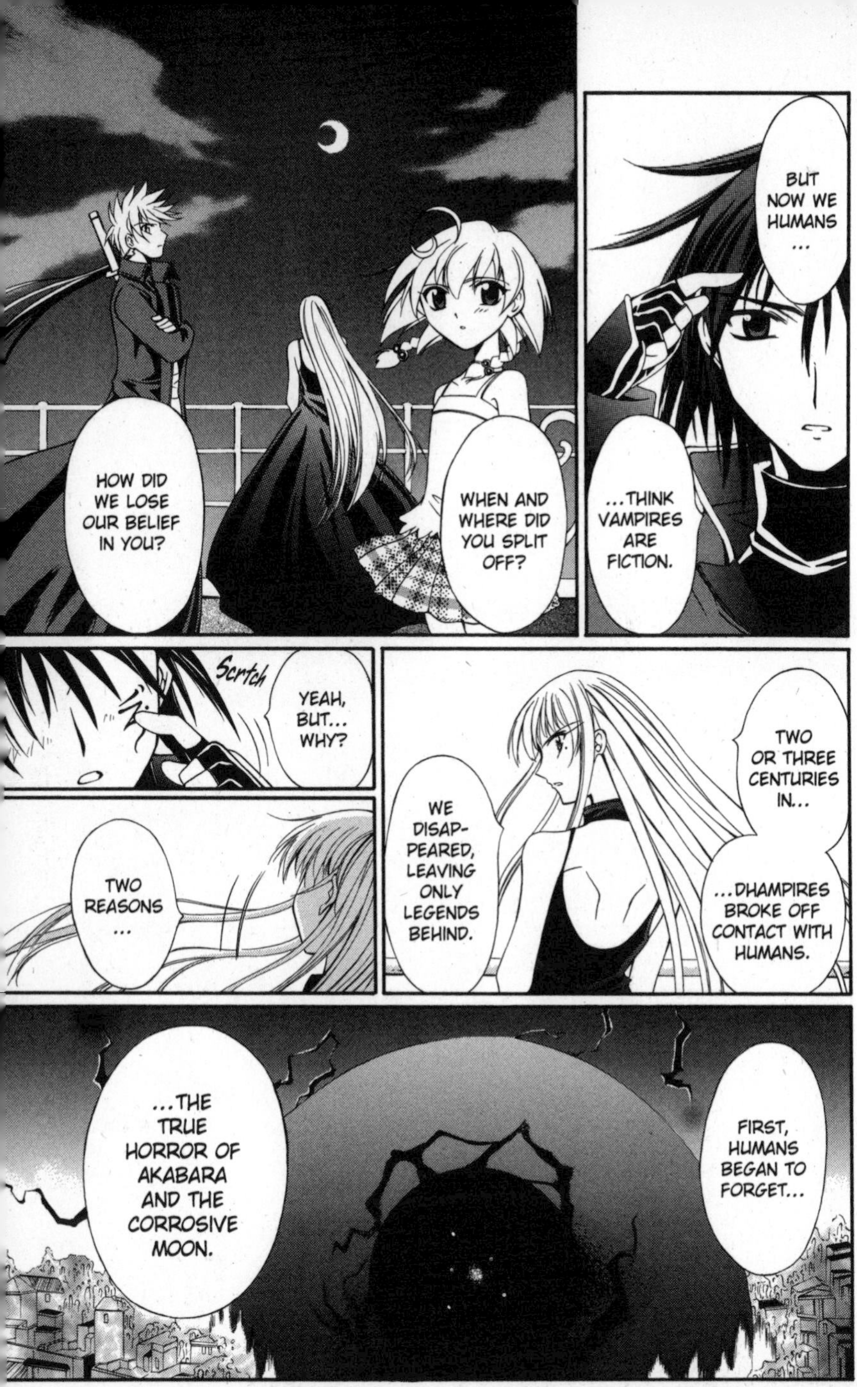
BUT NOW WE HUMANS ...
...THINK VAMPIRES ARE FICTION.
WHEN AND WHERE DID YOU SPLIT OFF?
HOW DID WE LOSE OUR BELIEF IN YOU?
TWO OR THREE CENTURIES IN...
...DHAMPIRES BROKE OFF CONTACT WITH HUMANS.
WE DISAP-PEARED, LEAVING ONLY LEGENDS BEHIND.
Scrtch
YEAH, BUT... WHY?
TWO REASONS ...
FIRST, HUMANS BEGAN TO FORGET...
...THE TRUE HORROR OF AKABARA AND THE CORROSIVE MOON.

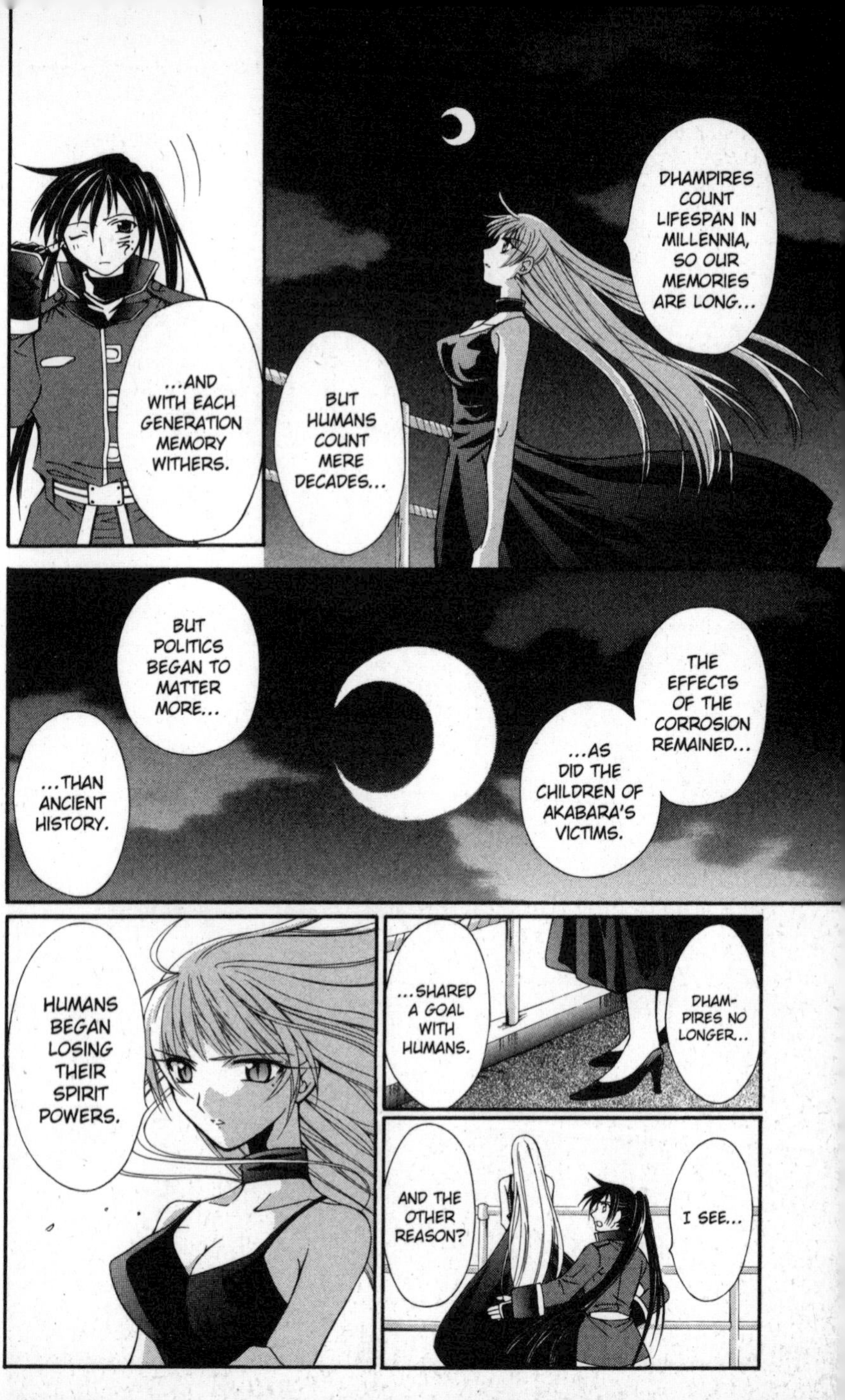
DHAMPIRES COUNT LIFESPAN IN MILLENNIA, SO OUR MEMORIES ARE LONG...
BUT HUMANS COUNT MERE DECADES...
...AND WITH EACH GENERATION MEMORY WITHERS.
THE EFFECTS OF THE CORROSION REMAINED...
...AS DID THE CHILDREN OF AKABARA'S VICTIMS.
BUT POLITICS BEGAN TO MATTER MORE...
...THAN ANCIENT HISTORY.
DHAMPIRES NO LONGER...
...SHARED A GOAL WITH HUMANS.
I SEE...
AND THE OTHER REASON?
HUMANS BEGAN LOSING THEIR SPIRIT POWERS.

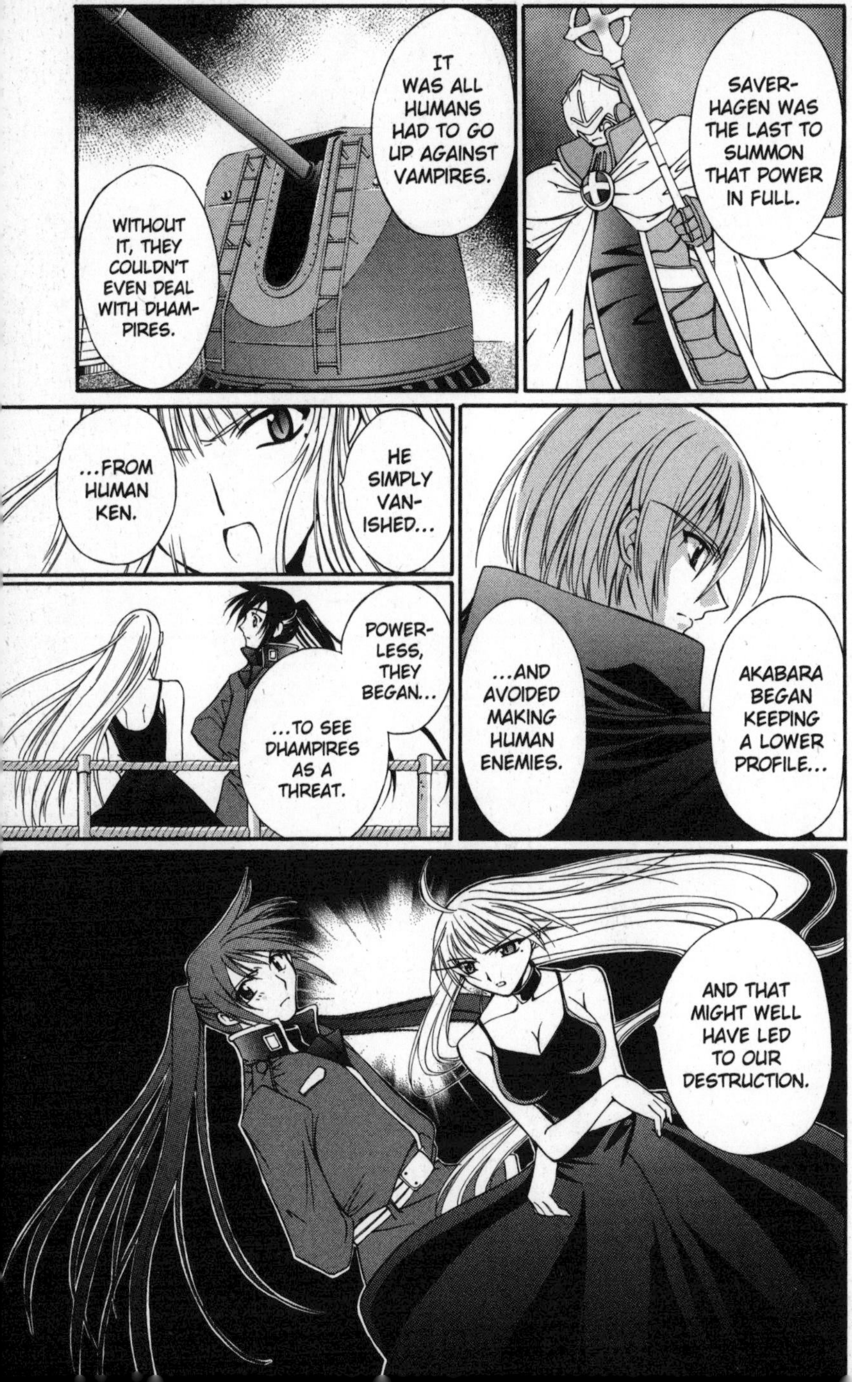
SAVER-HAGEN WAS THE LAST TO SUMMON THAT POWER IN FULL.
IT WAS ALL HUMANS HAD TO GO UP AGAINST VAMPIRES.
WITHOUT IT, THEY COULDN'T EVEN DEAL WITH DHAM-PIRES.
AKABARA BEGAN KEEPING A LOWER PROFILE...
...AND AVOIDED MAKING HUMAN ENEMIES.
HE SIMPLY VAN-ISHED...
...FROM HUMAN KEN.
POWER-LESS, THEY BEGAN...
...TO SEE DHAMPIRES AS A THREAT.
AND THAT MIGHT WELL HAVE LED TO OUR DESTRUCTION.

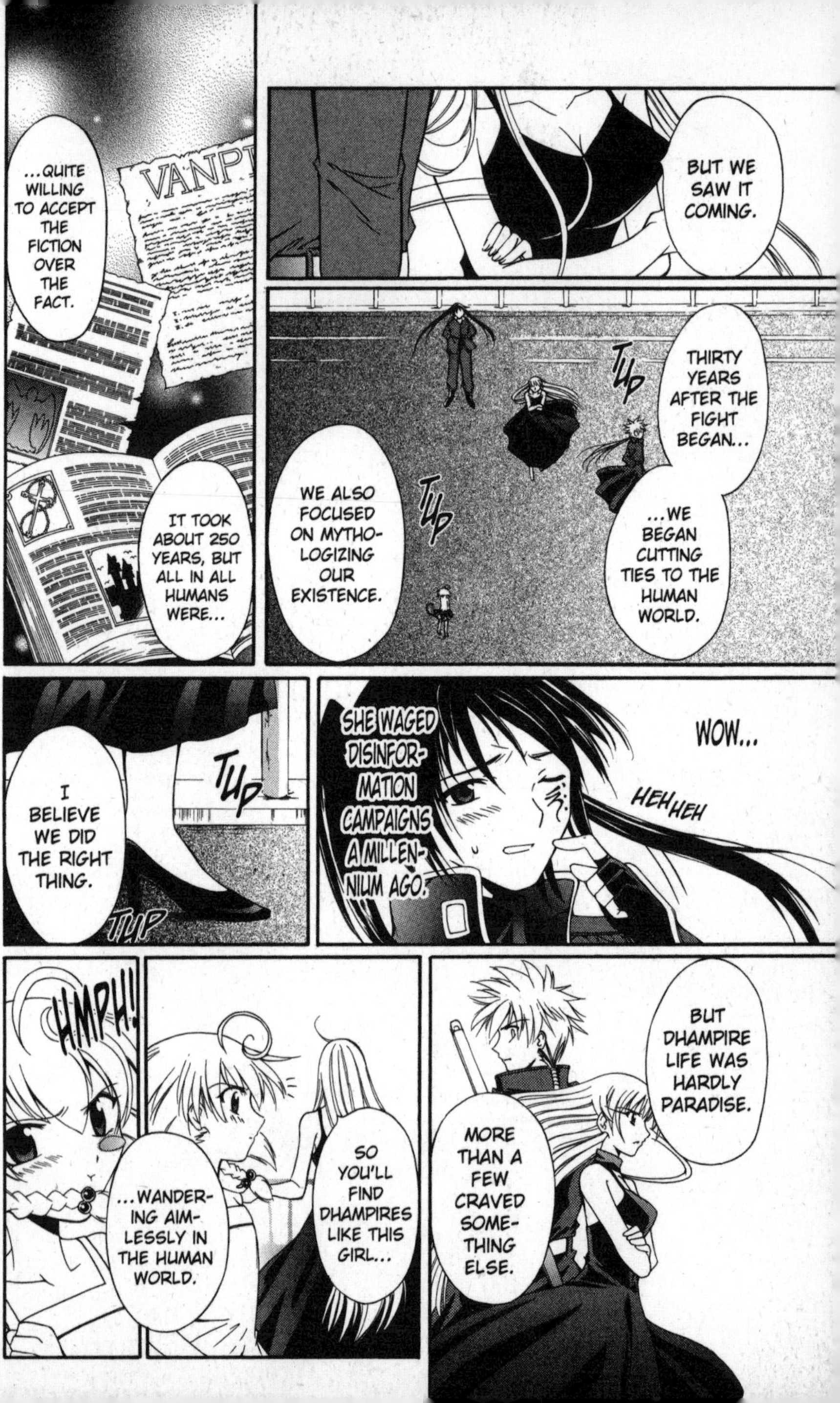
BUT WE SAW IT COMING.
THIRTY YEARS AFTER THE FIGHT BEGAN...
...WE BEGAN CUTTING TIES TO THE HUMAN WORLD.
TUP
TUP
WE ALSO FOCUSED ON MYTHOLOGIZING OUR EXISTENCE.
IT TOOK ABOUT 250 YEARS, BUT ALL IN ALL HUMANS WERE...
...QUITE WILLING TO ACCEPT THE FICTION OVER THE FACT.
WOW...
HEH HEH
SHE WAGED DISINFORMATION CAMPAIGNS A MILLENNIUM AGO.
TUP
I BELIEVE WE DID THE RIGHT THING.
TUP
BUT DHAMPIRE LIFE WAS HARDLY PARADISE.
MORE THAN A FEW CRAVED SOMETHING ELSE.
SO YOU'LL FIND DHAMPIRES LIKE THIS GIRL...
...WANDERING AIMLESSLY IN THE HUMAN WORLD.
HMPH!!

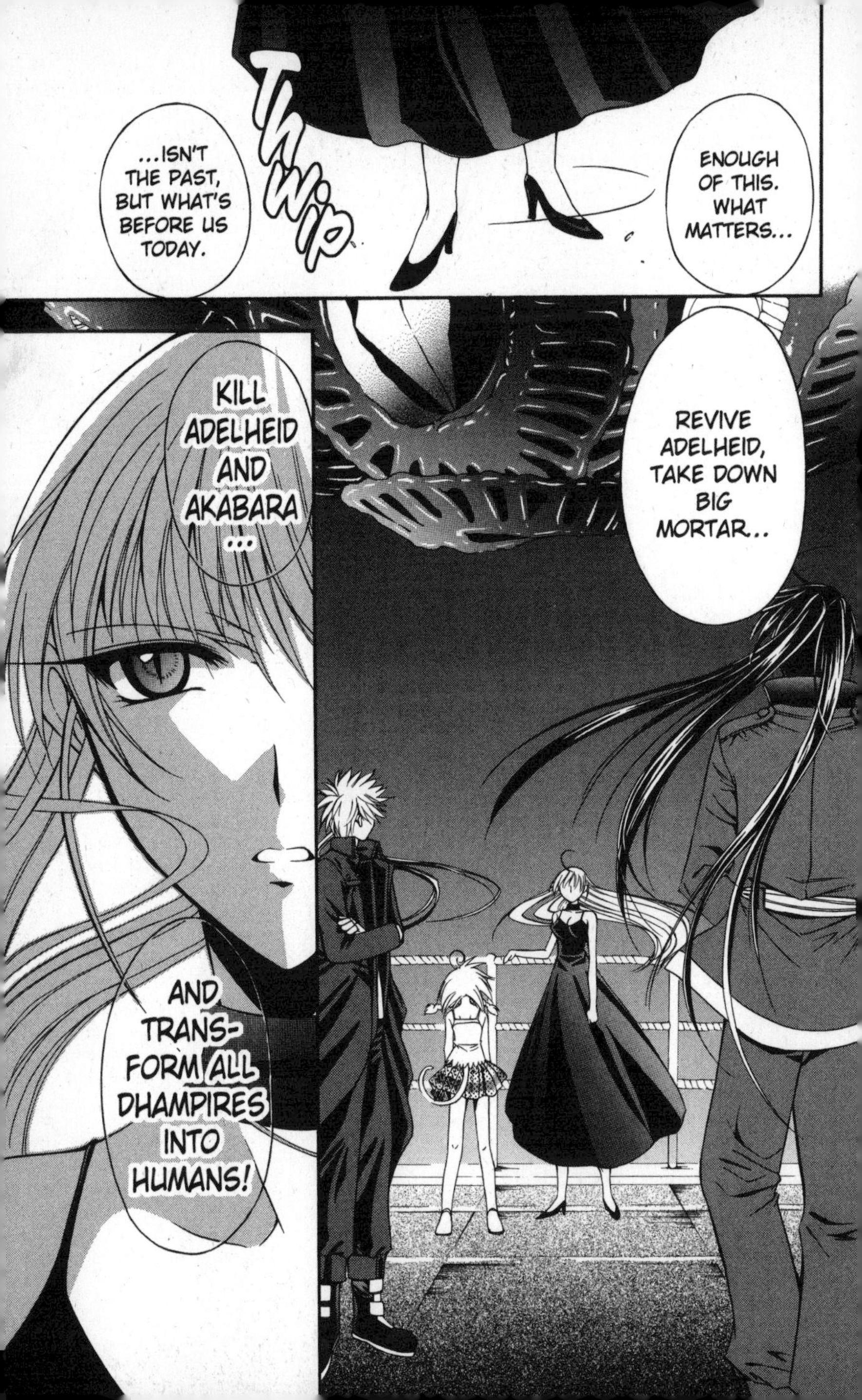
ENOUGH OF THIS. WHAT MATTERS...
THWIP
...ISN'T THE PAST, BUT WHAT'S BEFORE US TODAY.
REVIVE ADELHEID, TAKE DOWN BIG MORTAR...
KILL ADELHEID AND AKABARA...
AND TRANS-FORM ALL DHAMPIRES INTO HUMANS!

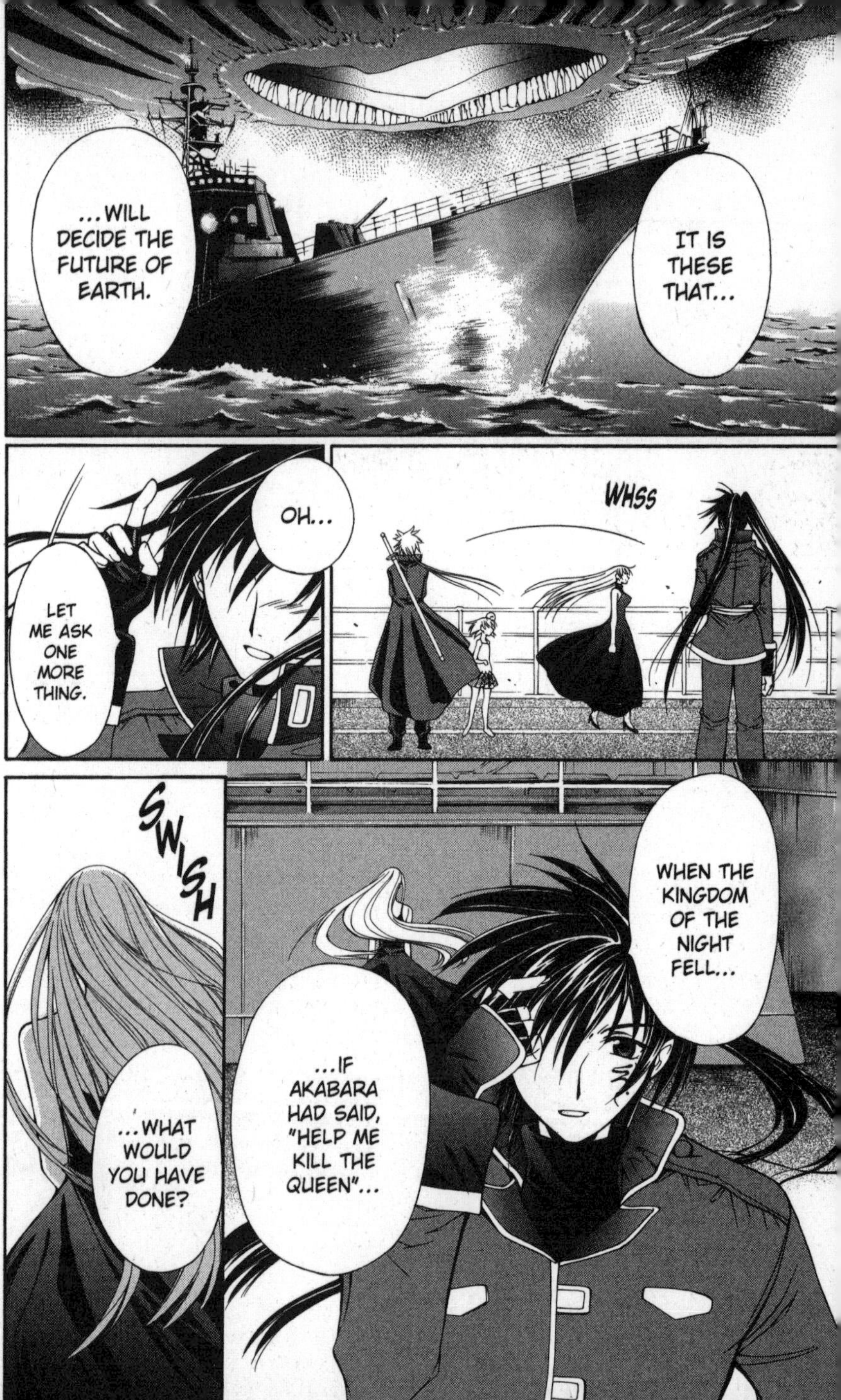
IT IS THESE THAT...
...WILL DECIDE THE FUTURE OF EARTH.
WHSS
OH...
LET ME ASK ONE MORE THING.
WHEN THE KINGDOM OF THE NIGHT FELL...
...IF AKABARA HAD SAID, "HELP ME KILL THE QUEEN"...
SWISH
...WHAT WOULD YOU HAVE DONE?

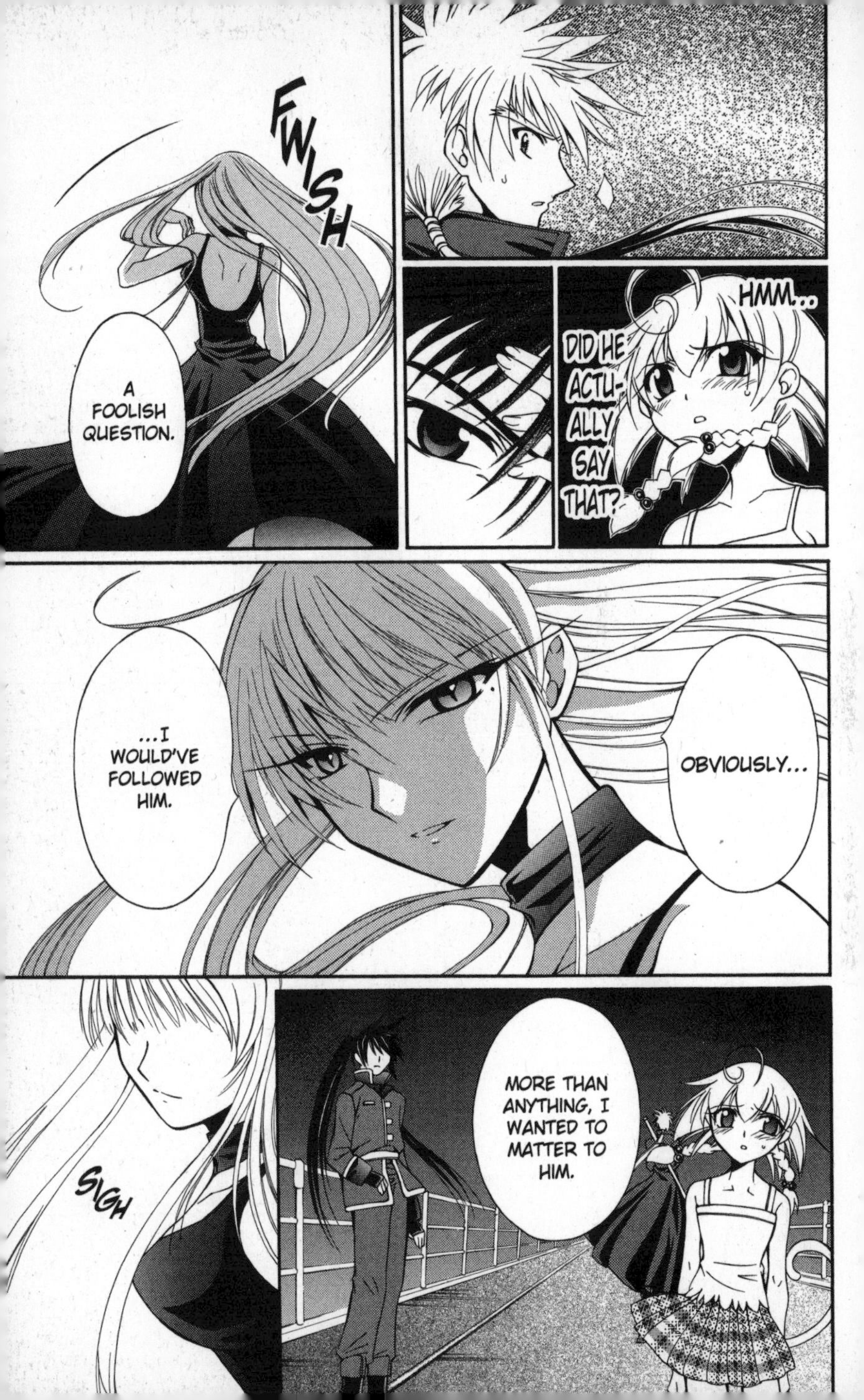
HMM...
DID HE ACTU-ALLY SAY THAT?
FWISH
A FOOLISH QUESTION.
OBVIOUSLY...
...I WOULD'VE FOLLOWED HIM.
MORE THAN ANYTHING, I WANTED TO MATTER TO HIM.
SIGH

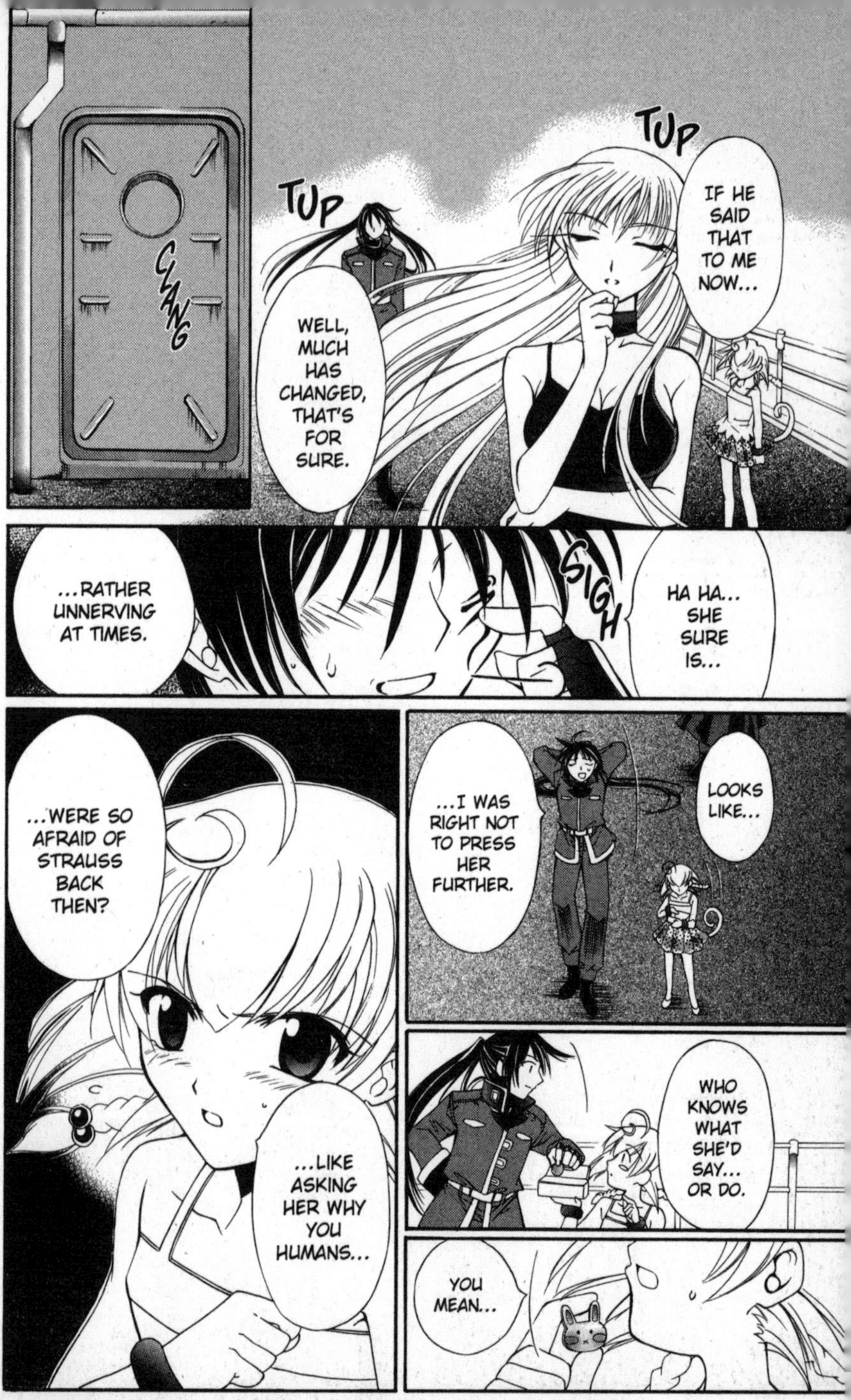
TUP
IF HE SAID THAT TO ME NOW...
TUP
WELL, MUCH HAS CHANGED, THAT'S FOR SURE.
CLANG
HA HA... SHE SURE IS...
SIGH
...RATHER UNNERVING AT TIMES.
LOOKS LIKE...
...I WAS RIGHT NOT TO PRESS HER FURTHER.
WHO KNOWS WHAT SHE'D SAY... OR DO.
YOU MEAN...
...LIKE ASKING HER WHY YOU HUMANS...
...WERE SO AFRAID OF STRAUSS BACK THEN?

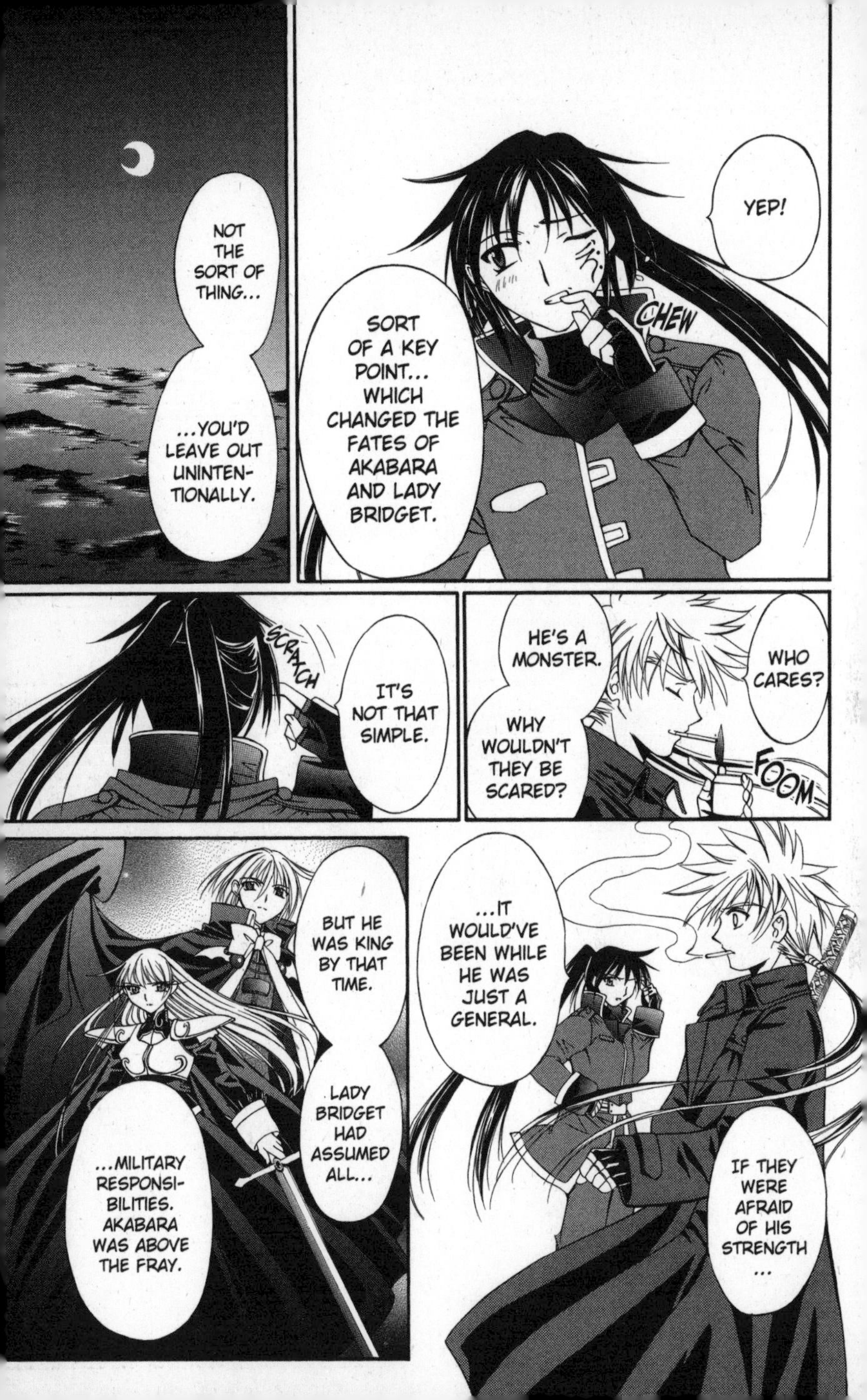
YEP!
CHEW
SORT OF A KEY POINT... WHICH CHANGED THE FATES OF AKABARA AND LADY BRIDGET.
NOT THE SORT OF THING...
...YOU'D LEAVE OUT UNINTEN-TIONALLY.
WHO CARES?
HE'S A MONSTER.
WHY WOULDN'T THEY BE SCARED?
FOOM
SCRATCH
IT'S NOT THAT SIMPLE.
IF THEY WERE AFRAID OF HIS STRENGTH...
...IT WOULD'VE BEEN WHILE HE WAS JUST A GENERAL.
BUT HE WAS KING BY THAT TIME.
LADY BRIDGET HAD ASSUMED ALL...
...MILITARY RESPONSI-BILITIES. AKABARA WAS ABOVE THE FRAY.

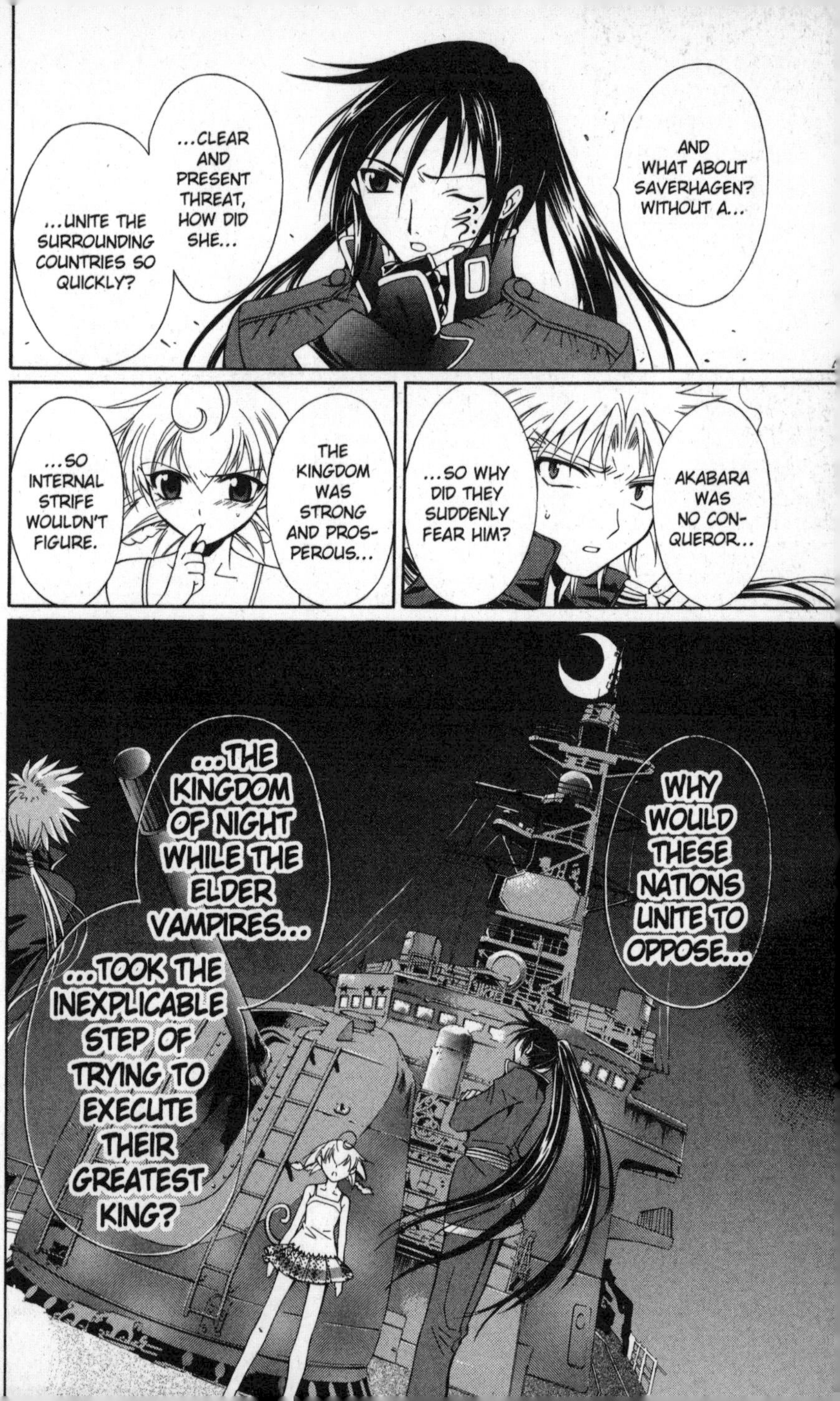
AND WHAT ABOUT SAVERHAGEN? WITHOUT A...
...CLEAR AND PRESENT THREAT, HOW DID SHE...
...UNITE THE SURROUNDING COUNTRIES SO QUICKLY?
AKABARA WAS NO CONQUEROR...
...SO WHY DID THEY SUDDENLY FEAR HIM?
THE KINGDOM WAS STRONG AND PROSPEROUS...
...SO INTERNAL STRIFE WOULDN'T FIGURE.
WHY WOULD THESE NATIONS UNITE TO OPPOSE...
...THE KINGDOM OF NIGHT WHILE THE ELDER VAMPIRES...
...TOOK THE INEXPLICABLE STEP OF TRYING TO EXECUTE THEIR GREATEST KING?

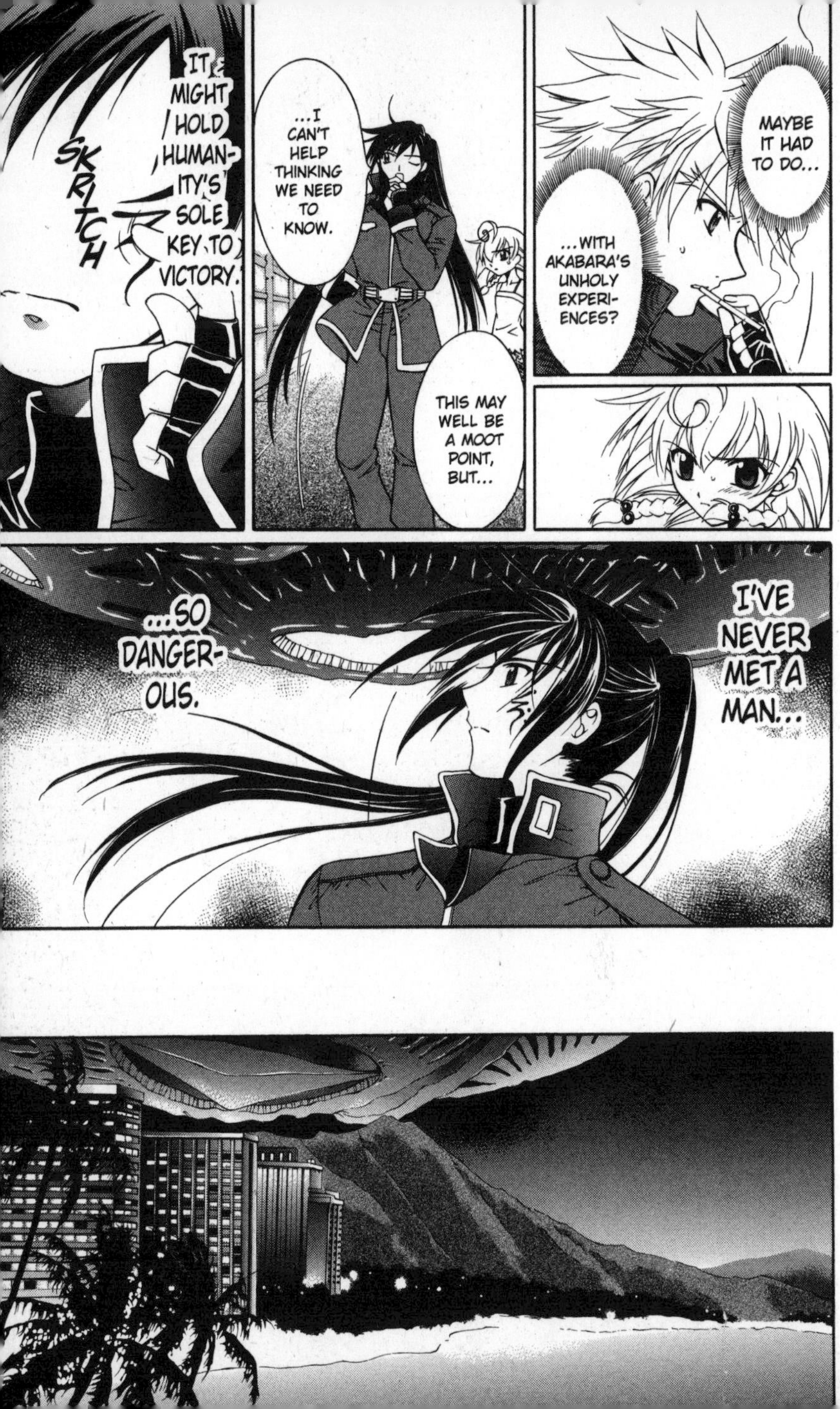
MAYBE IT HAD TO DO...
...WITH AKABARA'S UNHOLY EXPERIENCES?
THIS MAY WELL BE A MOOT POINT, BUT...
...I CAN'T HELP THINKING WE NEED TO KNOW.
IT MIGHT HOLD HUMANITY'S SOLE KEY TO VICTORY.
SKRITCH
I'VE NEVER MET A MAN...
...SO DANGEROUS.

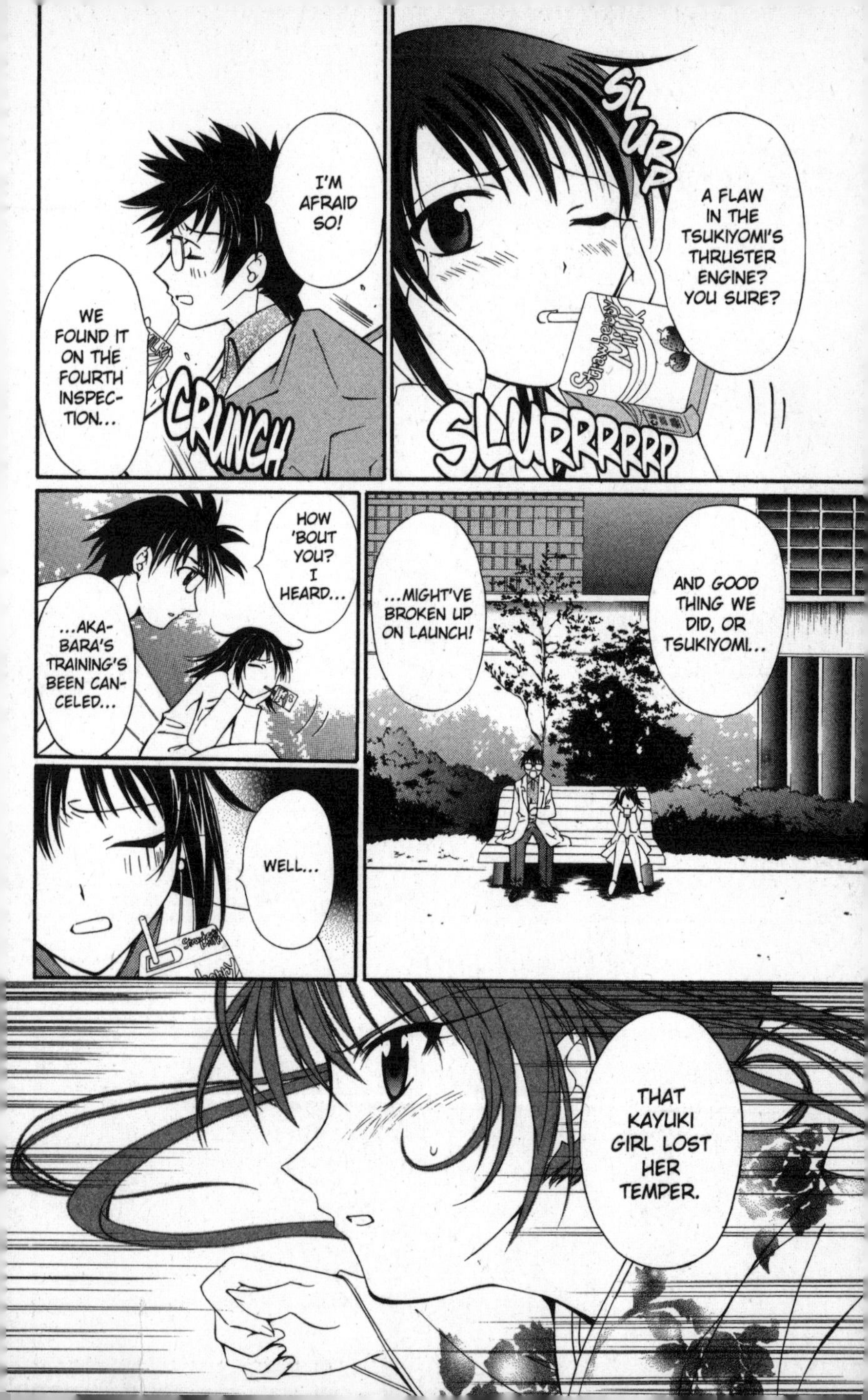
SLURP
A FLAW IN THE TSUKIYOMI'S THRUSTER ENGINE? YOU SURE?
SLURRRRRP
I'M AFRAID SO!
WE FOUND IT ON THE FOURTH INSPEC-TION...
CRUNCH
AND GOOD THING WE DID, OR TSUKIYOMI...
...MIGHT'VE BROKEN UP ON LAUNCH!
HOW 'BOUT YOU? I HEARD...
...AKA-BARA'S TRAINING'S BEEN CAN-CELED...
WELL...
THAT KAYUKI GIRL LOST HER TEMPER.

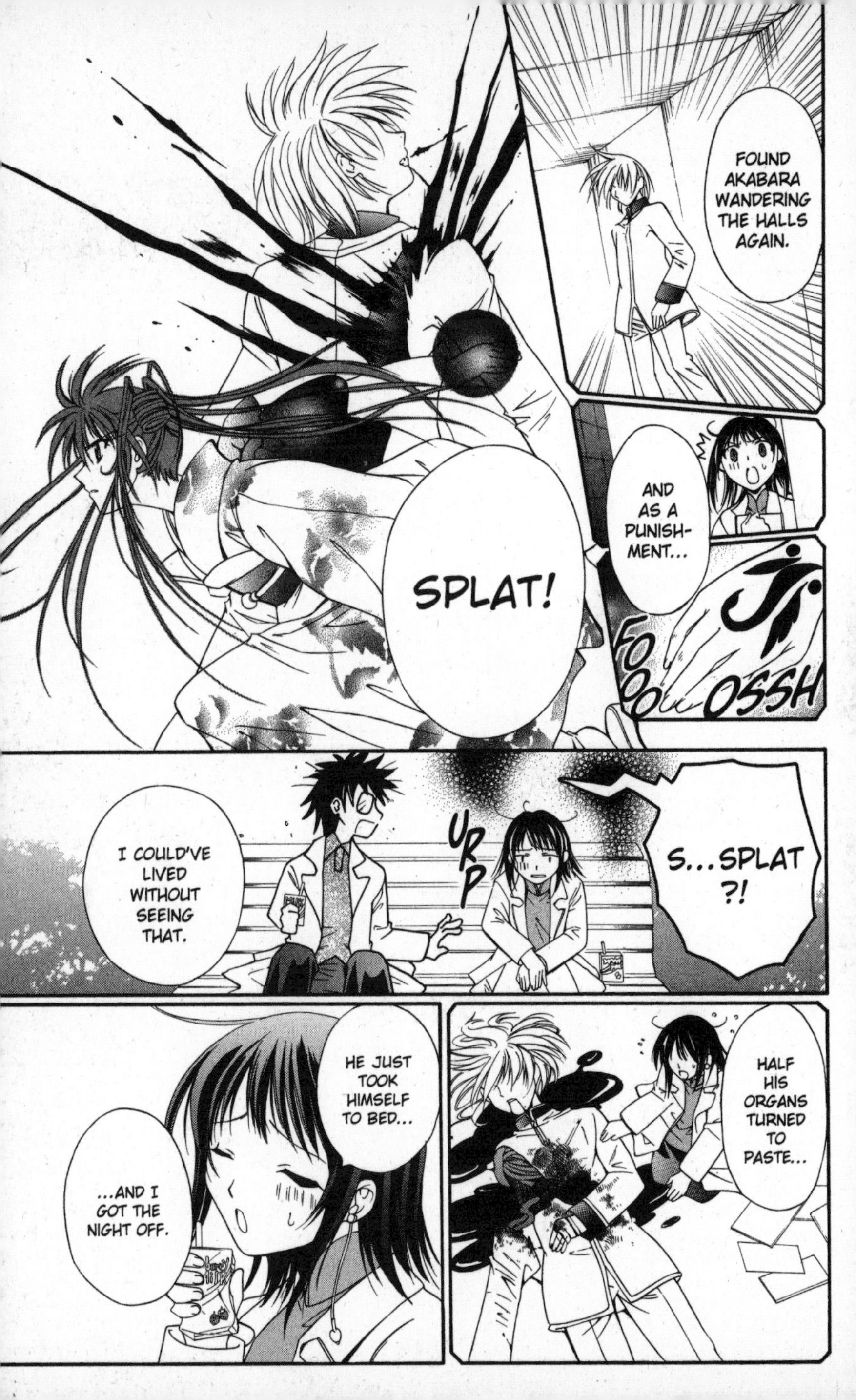
FOUND AKABARA WANDERING THE HALLS AGAIN.
AND AS A PUNISH-MENT...
FOOOOOSSH
SPLAT!
S...SPLAT?!
URP
I COULD'VE LIVED WITHOUT SEEING THAT.
HALF HIS ORGANS TURNED TO PASTE...
HE JUST TOOK HIMSELF TO BED...
...AND I GOT THE NIGHT OFF.

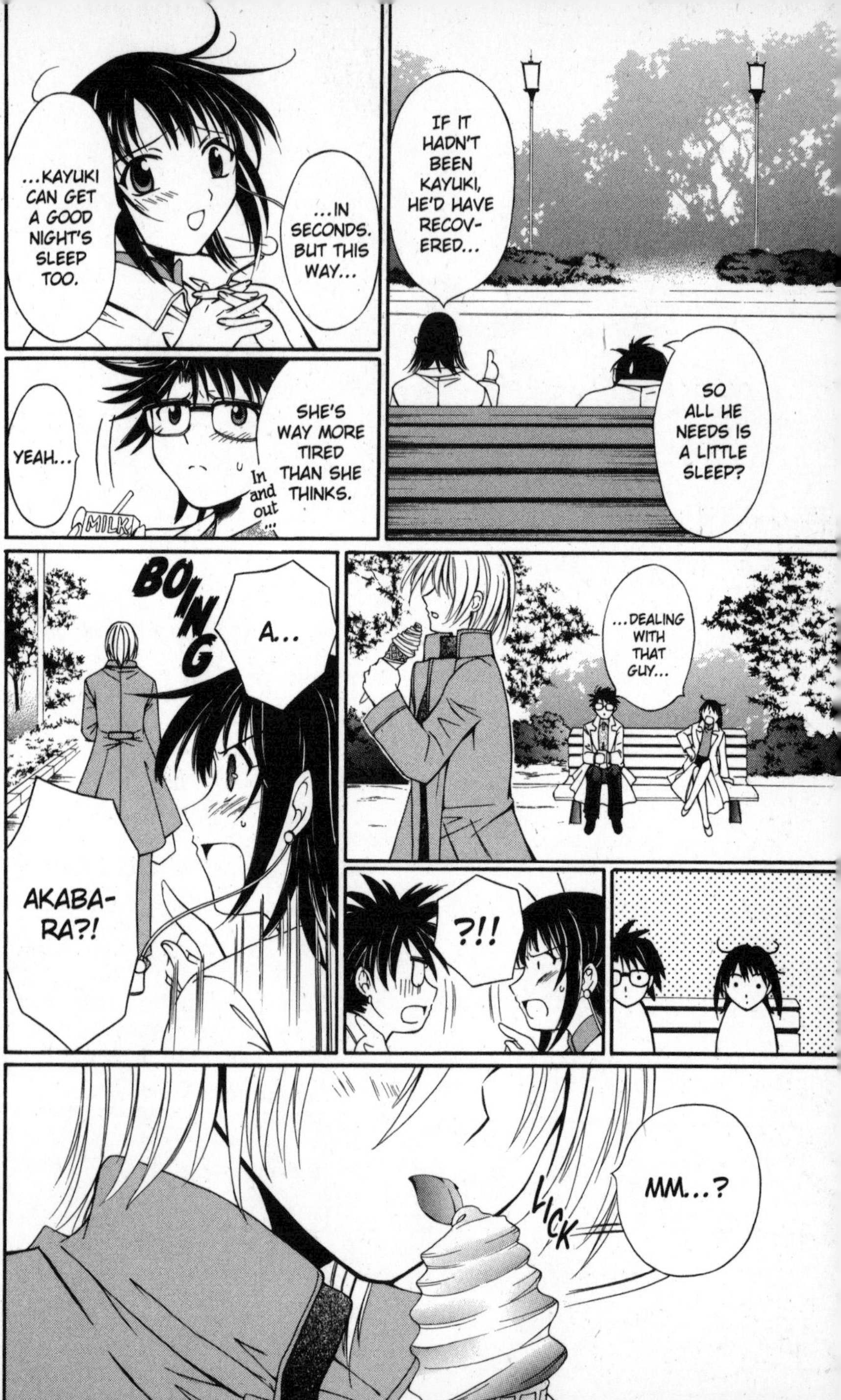

SO ALL HE NEEDS IS A LITTLE SLEEP?
IF IT HADN'T BEEN KAYUKI, HE'D HAVE RECOVERED...
...IN SECONDS. BUT THIS WAY...
...KAYUKI CAN GET A GOOD NIGHT'S SLEEP TOO.
SHE'S WAY MORE TIRED THAN SHE THINKS.
In and out ...
YEAH...
MILK
...DEALING WITH THAT GUY...
?!!
A...
BOING
AKABARA?!
MM...?
LICK

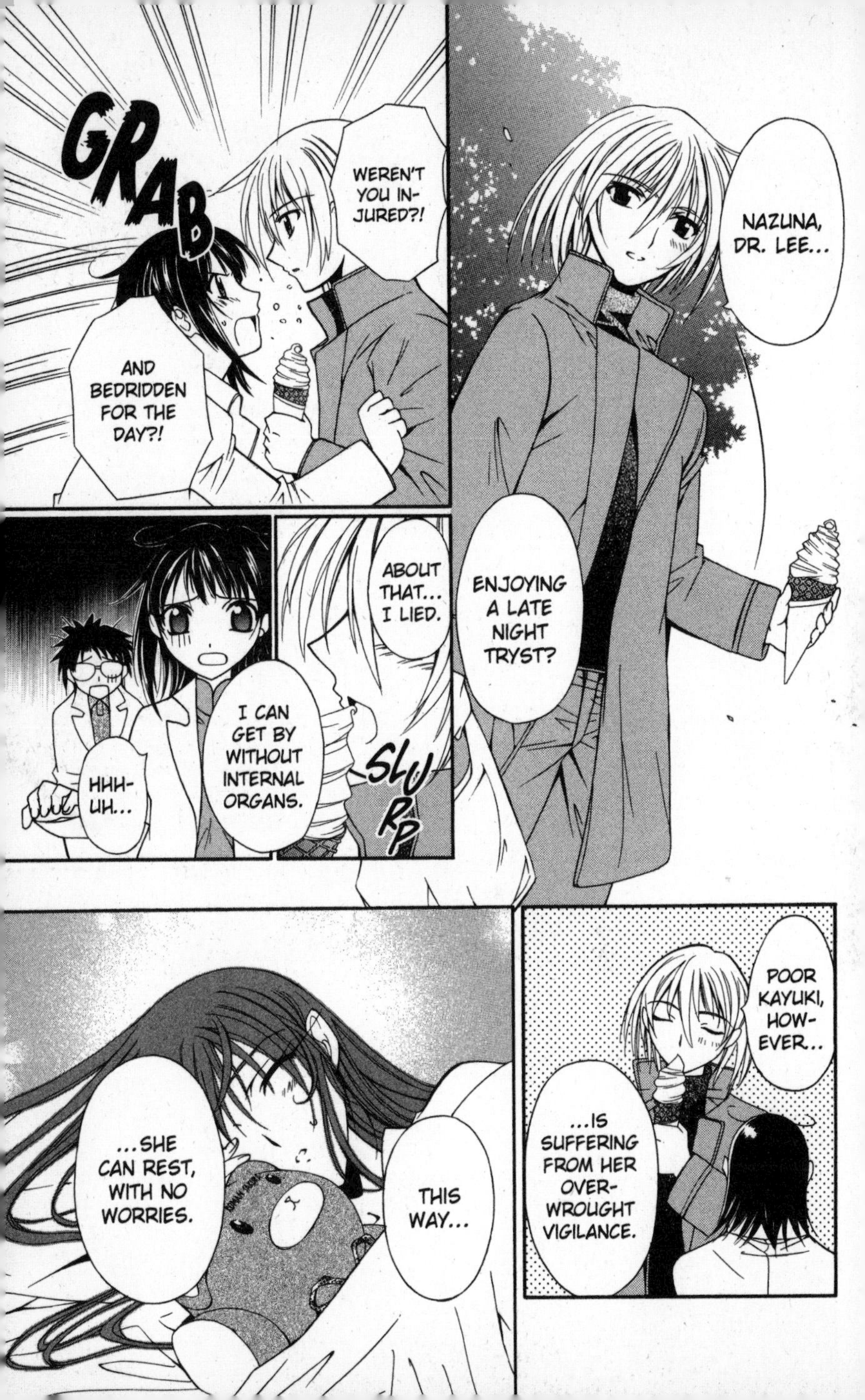
NAZUNA, DR. LEE...
ENJOYING A LATE NIGHT TRYST?
GRAB
WEREN'T YOU IN-JURED?!
AND BEDRIDDEN FOR THE DAY?!
ABOUT THAT... I LIED.
SLURP
I CAN GET BY WITHOUT INTERNAL ORGANS.
HHH-UH...
POOR KAYUKI, HOW-EVER...
...IS SUFFERING FROM HER OVER-WROUGHT VIGILANCE.
THIS WAY...
...SHE CAN REST, WITH NO WORRIES.

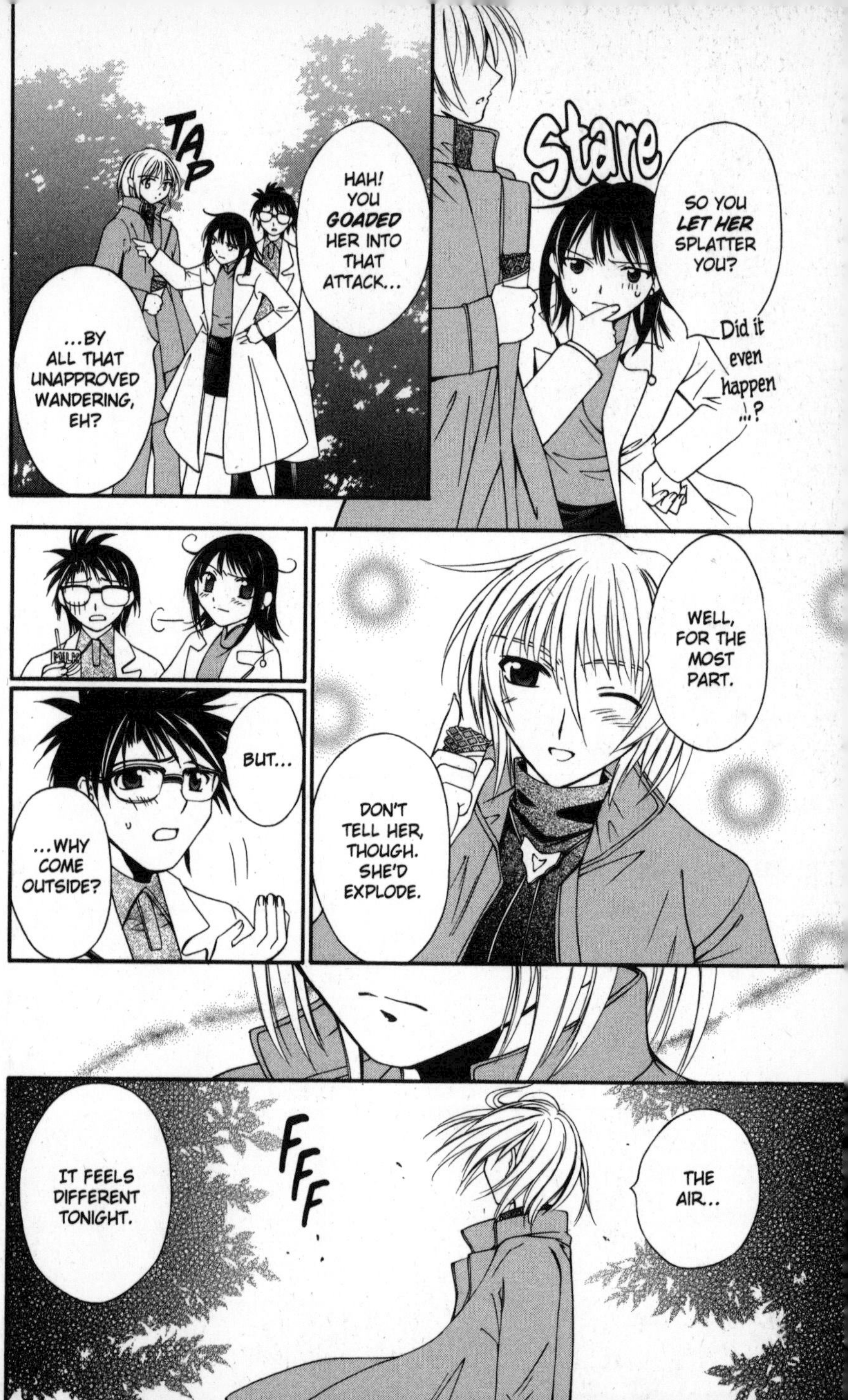
stare
SO YOU *LET HER* SPLATTER YOU?
Did it even happen ...?
TAP
HAH! YOU *GOADED* HER INTO THAT ATTACK...
...BY ALL THAT UNAPPROVED WANDERING, EH?
WELL, FOR THE MOST PART.
DON'T TELL HER, THOUGH. SHE'D EXPLODE.
MILK
BUT...
...WHY COME OUTSIDE?
THE AIR..
FFF
IT FEELS DIFFERENT TONIGHT.

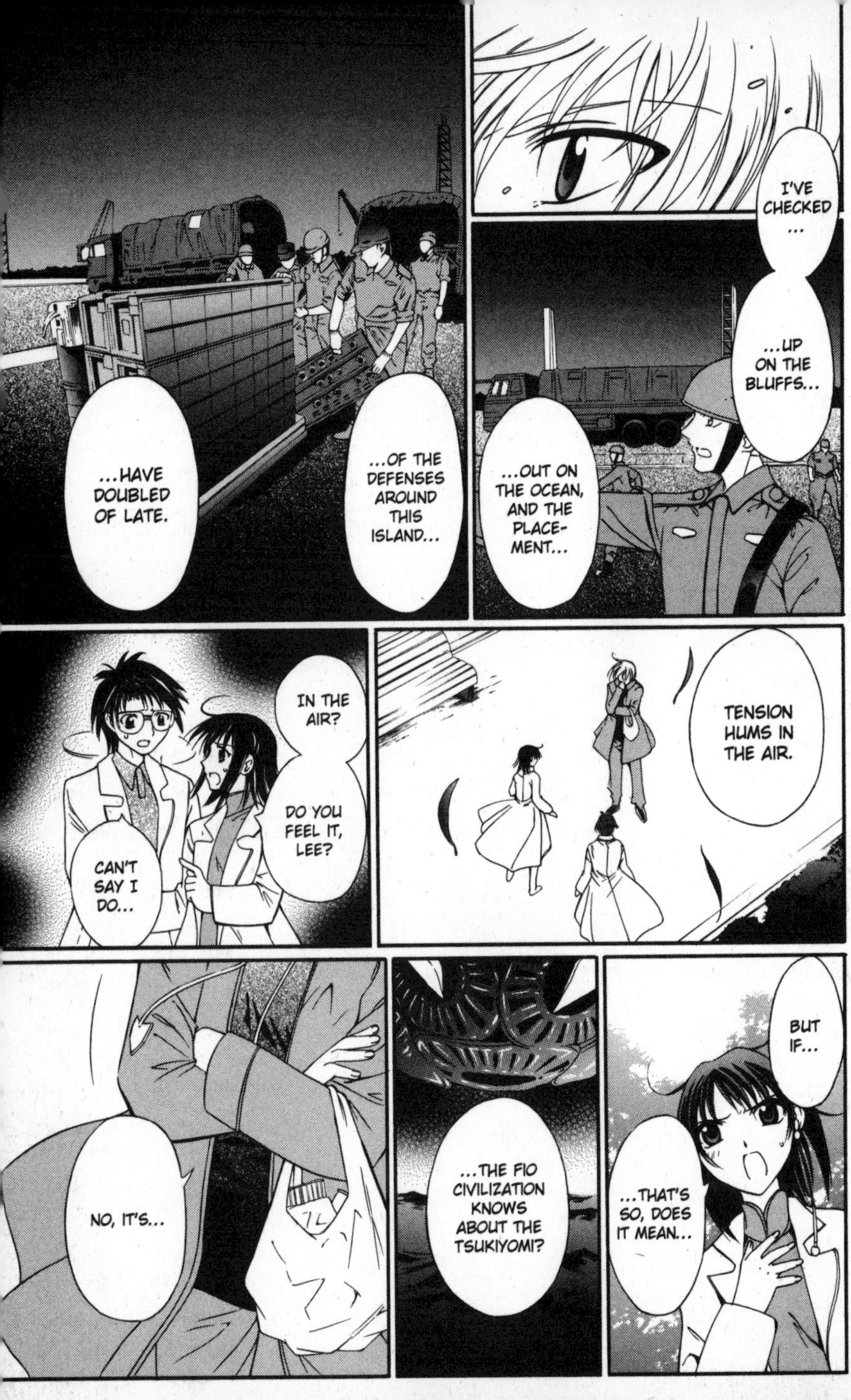
I'VE CHECKED...
...UP ON THE BLUFFS...
...OUT ON THE OCEAN, AND THE PLACE-MENT...
...OF THE DEFENSES AROUND THIS ISLAND...
...HAVE DOUBLED OF LATE.
TENSION HUMS IN THE AIR.
IN THE AIR?
DO YOU FEEL IT, LEE?
CAN'T SAY I DO...
BUT IF...
...THAT'S SO, DOES IT MEAN...
...THE FIO CIVILIZATION KNOWS ABOUT THE TSUKIYOMI?
NO, IT'S...

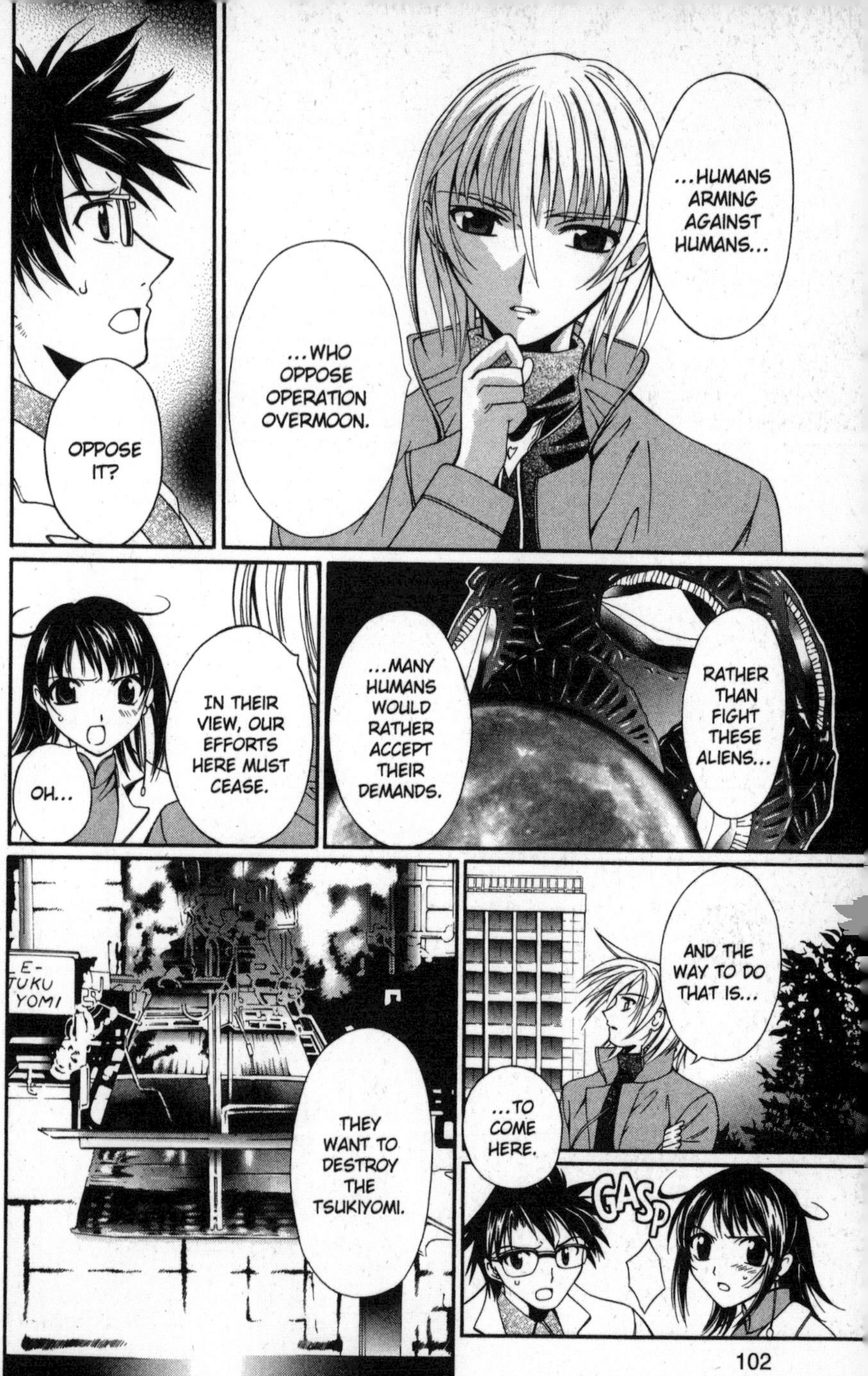
...HUMANS ARMING AGAINST HUMANS...
...WHO OPPOSE OPERATION OVERMOON.
OPPOSE IT?
RATHER THAN FIGHT THESE ALIENS...
...MANY HUMANS WOULD RATHER ACCEPT THEIR DEMANDS.
IN THEIR VIEW, OUR EFFORTS HERE MUST CEASE.
OH...
AND THE WAY TO DO THAT IS...
...TO COME HERE.
GASP
THEY WANT TO DESTROY THE TSUKIYOMI.

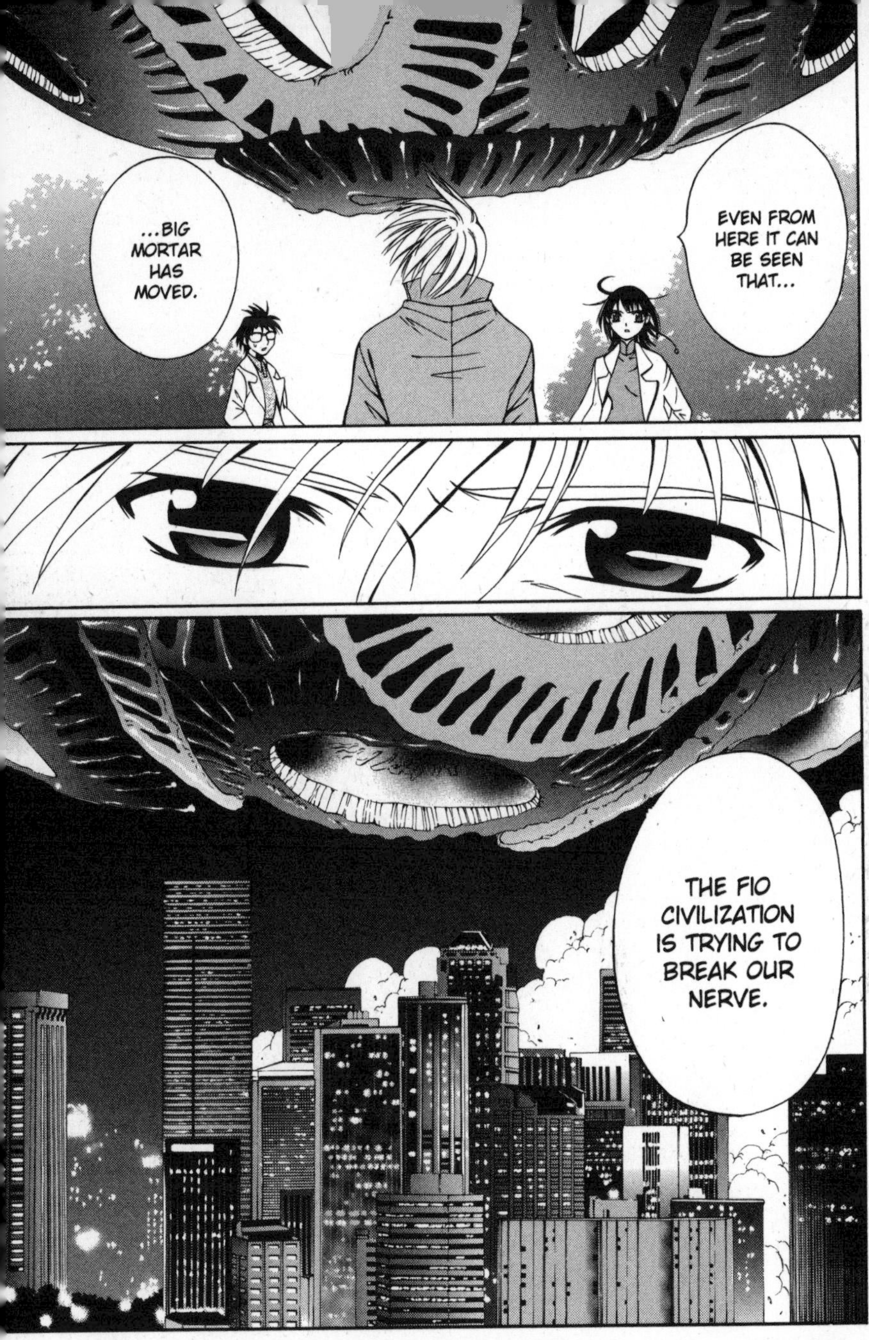
EVEN FROM HERE IT CAN BE SEEN THAT...
...BIG MORTAR HAS MOVED.
THE FIO CIVILIZATION IS TRYING TO BREAK OUR NERVE.

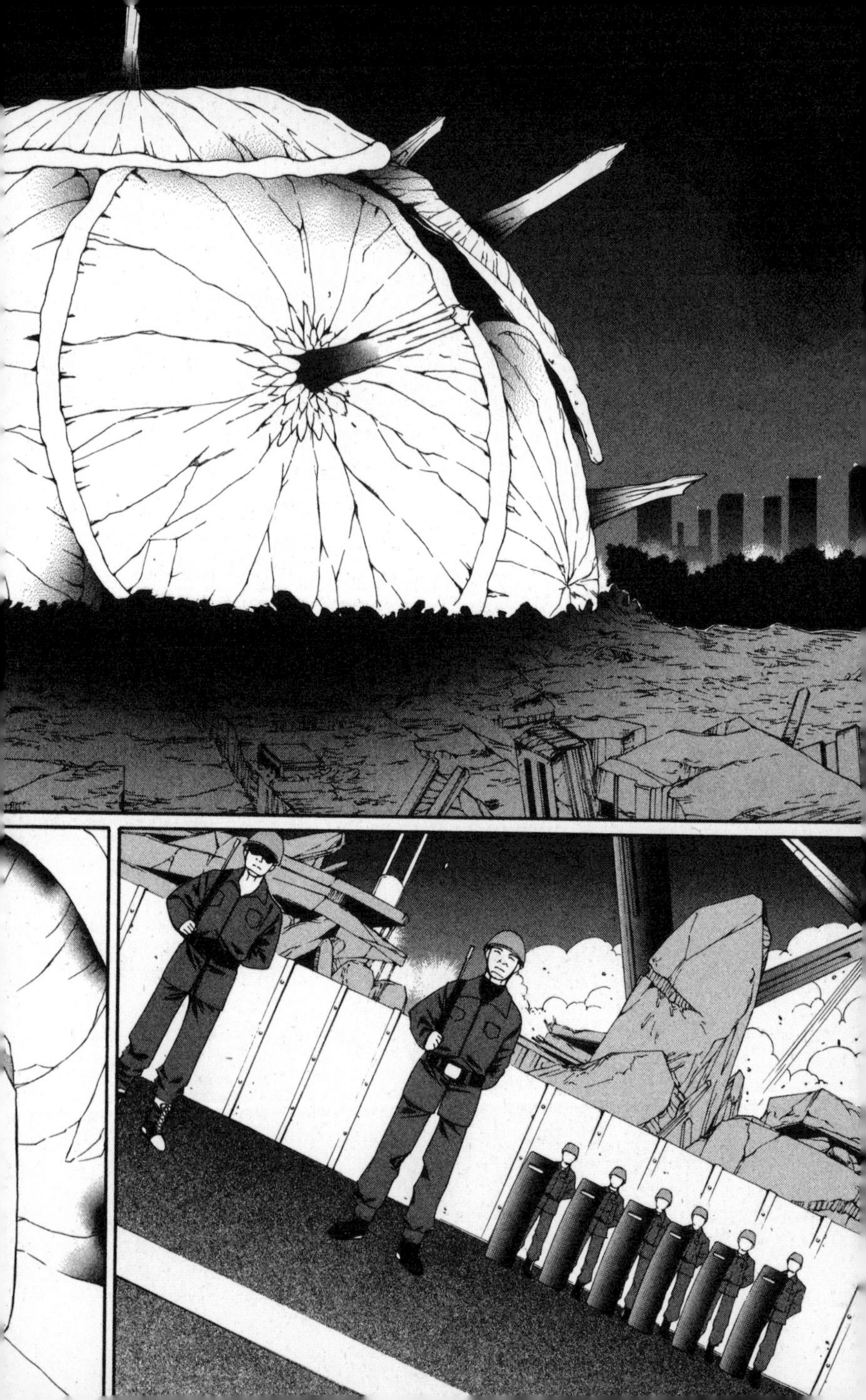

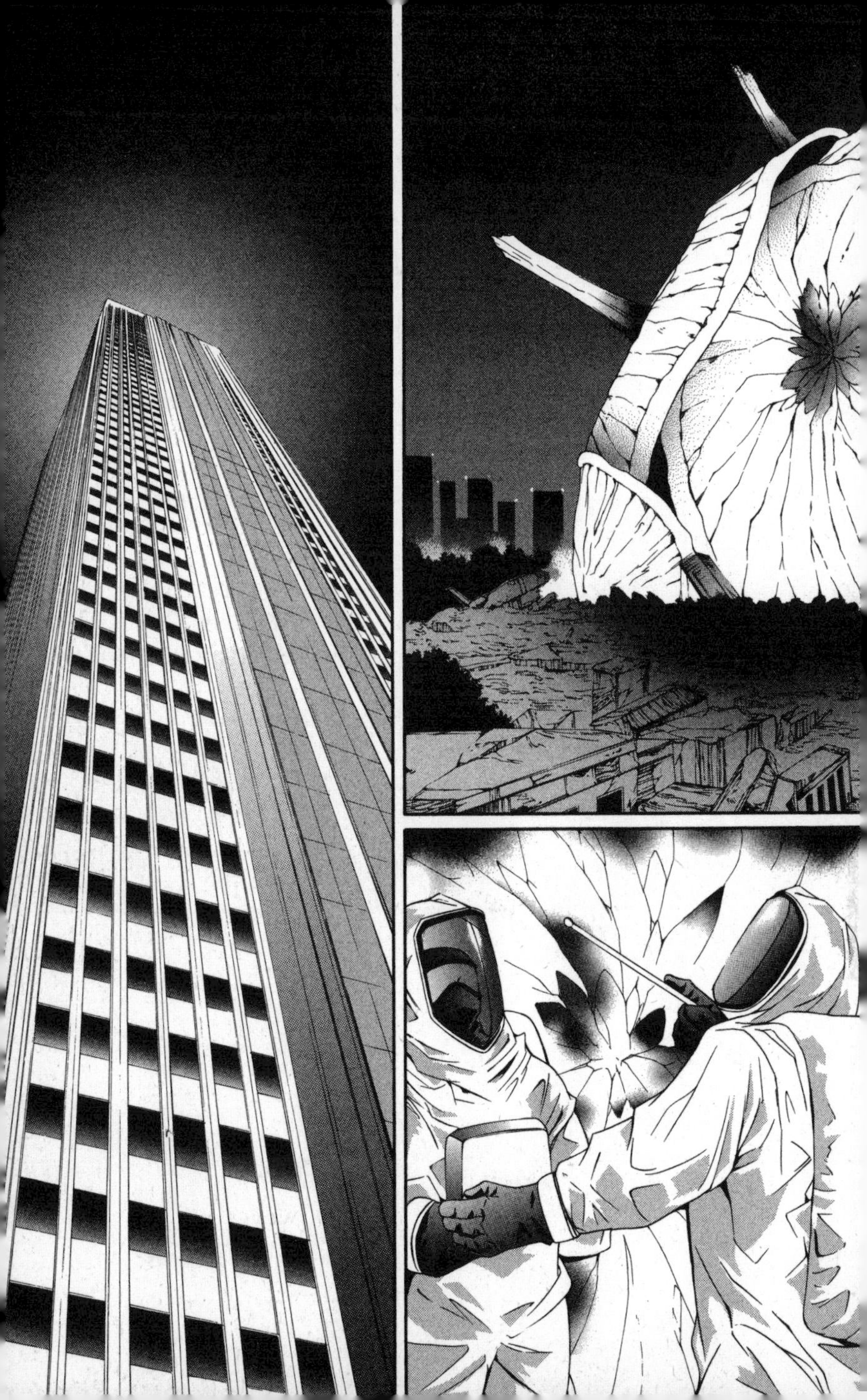

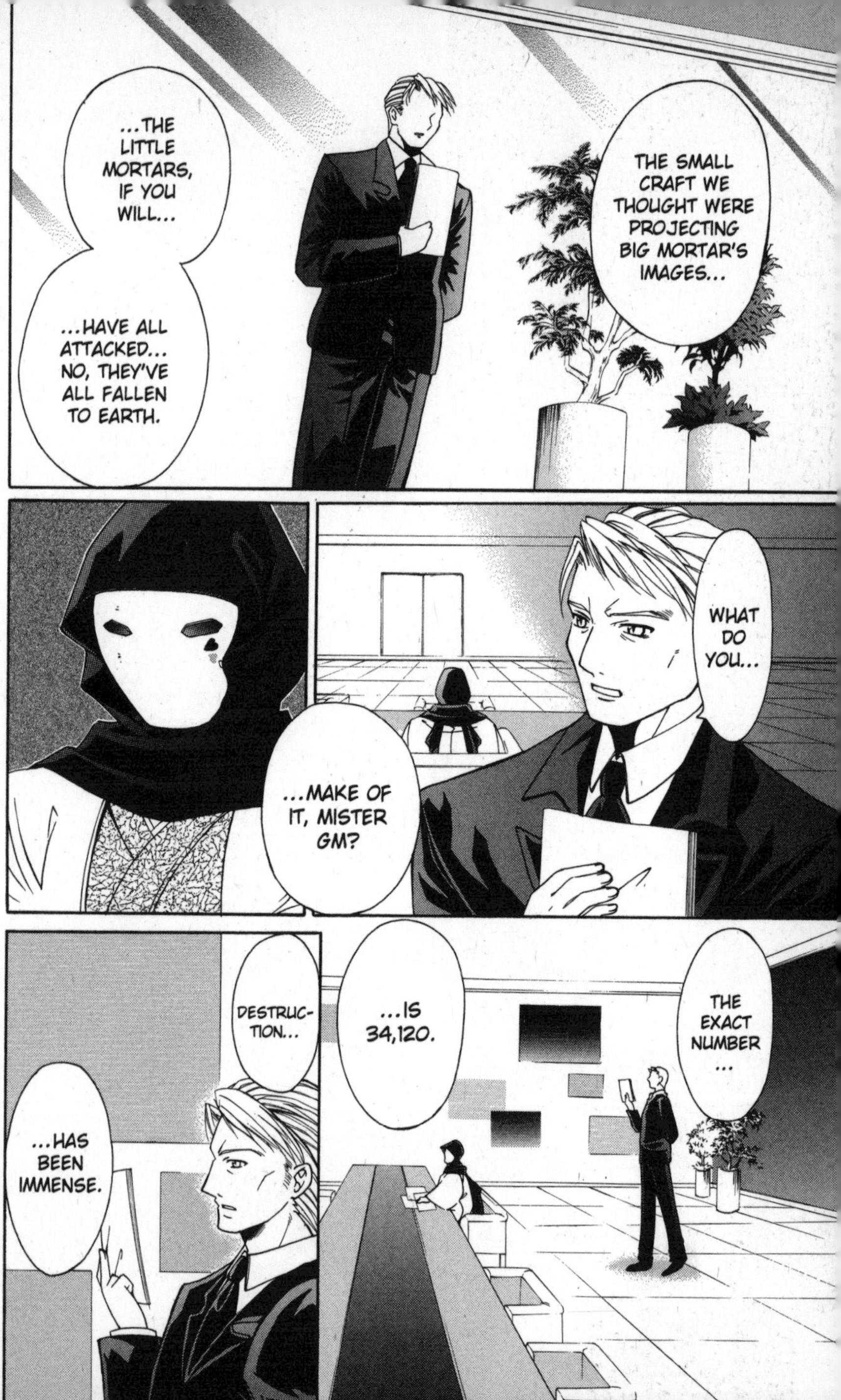
THE SMALL CRAFT WE THOUGHT WERE PROJECTING BIG MORTAR'S IMAGES...
...THE LITTLE MORTARS, IF YOU WILL...
...HAVE ALL ATTACKED... NO, THEY'VE ALL FALLEN TO EARTH.
WHAT DO YOU...
...MAKE OF IT, MISTER GM?
THE EXACT NUMBER ...
...IS 34,120.
DESTRUC-TION...
...HAS BEEN IMMENSE.

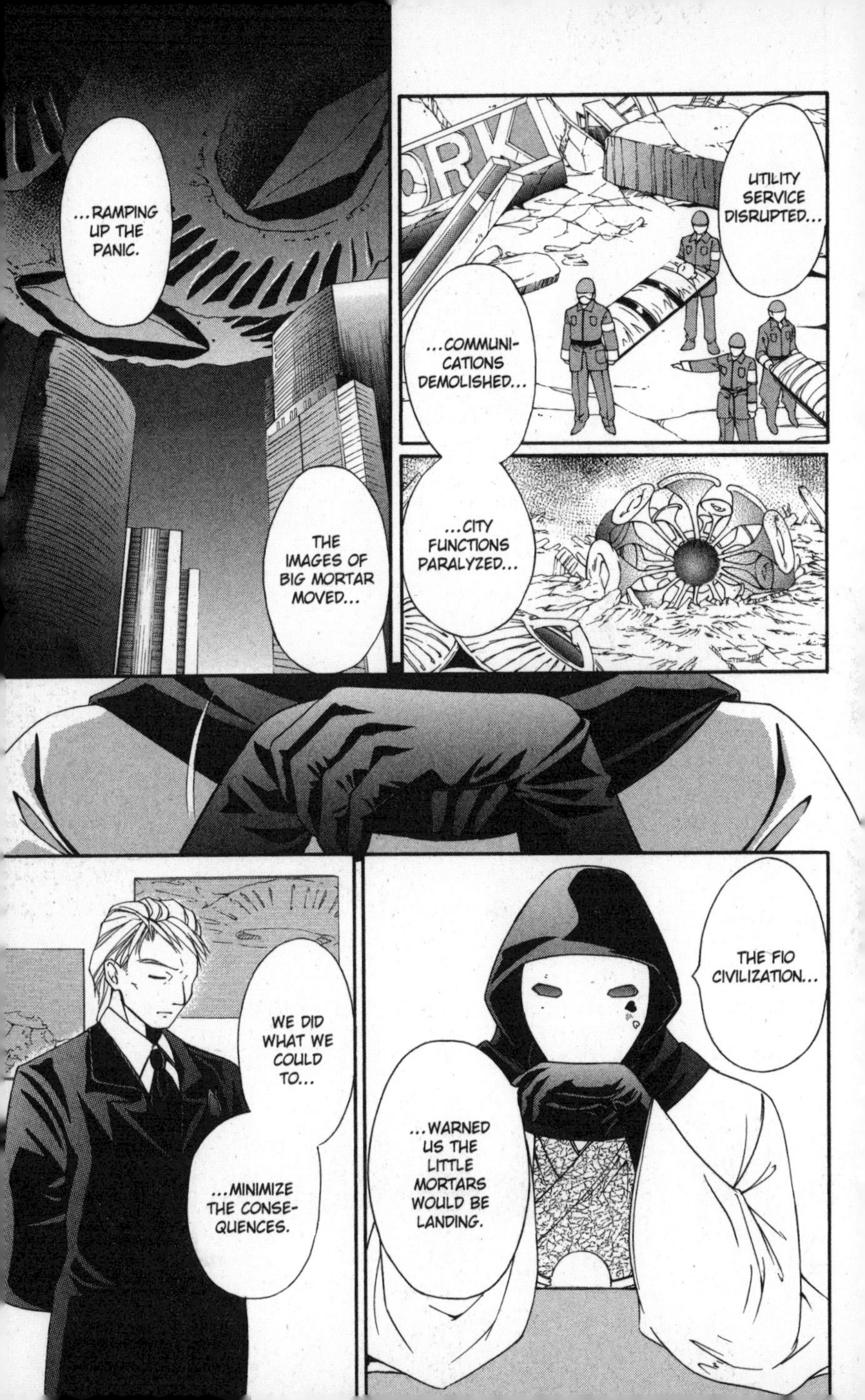
UTILITY SERVICE DISRUPTED...
...COMMUNI-CATIONS DEMOLISHED...
...CITY FUNCTIONS PARALYZED...
THE IMAGES OF BIG MORTAR MOVED...
...RAMPING UP THE PANIC.
THE FIO CIVILIZATION...
...WARNED US THE LITTLE MORTARS WOULD BE LANDING.
WE DID WHAT WE COULD TO...
...MINIMIZE THE CONSE-QUENCES.

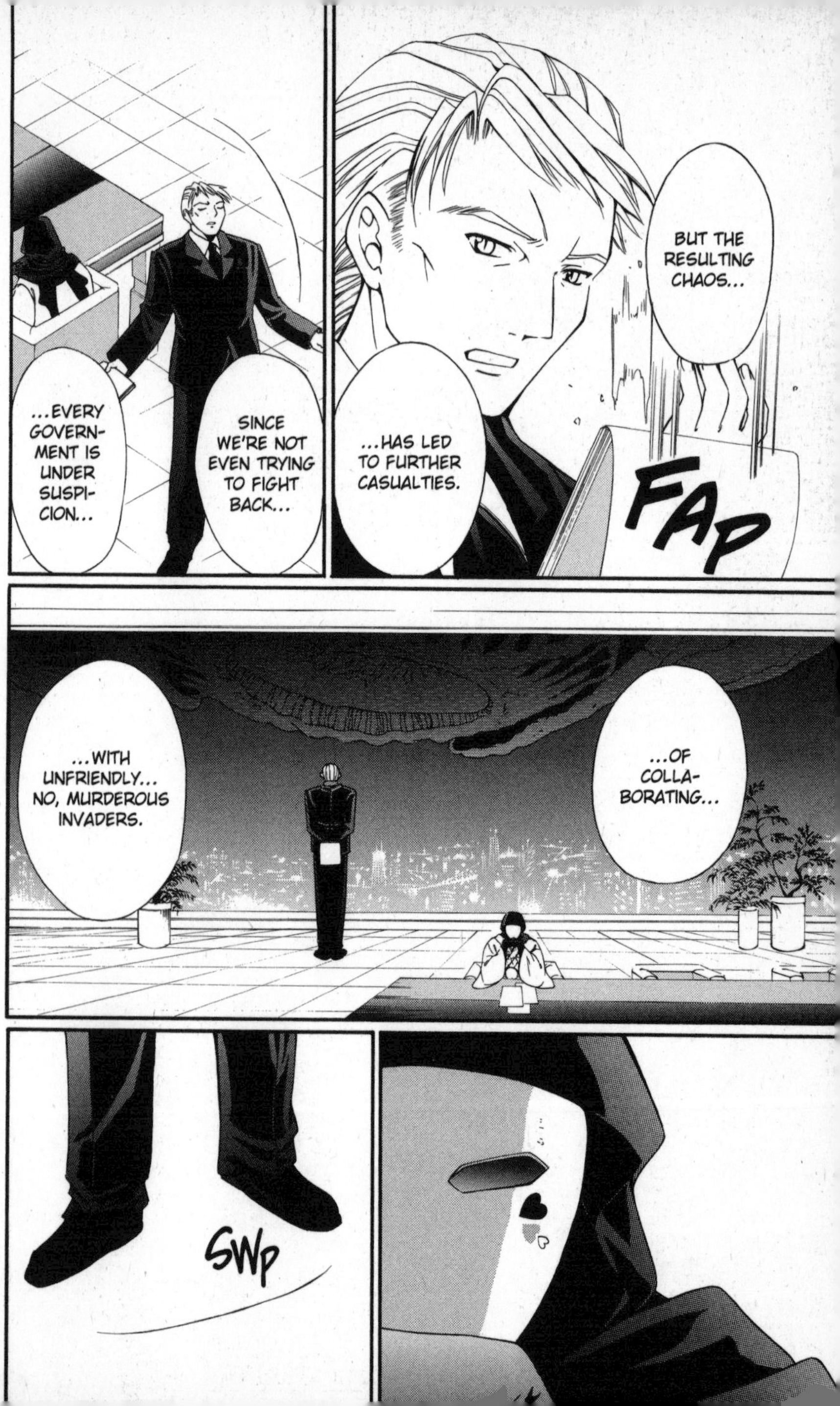
BUT THE RESULTING CHAOS...
...HAS LED TO FURTHER CASUALTIES.
FAP
SINCE WE'RE NOT EVEN TRYING TO FIGHT BACK...
...EVERY GOVERNMENT IS UNDER SUSPICION...
...OF COLLABORATING...
...WITH UNFRIENDLY... NO, MURDEROUS INVADERS.
SWP

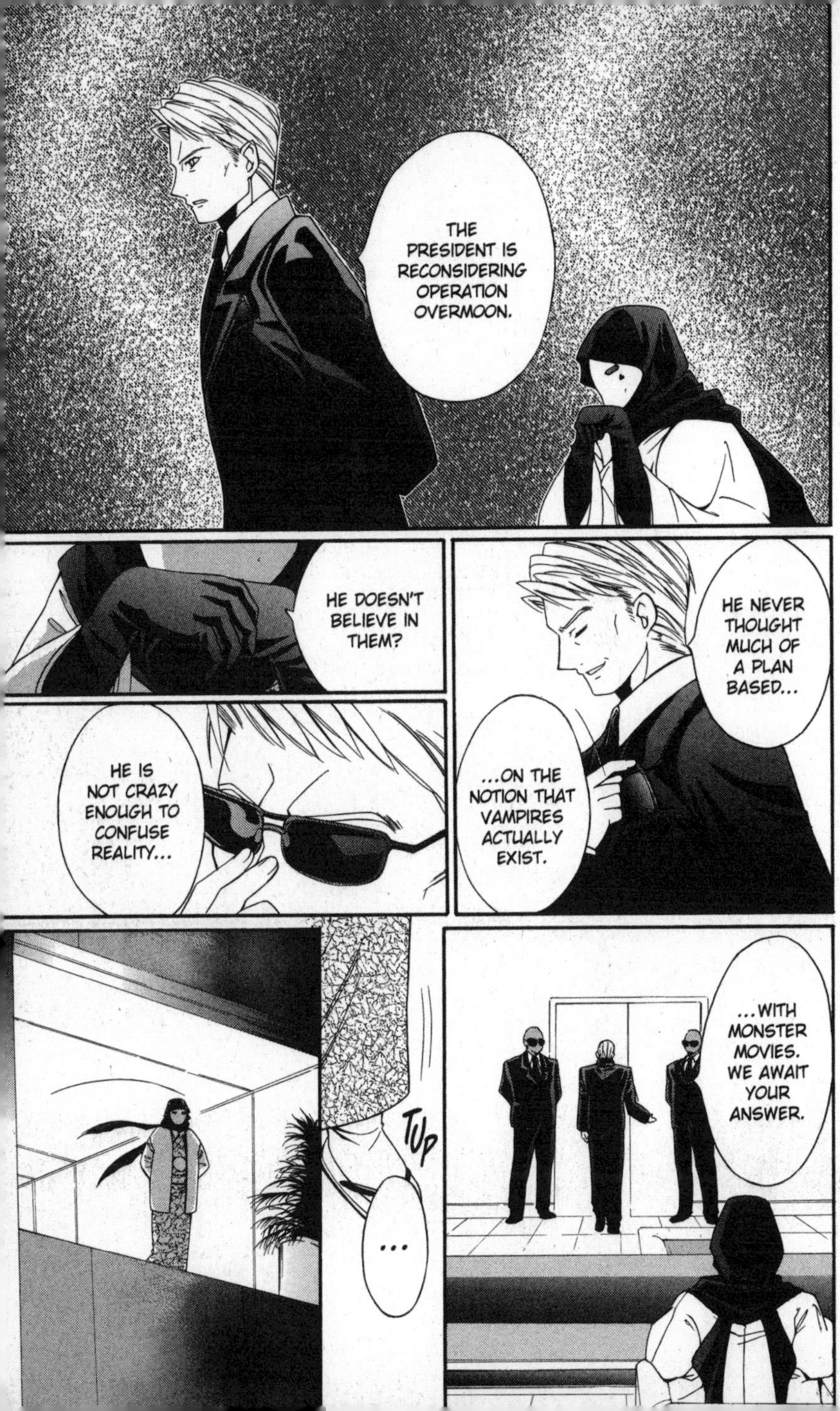
THE PRESIDENT IS RECONSIDERING OPERATION OVERMOON.
HE NEVER THOUGHT MUCH OF A PLAN BASED...
...ON THE NOTION THAT VAMPIRES ACTUALLY EXIST.
HE DOESN'T BELIEVE IN THEM?
HE IS NOT CRAZY ENOUGH TO CONFUSE REALITY...
...WITH MONSTER MOVIES. WE AWAIT YOUR ANSWER.
TUP
...

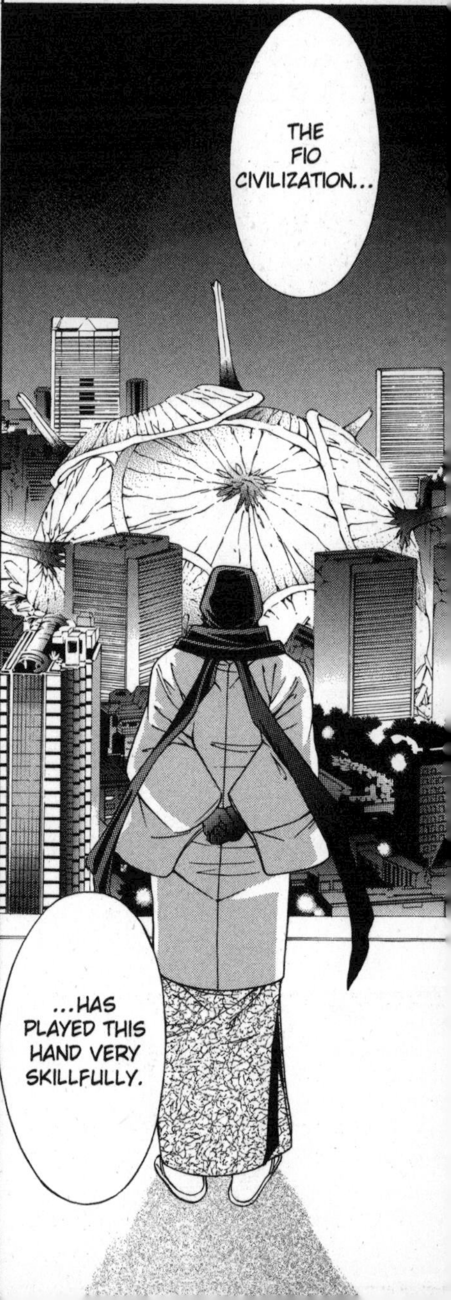
THE FIO CIVILIZATION...
...HAS PLAYED THIS HAND VERY SKILLFULLY.
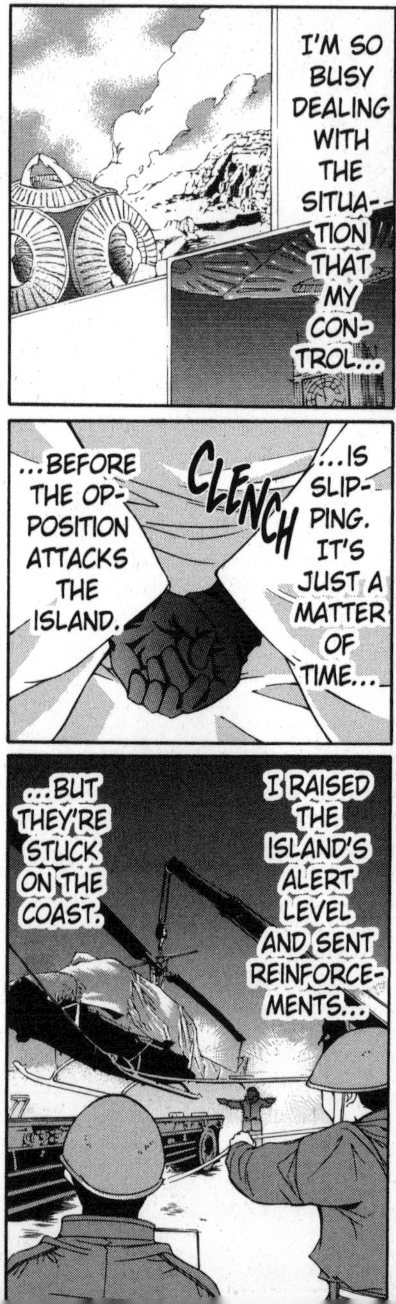
I'M SO BUSY DEALING WITH THE SITUATION THAT MY CONTROL...
...IS SLIPPING. IT'S JUST A MATTER OF TIME...
CLENCH
...BEFORE THE OPPOSITION ATTACKS THE ISLAND.
I RAISED THE ISLAND'S ALERT LEVEL AND SENT REINFORCEMENTS...
...BUT THEY'RE STUCK ON THE COAST.

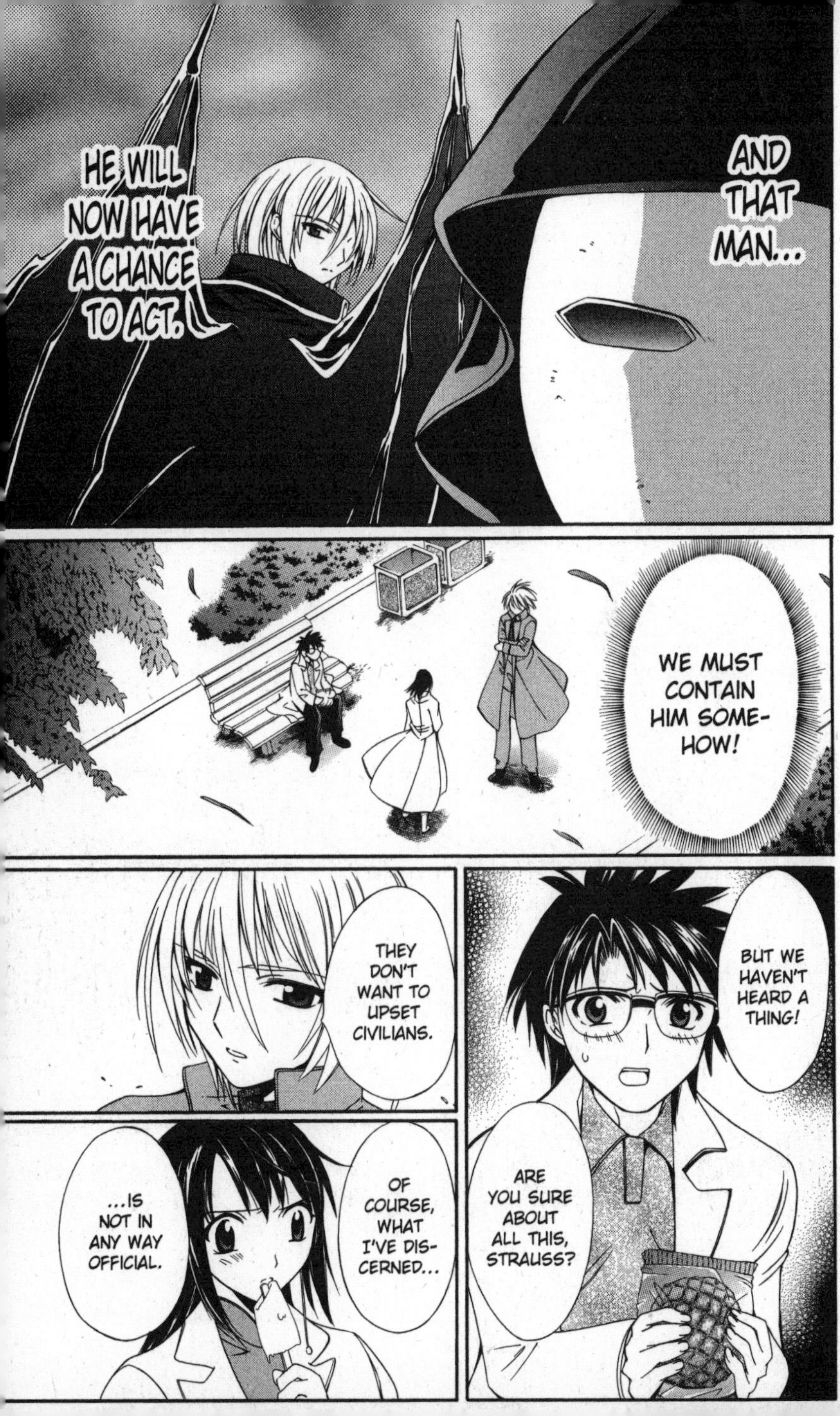
AND THAT MAN...
HE WILL NOW HAVE A CHANCE TO ACT.
WE MUST CONTAIN HIM SOME-HOW!
BUT WE HAVEN'T HEARD A THING!
ARE YOU SURE ABOUT ALL THIS, STRAUSS?
THEY DON'T WANT TO UPSET CIVILIANS.
OF COURSE, WHAT I'VE DIS-CERNED...
...IS NOT IN ANY WAY OFFICIAL.

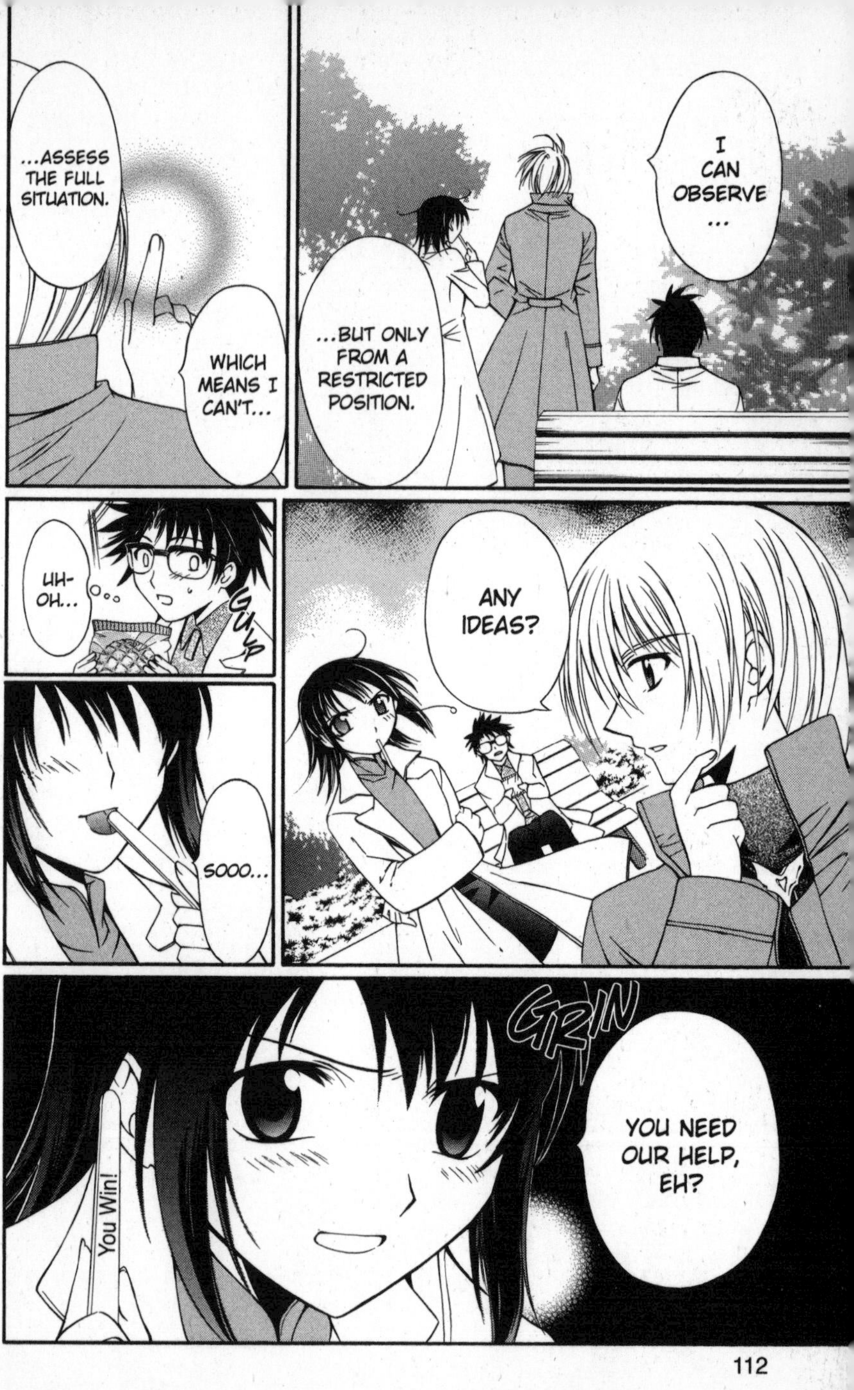
I CAN OBSERVE ...
...BUT ONLY FROM A RESTRICTED POSITION.
WHICH MEANS I CAN'T...
...ASSESS THE FULL SITUATION.
ANY IDEAS?
UH-OH...
GULP
SOOO...
GRIN
YOU NEED OUR HELP, EH?
You Win!

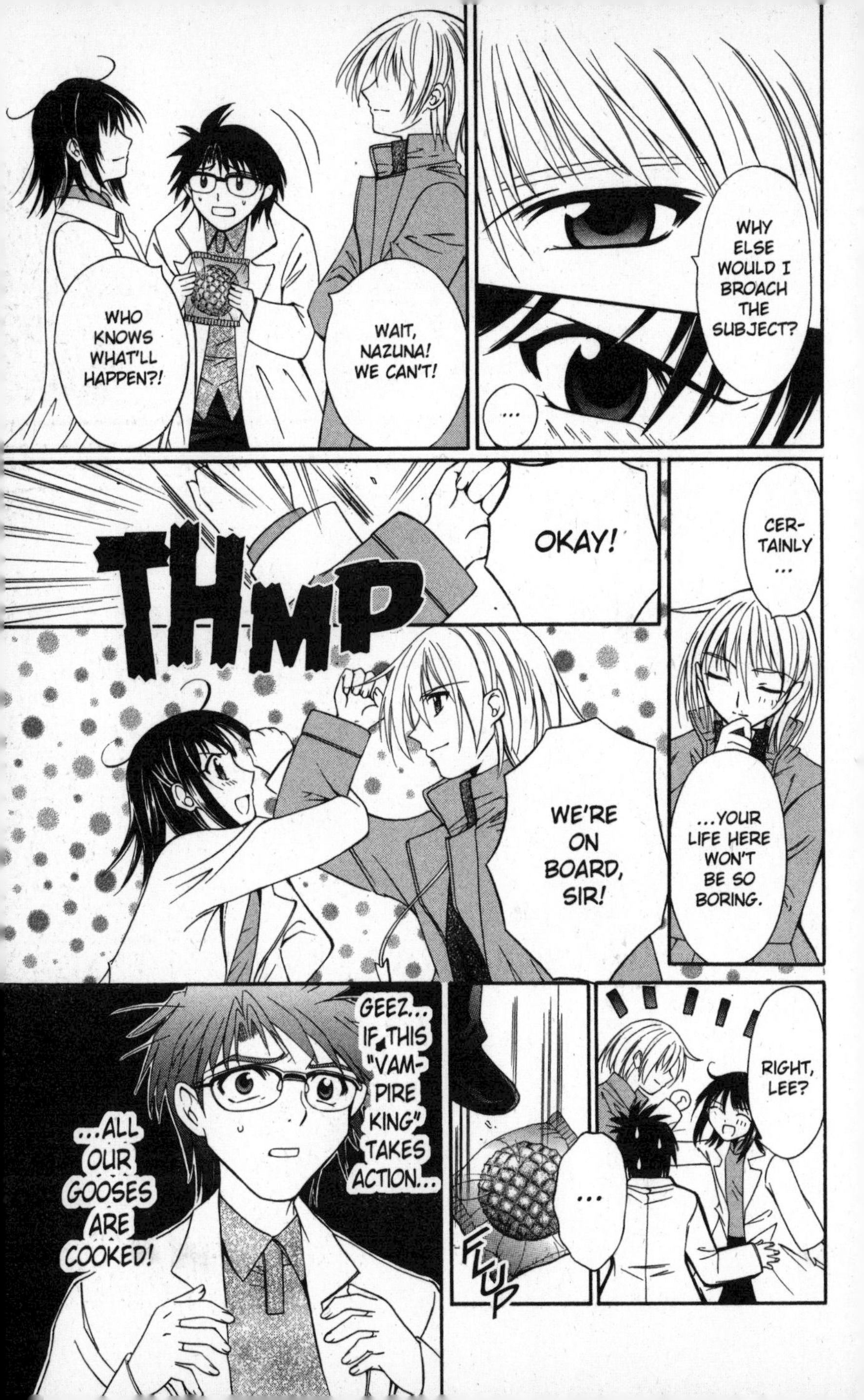
WHY ELSE WOULD I BROACH THE SUBJECT?
...
WAIT, NAZUNA! WE CAN'T!
WHO KNOWS WHAT'LL HAPPEN?!
CER-TAINLY...
...YOUR LIFE HERE WON'T BE SO BORING.
OKAY!
THMP
WE'RE ON BOARD, SIR!
RIGHT, LEE?
...
FLUP
GEEZ... IF THIS "VAM-PIRE KING" TAKES ACTION...
...ALL OUR GOOSES ARE COOKED!

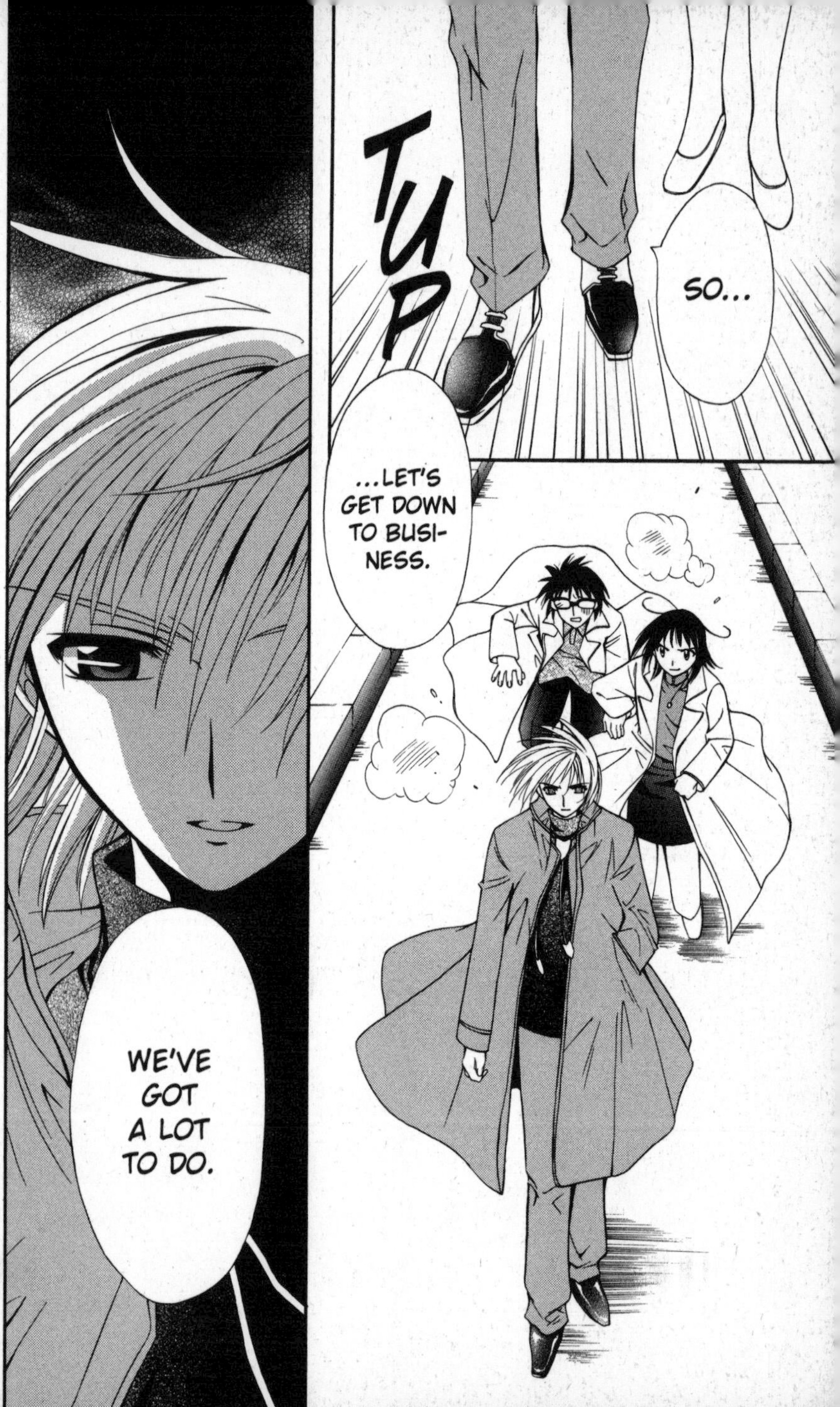
SO...
TUP
...LET'S GET DOWN TO BUSI-NESS.
WE'VE GOT A LOT TO DO.

THE RECORD OF A

FALLEN VAMPIRE

THE RECORD OF A
FALLEN VAMPIRE

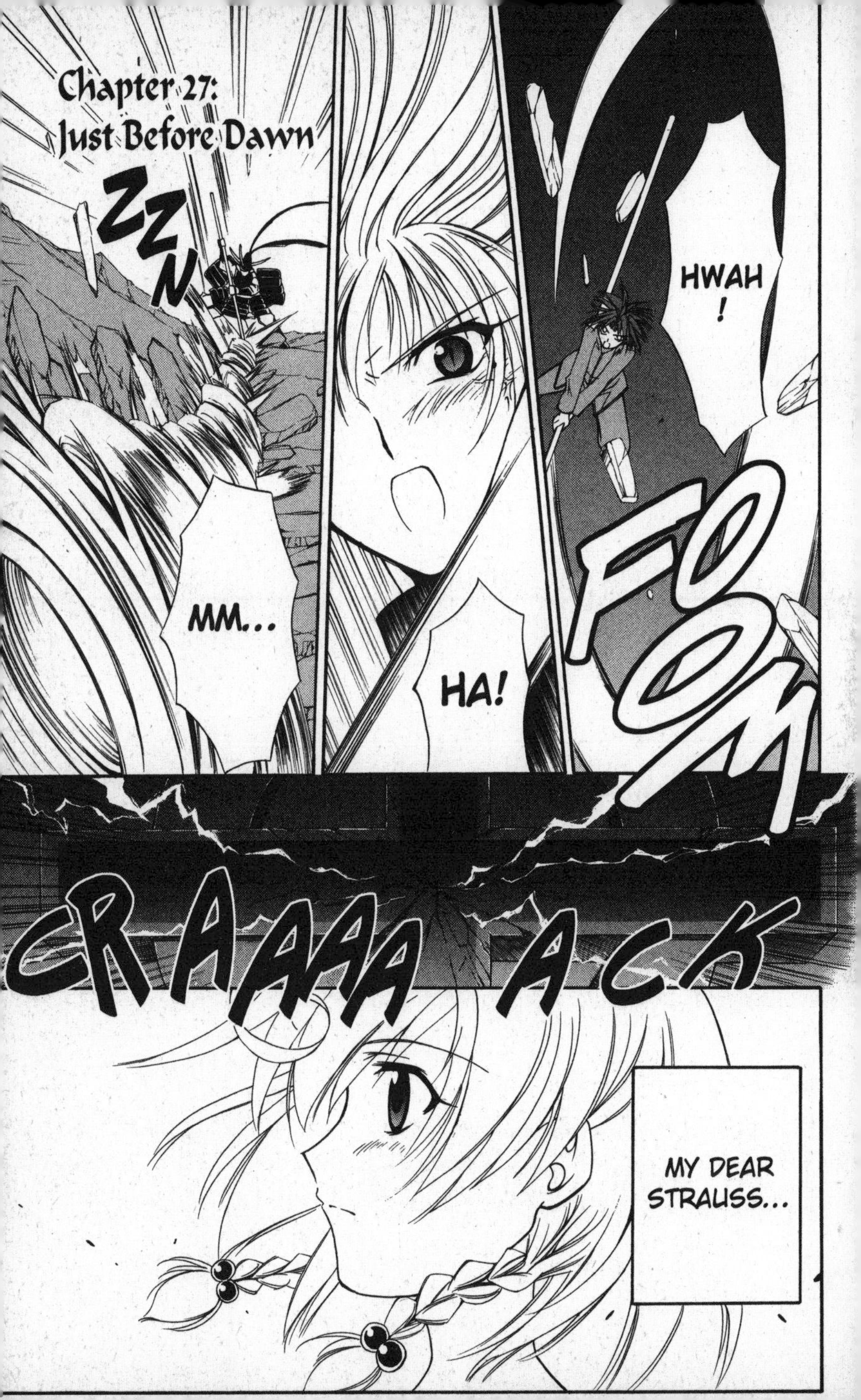
HWAH!
FOOM
HA!
Chapter 27: Just Before Dawn
ZZZN
MM...
CRAAAAACK
MY DEAR STRAUSS...

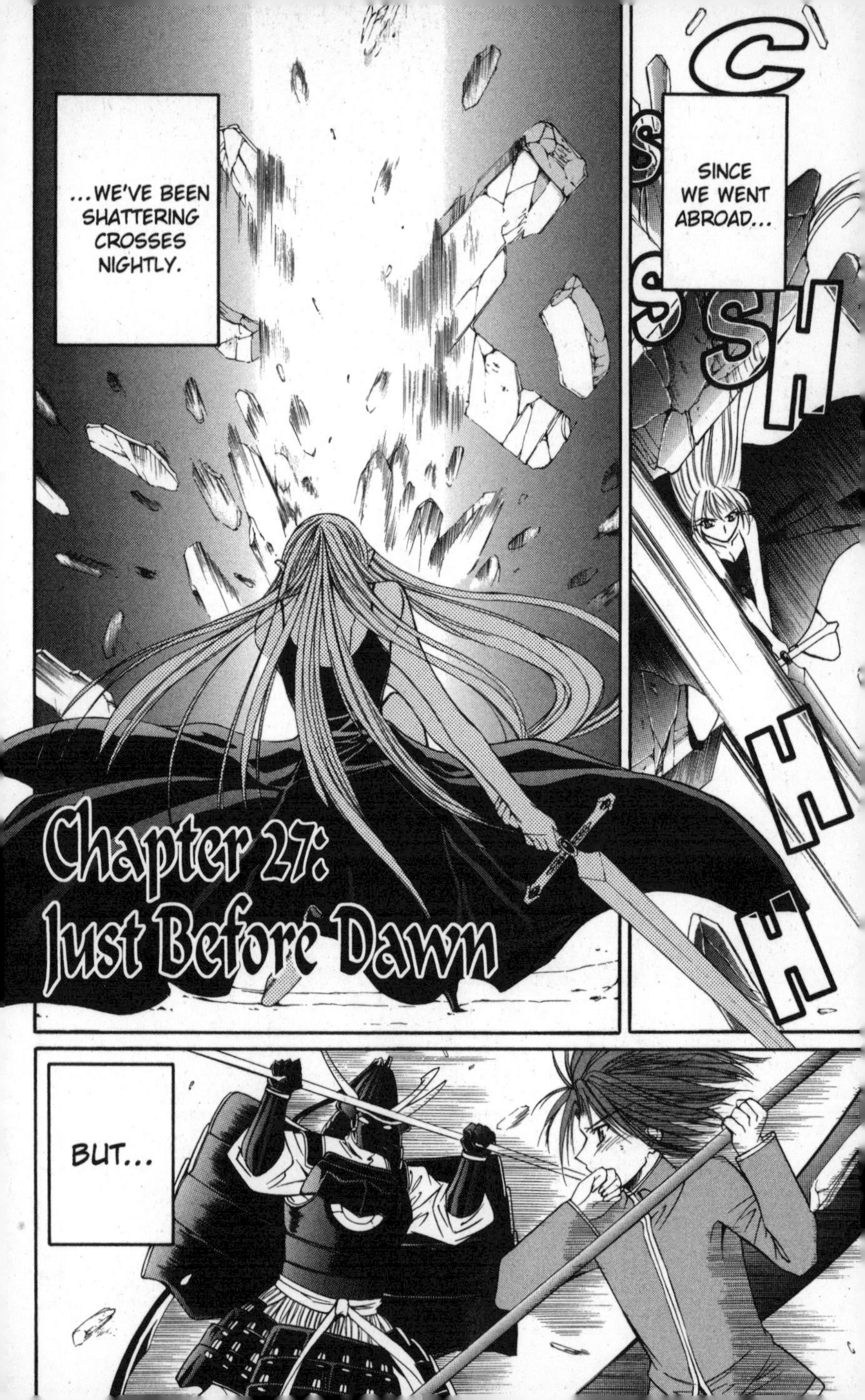
SINCE WE WENT ABROAD...
CSSSHHHH
...WE'VE BEEN SHATTERING CROSSES NIGHTLY.
Chapter 27: Just Before Dawn
BUT...

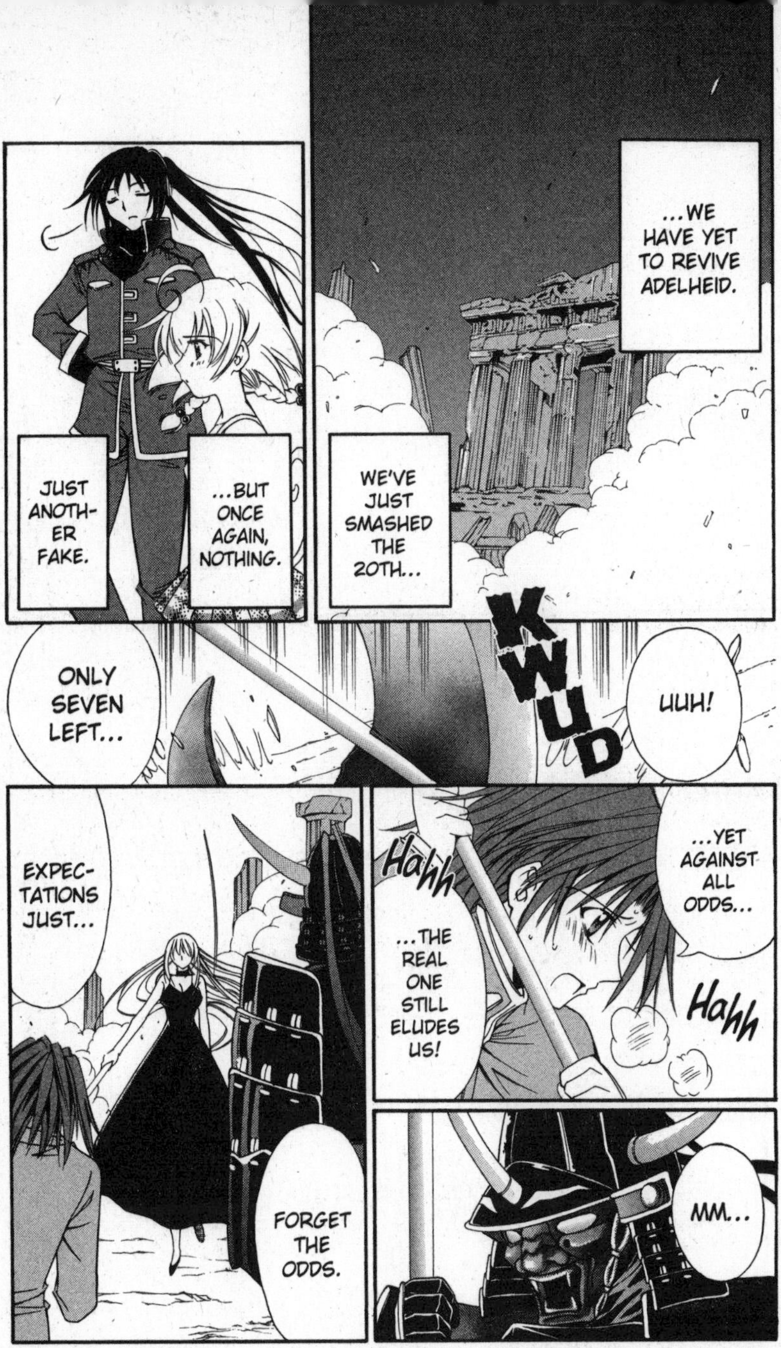
...WE HAVE YET TO REVIVE ADELHEID.
WE'VE JUST SMASHED THE 20TH...
...BUT ONCE AGAIN, NOTHING.
JUST ANOTH-ER FAKE.
UUH!
KWUD
ONLY SEVEN LEFT...
...YET AGAINST ALL ODDS...
Hahh
...THE REAL ONE STILL ELUDES US!
Hahh
MM...
EXPECTATIONS JUST...
FORGET THE ODDS.

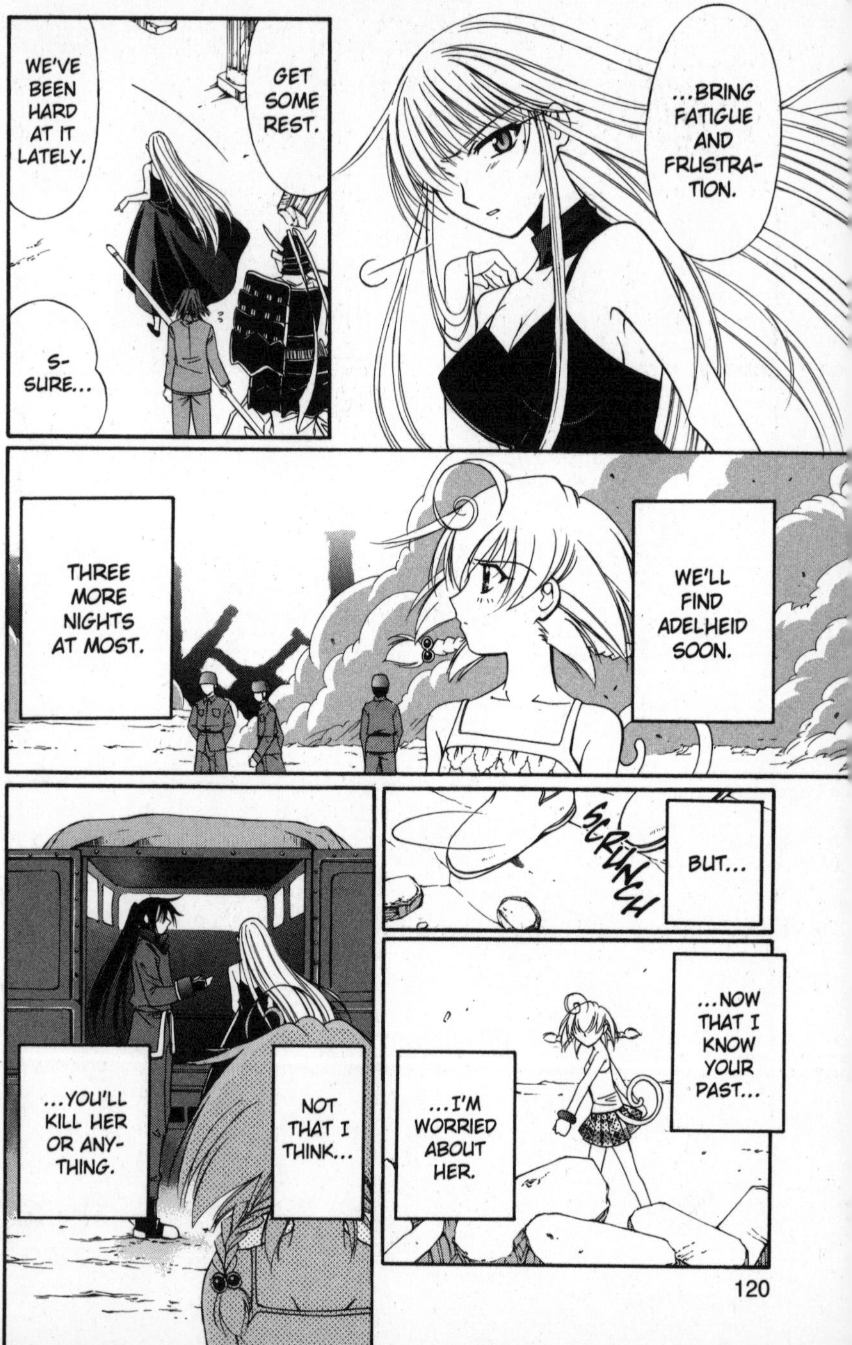
...BRING FATIGUE AND FRUSTRA-TION.
GET SOME REST.
WE'VE BEEN HARD AT IT LATELY.
S-SURE...
WE'LL FIND ADELHEID SOON.
THREE MORE NIGHTS AT MOST.
SCRUNCH
BUT...
...NOW THAT I KNOW YOUR PAST...
...I'M WORRIED ABOUT HER.
NOT THAT I THINK...
...YOU'LL KILL HER OR ANY-THING.

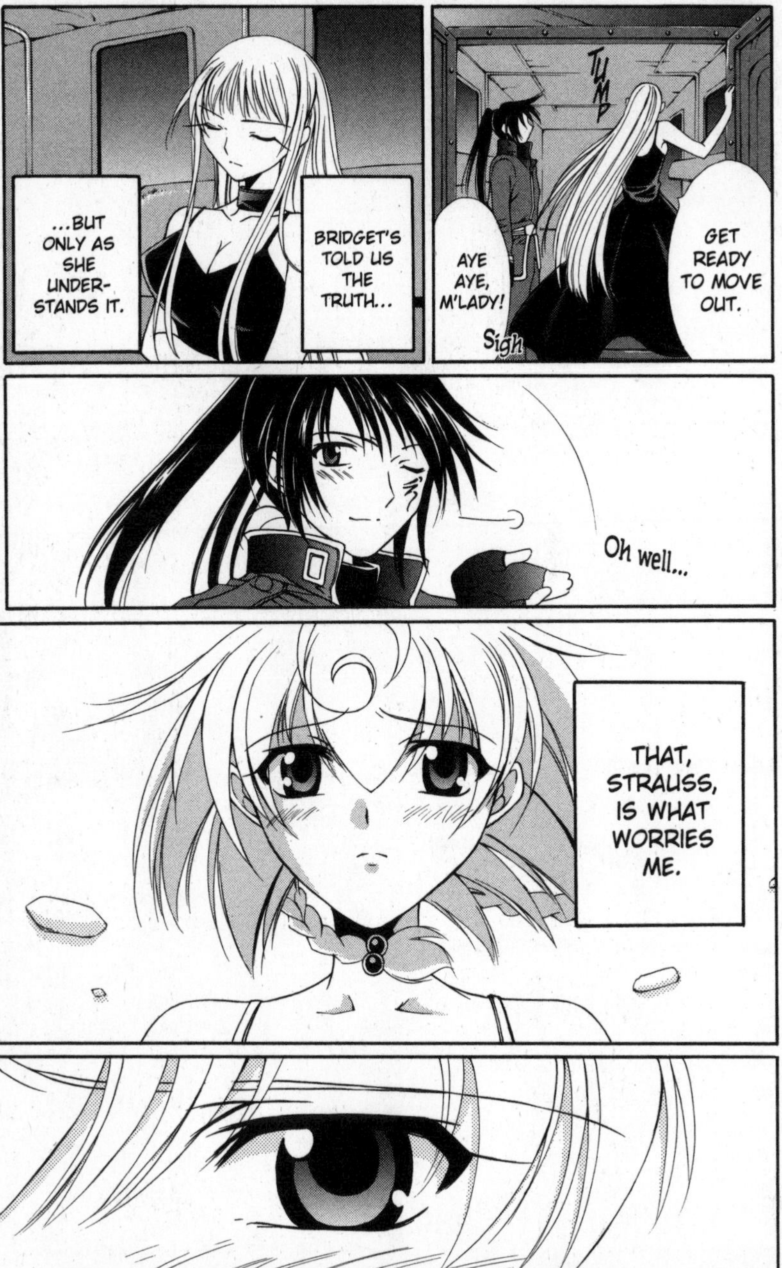
TUMP
GET READY TO MOVE OUT.
AYE AYE, M'LADY!
Sigh
BRIDGET'S TOLD US THE TRUTH...
...BUT ONLY AS SHE UNDERSTANDS IT.
Oh well...
THAT, STRAUSS, IS WHAT WORRIES ME.

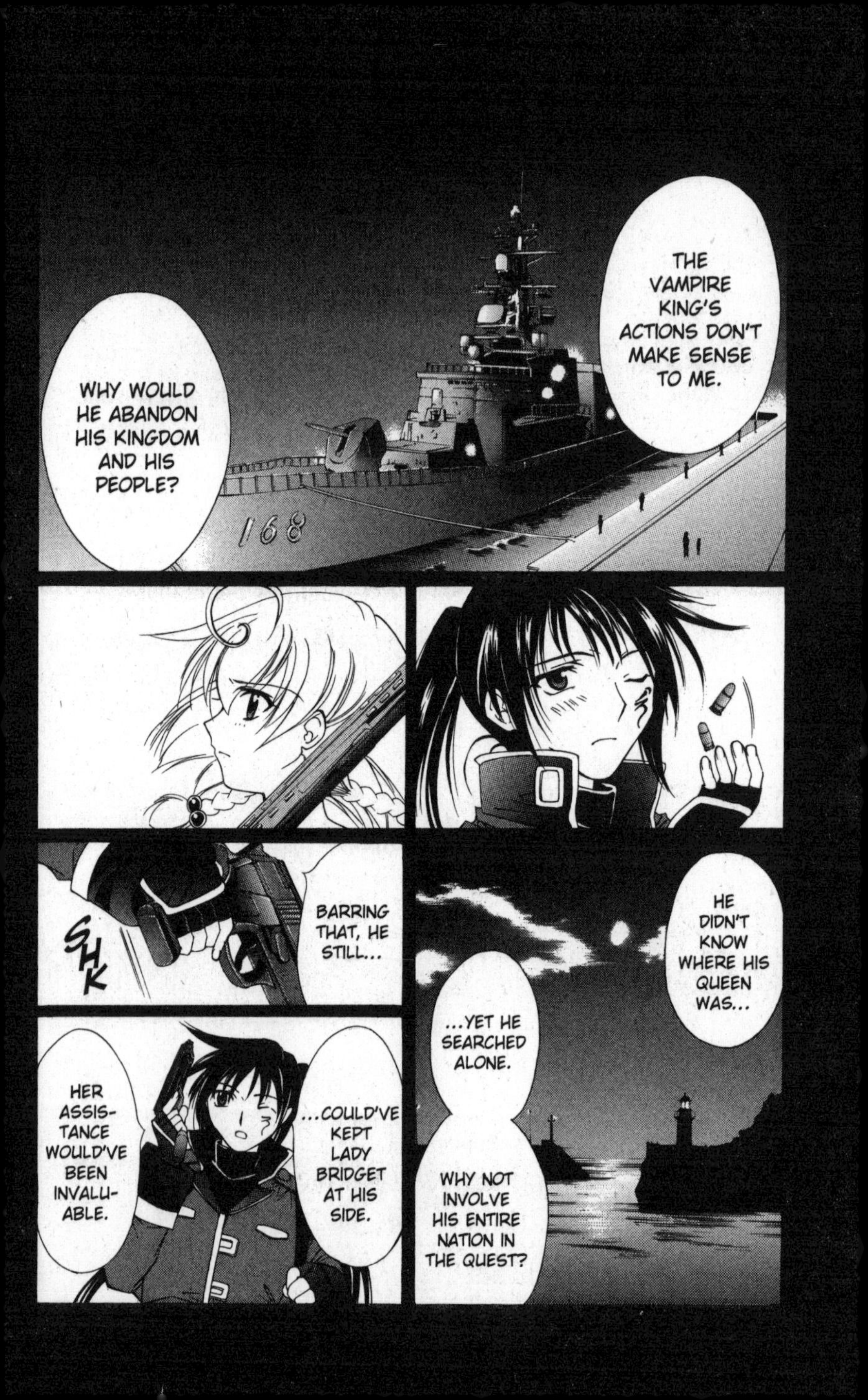
THE VAMPIRE KING'S ACTIONS DON'T MAKE SENSE TO ME.
WHY WOULD HE ABANDON HIS KINGDOM AND HIS PEOPLE?
168
HE DIDN'T KNOW WHERE HIS QUEEN WAS...
...YET HE SEARCHED ALONE.
WHY NOT INVOLVE HIS ENTIRE NATION IN THE QUEST?
BARRING THAT, HE STILL...
SHK
...COULD'VE KEPT LADY BRIDGET AT HIS SIDE.
HER ASSISTANCE WOULD'VE BEEN INVALUABLE.

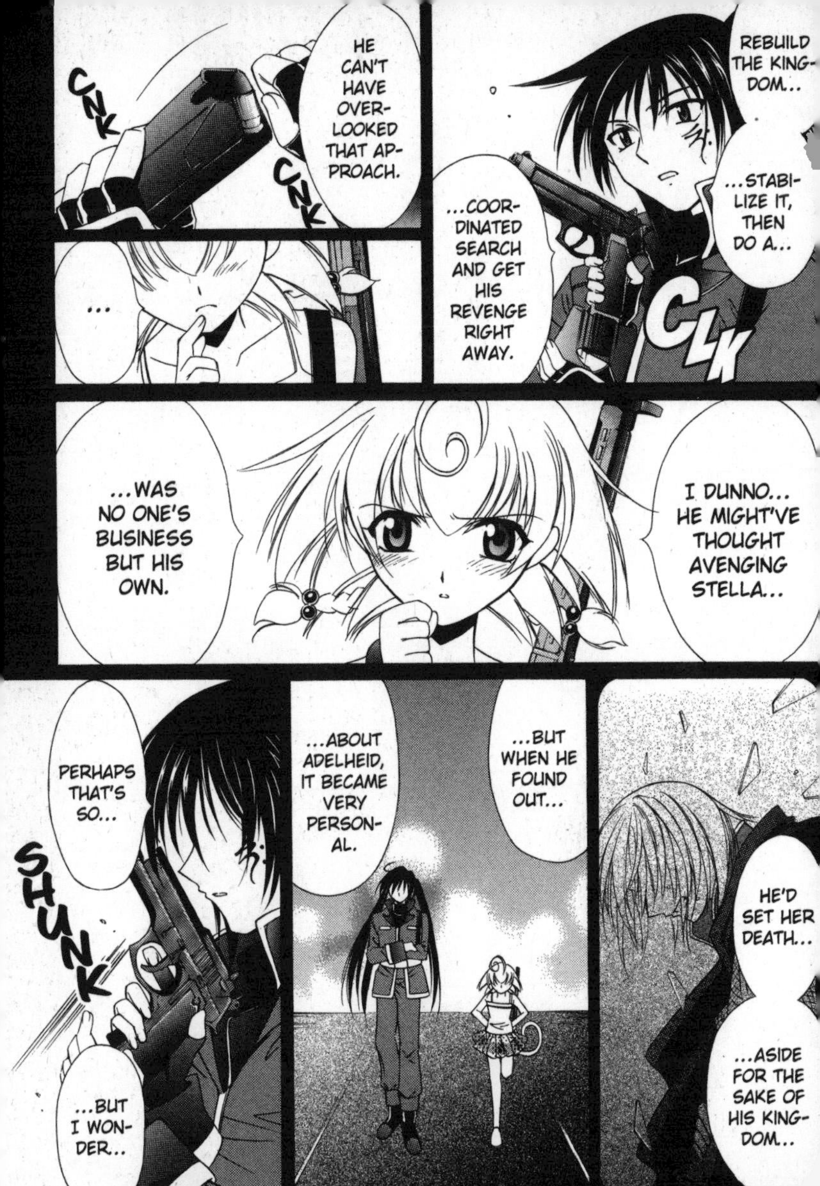
REBUILD THE KINGDOM...
...STABILIZE IT, THEN DO A...
...COORDINATED SEARCH AND GET HIS REVENGE RIGHT AWAY.
CLK
HE CAN'T HAVE OVERLOOKED THAT APPROACH.
CNK
CNK
...
I DUNNO... HE MIGHT'VE THOUGHT AVENGING STELLA...
...WAS NO ONE'S BUSINESS BUT HIS OWN.
HE'D SET HER DEATH...
...ASIDE FOR THE SAKE OF HIS KINGDOM...
...BUT WHEN HE FOUND OUT...
...ABOUT ADELHEID, IT BECAME VERY PERSONAL.
PERHAPS THAT'S SO...
SHUNK
...BUT I WONDER...

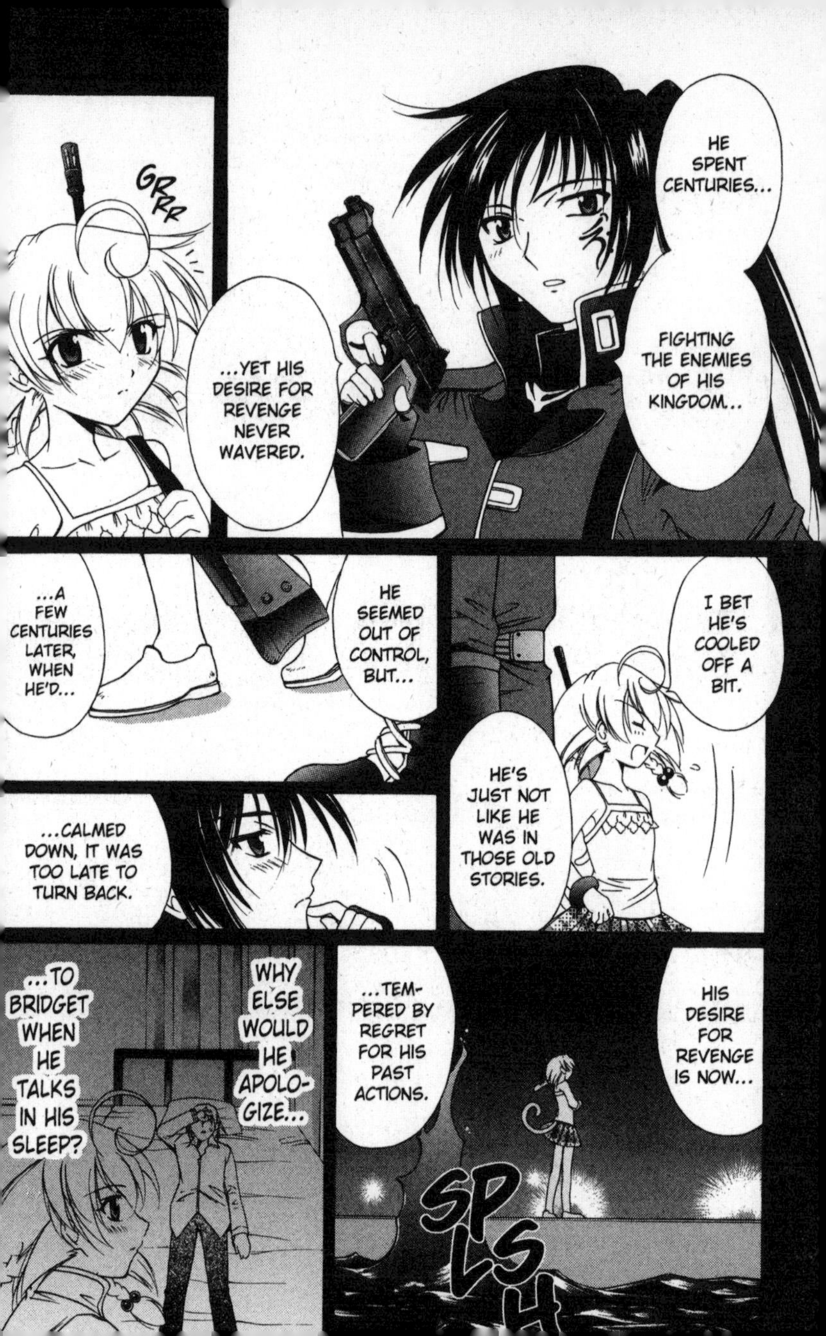
HE SPENT CENTURIES...
FIGHTING THE ENEMIES OF HIS KINGDOM...
...YET HIS DESIRE FOR REVENGE NEVER WAVERED.
GRRR
I BET HE'S COOLED OFF A BIT.
HE'S JUST NOT LIKE HE WAS IN THOSE OLD STORIES.
HE SEEMED OUT OF CONTROL, BUT...
...A FEW CENTURIES LATER, WHEN HE'D...
...CALMED DOWN, IT WAS TOO LATE TO TURN BACK.
HIS DESIRE FOR REVENGE IS NOW...
...TEMPERED BY REGRET FOR HIS PAST ACTIONS.
SPLSH
WHY ELSE WOULD HE APOLOGIZE...
...TO BRIDGET WHEN HE TALKS IN HIS SLEEP?

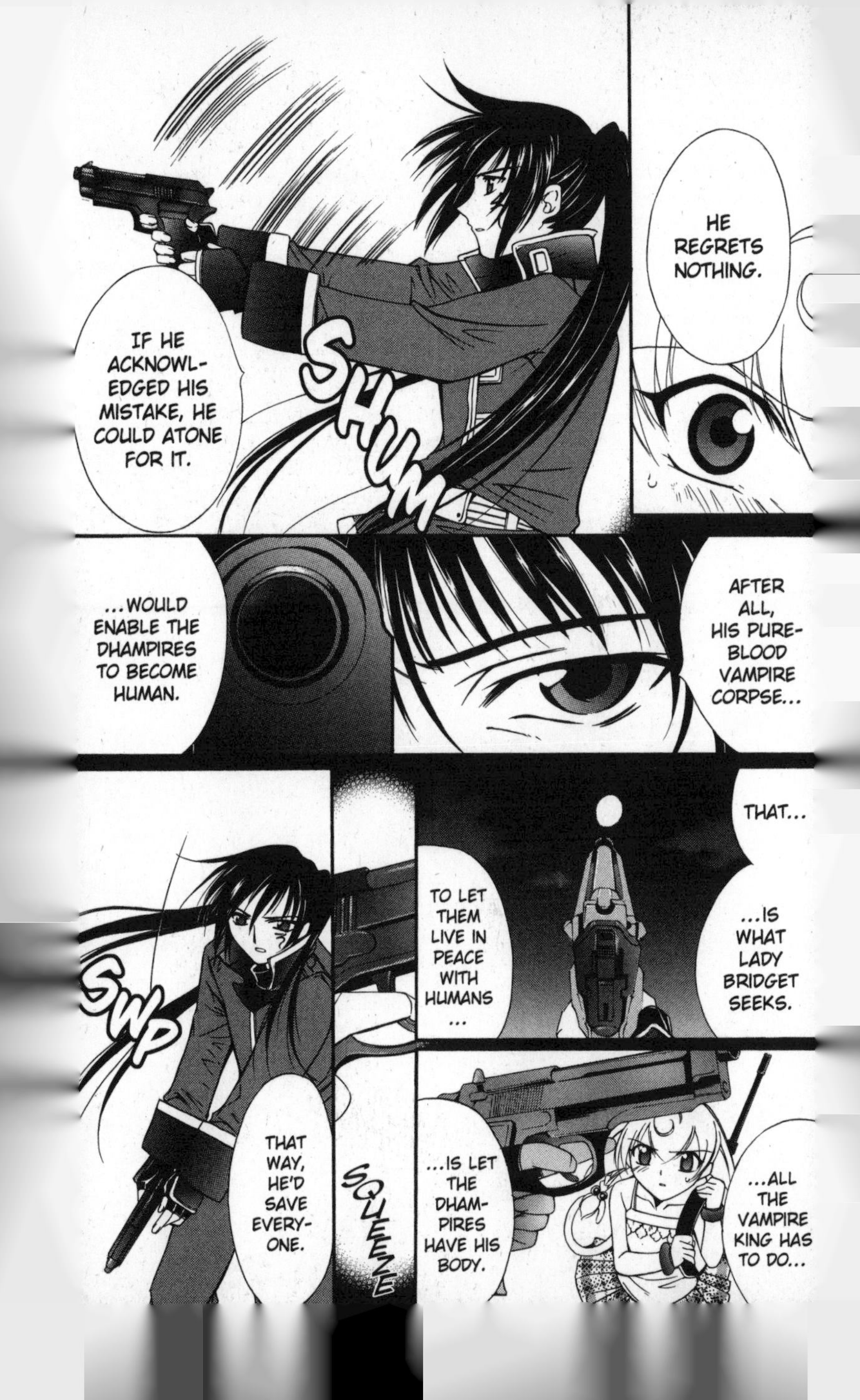
HE REGRETS NOTHING.
IF HE ACKNOWL-EDGED HIS MISTAKE, HE COULD ATONE FOR IT.
SHUM
AFTER ALL, HIS PURE-BLOOD VAMPIRE CORPSE...
...WOULD ENABLE THE DHAMPIRES TO BECOME HUMAN.
THAT...
...IS WHAT LADY BRIDGET SEEKS.
TO LET THEM LIVE IN PEACE WITH HUMANS...
...ALL THE VAMPIRE KING HAS TO DO...
...IS LET THE DHAM-PIRES HAVE HIS BODY.
SQUEEZE
SWP
THAT WAY, HE'D SAVE EVERY-ONE.

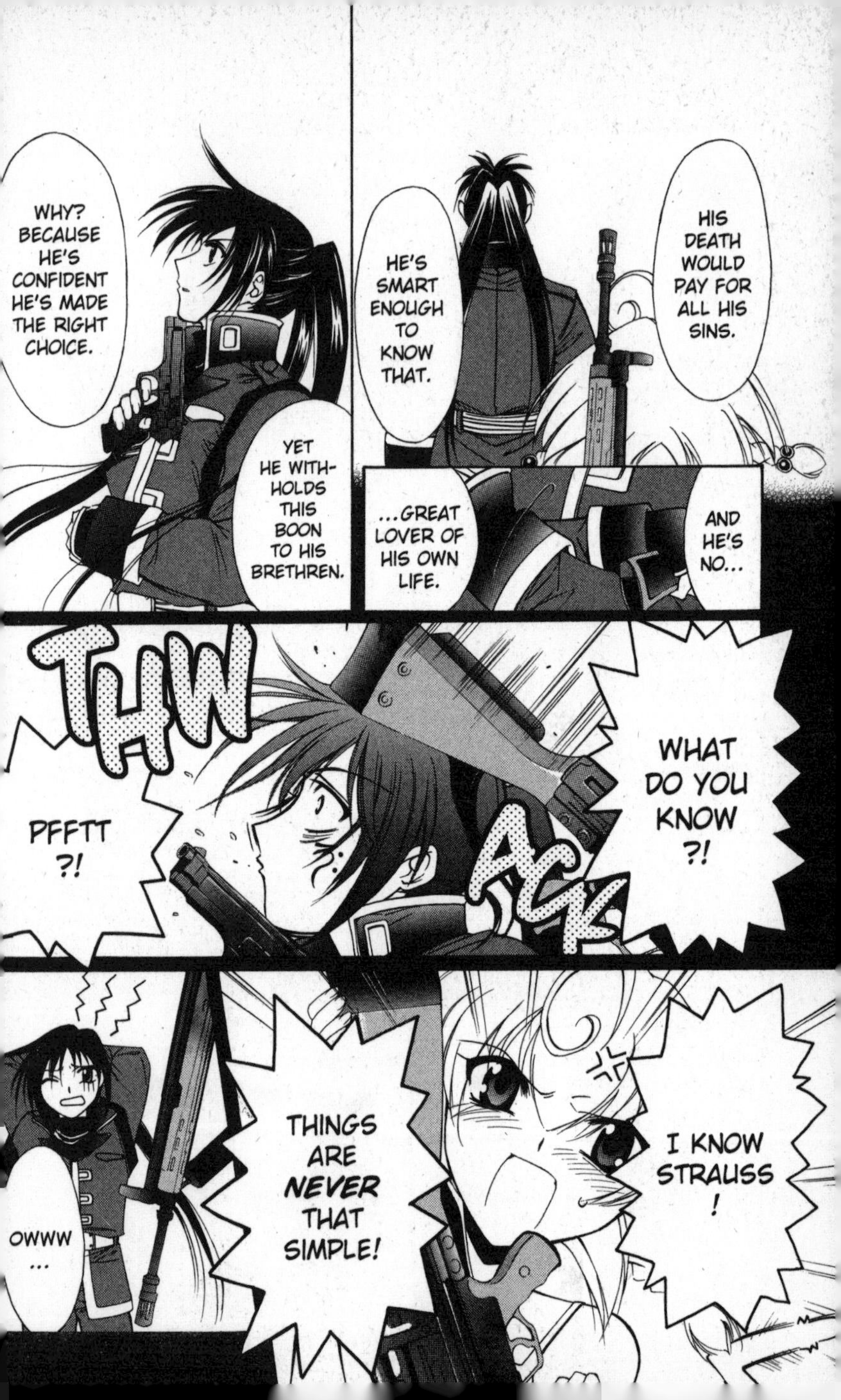

HIS DEATH WOULD PAY FOR ALL HIS SINS.
HE'S SMART ENOUGH TO KNOW THAT.
AND HE'S NO...
...GREAT LOVER OF HIS OWN LIFE.
WHY? BECAUSE HE'S CONFIDENT HE'S MADE THE RIGHT CHOICE.
YET HE WITH-HOLDS THIS BOON TO HIS BRETHREN.
WHAT DO YOU KNOW ?!
THWACK
PFFTT ?!
I KNOW STRAUSS !
THINGS ARE *NEVER* THAT SIMPLE!
OWWW ...

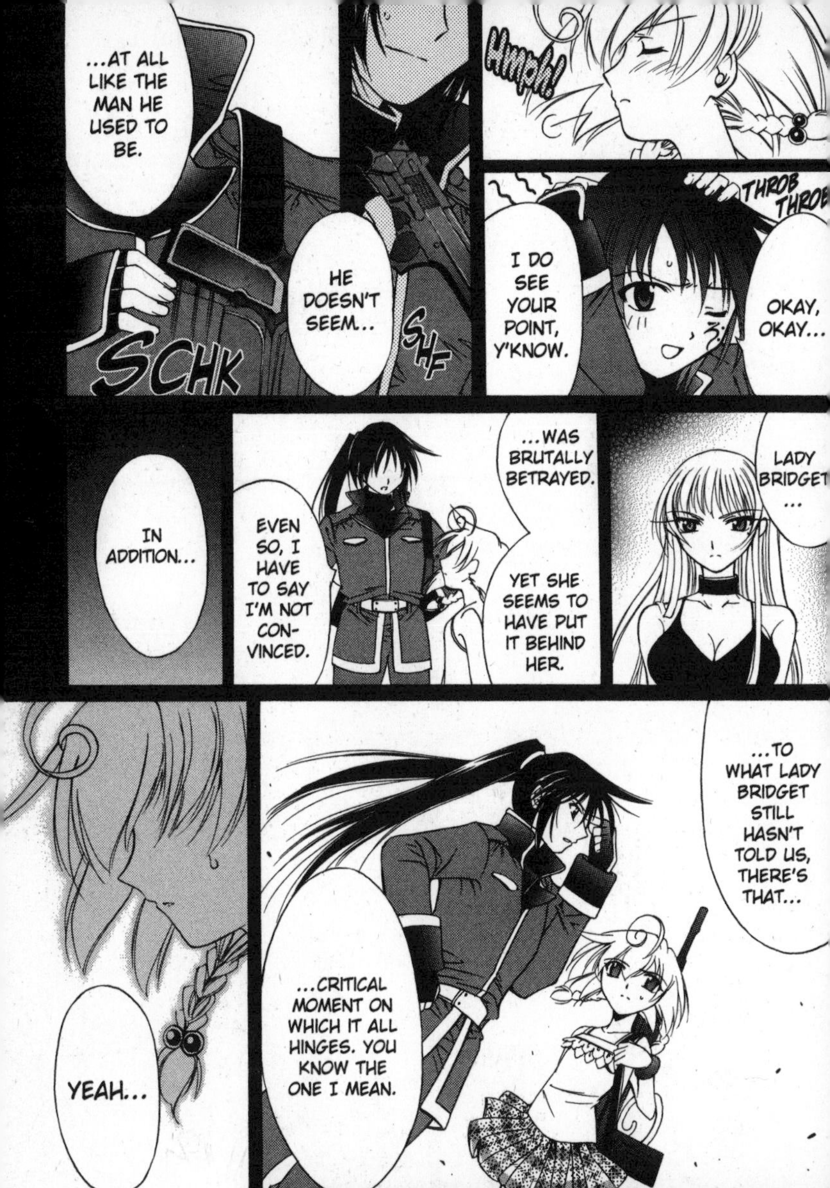
HMPH!
THROB THRO
OKAY, OKAY...
I DO SEE YOUR POINT, Y'KNOW.
HE DOESN'T SEEM...
SHF
...AT ALL LIKE THE MAN HE USED TO BE.
SCHK
LADY BRIDGET...
...WAS BRUTALLY BETRAYED.
YET SHE SEEMS TO HAVE PUT IT BEHIND HER.
EVEN SO, I HAVE TO SAY I'M NOT CON-VINCED.
IN ADDITION...
...TO WHAT LADY BRIDGET STILL HASN'T TOLD US, THERE'S THAT...
...CRITICAL MOMENT ON WHICH IT ALL HINGES. YOU KNOW THE ONE I MEAN.
YEAH...

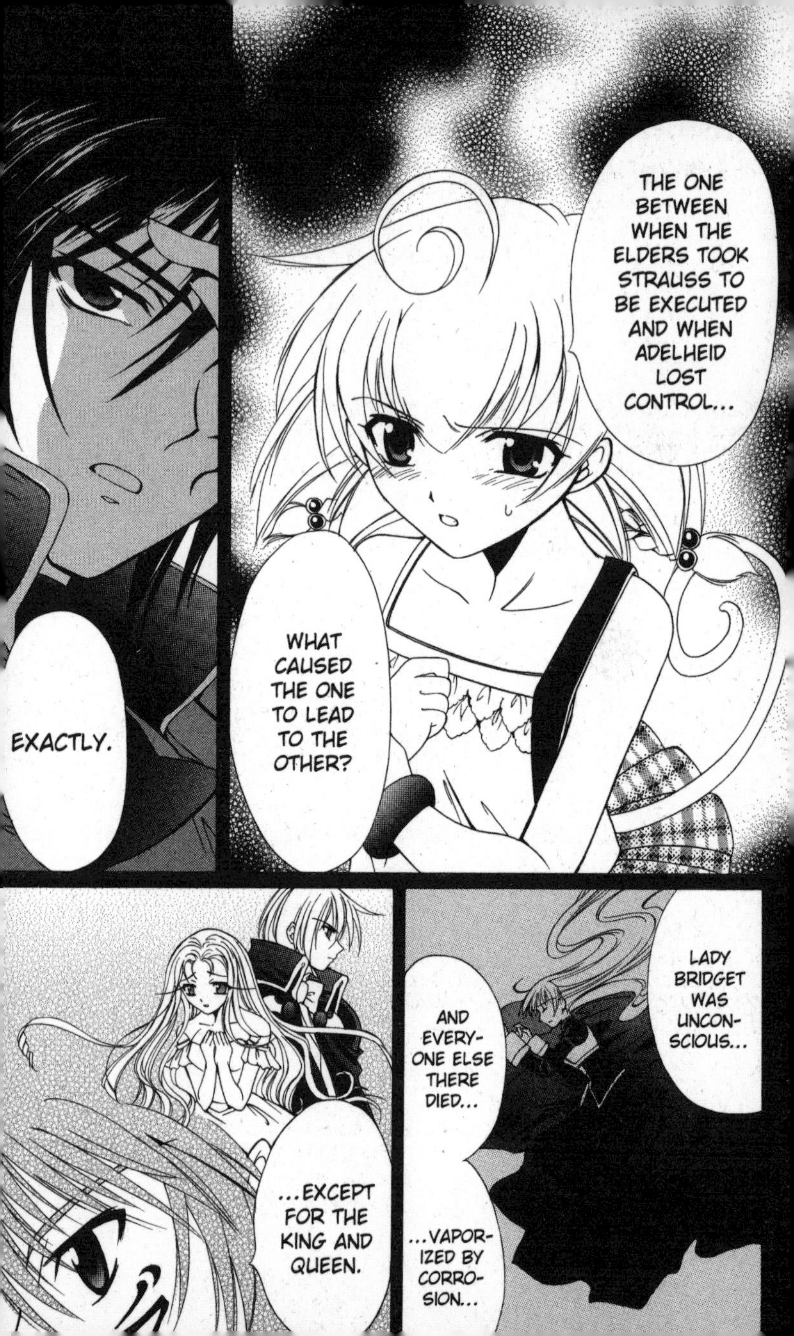
THE ONE BETWEEN WHEN THE ELDERS TOOK STRAUSS TO BE EXECUTED AND WHEN ADELHEID LOST CONTROL...
WHAT CAUSED THE ONE TO LEAD TO THE OTHER?
EXACTLY.
LADY BRIDGET WAS UNCON-SCIOUS...
AND EVERY-ONE ELSE THERE DIED...
...VAPOR-IZED BY CORRO-SION...
...EXCEPT FOR THE KING AND QUEEN.

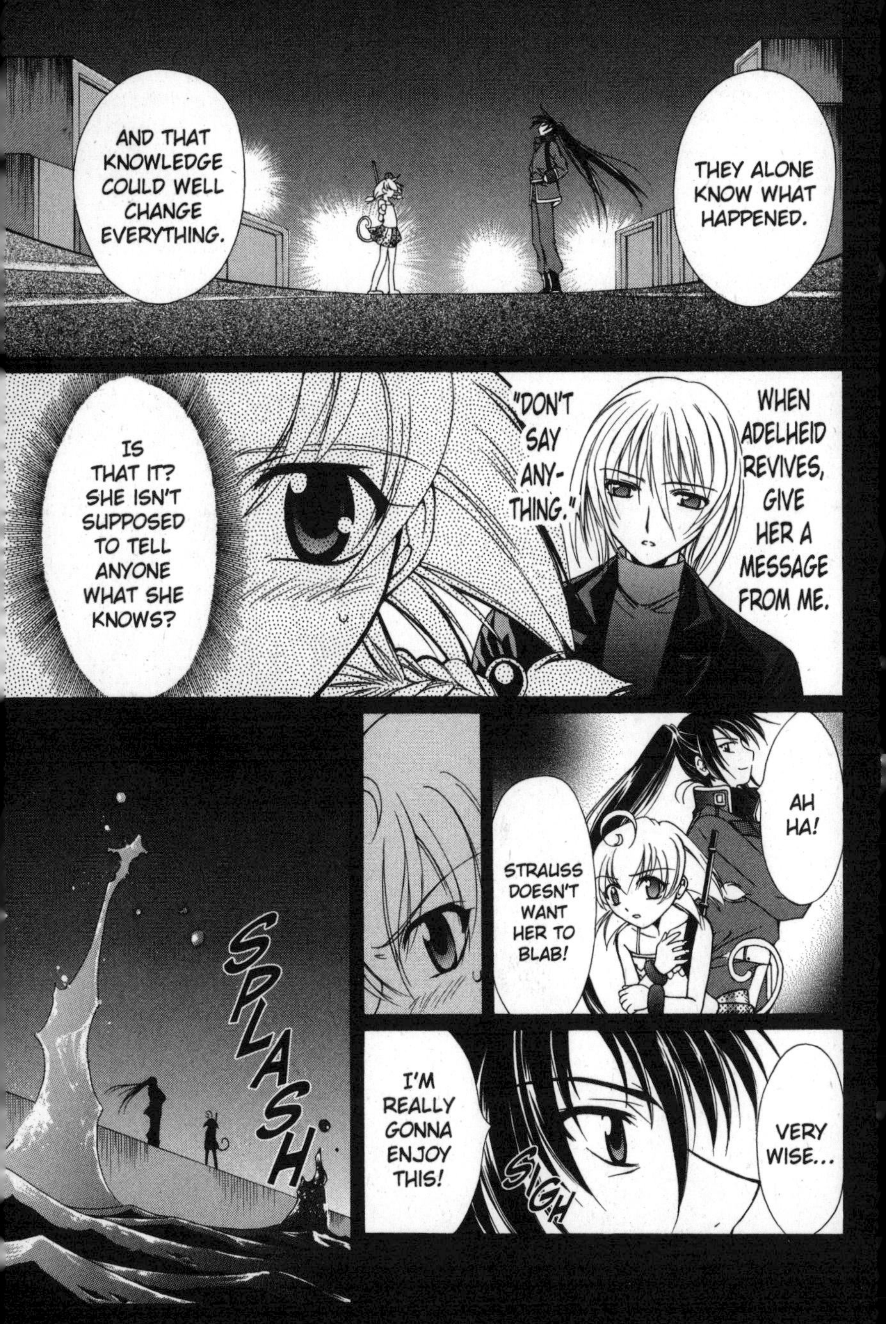
THEY ALONE KNOW WHAT HAPPENED.
AND THAT KNOWLEDGE COULD WELL CHANGE EVERYTHING.
WHEN ADELHEID REVIVES, GIVE HER A MESSAGE FROM ME.
"DON'T SAY ANY-THING."
IS THAT IT? SHE ISN'T SUPPOSED TO TELL ANYONE WHAT SHE KNOWS?
AH HA!
STRAUSS DOESN'T WANT HER TO BLAB!
VERY WISE...
SIGH
I'M REALLY GONNA ENJOY THIS!
SPLASH

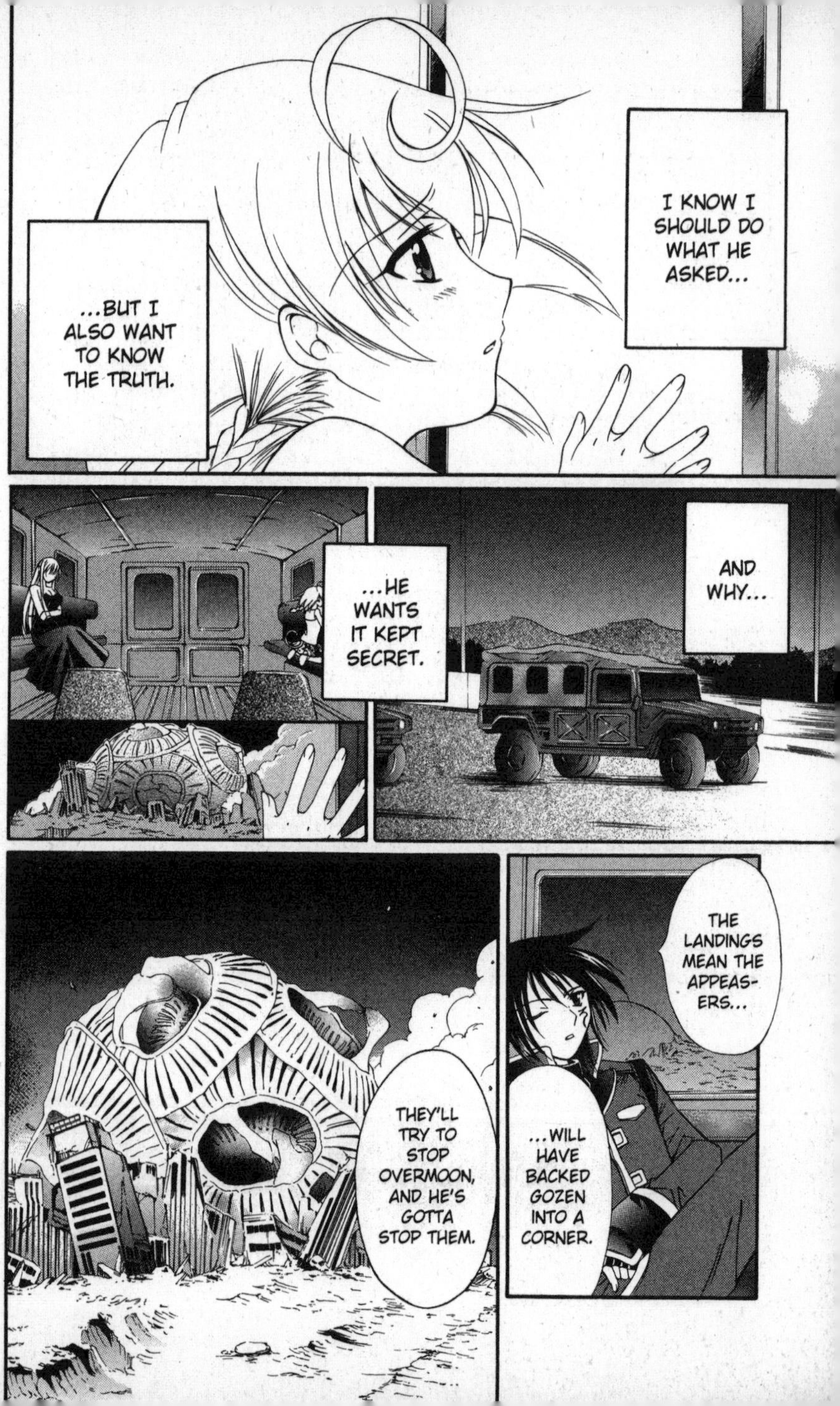
I KNOW I SHOULD DO WHAT HE ASKED...
...BUT I ALSO WANT TO KNOW THE TRUTH.
AND WHY...
...HE WANTS IT KEPT SECRET.
THE LANDINGS MEAN THE APPEAS-ERS...
...WILL HAVE BACKED GOZEN INTO A CORNER.
THEY'LL TRY TO STOP OVERMOON, AND HE'S GOTTA STOP THEM.

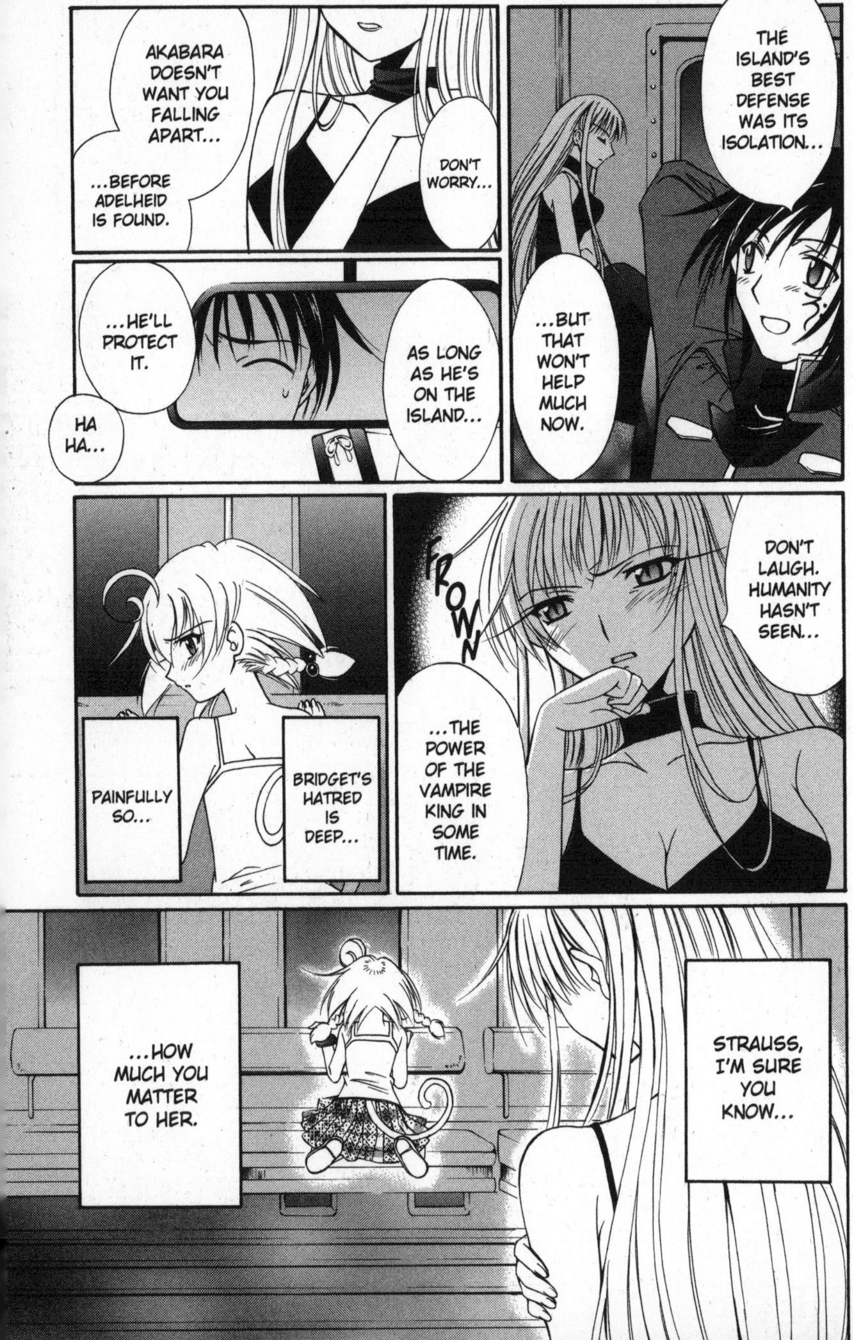
THE ISLAND'S BEST DEFENSE WAS ITS ISOLATION...
...BUT THAT WON'T HELP MUCH NOW.
AKABARA DOESN'T WANT YOU FALLING APART...
...BEFORE ADELHEID IS FOUND.
DON'T WORRY...
AS LONG AS HE'S ON THE ISLAND...
...HE'LL PROTECT IT.
HA HA...
FROWN
DON'T LAUGH. HUMANITY HASN'T SEEN...
...THE POWER OF THE VAMPIRE KING IN SOME TIME.
BRIDGET'S HATRED IS DEEP...
PAINFULLY SO...
STRAUSS, I'M SURE YOU KNOW...
...HOW MUCH YOU MATTER TO HER.

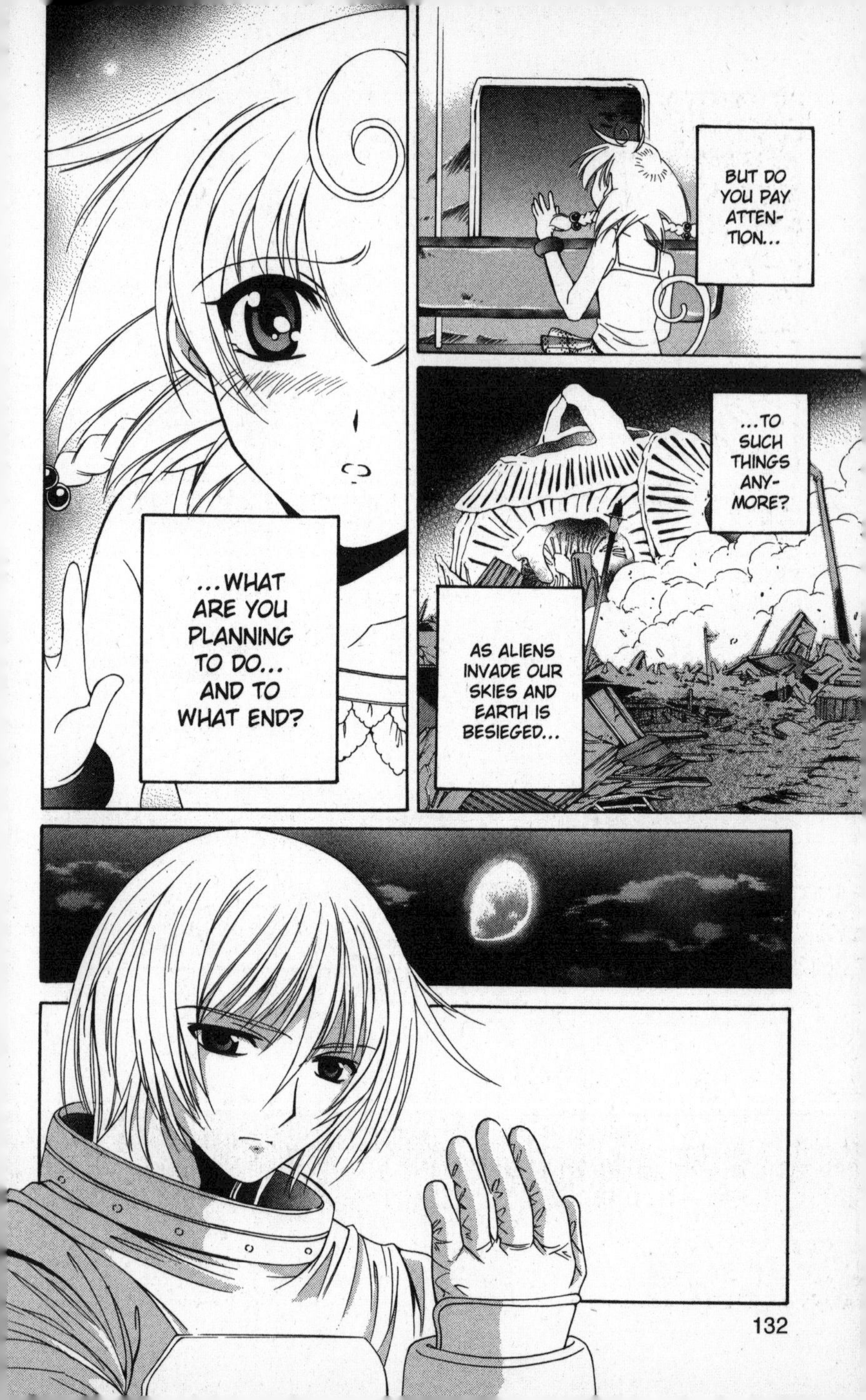
BUT DO YOU PAY ATTEN- TION...
...TO SUCH THINGS ANY- MORE?
AS ALIENS INVADE OUR SKIES AND EARTH IS BESIEGED...
...WHAT ARE YOU PLANNING TO DO... AND TO WHAT END?

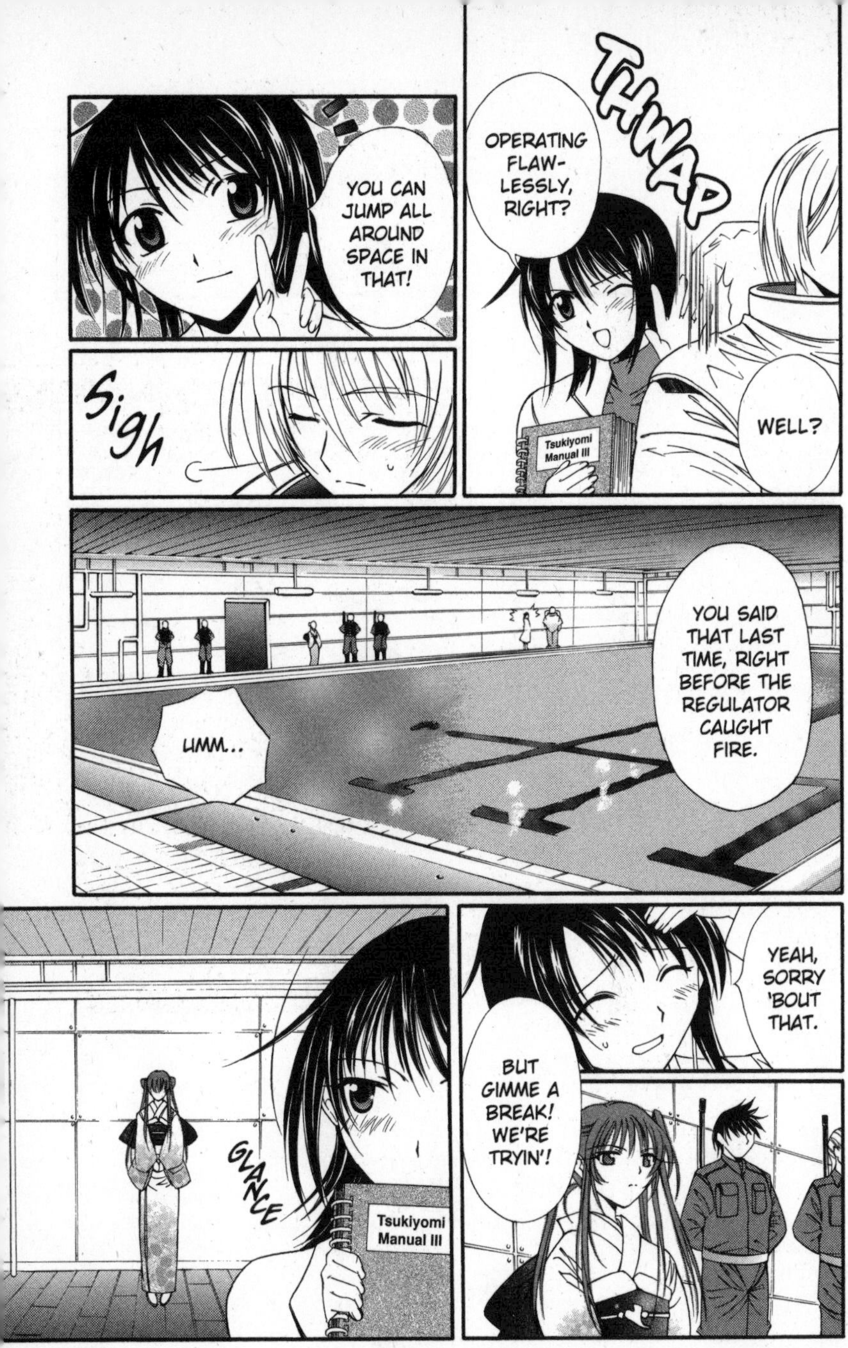
THWAP
OPERATING FLAW-LESSLY, RIGHT?
Tsukiyomi Manual III
WELL?
YOU CAN JUMP ALL AROUND SPACE IN THAT!
Sigh
YOU SAID THAT LAST TIME, RIGHT BEFORE THE REGULATOR CAUGHT FIRE.
UMM...
YEAH, SORRY 'BOUT THAT.
BUT GIMME A BREAK! WE'RE TRYIN'!
GLANCE
Tsukiyomi Manual III

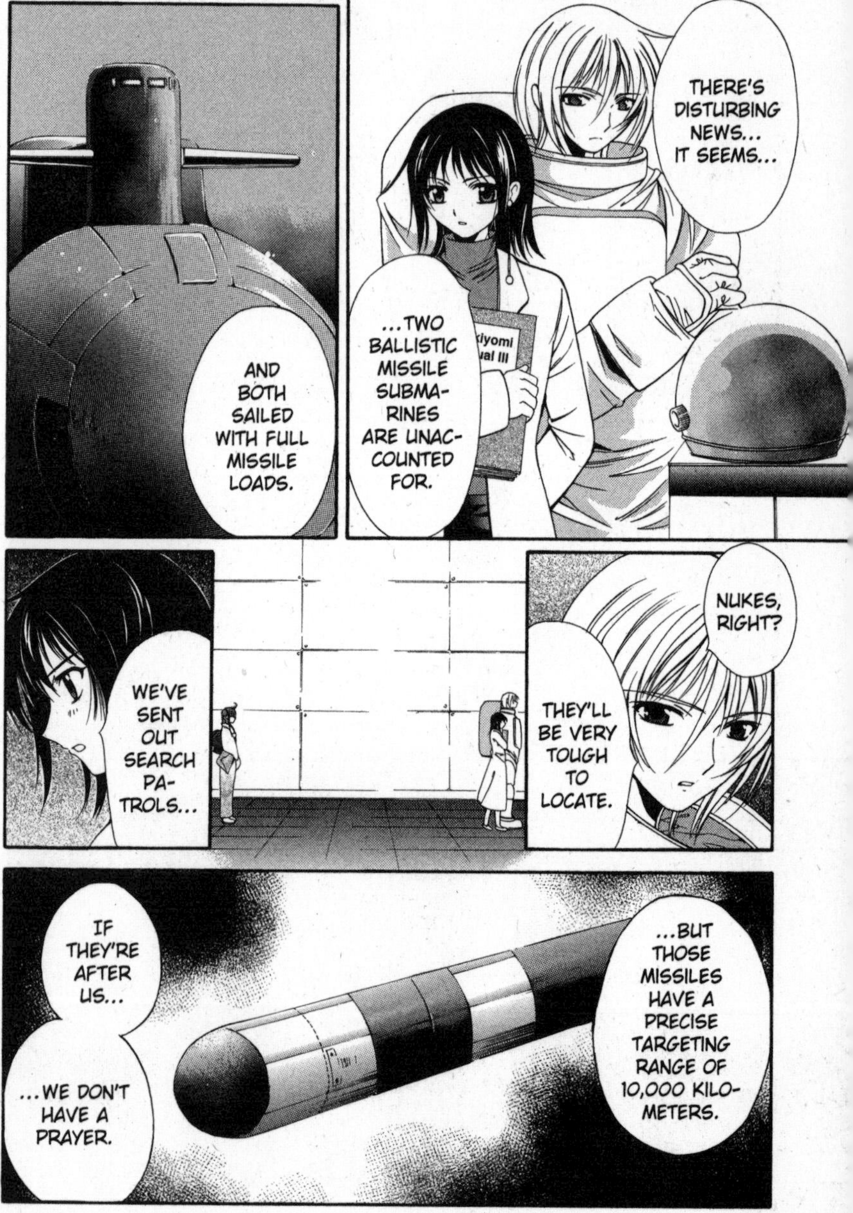
THERE'S DISTURBING NEWS... IT SEEMS...
...TWO BALLISTIC MISSILE SUBMARINES ARE UNACCOUNTED FOR.
AND BOTH SAILED WITH FULL MISSILE LOADS.
NUKES, RIGHT?
THEY'LL BE VERY TOUGH TO LOCATE.
WE'VE SENT OUT SEARCH PATROLS...
...BUT THOSE MISSILES HAVE A PRECISE TARGETING RANGE OF 10,000 KILOMETERS.
IF THEY'RE AFTER US...
...WE DON'T HAVE A PRAYER.

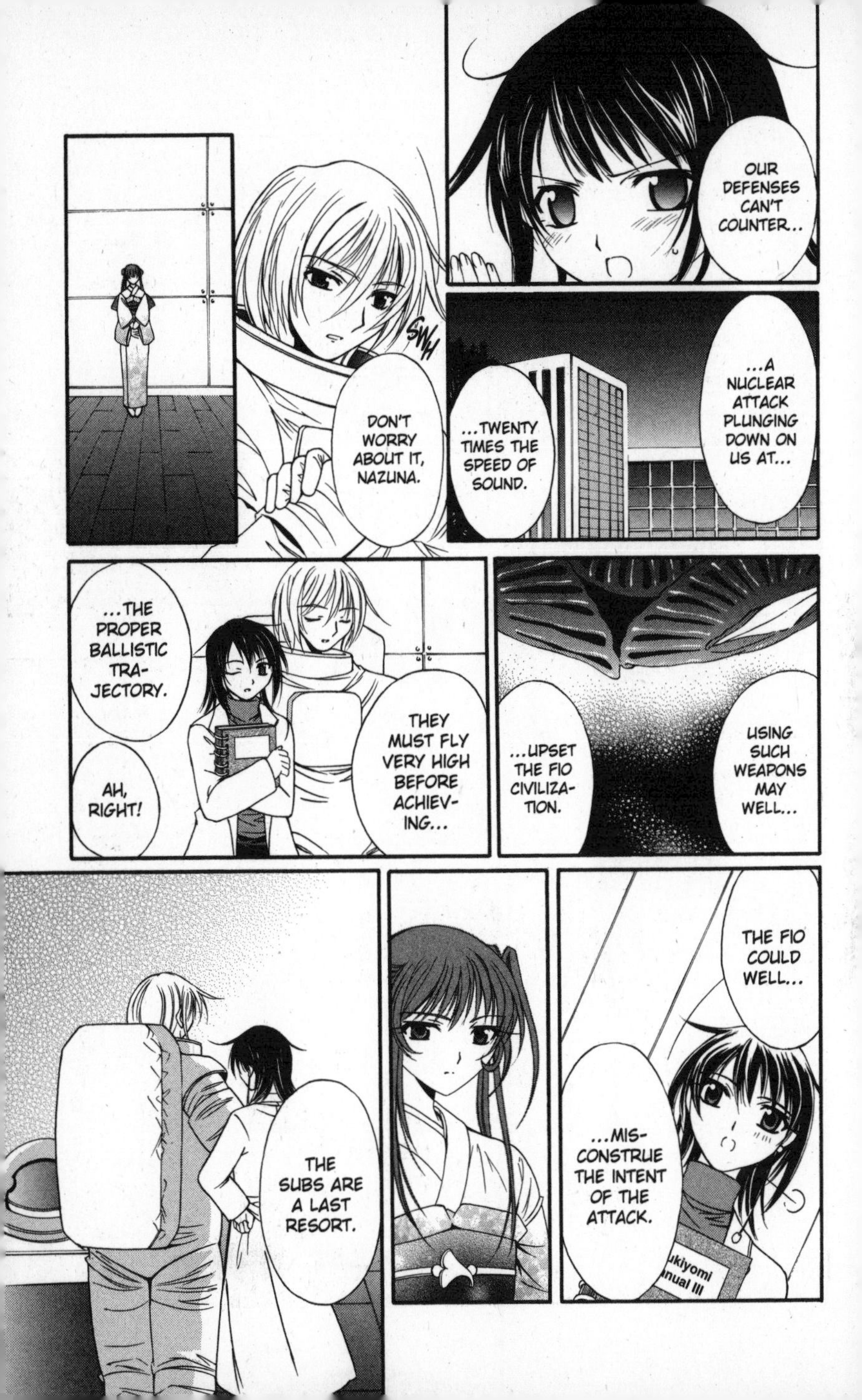
OUR DEFENSES CAN'T COUNTER...
...A NUCLEAR ATTACK PLUNGING DOWN ON US AT...
...TWENTY TIMES THE SPEED OF SOUND.
SWH
DON'T WORRY ABOUT IT, NAZUNA.
USING SUCH WEAPONS MAY WELL...
...UPSET THE FIO CIVILIZA-TION.
THEY MUST FLY VERY HIGH BEFORE ACHIEV-ING...
...THE PROPER BALLISTIC TRA-JECTORY.
AH, RIGHT!
THE FIO COULD WELL...
...MIS-CONSTRUE THE INTENT OF THE ATTACK.
THE SUBS ARE A LAST RESORT.

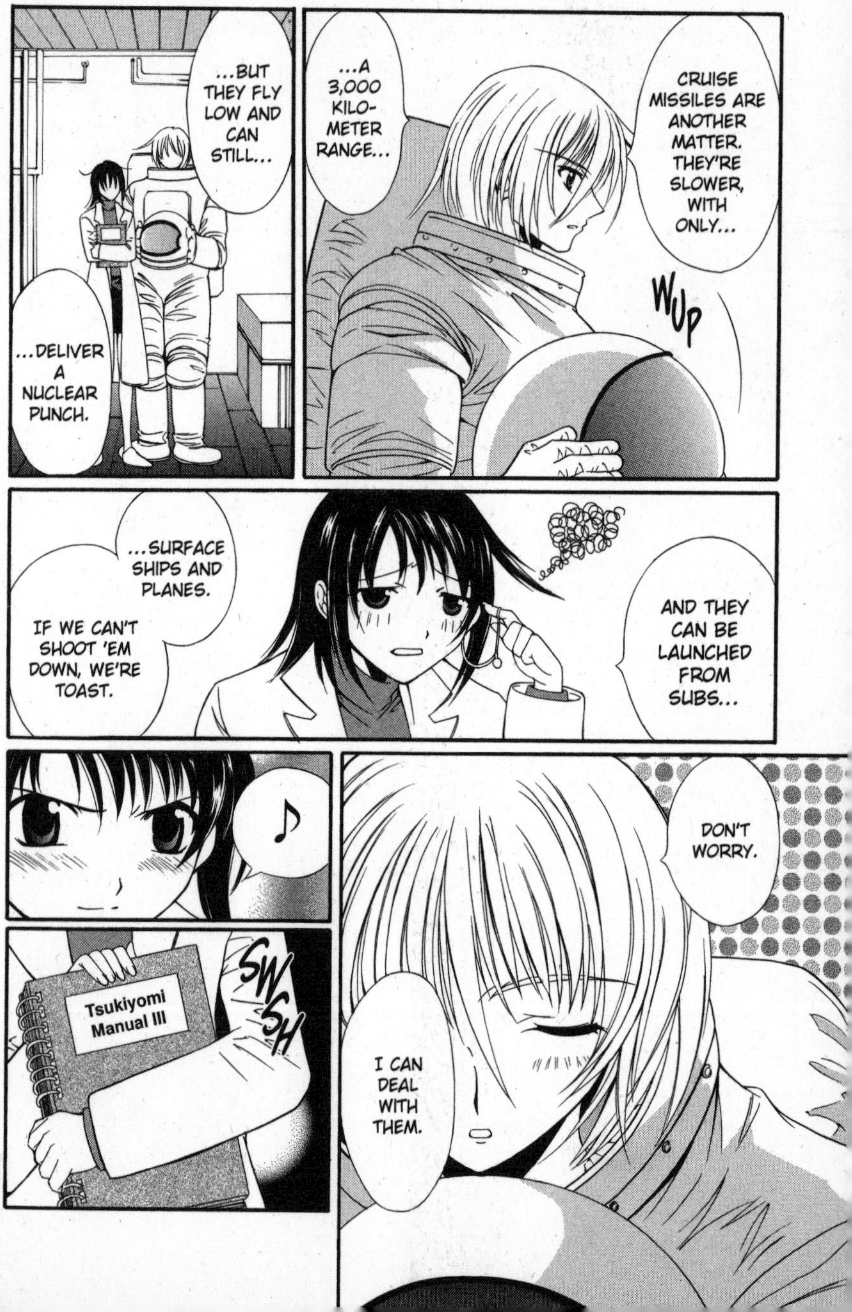
CRUISE MISSILES ARE ANOTHER MATTER. THEY'RE SLOWER, WITH ONLY...
WUP
...A 3,000 KILO-METER RANGE...
...BUT THEY FLY LOW AND CAN STILL...
...DELIVER A NUCLEAR PUNCH.
AND THEY CAN BE LAUNCHED FROM SUBS...
...SURFACE SHIPS AND PLANES.
IF WE CAN'T SHOOT 'EM DOWN, WE'RE TOAST.
DON'T WORRY.
I CAN DEAL WITH THEM.
♪
Tsukiyomi Manual III
SWSH

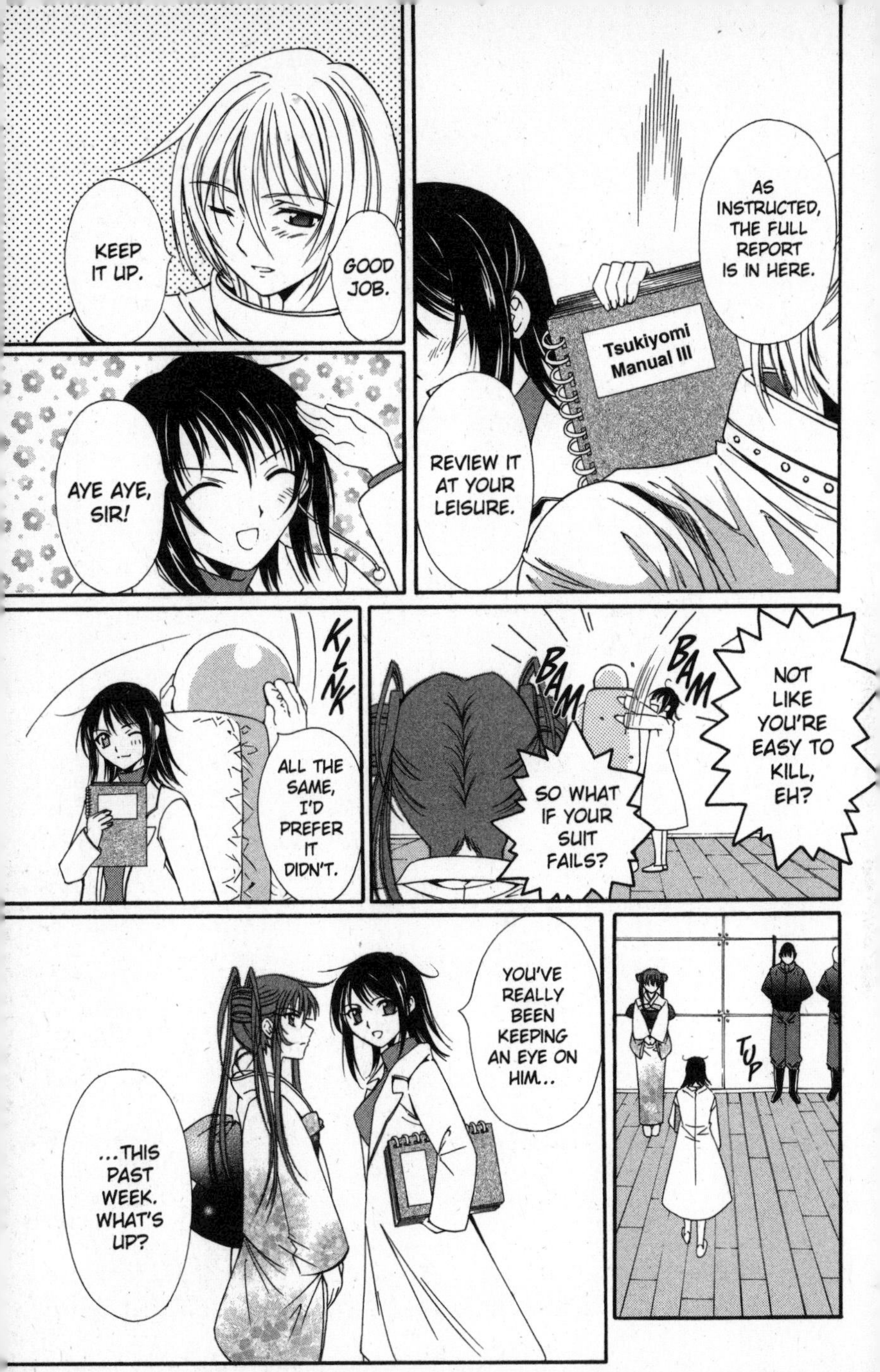
AS INSTRUCTED, THE FULL REPORT IS IN HERE.
Tsukiyomi Manual III
REVIEW IT AT YOUR LEISURE.
GOOD JOB.
KEEP IT UP.
AYE AYE, SIR!
BAM
BAM
NOT LIKE YOU'RE EASY TO KILL, EH?
SO WHAT IF YOUR SUIT FAILS?
KLNK
ALL THE SAME, I'D PREFER IT DIDN'T.
TUP
YOU'VE REALLY BEEN KEEPING AN EYE ON HIM...
...THIS PAST WEEK. WHAT'S UP?

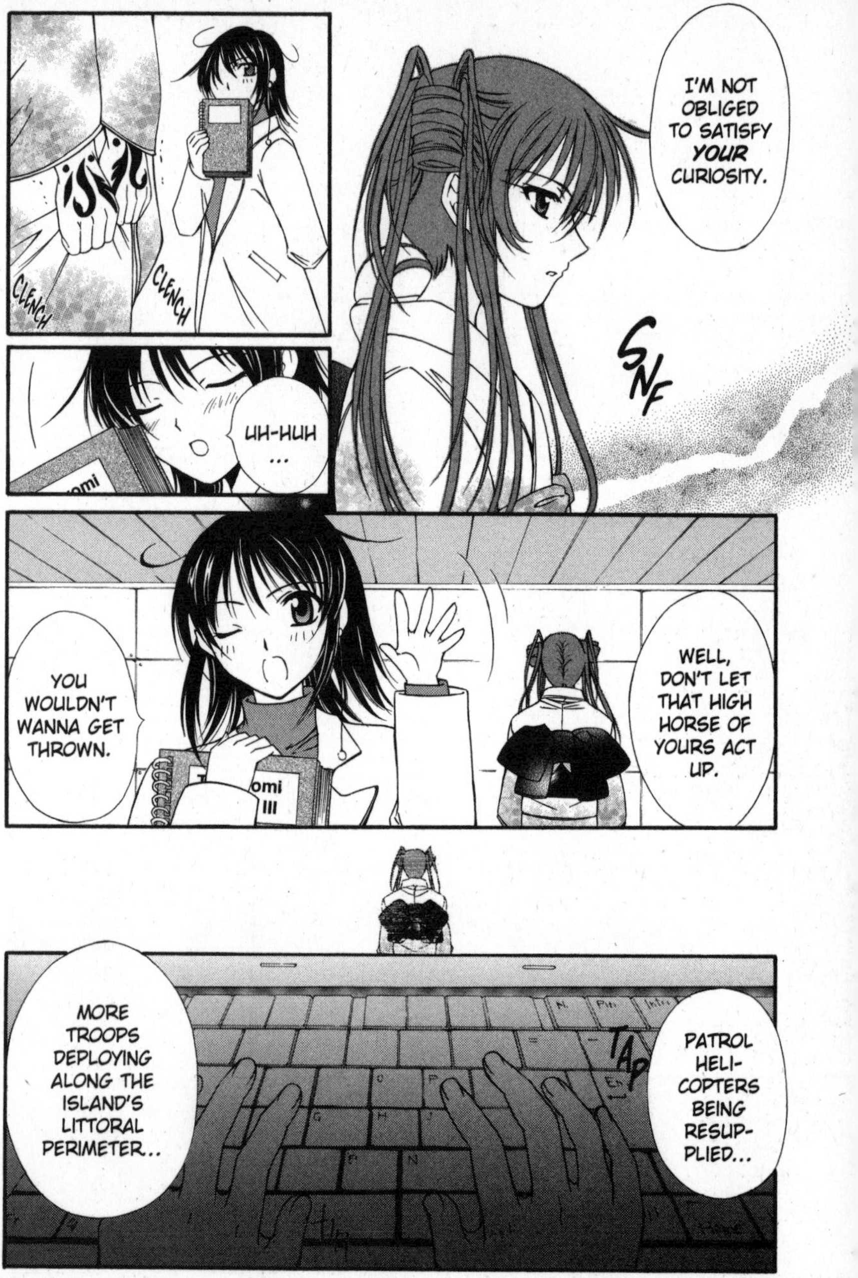
I'M NOT OBLIGED TO SATISFY *YOUR* CURIOSITY.
SNF
CLENCH
CLENCH
UH-HUH ...
WELL, DON'T LET THAT HIGH HORSE OF YOURS ACT UP.
YOU WOULDN'T WANNA GET THROWN.
PATROL HELI-COPTERS BEING RESUP-PLIED...
TAP
MORE TROOPS DEPLOYING ALONG THE ISLAND'S LITTORAL PERIMETER..

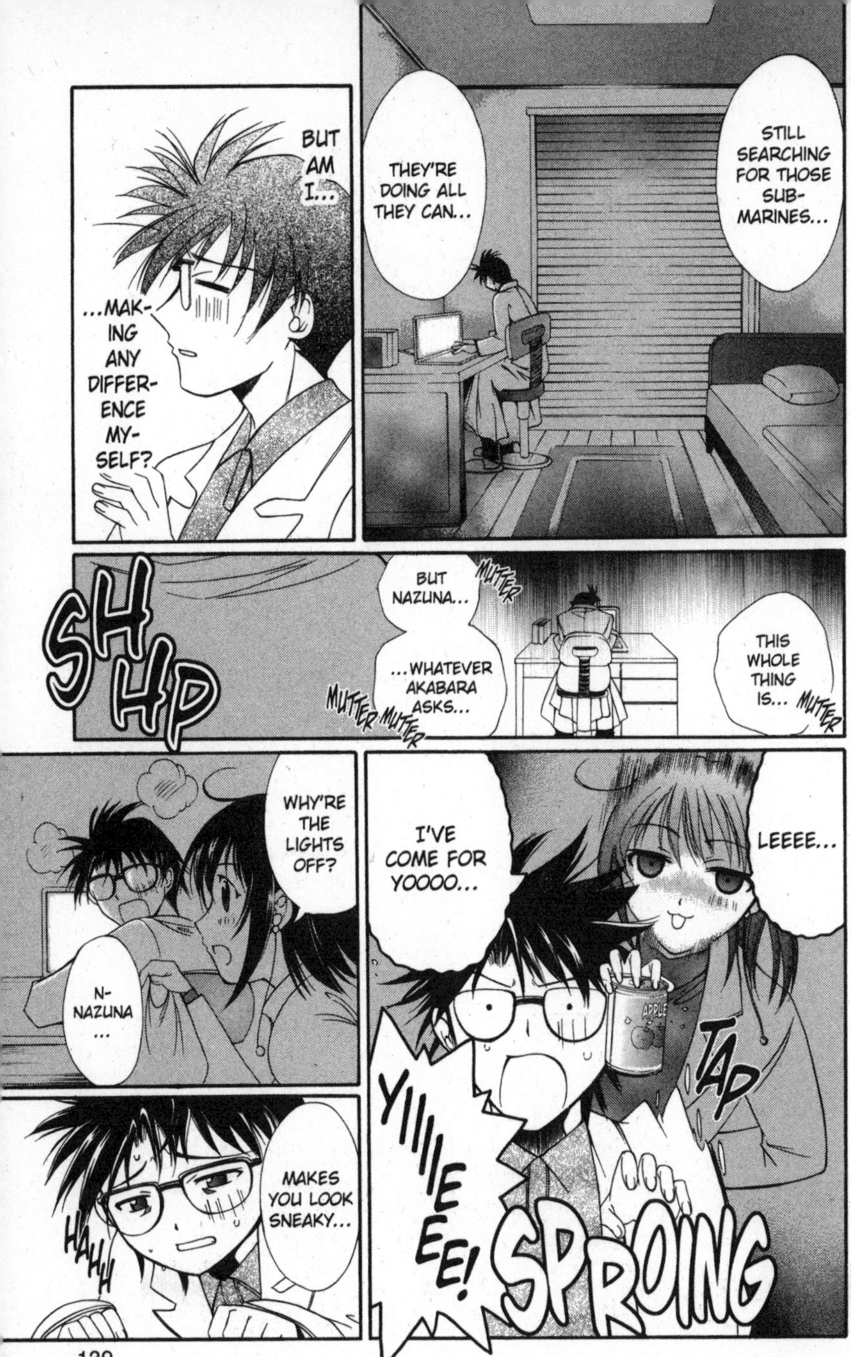
STILL SEARCHING FOR THOSE SUB-MARINES...
THEY'RE DOING ALL THEY CAN...
BUT AM I...
...MAKING ANY DIFFERENCE MYSELF?
THIS WHOLE THING IS...
MUTTER
BUT NAZUNA...
MUTTER
...WHATEVER AKABARA ASKS...
MUTTER MUTTER
SHHP
LEEEE...
I'VE COME FOR YOOOO...
TAP
YIIIIEEEE!
SPROING
WHY'RE THE LIGHTS OFF?
N-NAZUNA...
MAKES YOU LOOK SNEAKY...
HAHH

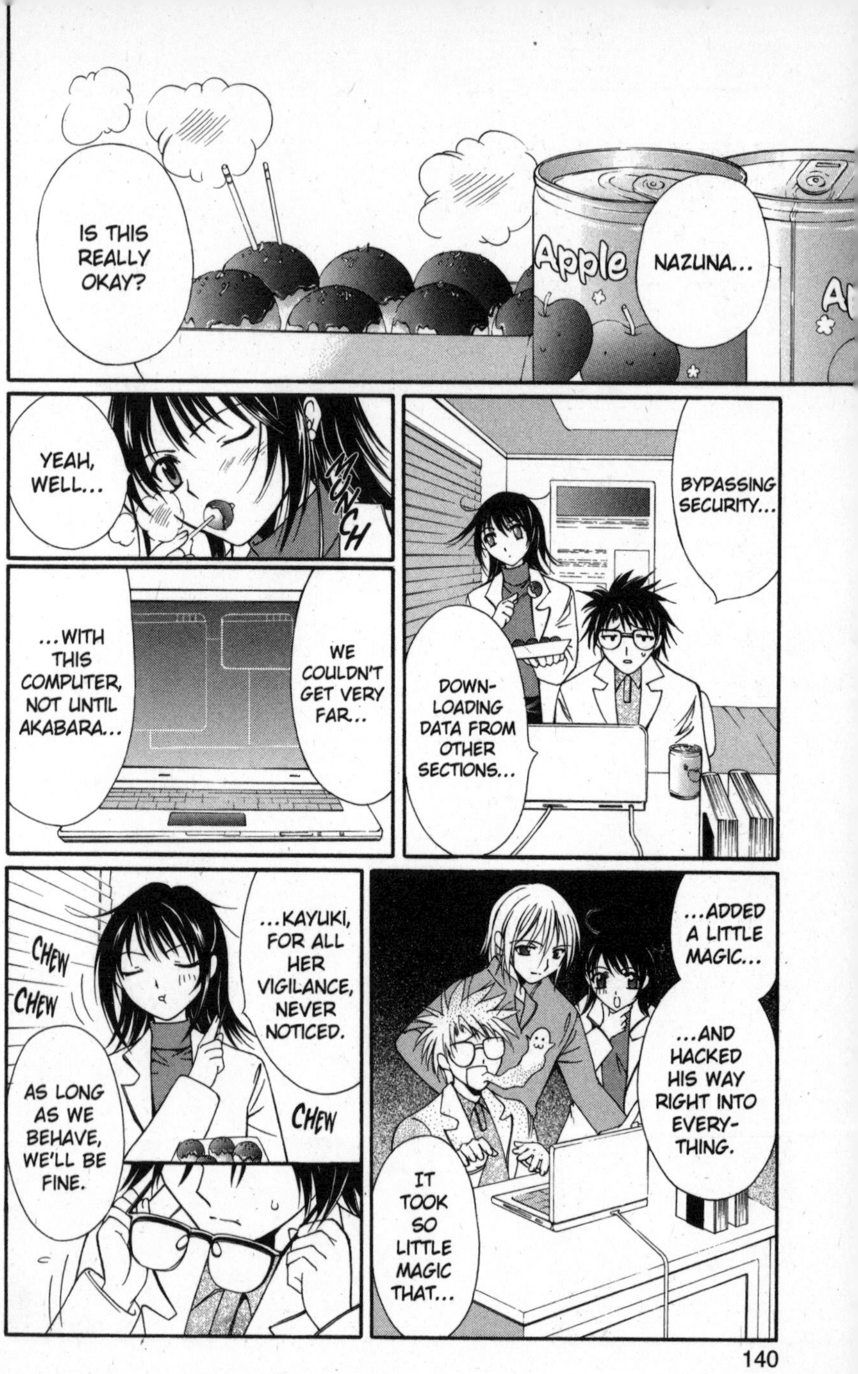
NAZUNA...
IS THIS REALLY OKAY?
BYPASSING SECURITY...
DOWN-LOADING DATA FROM OTHER SECTIONS...
YEAH, WELL...
MUNCH
WE COULDN'T GET VERY FAR...
...WITH THIS COMPUTER, NOT UNTIL AKABARA...
...ADDED A LITTLE MAGIC...
...AND HACKED HIS WAY RIGHT INTO EVERY-THING.
IT TOOK SO LITTLE MAGIC THAT...
...KAYUKI, FOR ALL HER VIGILANCE, NEVER NOTICED.
CHEW
CHEW
AS LONG AS WE BEHAVE, WE'LL BE FINE.
CHEW

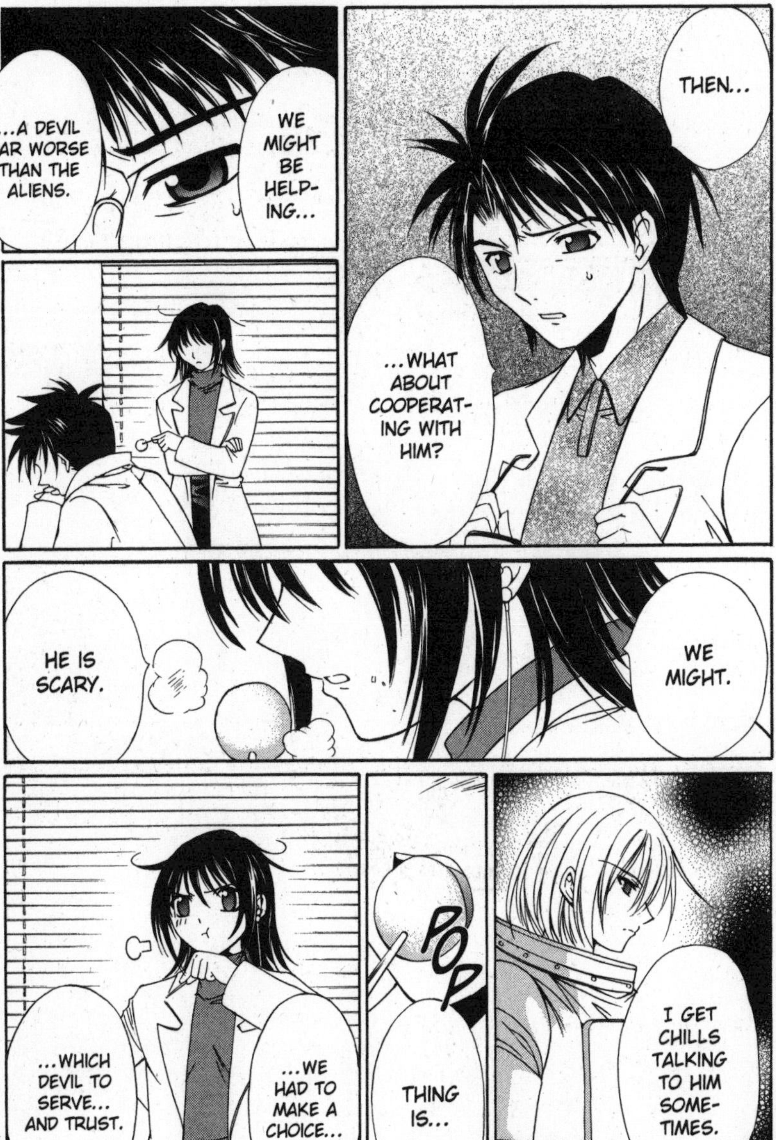
THEN...
...WHAT ABOUT COOPERATING WITH HIM?
WE MIGHT BE HELPING...
...A DEVIL FAR WORSE THAN THE ALIENS.
WE MIGHT.
HE IS SCARY.
I GET CHILLS TALKING TO HIM SOMETIMES.
POP
THING IS...
...WE HAD TO MAKE A CHOICE...
...WHICH DEVIL TO SERVE... AND TRUST.

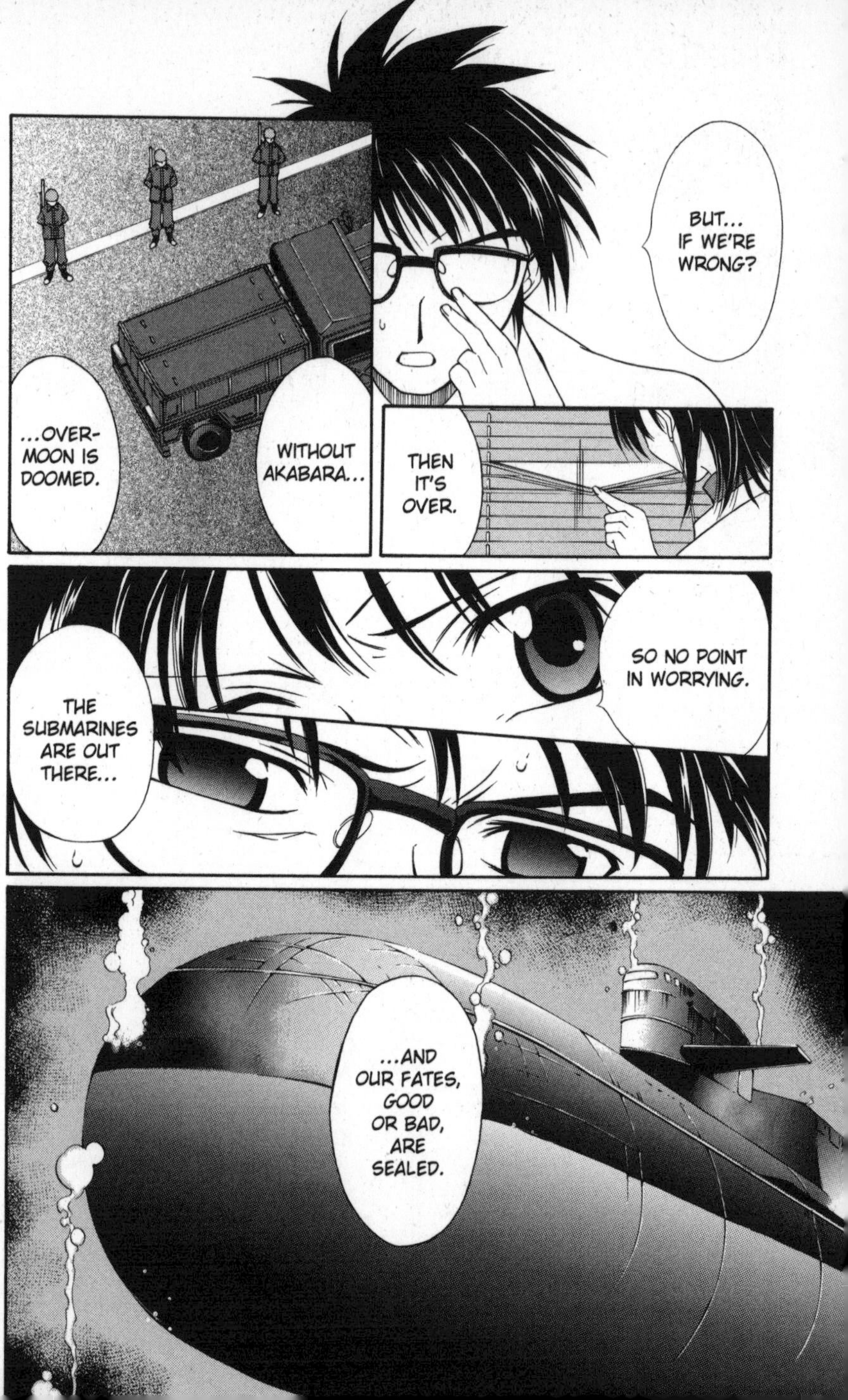
BUT... IF WE'RE WRONG?
THEN IT'S OVER.
WITHOUT AKABARA...
...OVER-MOON IS DOOMED.
SO NO POINT IN WORRYING.
THE SUBMARINES ARE OUT THERE...
...AND OUR FATES, GOOD OR BAD, ARE SEALED.

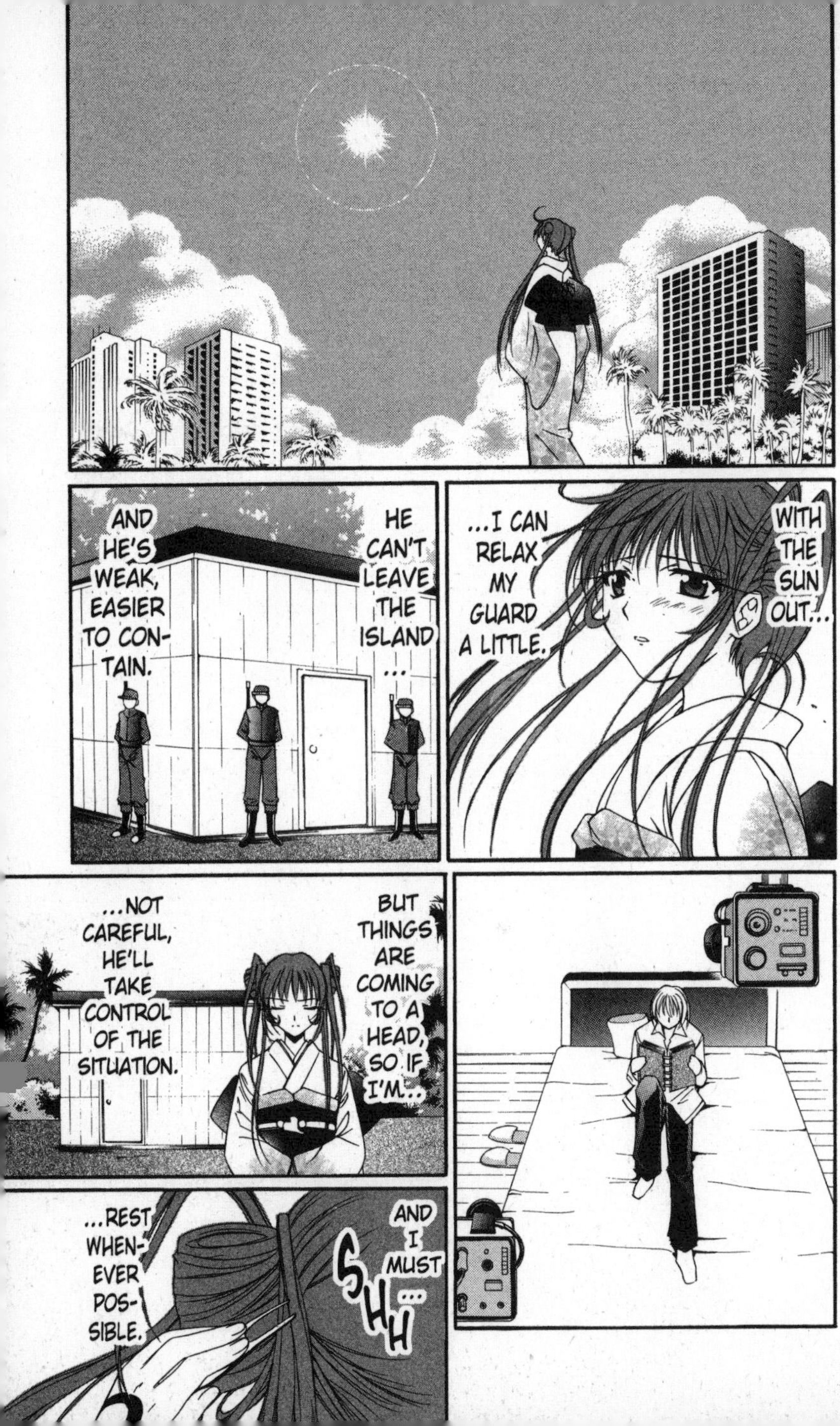
WITH THE SUN OUT...
...I CAN RELAX MY GUARD A LITTLE.
HE CAN'T LEAVE THE ISLAND...
AND HE'S WEAK, EASIER TO CON-TAIN.
BUT THINGS ARE COMING TO A HEAD, SO IF I'M...
...NOT CAREFUL, HE'LL TAKE CONTROL OF THE SITUATION.
AND I MUST...
SHH
...REST WHEN-EVER POS-SIBLE.

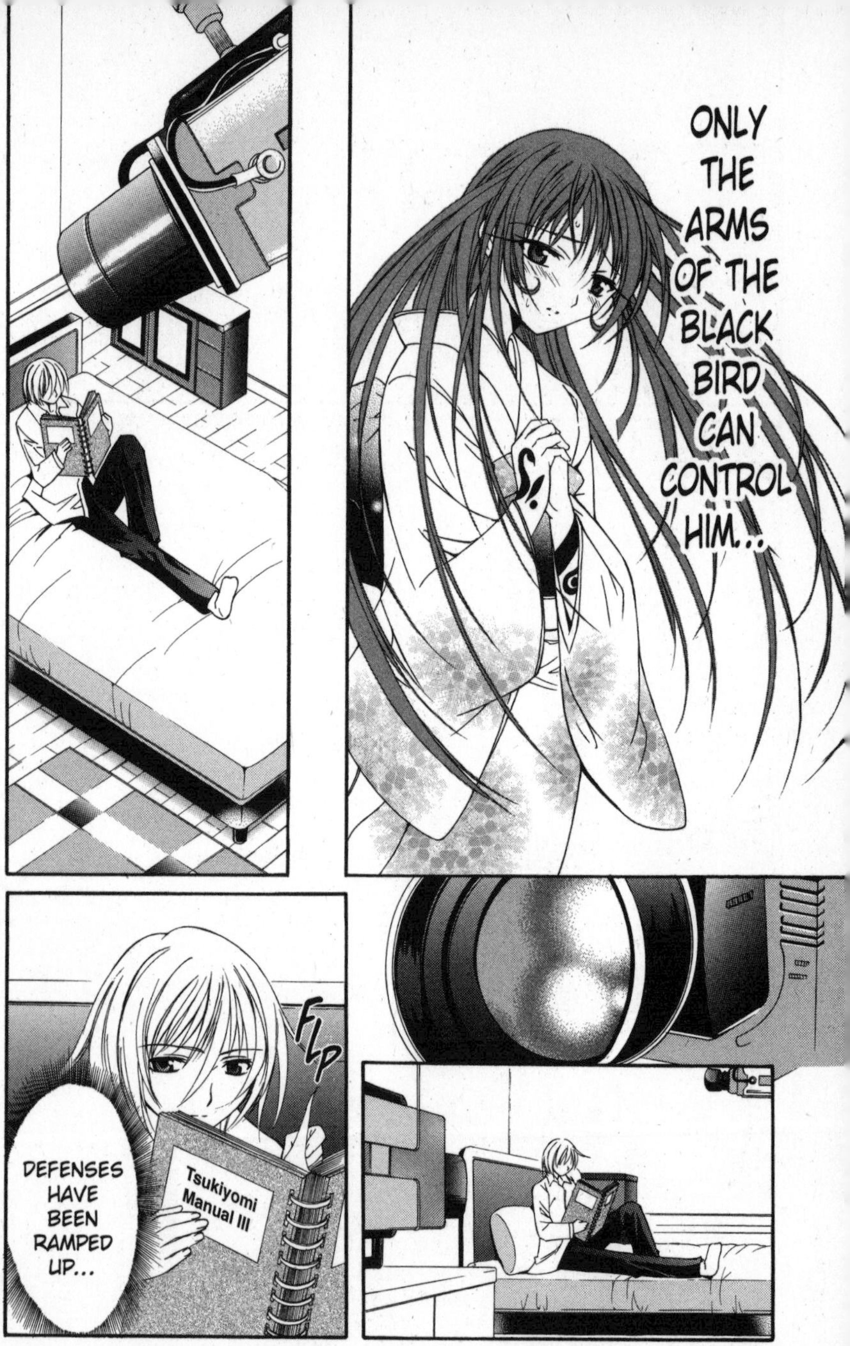
ONLY THE ARMS OF THE BLACK BIRD CAN CONTROL HIM...
FLP
DEFENSES HAVE BEEN RAMPED UP...
Tsukiyomi Manual III

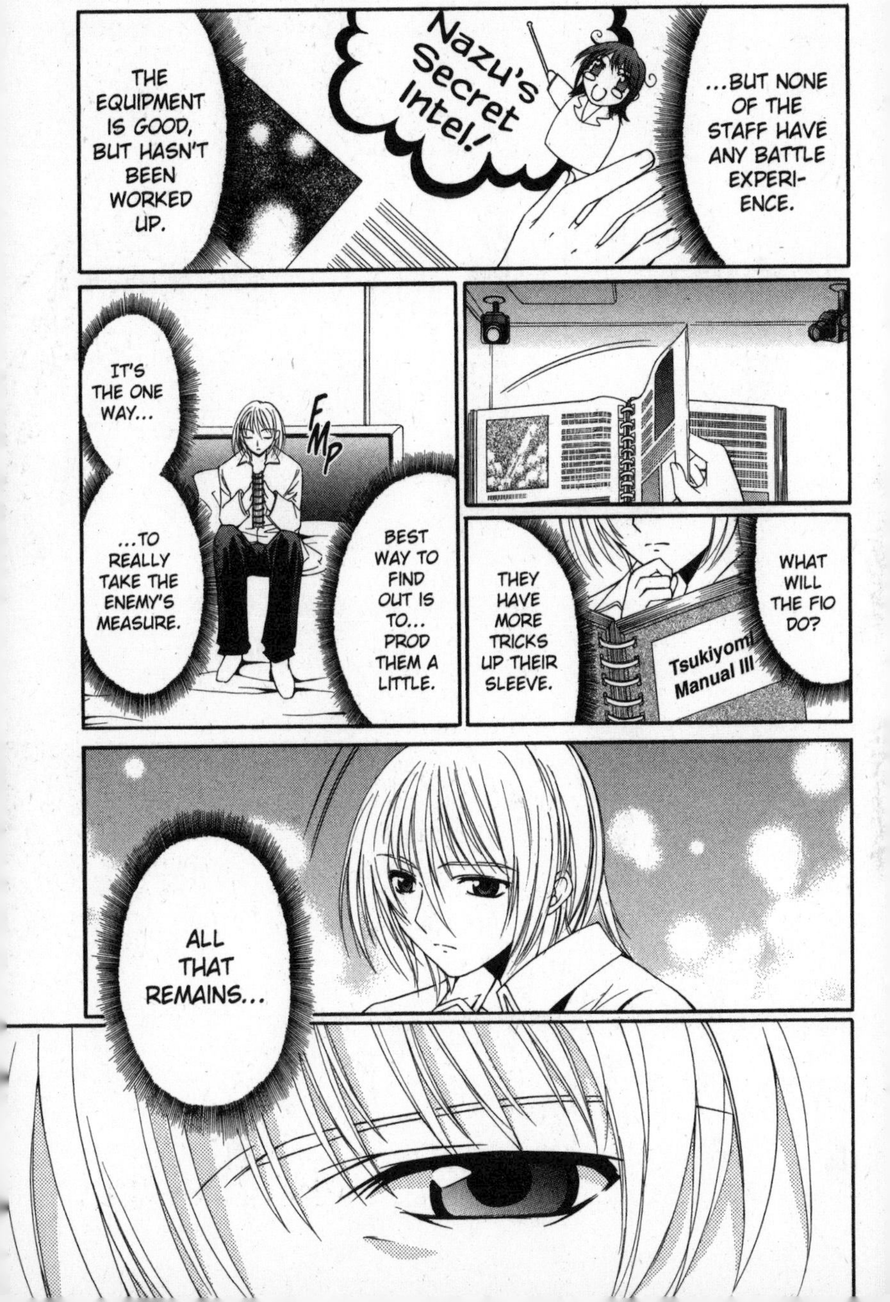
...BUT NONE OF THE STAFF HAVE ANY BATTLE EXPERIENCE.
Nazu's Secret Intel!
THE EQUIPMENT IS GOOD, BUT HASN'T BEEN WORKED UP.
WHAT WILL THE FIO DO?
Tsukiyomi Manual III
THEY HAVE MORE TRICKS UP THEIR SLEEVE.
BEST WAY TO FIND OUT IS TO... PROD THEM A LITTLE.
FMP
IT'S THE ONE WAY...
...TO REALLY TAKE THE ENEMY'S MEASURE.
ALL THAT REMAINS...

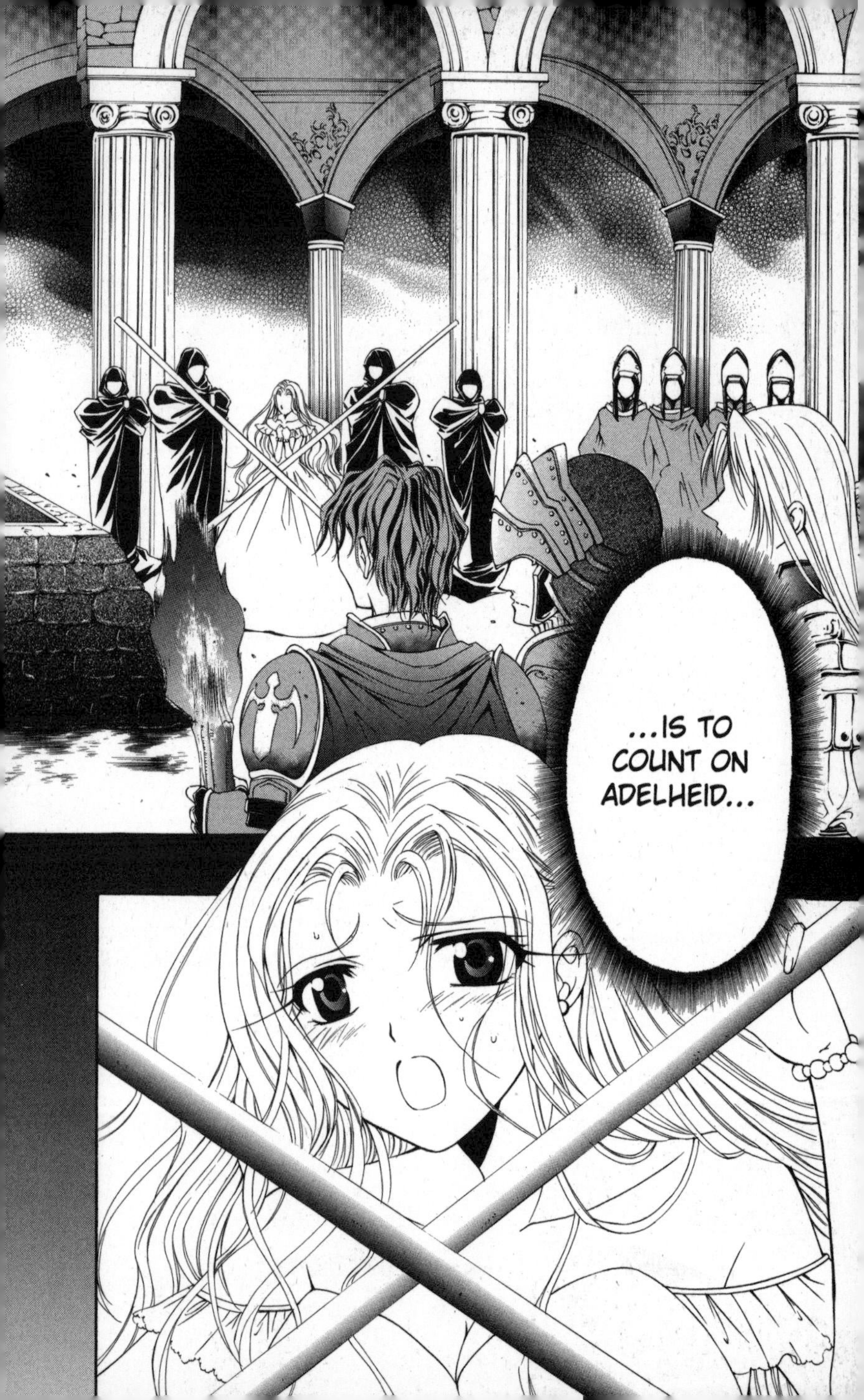
...IS TO COUNT ON ADELHEID...

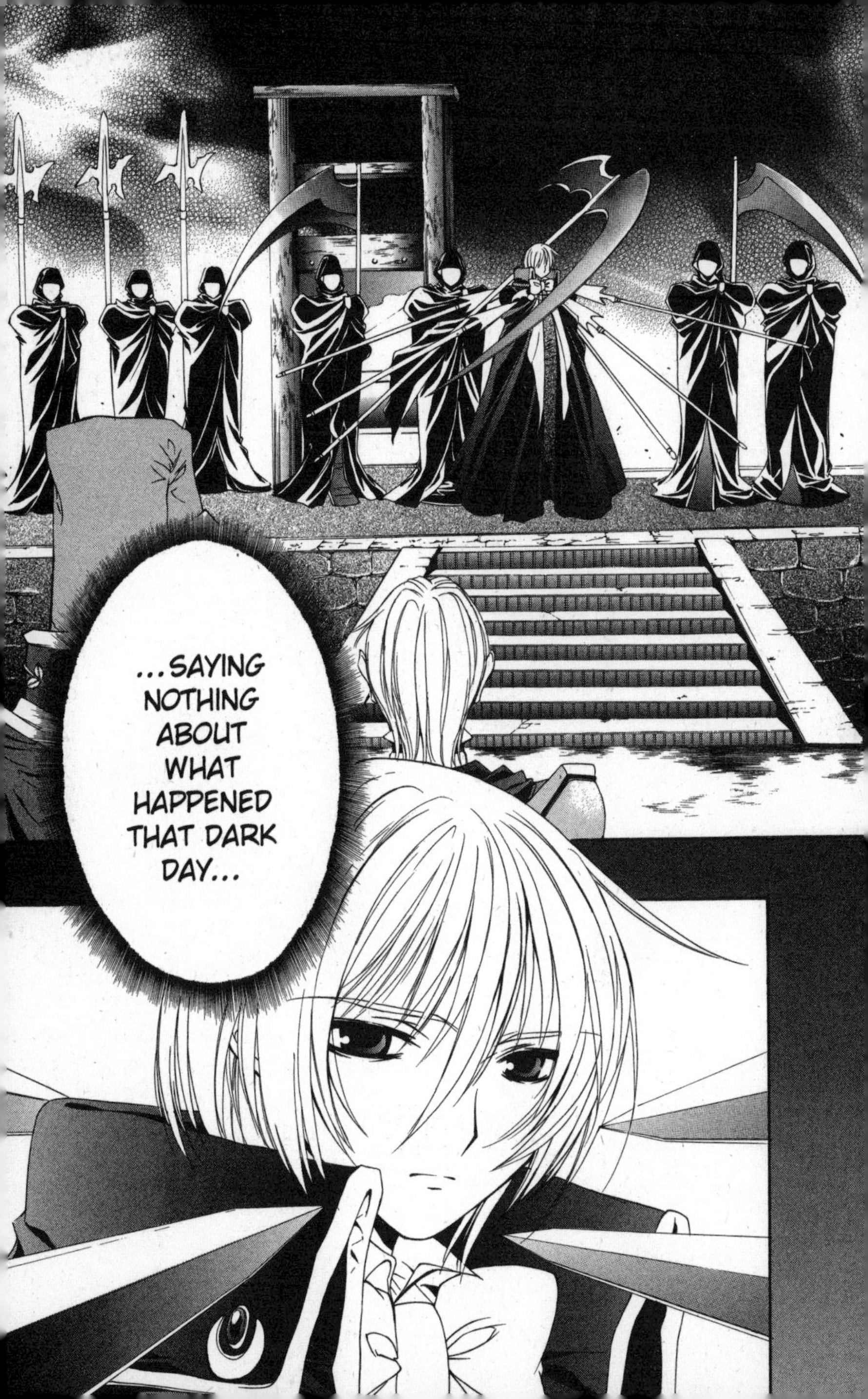
...SAYING NOTHING ABOUT WHAT HAPPENED THAT DARK DAY...

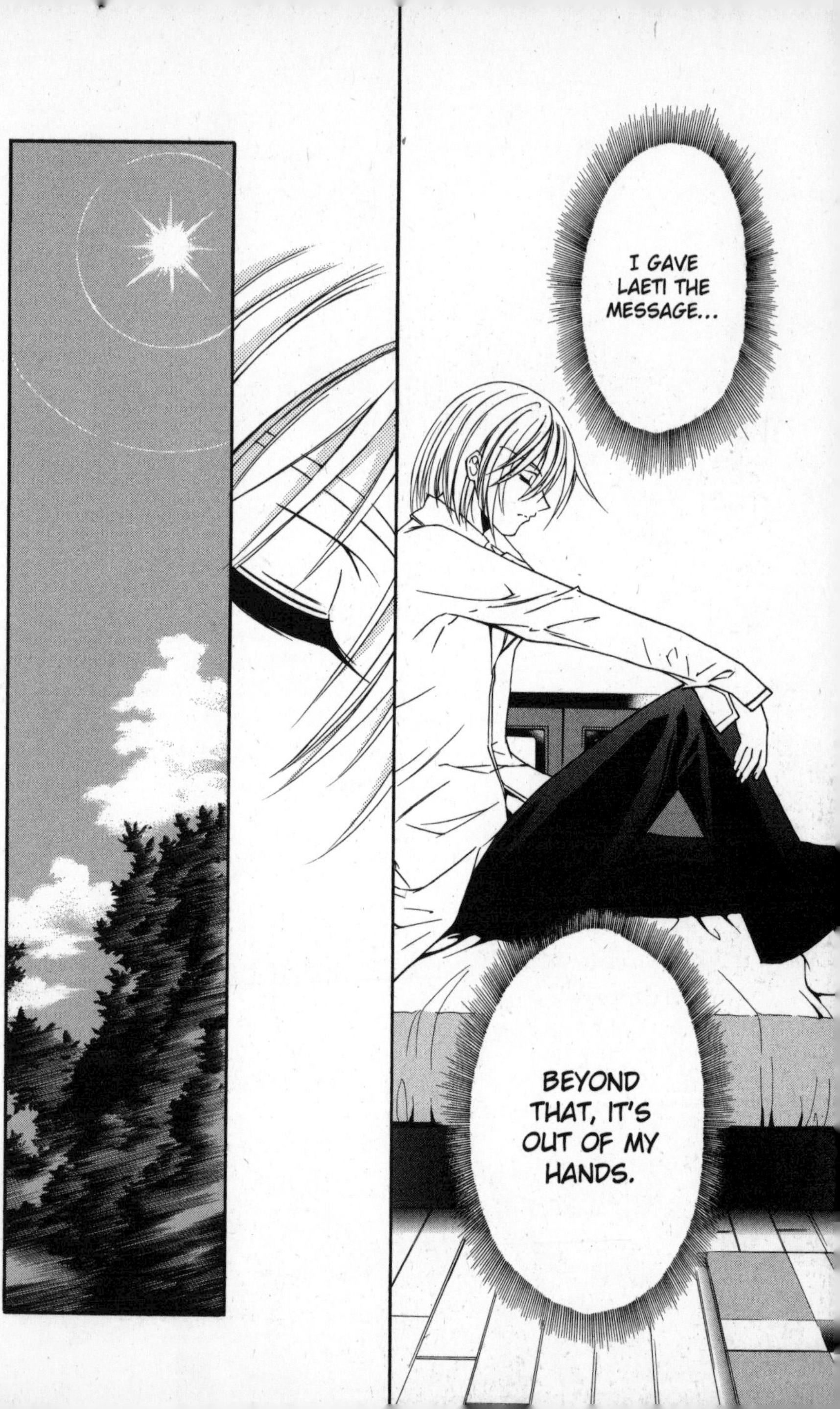
I GAVE LAETI THE MESSAGE...
BEYOND THAT, IT'S OUT OF MY HANDS.

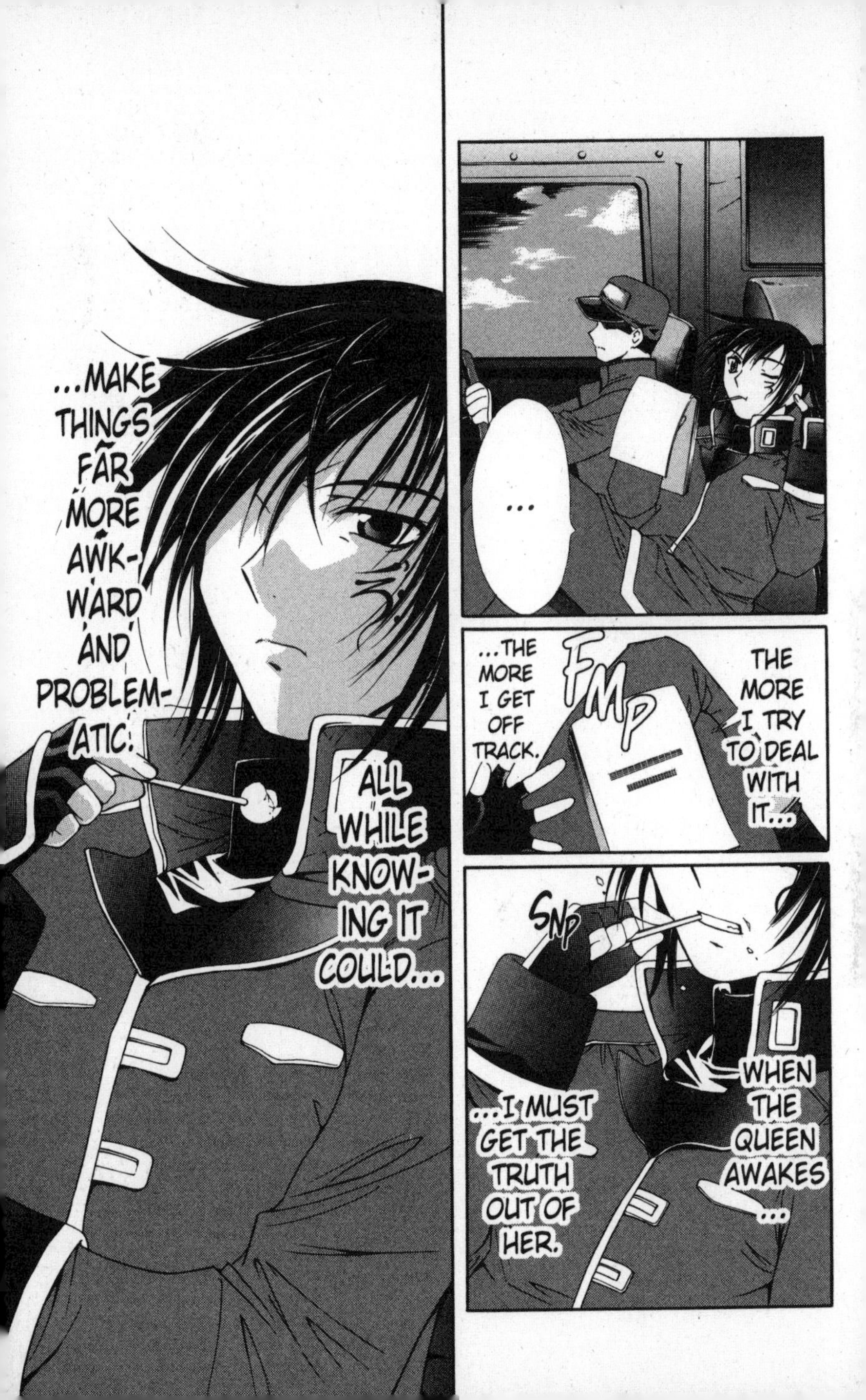
...
THE MORE I TRY TO DEAL WITH IT...
FMP
...THE MORE I GET OFF TRACK.
SNP
WHEN THE QUEEN AWAKES...
...I MUST GET THE TRUTH OUT OF HER.
ALL WHILE KNOWING IT COULD...
...MAKE THINGS FAR MORE AWK-WARD AND PROBLEM-ATIC.

THE RECORD OF A

FALLEN VAMPIRE

Chapter 28:
The One Called Akabara

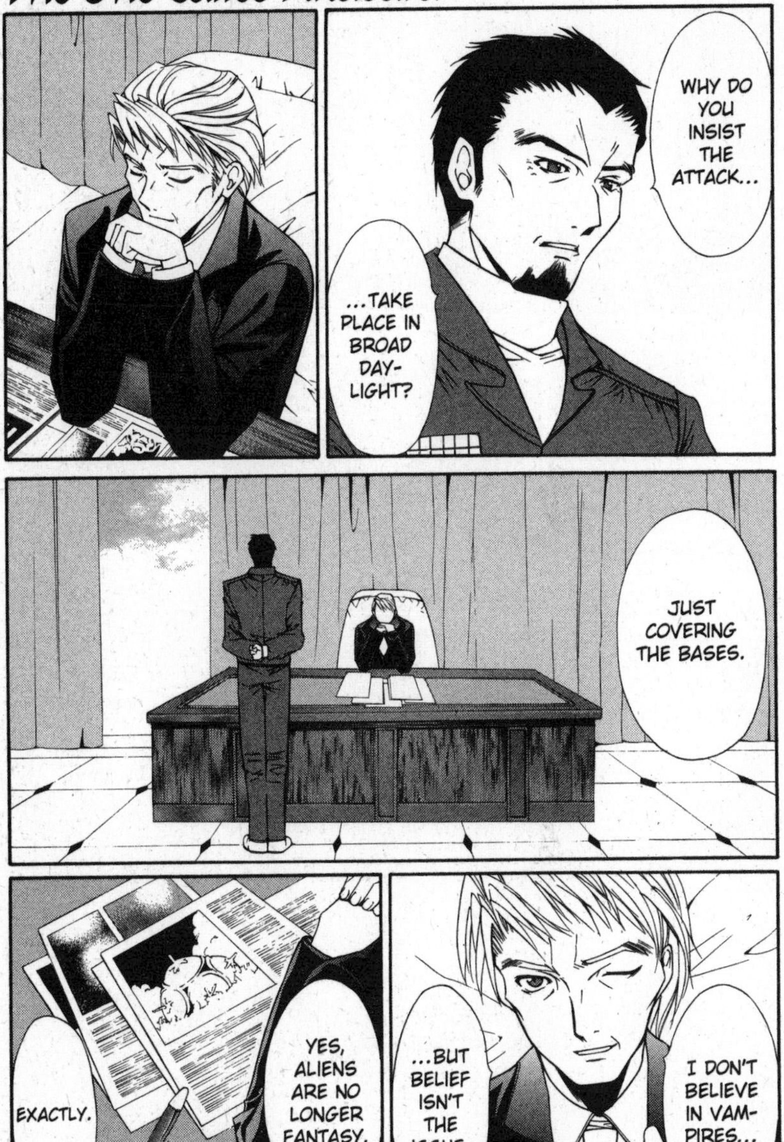
WHY DO YOU INSIST THE ATTACK...
...TAKE PLACE IN BROAD DAY-LIGHT?
JUST COVERING THE BASES.
I DON'T BELIEVE IN VAM-PIRES...
...BUT BELIEF ISN'T THE ISSUE.
YES, ALIENS ARE NO LONGER FANTASY.
EXACTLY.

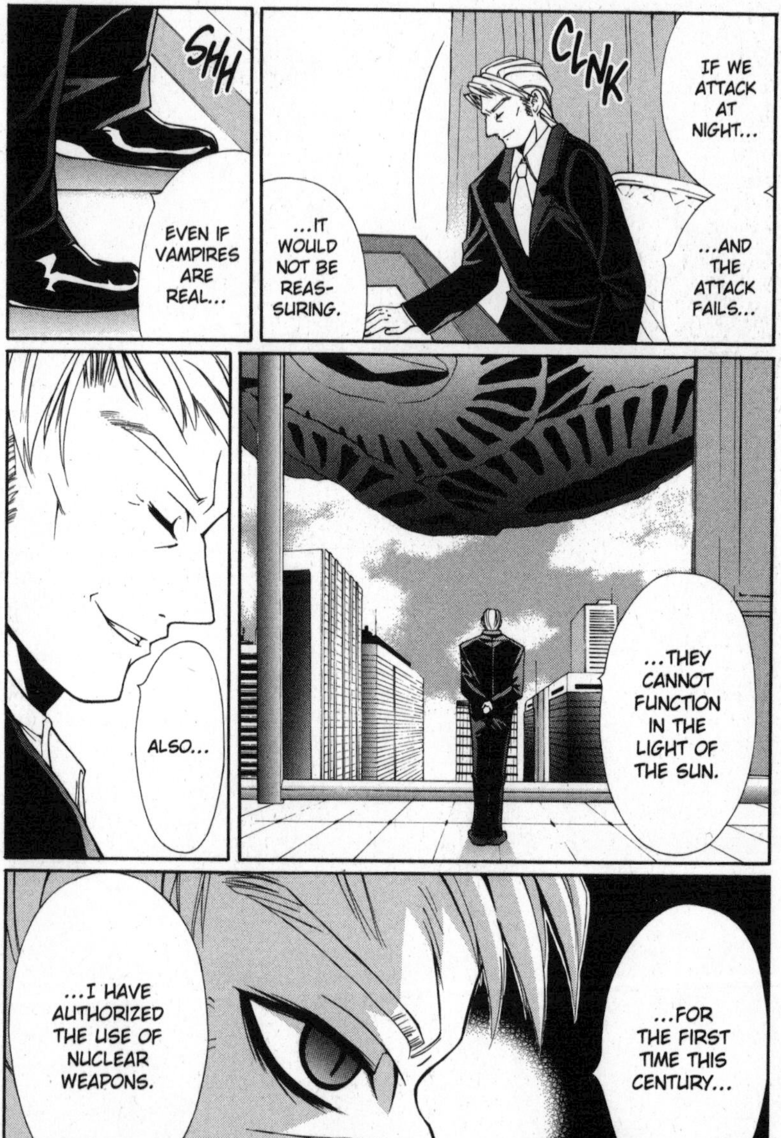
CLNK
IF WE ATTACK AT NIGHT...
...AND THE ATTACK FAILS...
...IT WOULD NOT BE REAS-SURING.
SHH
EVEN IF VAMPIRES ARE REAL...
...THEY CANNOT FUNCTION IN THE LIGHT OF THE SUN.
ALSO...
...FOR THE FIRST TIME THIS CENTURY...
...I HAVE AUTHORIZED THE USE OF NUCLEAR WEAPONS.

Chapter 28: The One Called Akabara

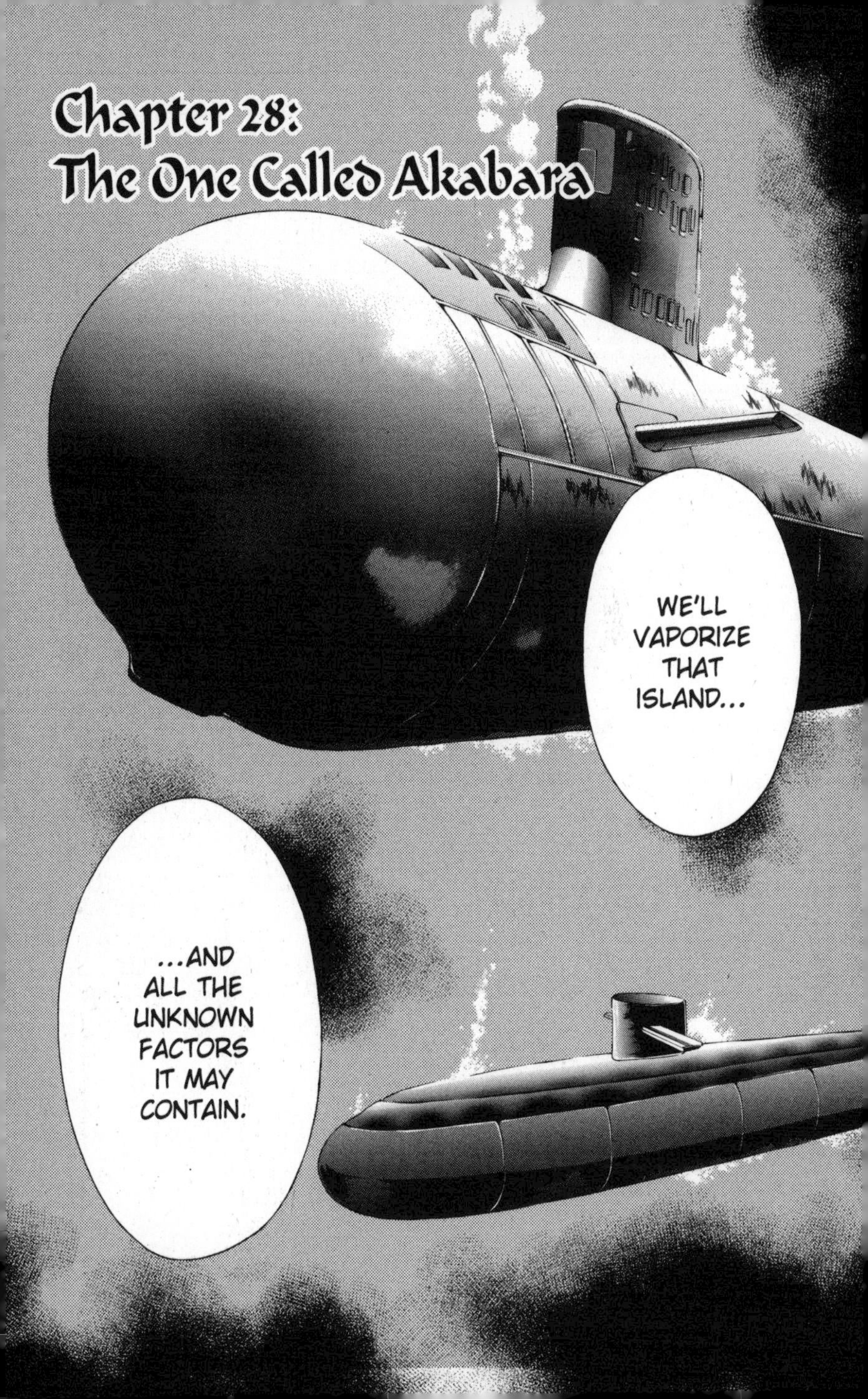
WE'LL VAPORIZE THAT ISLAND...
...AND ALL THE UNKNOWN FACTORS IT MAY CONTAIN.

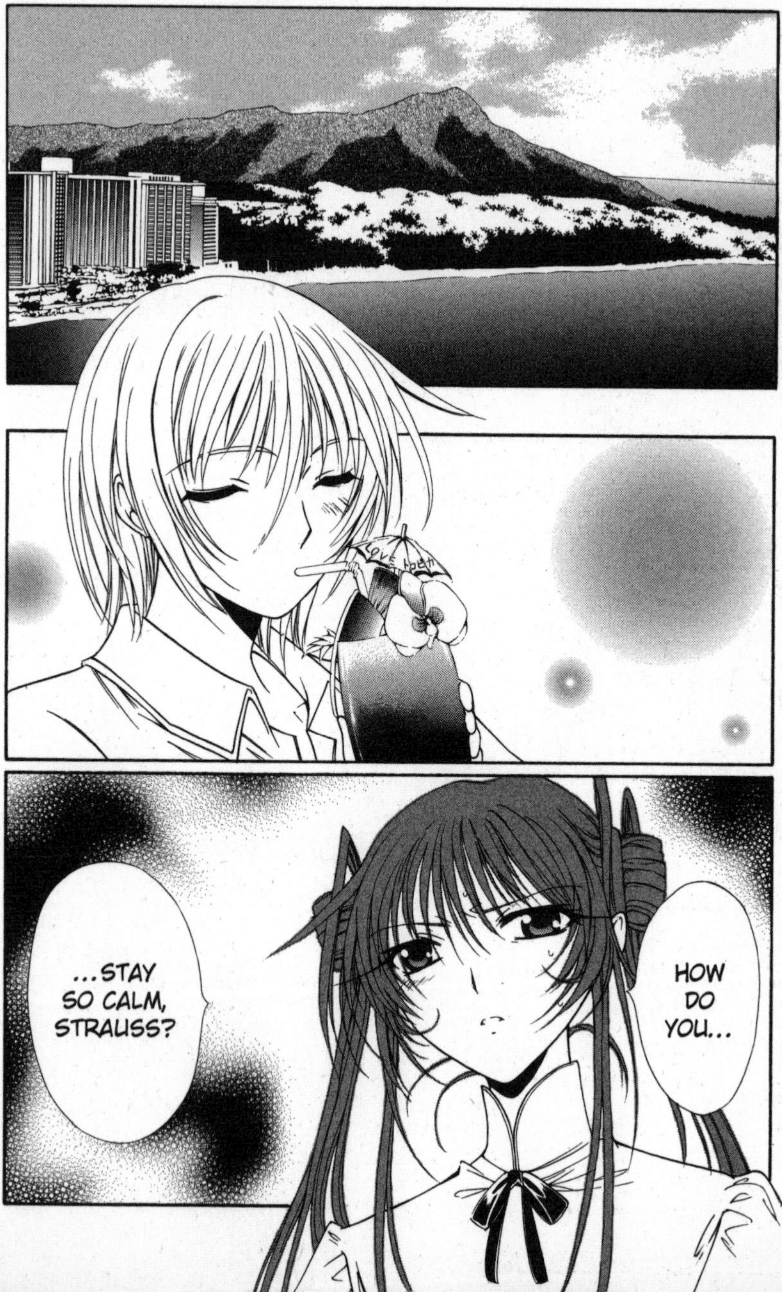
HOW DO YOU...
...STAY SO CALM, STRAUSS?

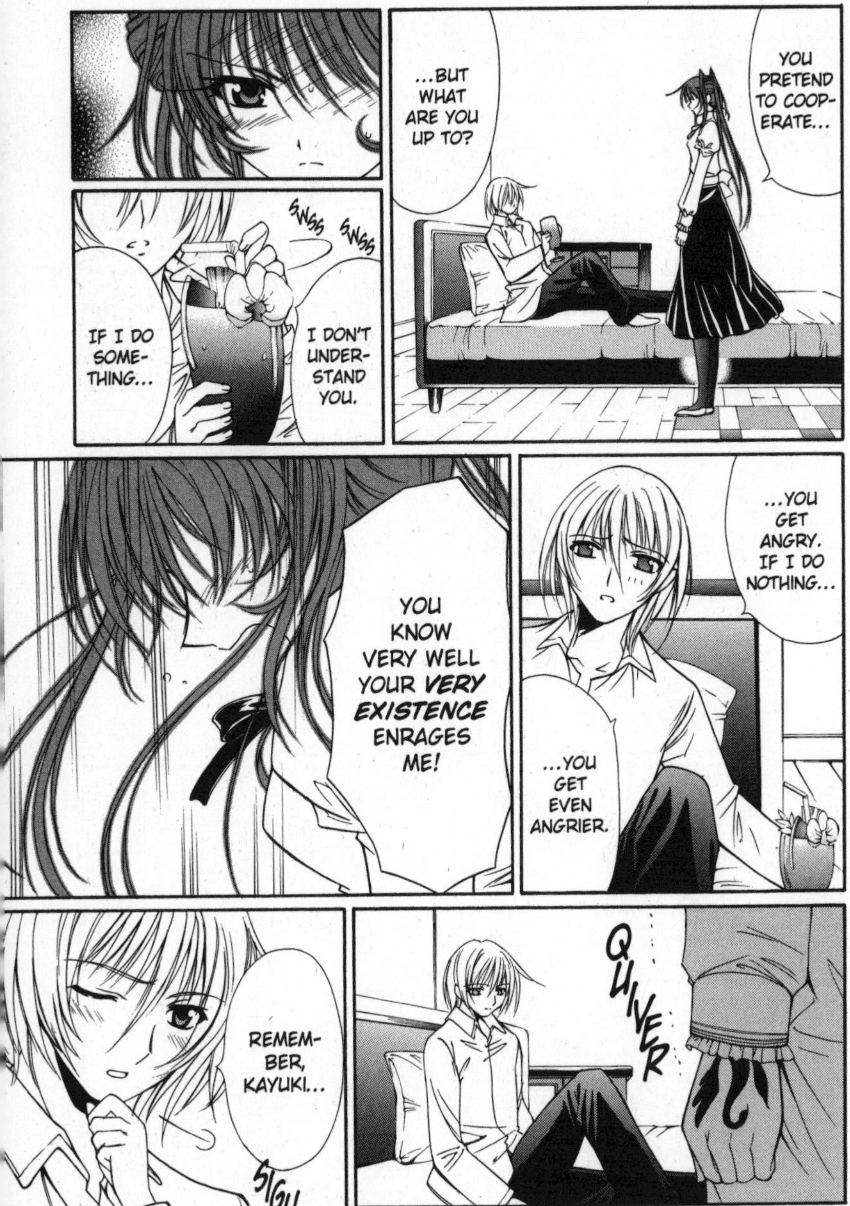
YOU PRETEND TO COOP-ERATE...
...BUT WHAT ARE YOU UP TO?
SNSS SNSS
I DON'T UNDER-STAND YOU.
IF I DO SOME-THING...
...YOU GET ANGRY. IF I DO NOTHING...
...YOU GET EVEN ANGRIER.
YOU KNOW VERY WELL YOUR ***VERY EXISTENCE*** ENRAGES ME!
QUIVER
REMEM-BER, KAYUKI...
SIGH

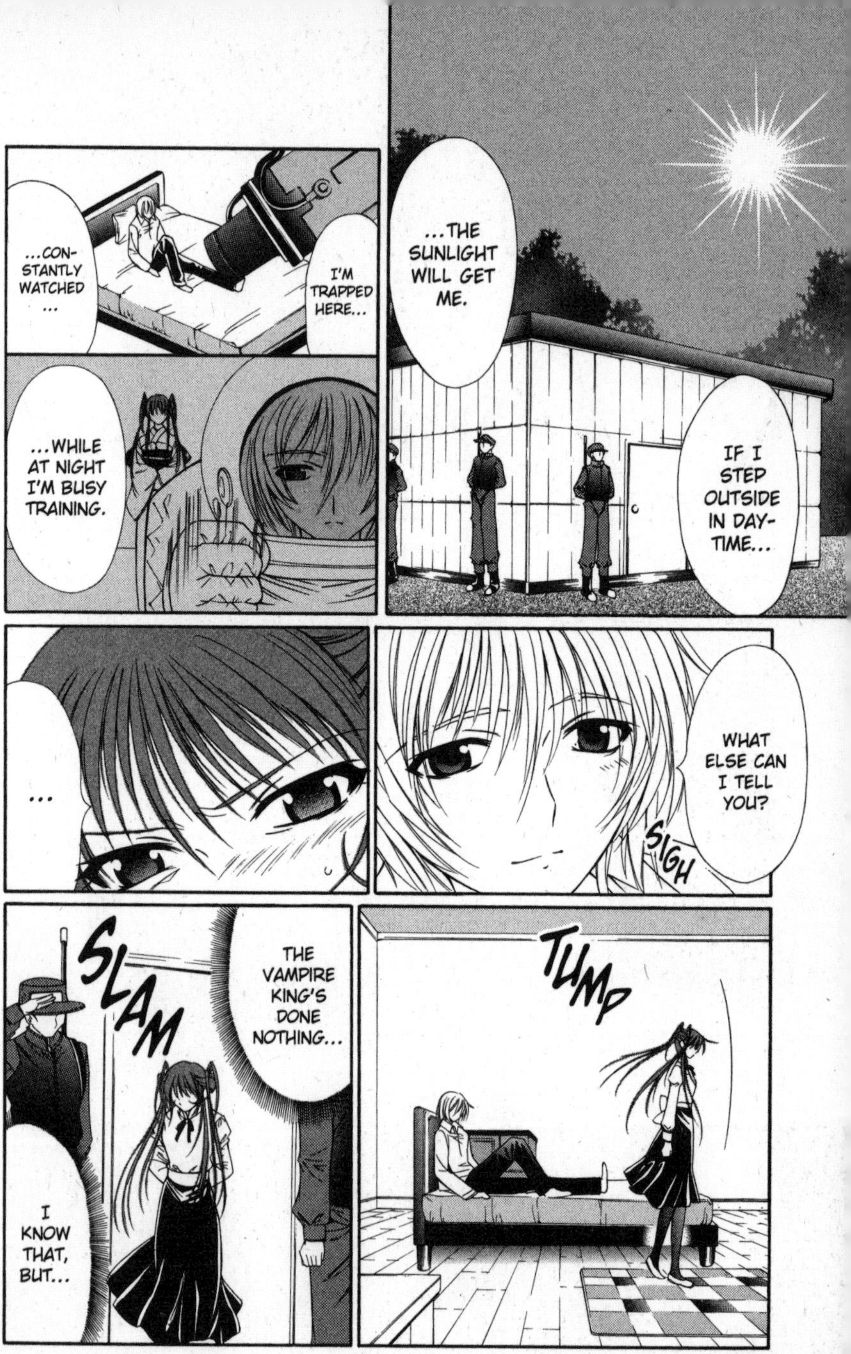
IF I STEP OUTSIDE IN DAY-TIME...
...THE SUNLIGHT WILL GET ME.
I'M TRAPPED HERE...
...CON-STANTLY WATCHED ...
...WHILE AT NIGHT I'M BUSY TRAINING.
WHAT ELSE CAN I TELL YOU?
SIGH
...
TUMP
THE VAMPIRE KING'S DONE NOTHING...
SLAM
I KNOW THAT, BUT...

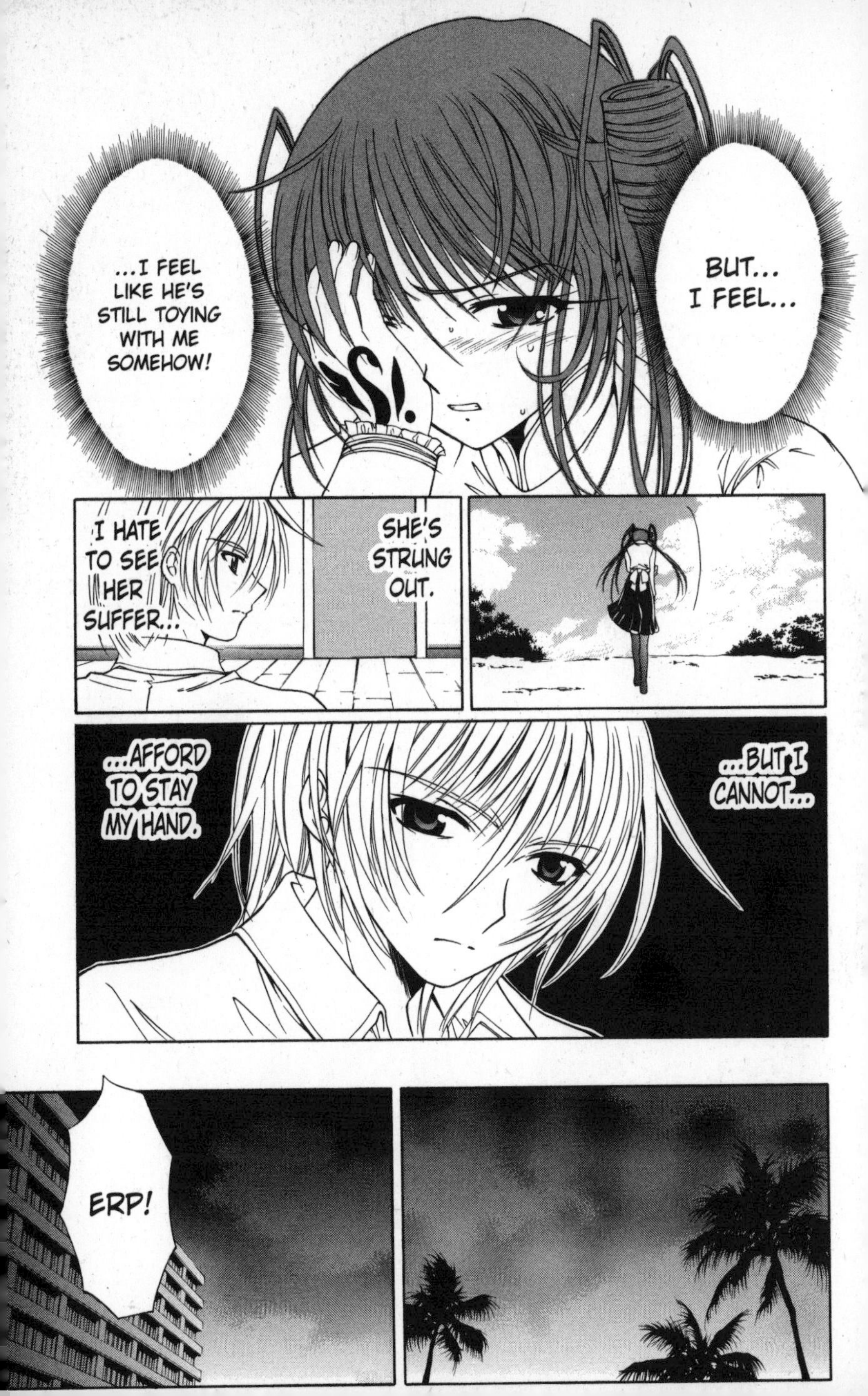
BUT... I FEEL...
...I FEEL LIKE HE'S STILL TOYING WITH ME SOMEHOW!
SHE'S STRUNG OUT.
I HATE TO SEE HER SUFFER...
...BUT I CANNOT...
...AFFORD TO STAY MY HAND.
ERP!

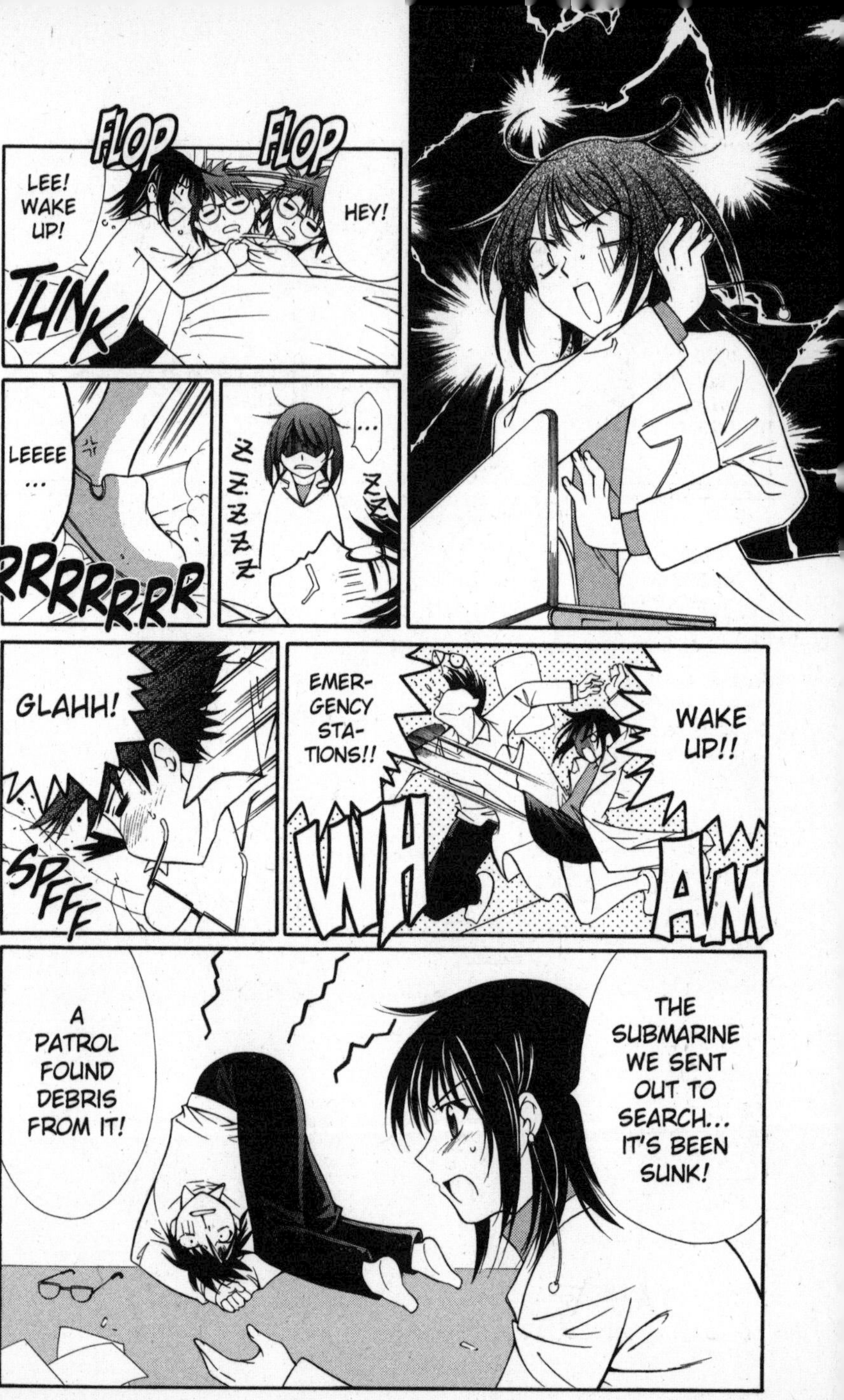
FLOP
HEY!
FLOP
LEE! WAKE UP!
THINK
...
ZZZ
ZZZZZZ
LEEEE...
RRRRRRR
WAKE UP!!
EMER-GENCY STA-TIONS!!
WHAM
GLAHH!
SPFFF
THE SUBMARINE WE SENT OUT TO SEARCH... IT'S BEEN SUNK!
A PATROL FOUND DEBRIS FROM IT!

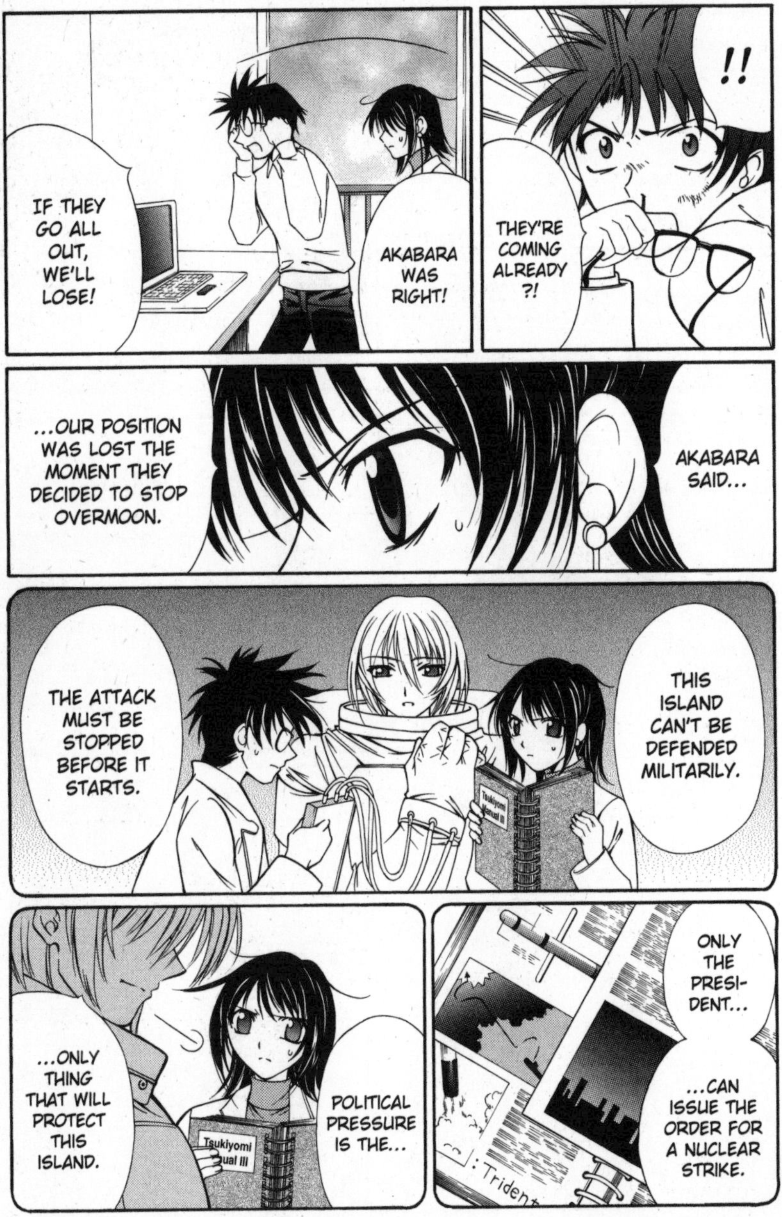
!!
THEY'RE COMING ALREADY?!
AKABARA WAS RIGHT!
IF THEY GO ALL OUT, WE'LL LOSE!
AKABARA SAID...
...OUR POSITION WAS LOST THE MOMENT THEY DECIDED TO STOP OVERMOON.
THIS ISLAND CAN'T BE DEFENDED MILITARILY.
Tsukiyomi Manual III
THE ATTACK MUST BE STOPPED BEFORE IT STARTS.
ONLY THE PRESI-DENT...
...CAN ISSUE THE ORDER FOR A NUCLEAR STRIKE.
POLITICAL PRESSURE IS THE...
...ONLY THING THAT WILL PROTECT THIS ISLAND.

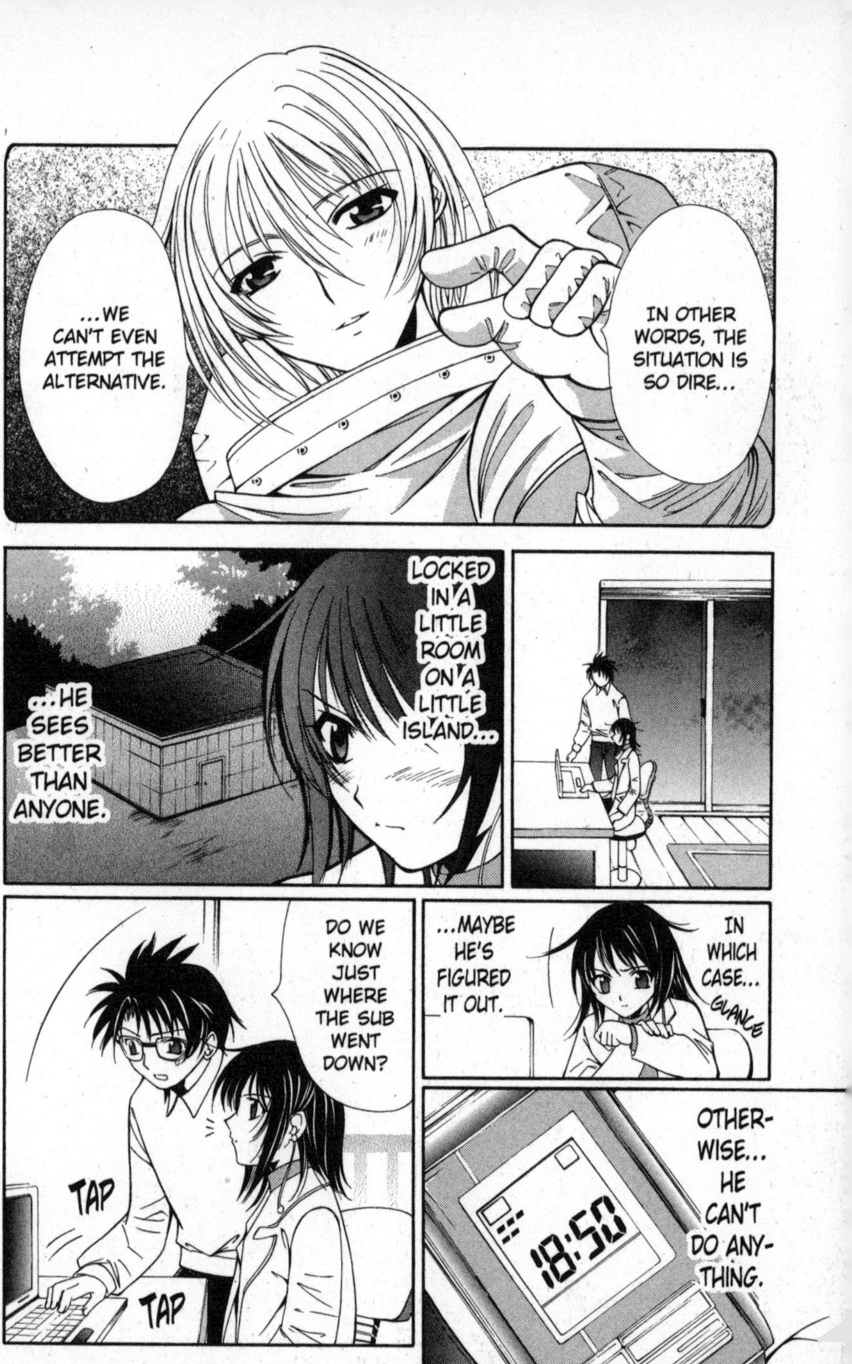
IN OTHER WORDS, THE SITUATION IS SO DIRE...
...WE CAN'T EVEN ATTEMPT THE ALTERNATIVE.
LOCKED IN A LITTLE ROOM ON A LITTLE ISLAND...
...HE SEES BETTER THAN ANYONE.
IN WHICH CASE...
GLANCE
...MAYBE HE'S FIGURED IT OUT.
OTHER-WISE... HE CAN'T DO ANY-THING.
18:50
DO WE KNOW JUST WHERE THE SUB WENT DOWN?
TAP
TAP

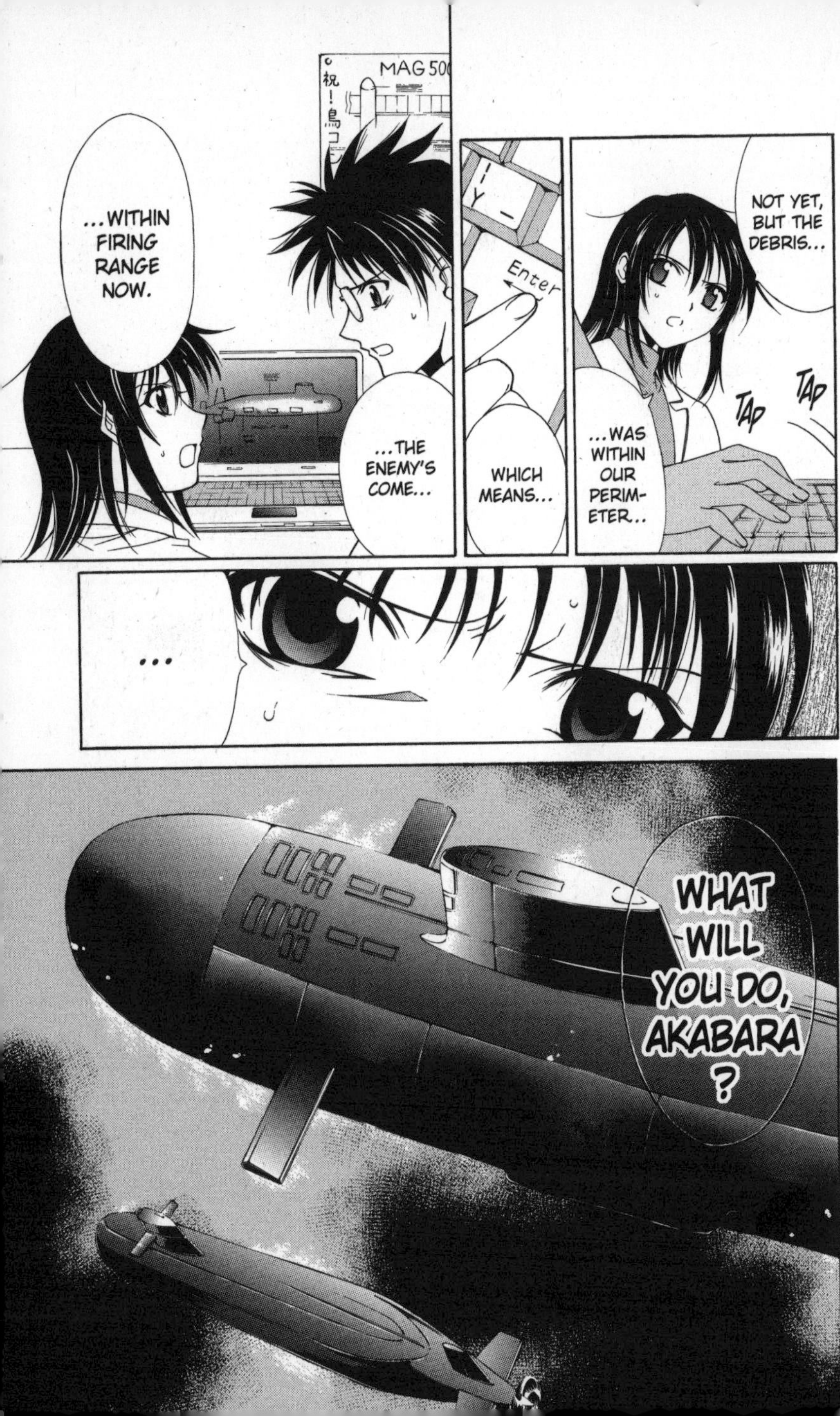
NOT YET, BUT THE DEBRIS...
TAP
TAP
...WAS WITHIN OUR PERIMETER...
Enter
WHICH MEANS...
MAG 50
祝!鳥コン
...THE ENEMY'S COME...
...WITHIN FIRING RANGE NOW.
...
WHAT WILL YOU DO, AKABARA?

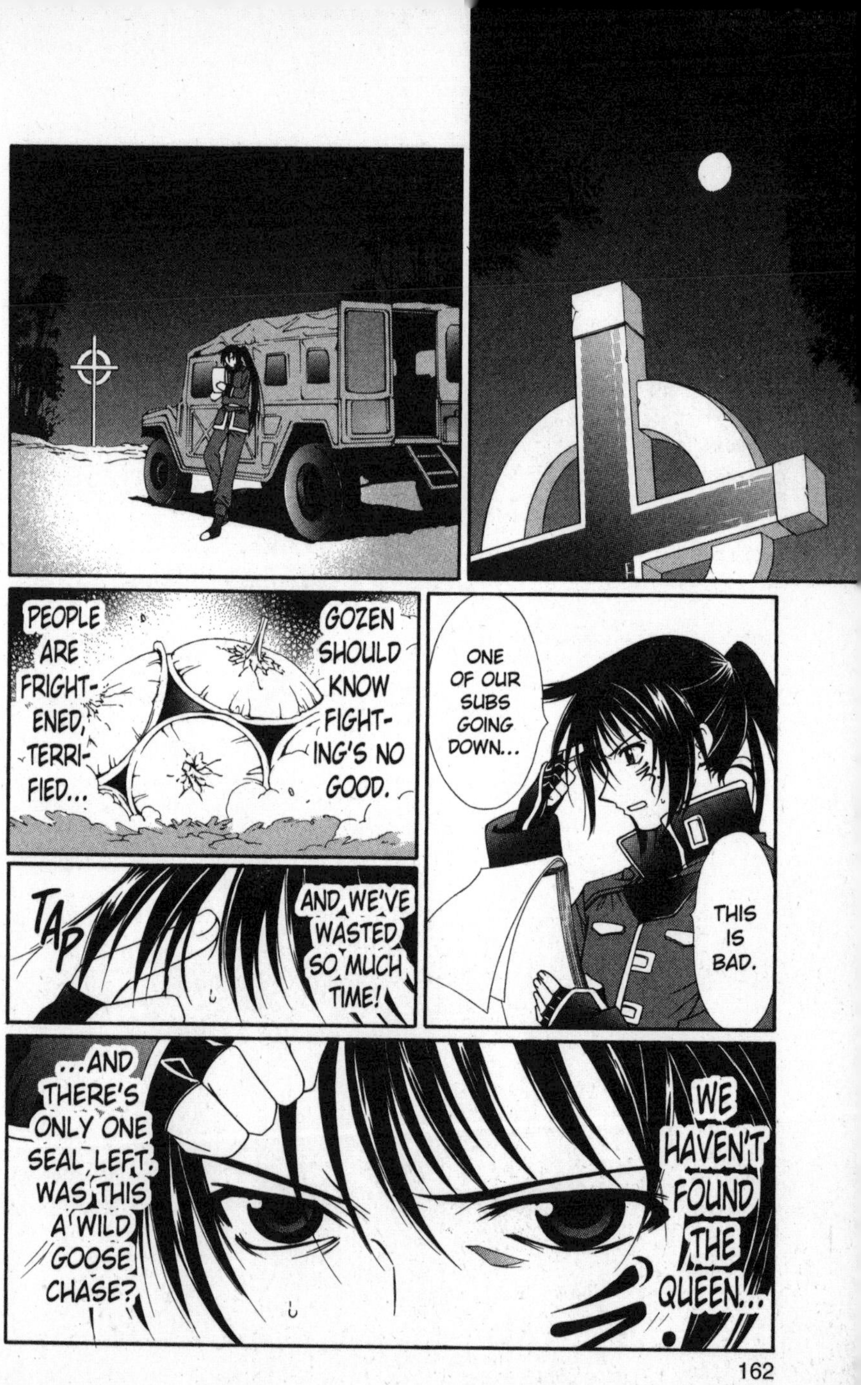
ONE OF OUR SUBS GOING DOWN...
THIS IS BAD.
GOZEN SHOULD KNOW FIGHT-ING'S NO GOOD.
PEOPLE ARE FRIGHT-ENED, TERRI-FIED...
AND WE'VE WASTED SO MUCH TIME!
TAP
WE HAVEN'T FOUND THE QUEEN...
...AND THERE'S ONLY ONE SEAL LEFT. WAS THIS A WILD GOOSE CHASE?

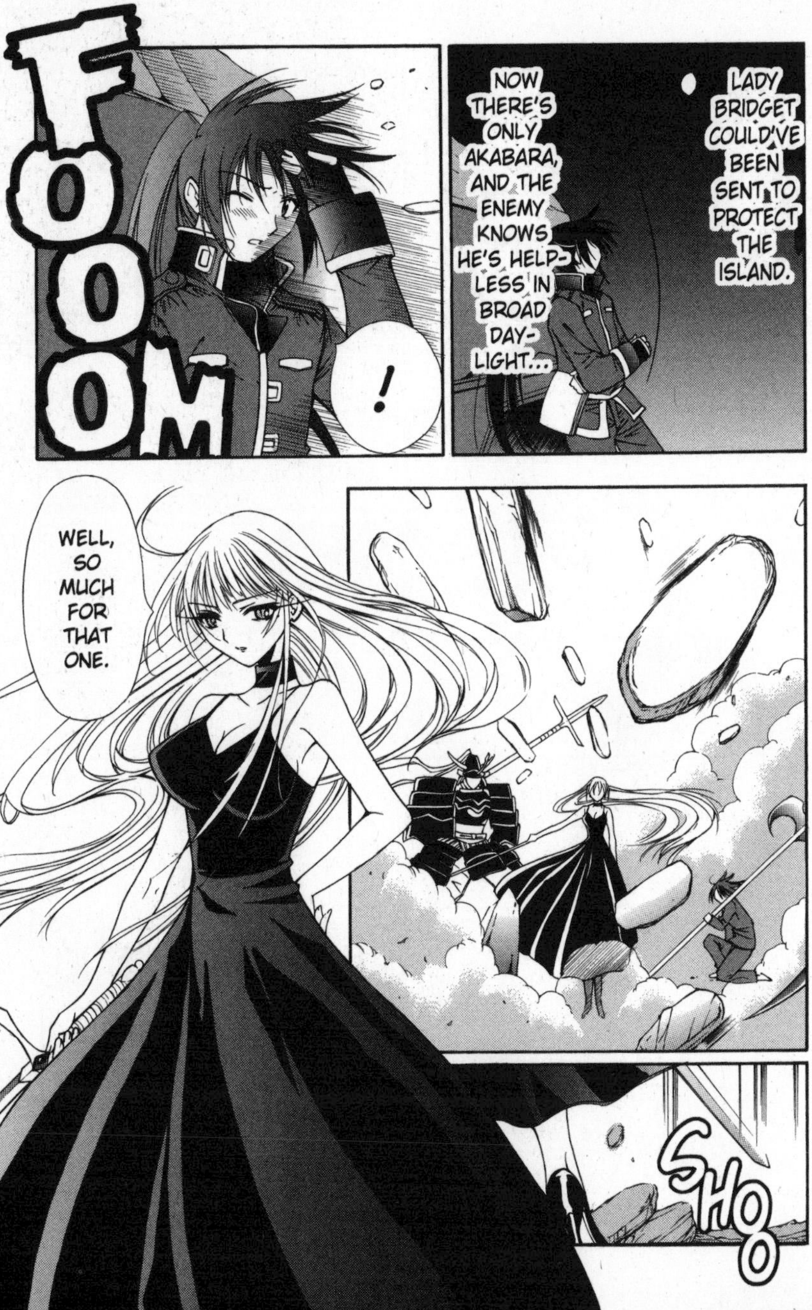
LADY BRIDGET COULD'VE BEEN SENT TO PROTECT THE ISLAND.
NOW THERE'S ONLY AKABARA, AND THE ENEMY KNOWS HE'S HELPLESS IN BROAD DAYLIGHT...
FOOOM
!
SHOO
WELL, SO MUCH FOR THAT ONE.

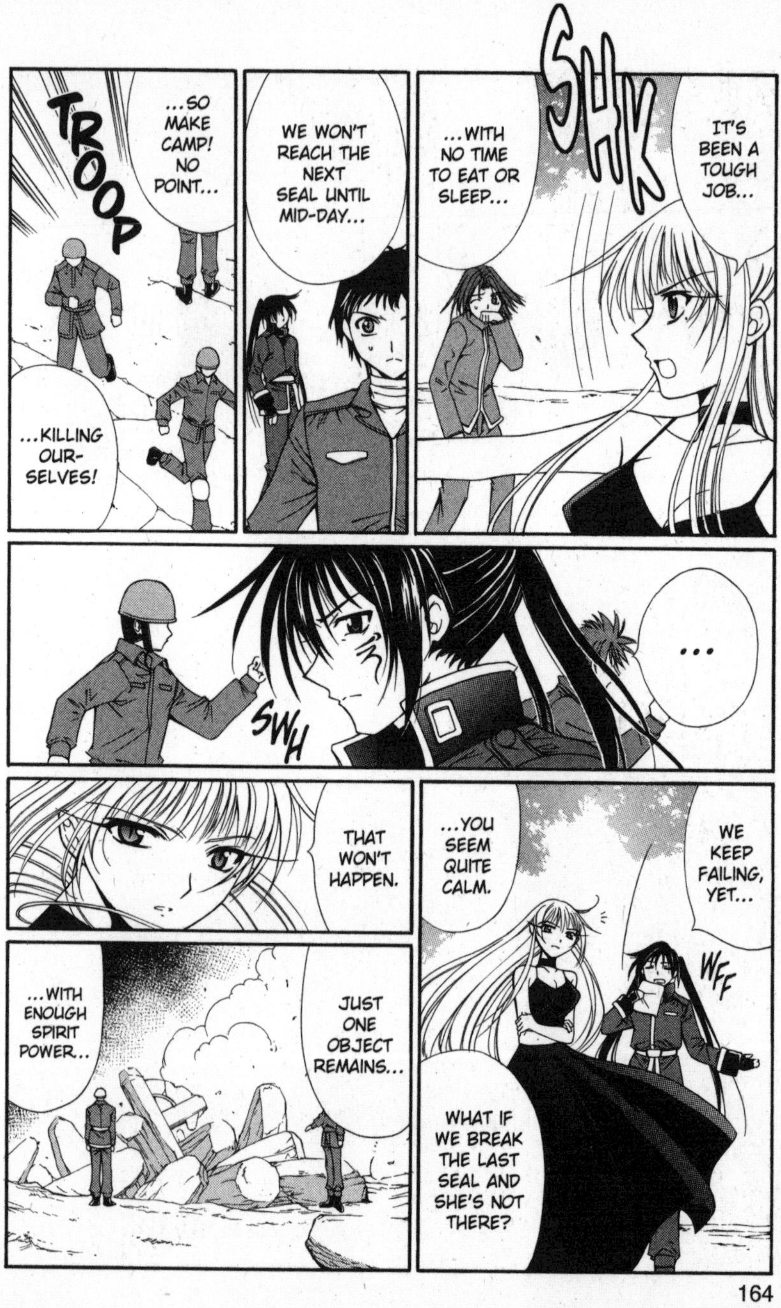
SHK
IT'S BEEN A TOUGH JOB...
...WITH NO TIME TO EAT OR SLEEP...
WE WON'T REACH THE NEXT SEAL UNTIL MID-DAY...
TROOP
...SO MAKE CAMP! NO POINT...
...KILLING OUR-SELVES!
...
SWH
WE KEEP FAILING, YET...
...YOU SEEM QUITE CALM.
WFF
WHAT IF WE BREAK THE LAST SEAL AND SHE'S NOT THERE?
THAT WON'T HAPPEN.
JUST ONE OBJECT REMAINS...
...WITH ENOUGH SPIRIT POWER...

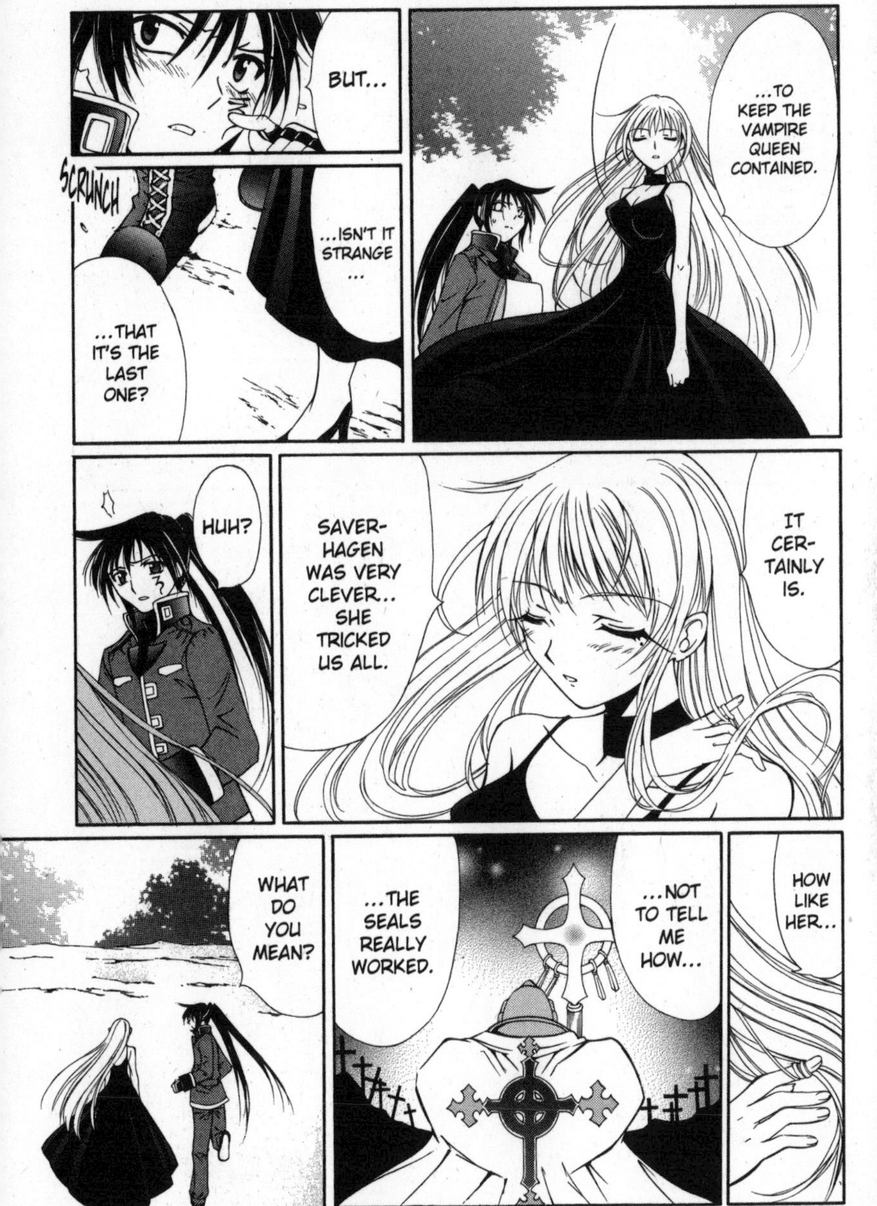
...TO KEEP THE VAMPIRE QUEEN CONTAINED.
BUT...
SCRUNCH
...ISN'T IT STRANGE ...
...THAT IT'S THE LAST ONE?
IT CERTAINLY IS.
SAVERHAGEN WAS VERY CLEVER... SHE TRICKED US ALL.
HUH?
HOW LIKE HER...
...NOT TO TELL ME HOW...
...THE SEALS REALLY WORKED.
WHAT DO YOU MEAN?

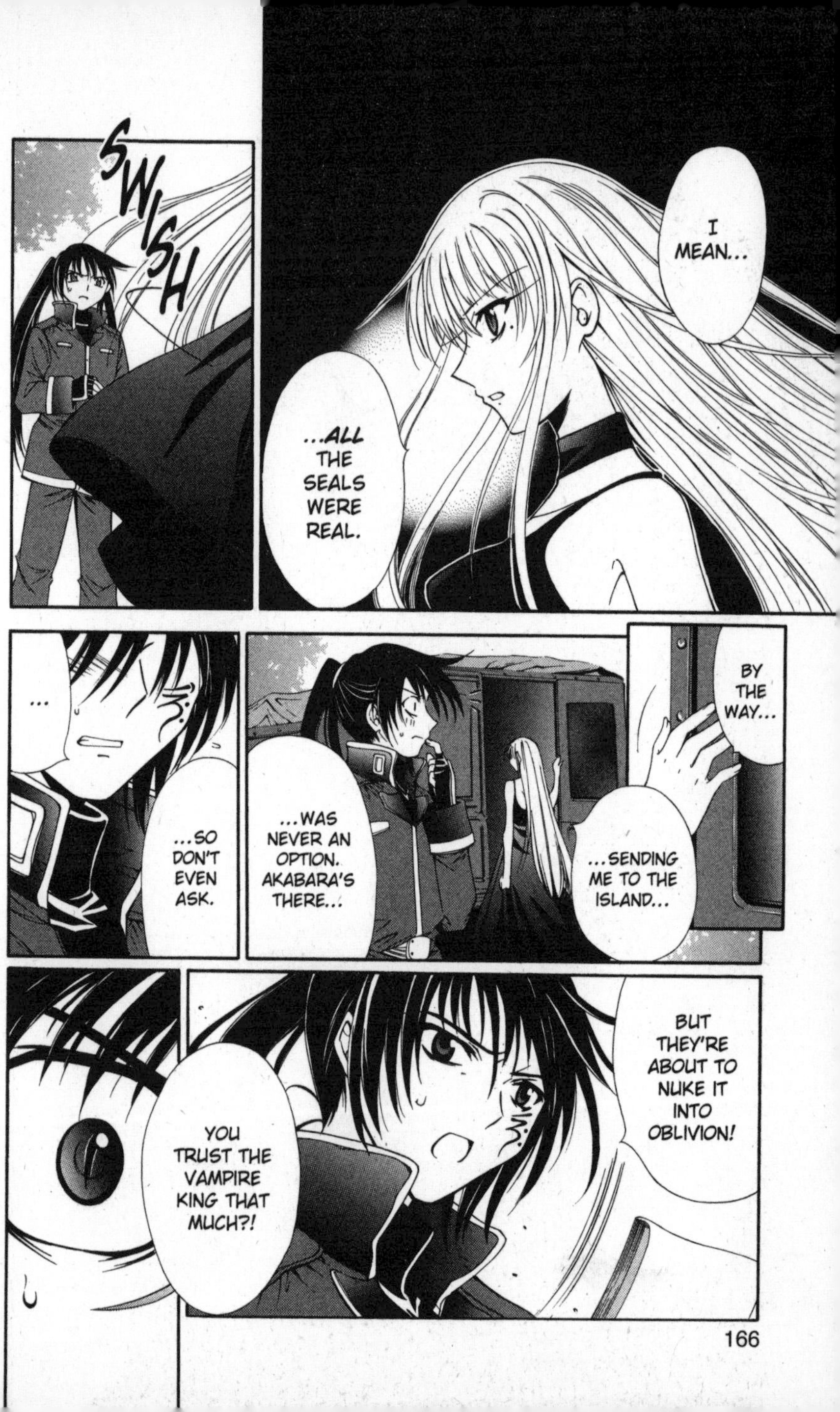
I MEAN...
...ALL THE SEALS WERE REAL.
SWISH
BY THE WAY...
...SENDING ME TO THE ISLAND...
...WAS NEVER AN OPTION. AKABARA'S THERE...
...
...SO DON'T EVEN ASK.
BUT THEY'RE ABOUT TO NUKE IT INTO OBLIVION!
YOU TRUST THE VAMPIRE KING THAT MUCH?!

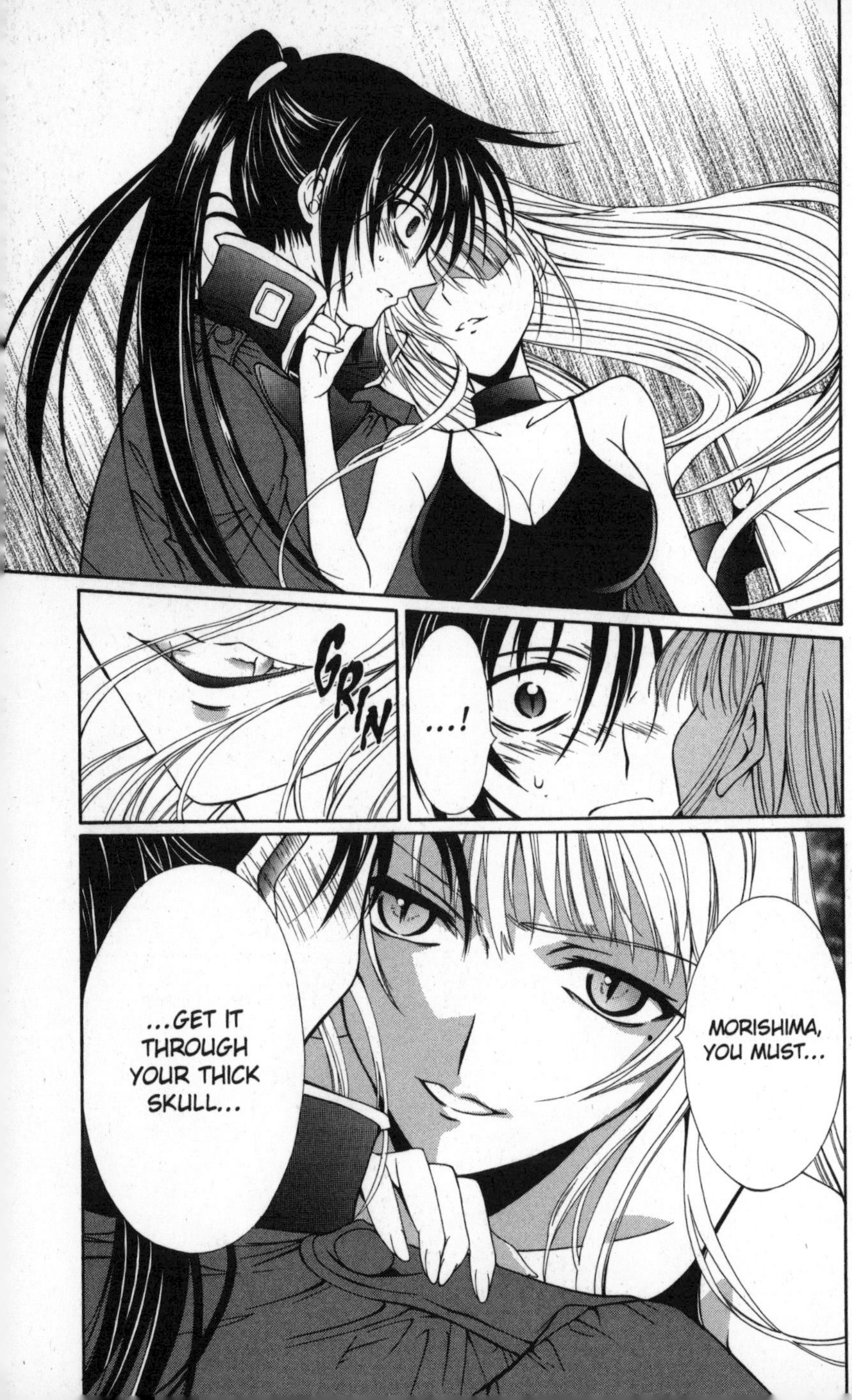
...!
GRIN
MORISHIMA, YOU MUST...
...GET IT THROUGH YOUR THICK SKULL...

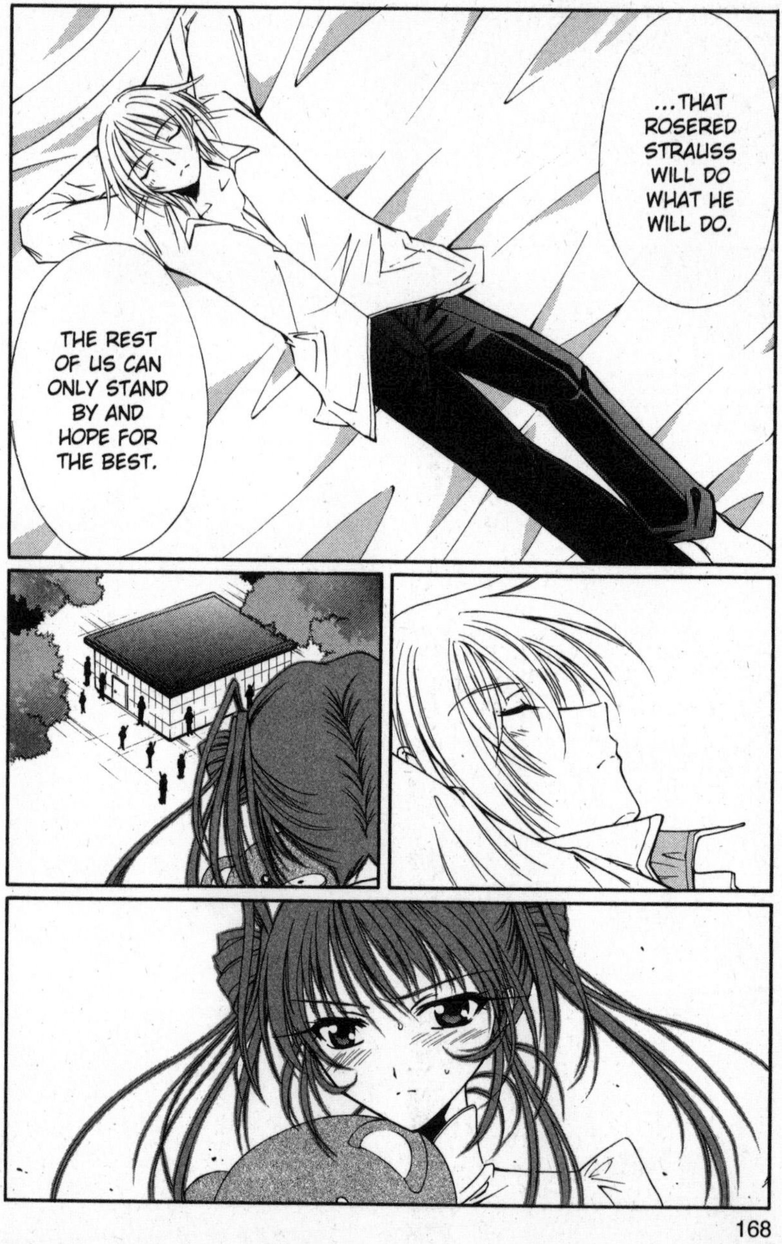
...THAT ROSERED STRAUSS WILL DO WHAT HE WILL DO.
THE REST OF US CAN ONLY STAND BY AND HOPE FOR THE BEST.

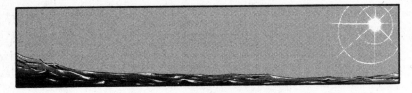

1:00 P.M., 2500 KILOMETERS FROM THE ISLAND...

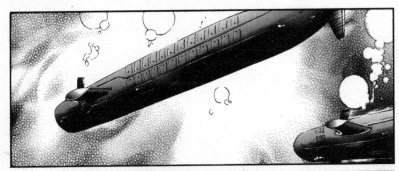

CRUISE MISSILES LAUNCH FROM TWO SUBMARINES...

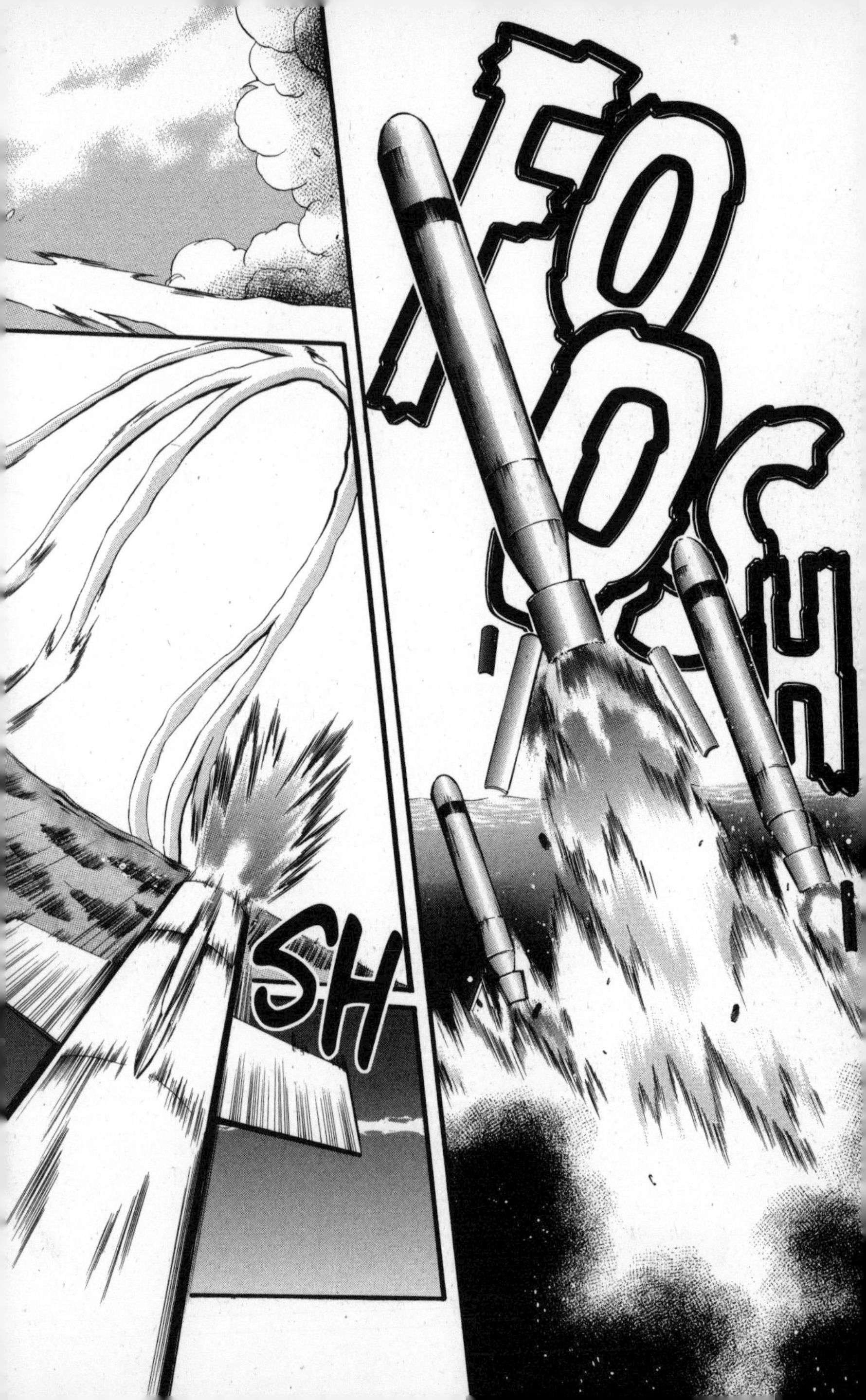
FOOSH
SH

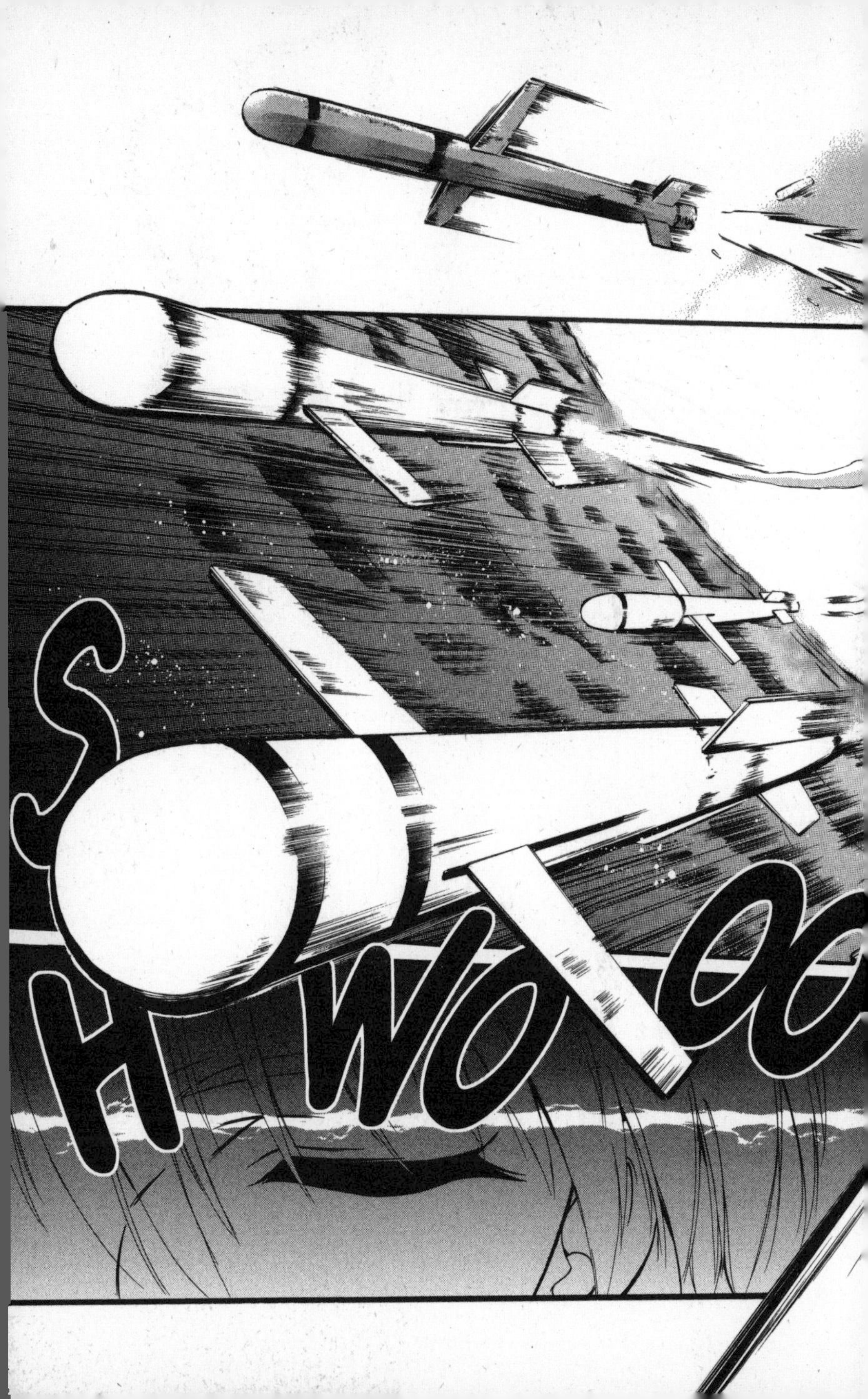
SHWOOO

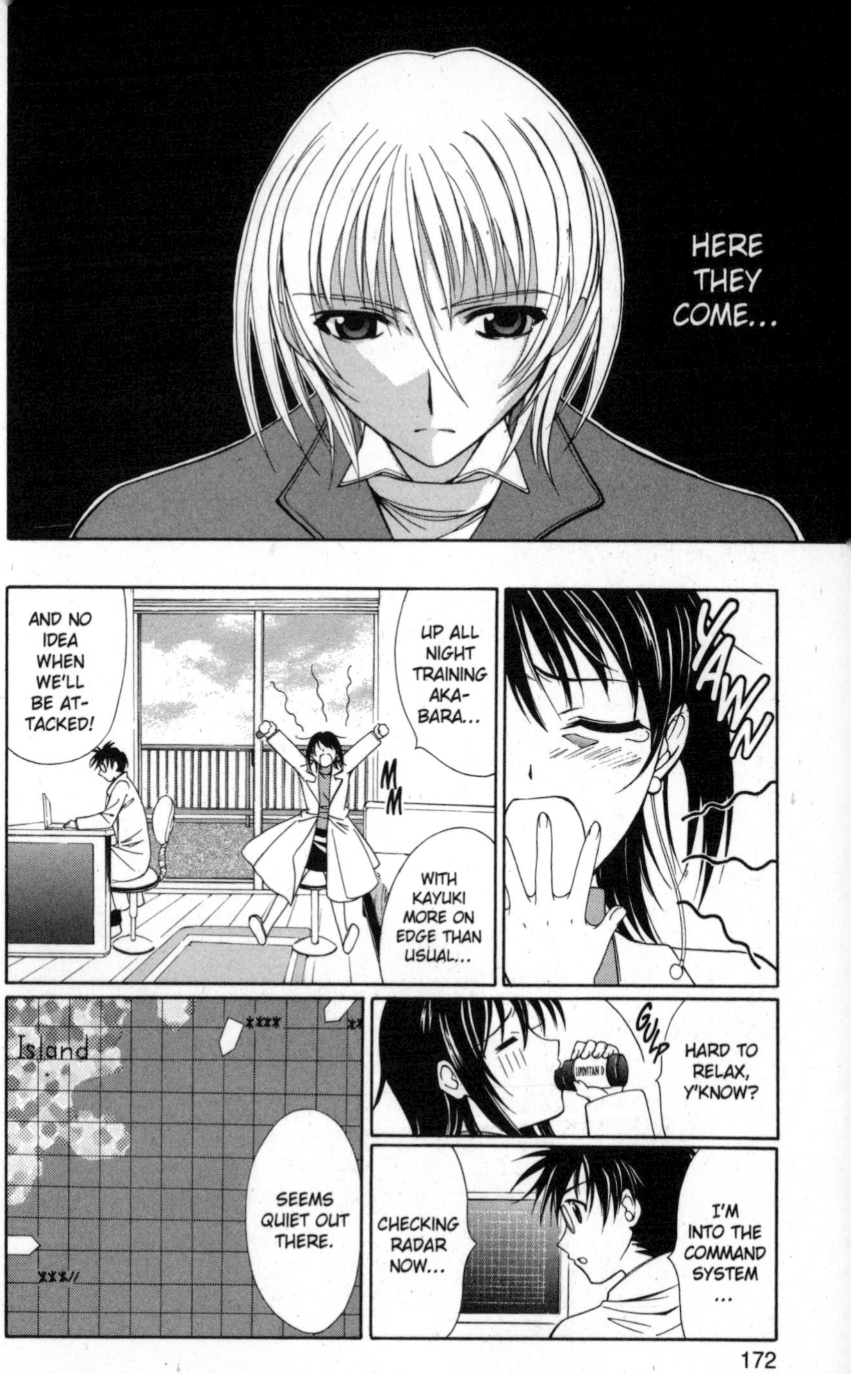
HERE THEY COME...
YAWWN
UP ALL NIGHT TRAINING AKA-BARA...
MM
WITH KAYUKI MORE ON EDGE THAN USUAL...
AND NO IDEA WHEN WE'LL BE AT-TACKED!
GULP
HARD TO RELAX, Y'KNOW?
I'M INTO THE COMMAND SYSTEM ...
CHECKING RADAR NOW...
Island
SEEMS QUIET OUT THERE.

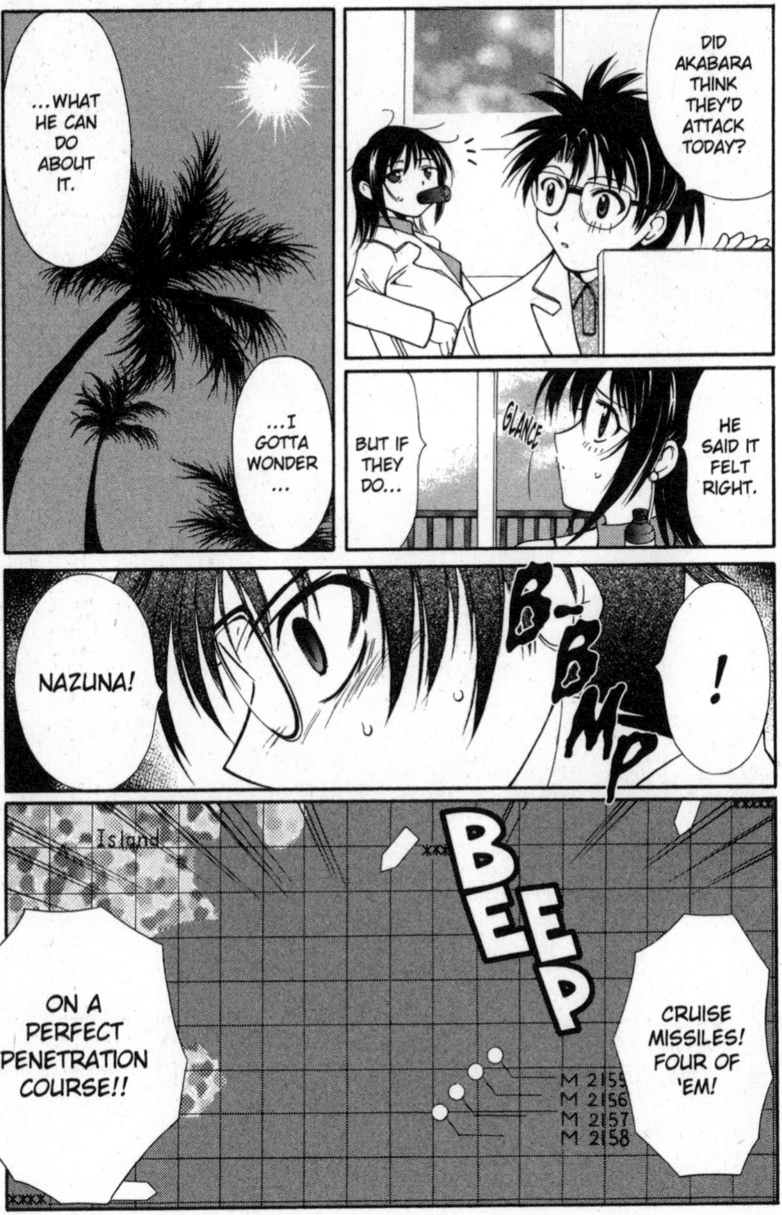
DID AKABARA THINK THEY'D ATTACK TODAY?
HE SAID IT FELT RIGHT.
GLANCE
BUT IF THEY DO...
...I GOTTA WONDER...
...WHAT HE CAN DO ABOUT IT.
!
B-BMP
NAZUNA!
Island
CRUISE MISSILES! FOUR OF 'EM!
BEEP
M 2155
M 2156
M 2157
M 2158
ON A PERFECT PENETRATION COURSE!!

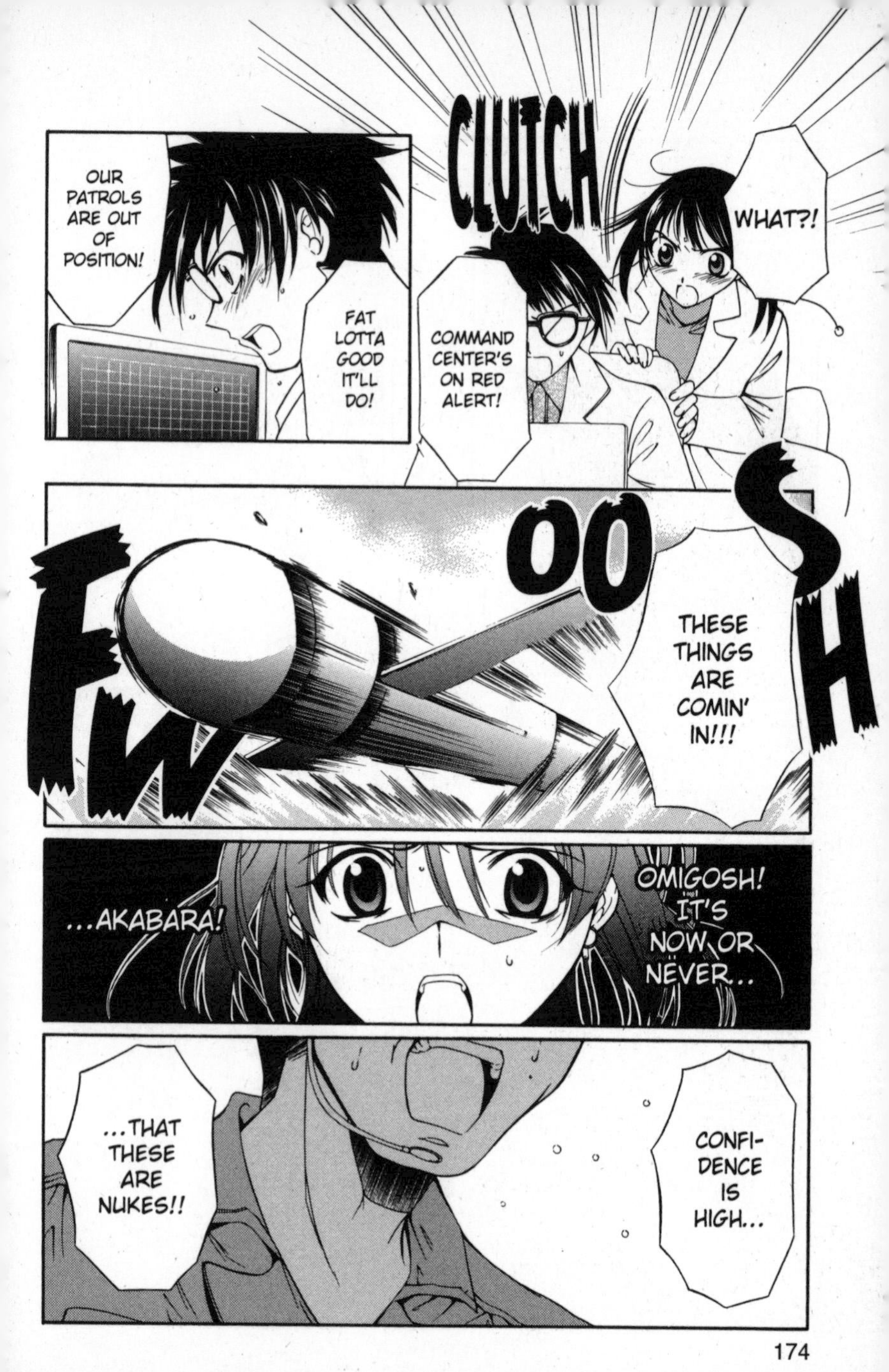
CLUTCH
WHAT?!
COMMAND CENTER'S ON RED ALERT!
FAT LOTTA GOOD IT'LL DO!
OUR PATROLS ARE OUT OF POSITION!
FWOOSH
THESE THINGS ARE COMIN' IN!!!
OMIGOSH! IT'S NOW OR NEVER...
...AKABARA!
CONFI-DENCE IS HIGH...
...THAT THESE ARE NUKES!!

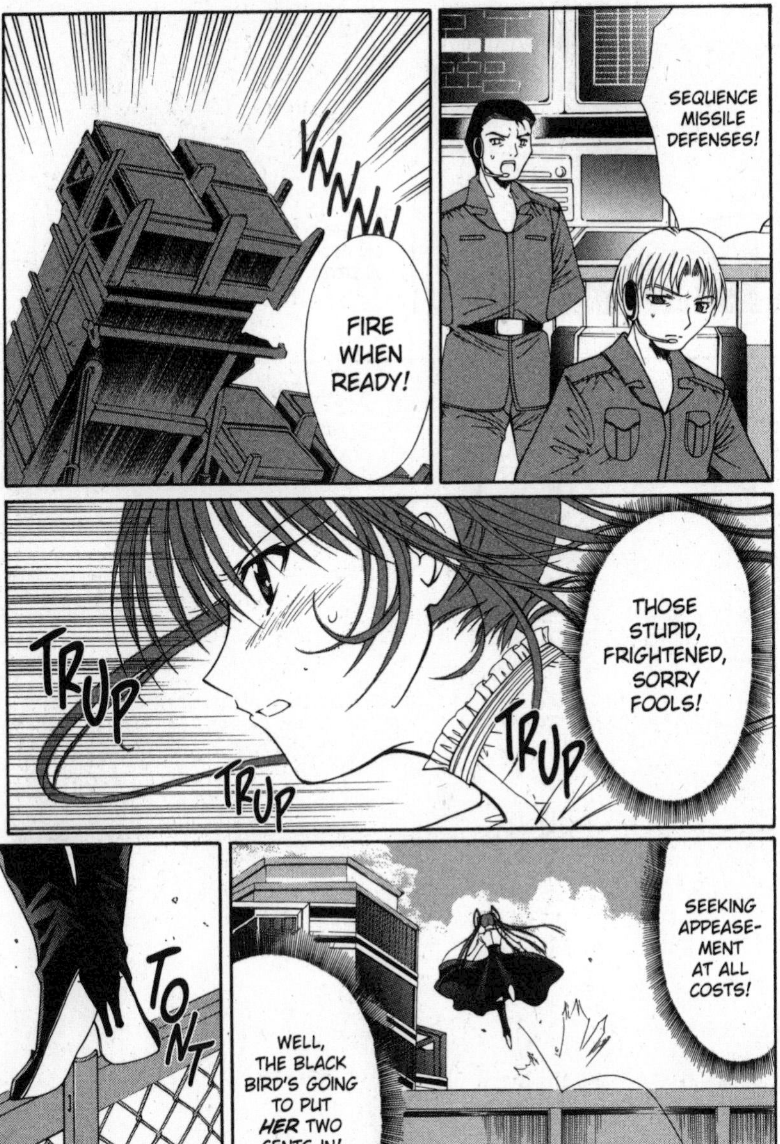
SEQUENCE MISSILE DEFENSES!
VNNNN
FIRE WHEN READY!
THOSE STUPID, FRIGHTENED, SORRY FOOLS!
TRUP
TRUP
TRUP
SEEKING APPEASE-MENT AT ALL COSTS!
WELL, THE BLACK BIRD'S GOING TO PUT *HER* TWO CENTS IN!
TONT

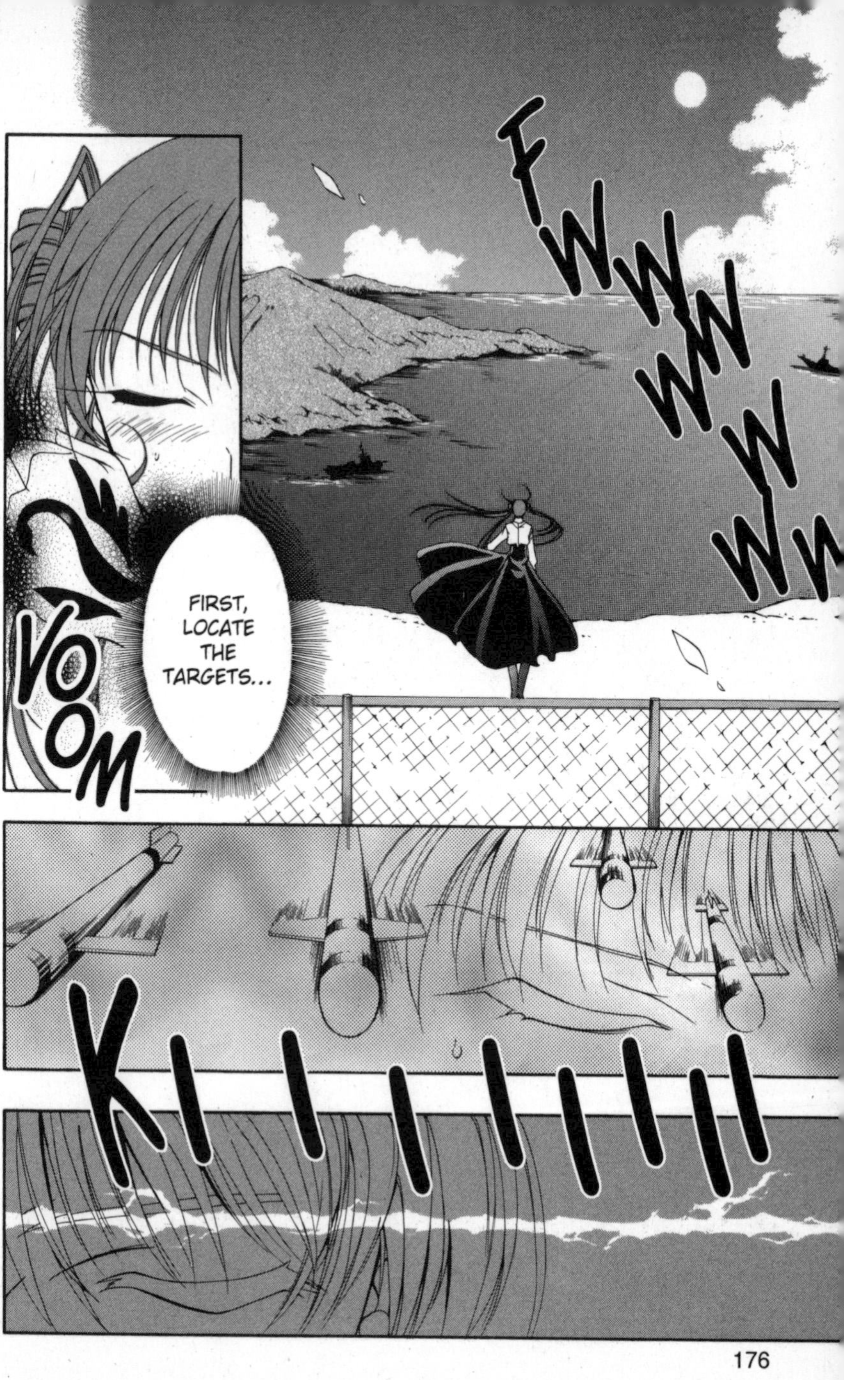
FWWWWWWWW
FIRST, LOCATE THE TARGETS...
VOOM
KIIIIIII

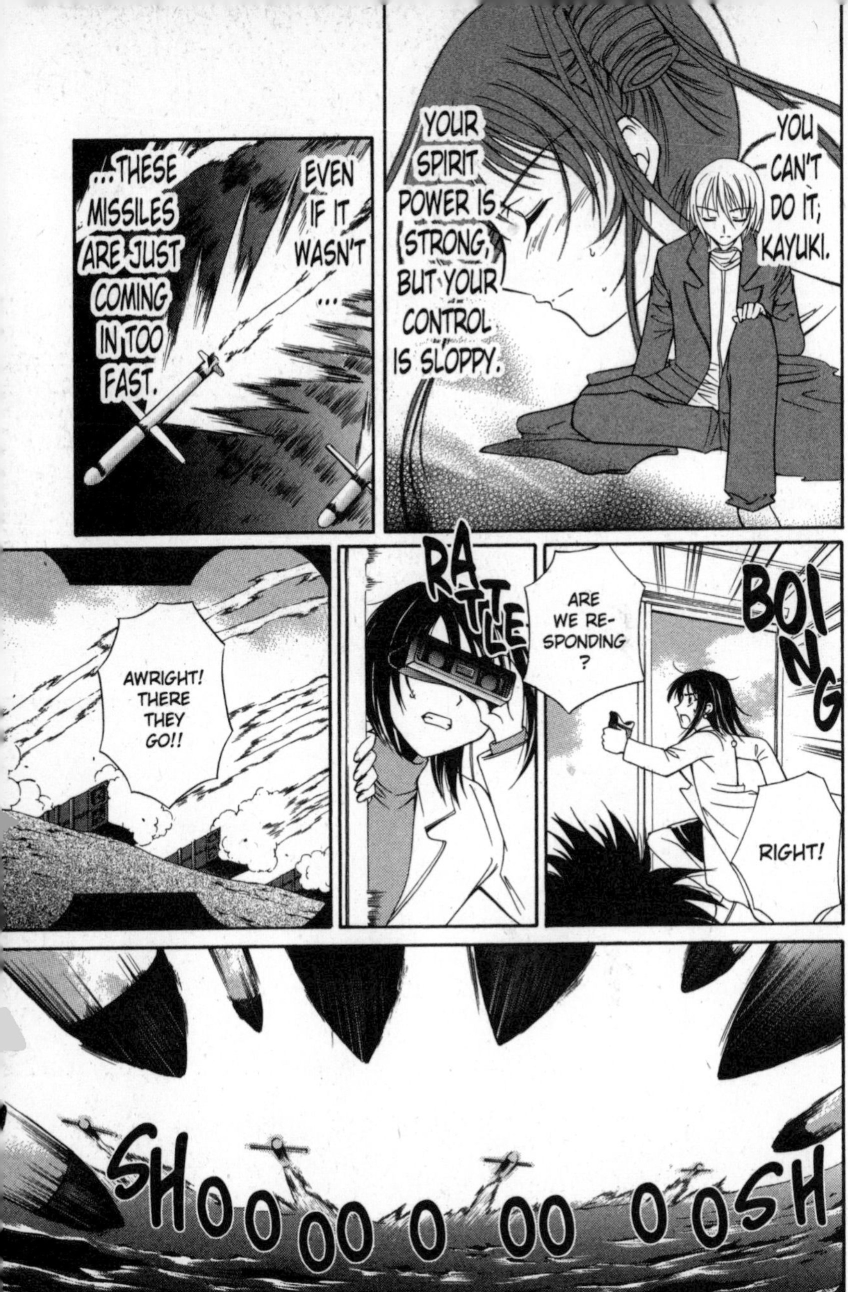
YOU CAN'T DO IT; KAYUKI.
YOUR SPIRIT POWER IS STRONG, BUT YOUR CONTROL IS SLOPPY.
EVEN IF IT WASN'T...
...THESE MISSILES ARE JUST COMING IN TOO FAST.
BOING
ARE WE RE-SPONDING?
RIGHT!
RATTLE
AWRIGHT! THERE THEY GO!!
SHOOOOOOOOOOSH

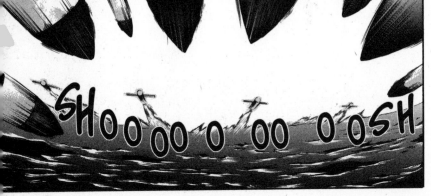

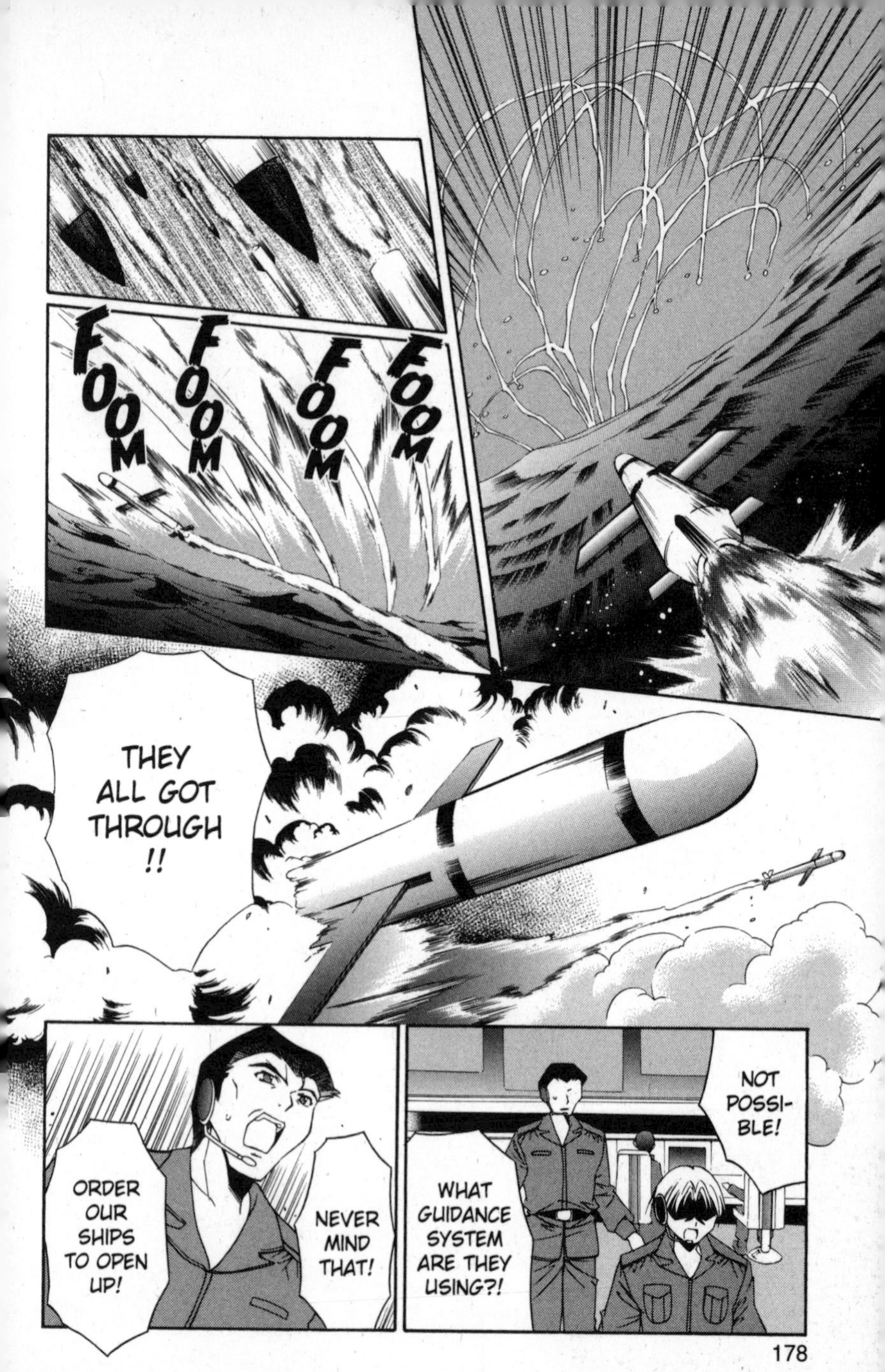
FOOM
FOOM
FOOM
FOOM
THEY ALL GOT THROUGH!!
NOT POSSI-BLE!
WHAT GUIDANCE SYSTEM ARE THEY USING?!
NEVER MIND THAT!
ORDER OUR SHIPS TO OPEN UP!

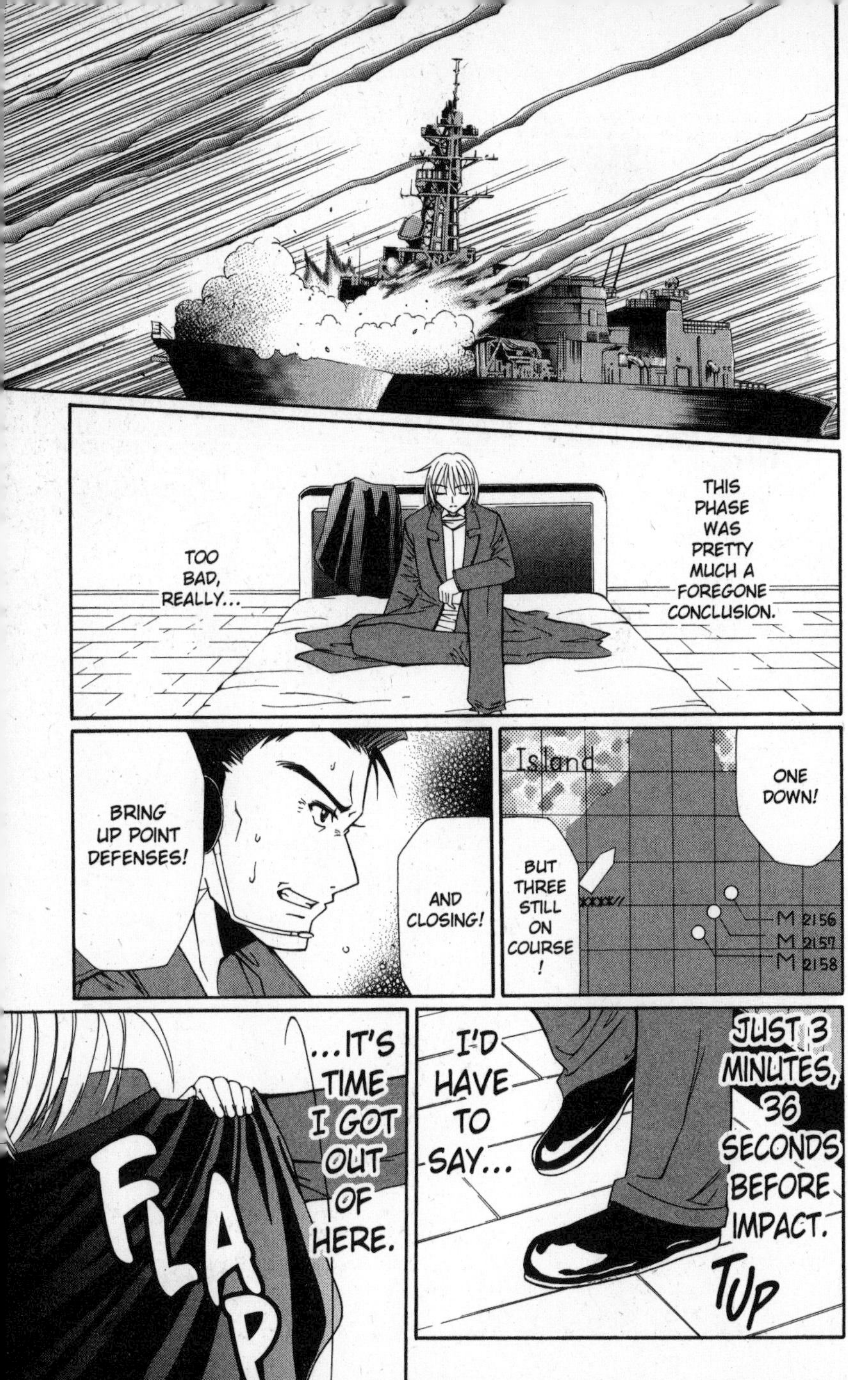
THIS PHASE WAS PRETTY MUCH A FOREGONE CONCLUSION.
TOO BAD, REALLY...
Island
ONE DOWN!
BUT THREE STILL ON COURSE!
M 2156
M 2157
M 2158
AND CLOSING!
BRING UP POINT DEFENSES!
JUST 3 MINUTES, 36 SECONDS BEFORE IMPACT.
I'D HAVE TO SAY...
TUP
...IT'S TIME I GOT OUT OF HERE.
FLAP

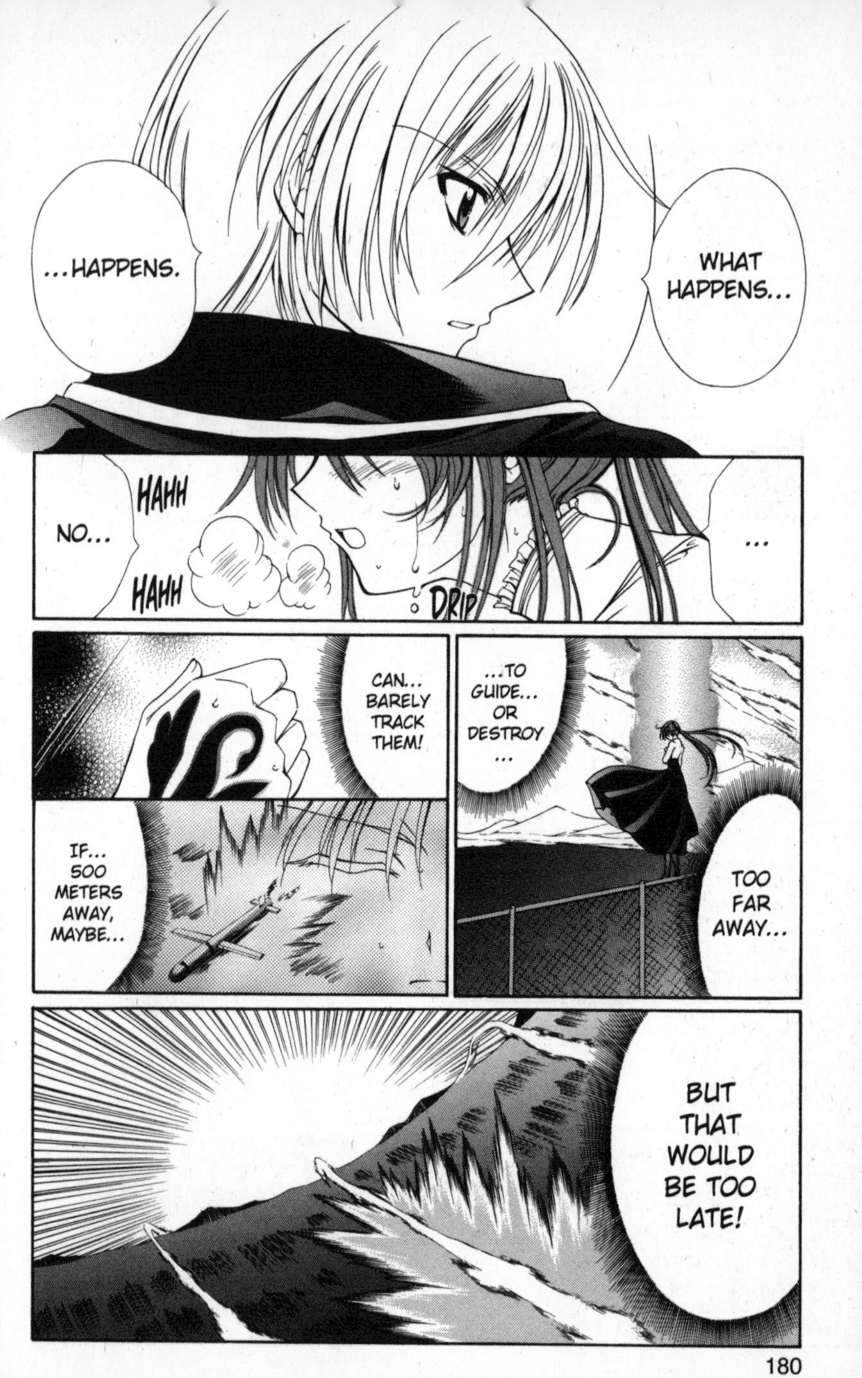
WHAT HAPPENS...
...HAPPENS.
...
HAHH
NO...
HAHH
DRIP
...TO GUIDE... OR DESTROY ...
TOO FAR AWAY...
CAN... BARELY TRACK THEM!
IF... 500 METERS AWAY, MAYBE...
BUT THAT WOULD BE TOO LATE!

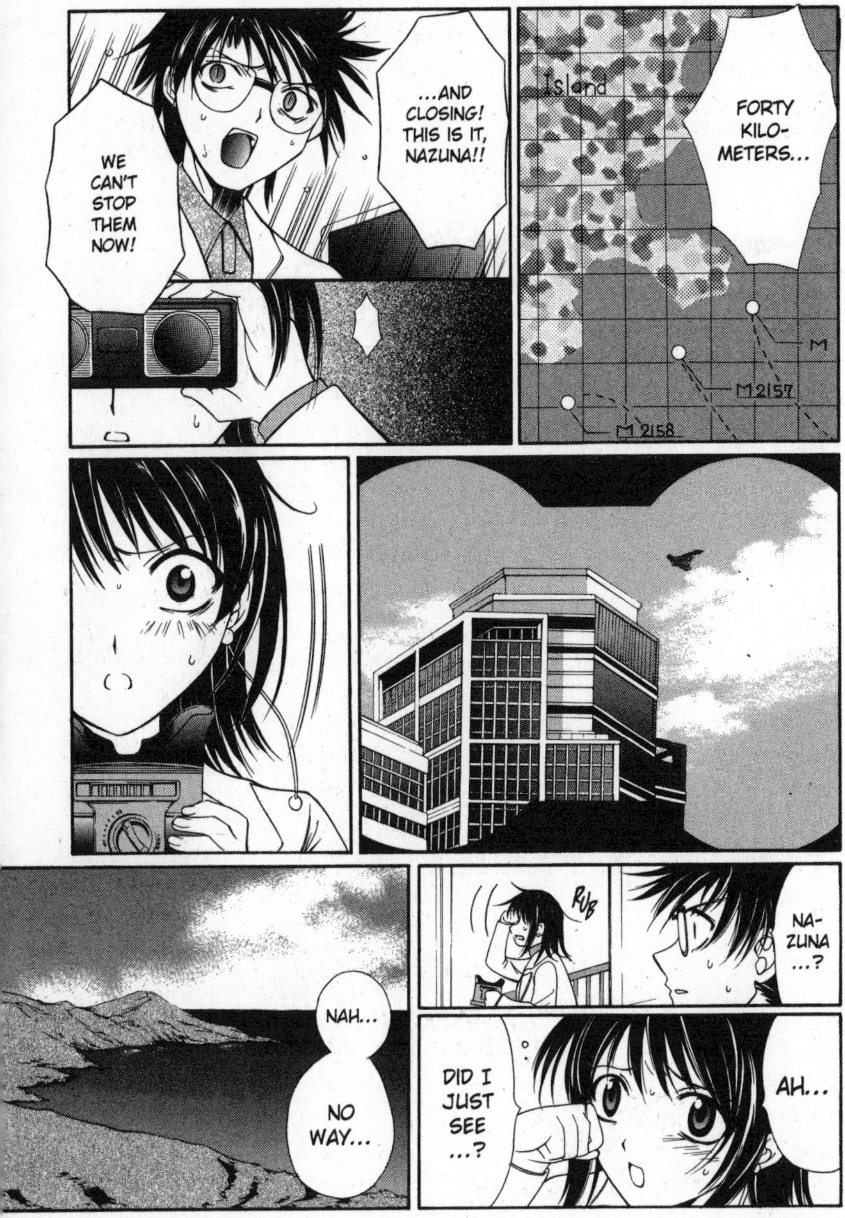
FORTY KILO-METERS...
Island
M
M 2157
M 2158
...AND CLOSING! THIS IS IT, NAZUNA!!
WE CAN'T STOP THEM NOW!
NA-ZUNA...?
RUB
AH...
DID I JUST SEE...?
NAH...
NO WAY...

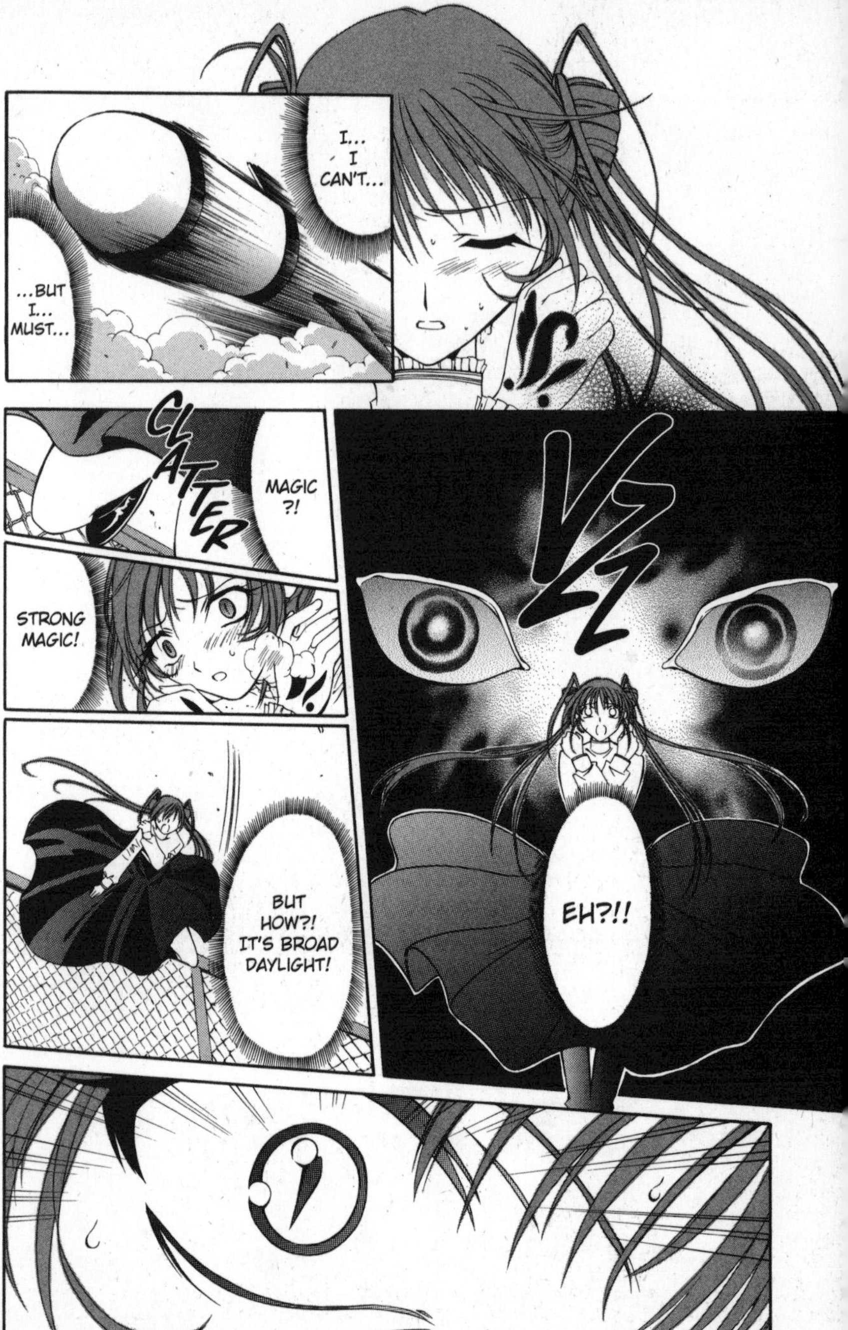

I... I CAN'T...
...BUT I... MUST...
VZZ
EH?!!
CLATTER
MAGIC?!
STRONG MAGIC!
BUT HOW?! IT'S BROAD DAYLIGHT!

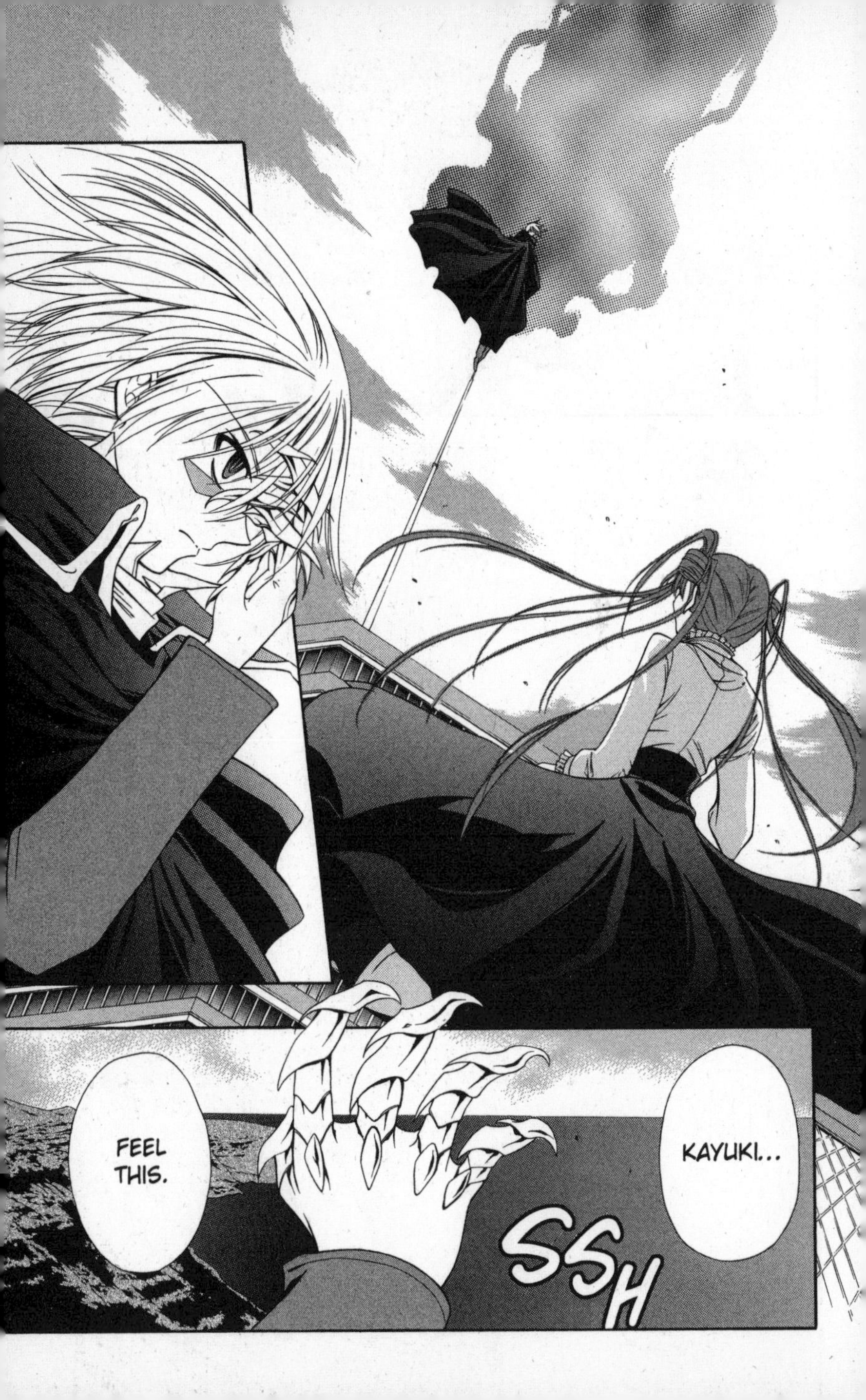
KAYUKI...
SSH
FEEL THIS.

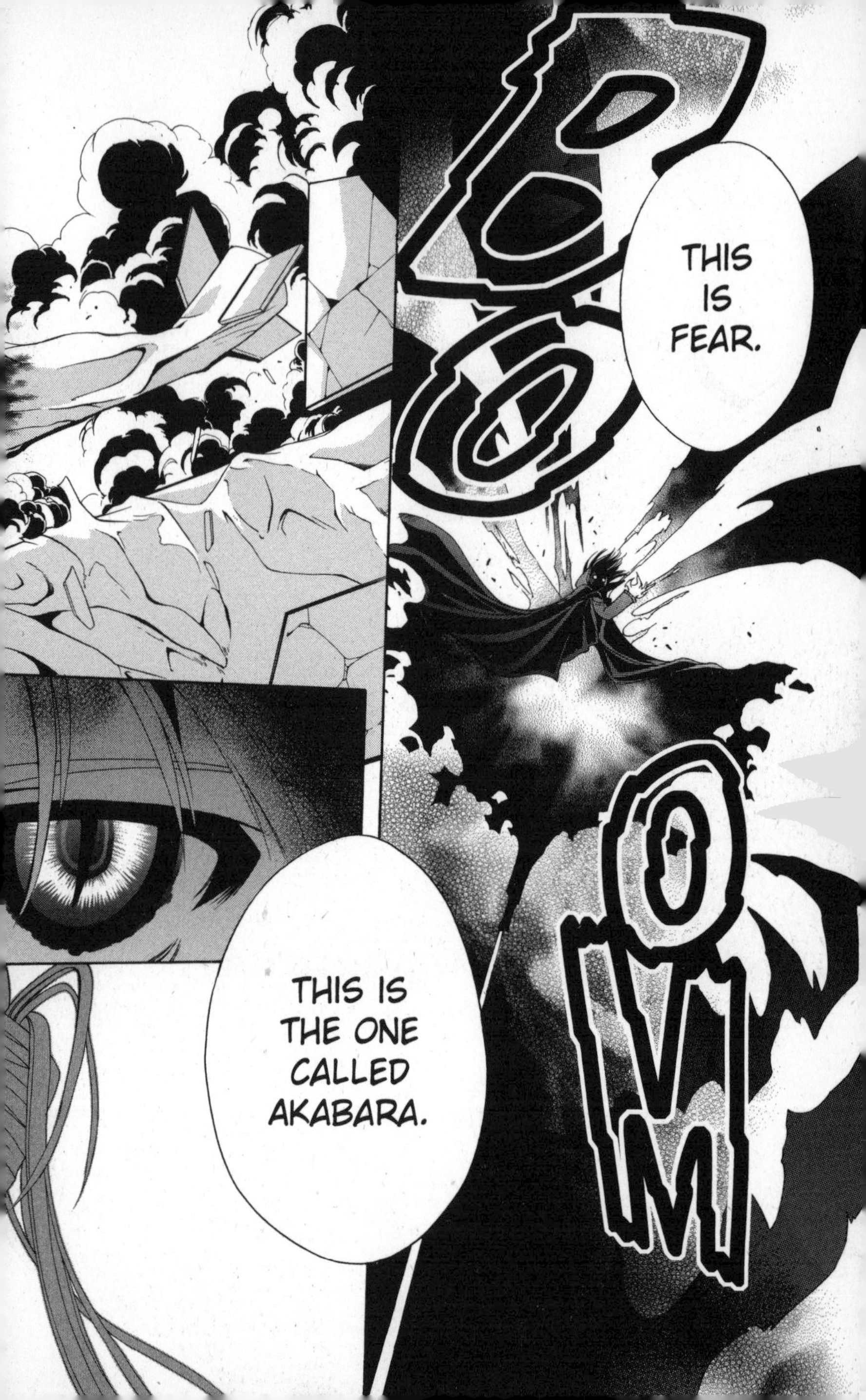
THIS IS FEAR.
DOOM
THIS IS THE ONE CALLED AKABARA.

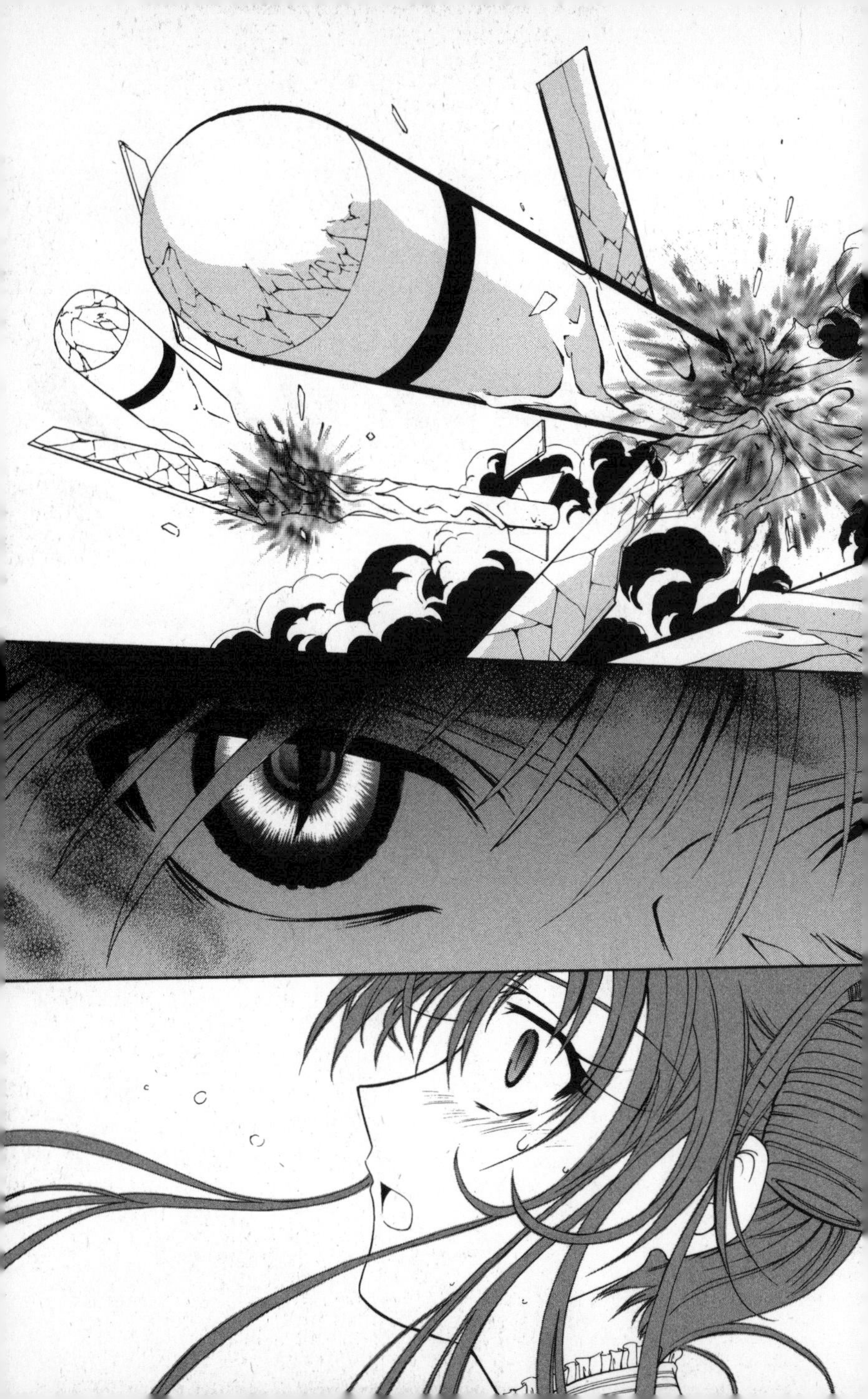

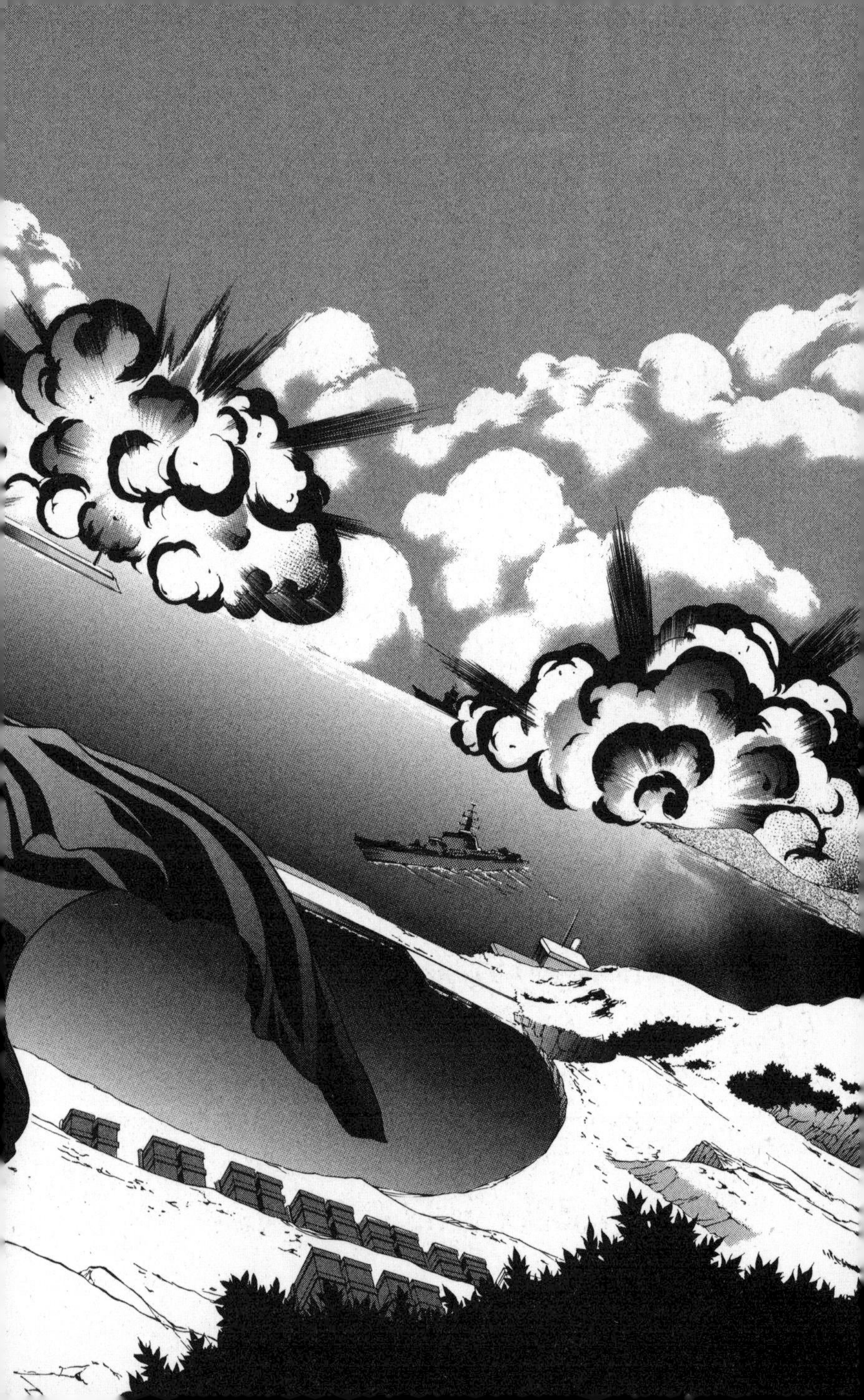

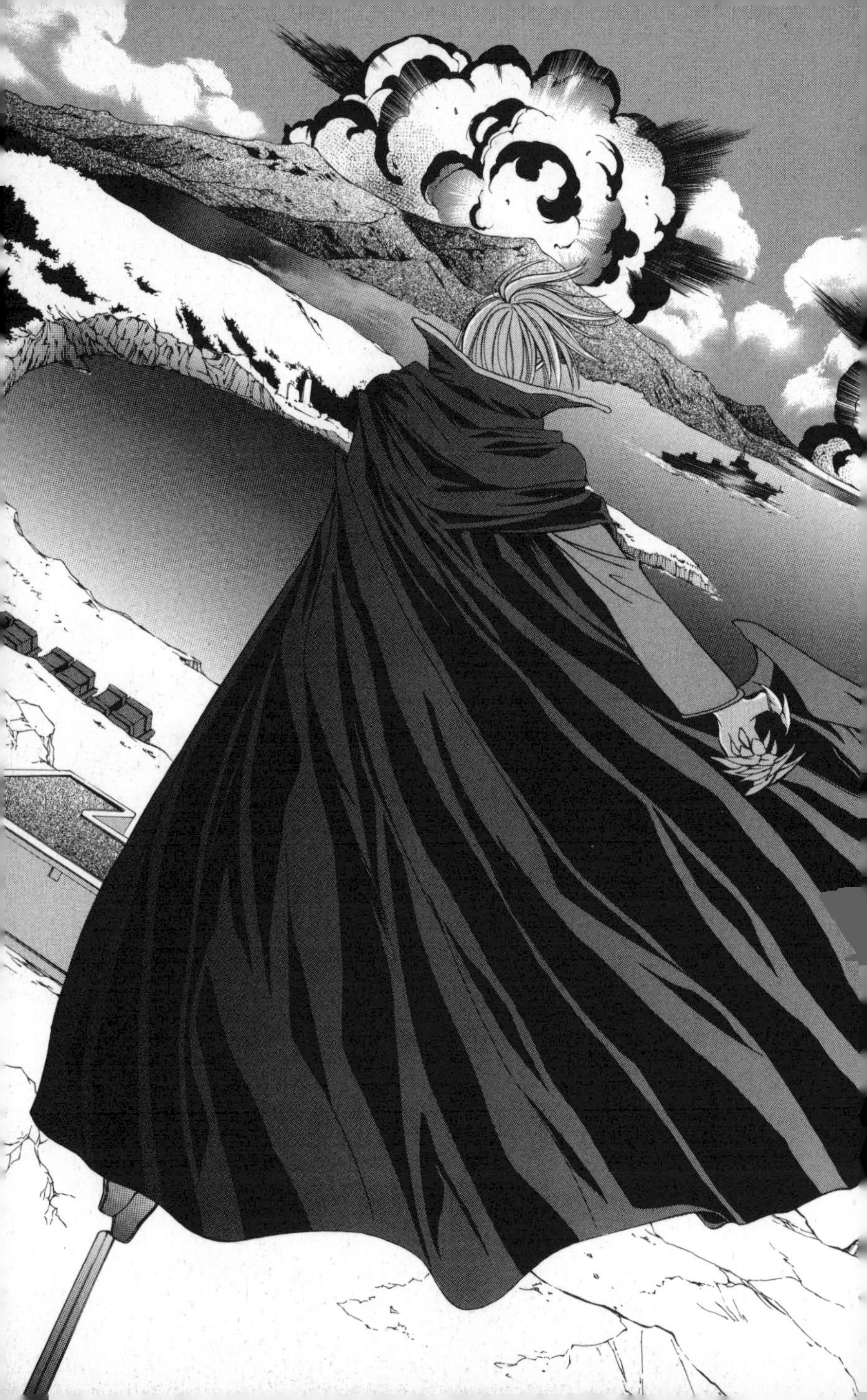

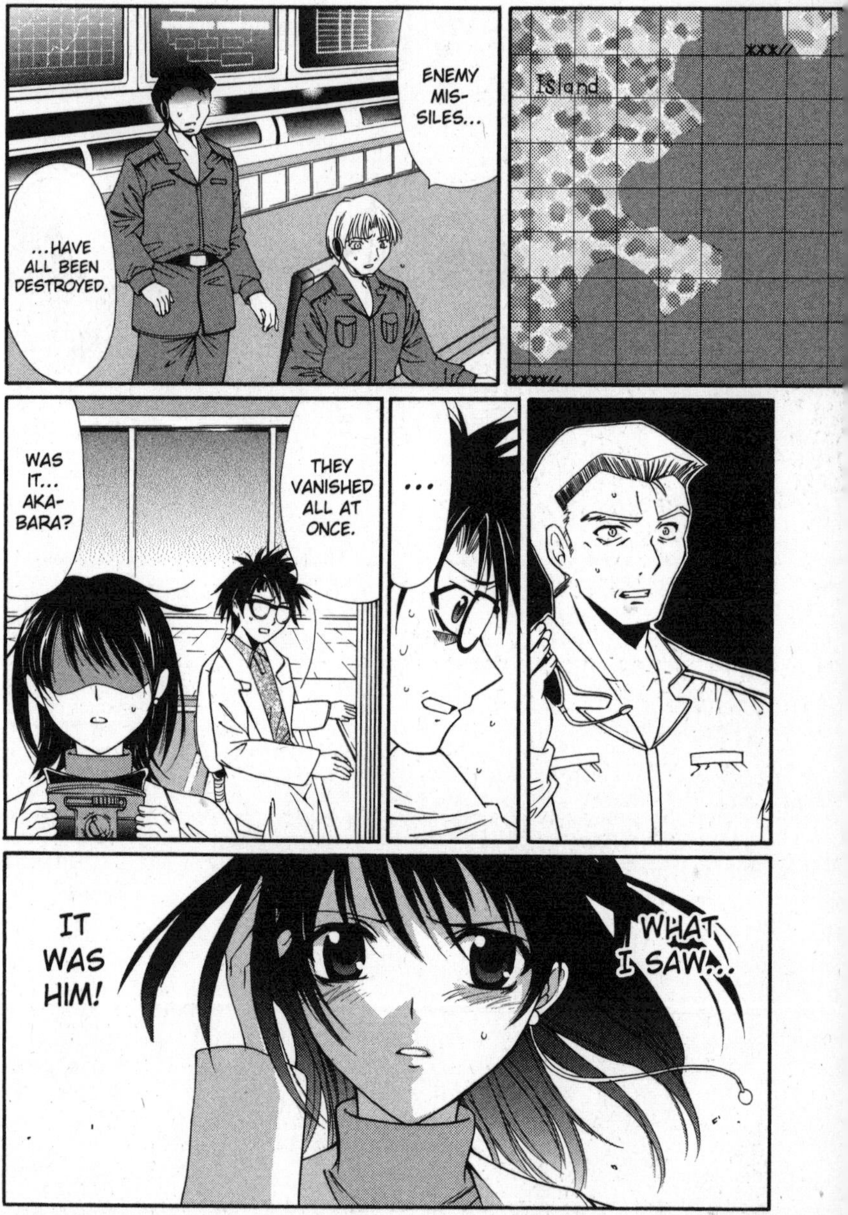
Island
XXX//
ENEMY MIS-SILES...
...HAVE ALL BEEN DESTROYED.
...
THEY VANISHED ALL AT ONCE.
WAS IT... AKA-BARA?
WHAT I SAW...
IT WAS HIM!

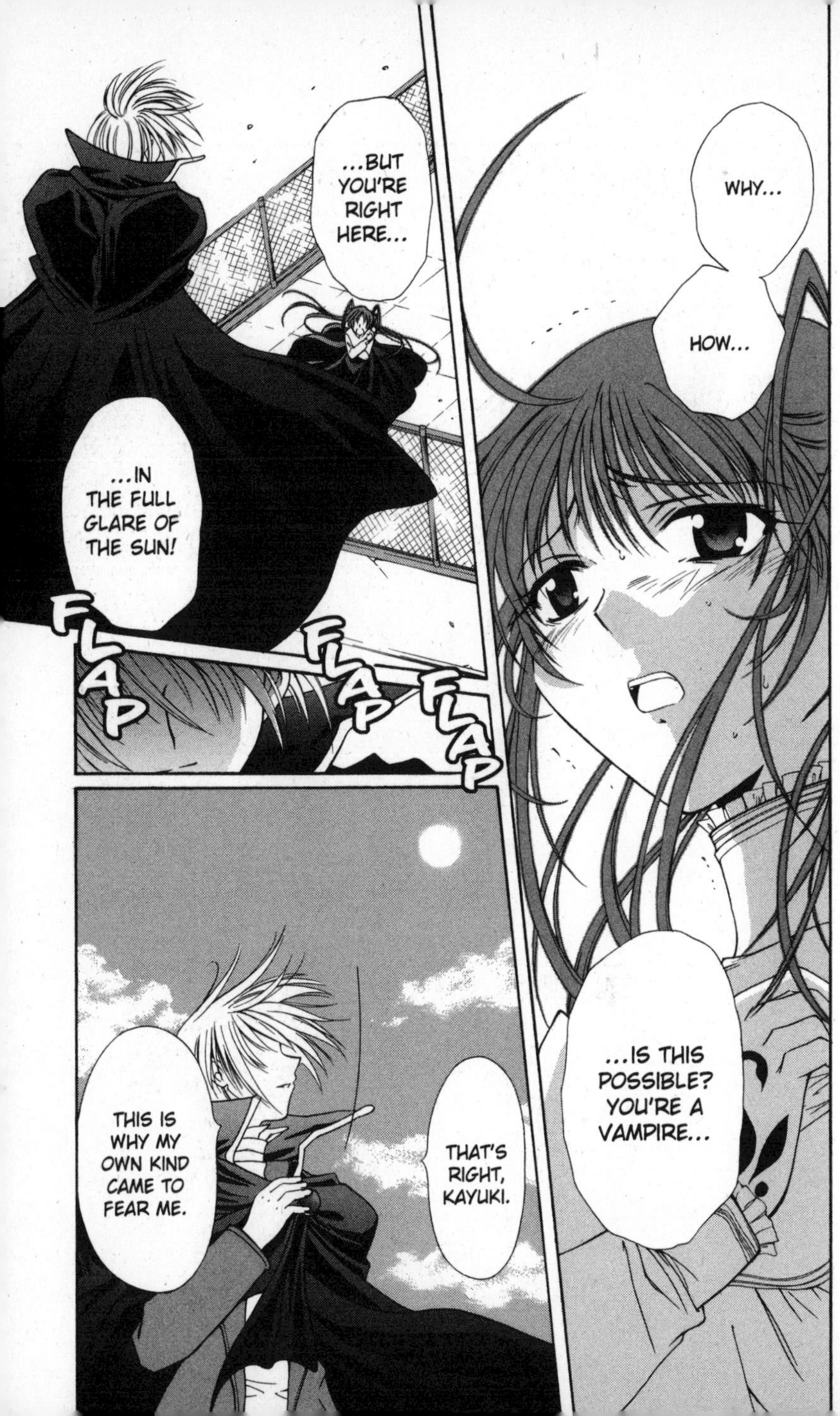
WHY...
HOW...
...IS THIS POSSIBLE? YOU'RE A VAMPIRE...
...BUT YOU'RE RIGHT HERE...
...IN THE FULL GLARE OF THE SUN!
FLAP
FLAP
FLAP
FLAP
THAT'S RIGHT, KAYUKI.
THIS IS WHY MY OWN KIND CAME TO FEAR ME.

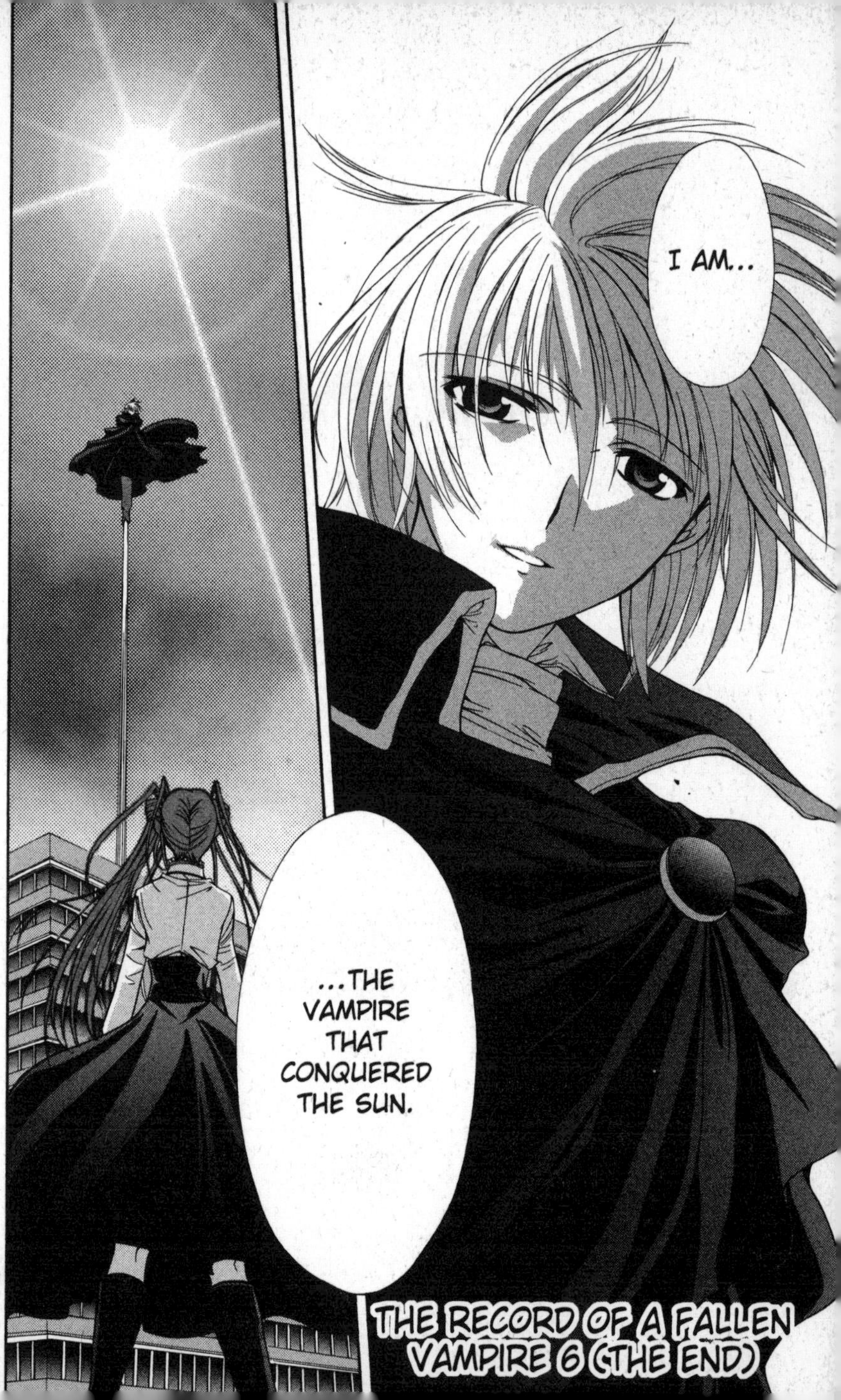
I AM...
...THE VAMPIRE THAT CONQUERED THE SUN.
THE RECORD OF A FALLEN VAMPIRE 6 (THE END)

THE RECORD OF A

FALLEN VAMPIRE

ILLUSTRATION OF

THE RECORD OF A

FALLEN VAMPIRE

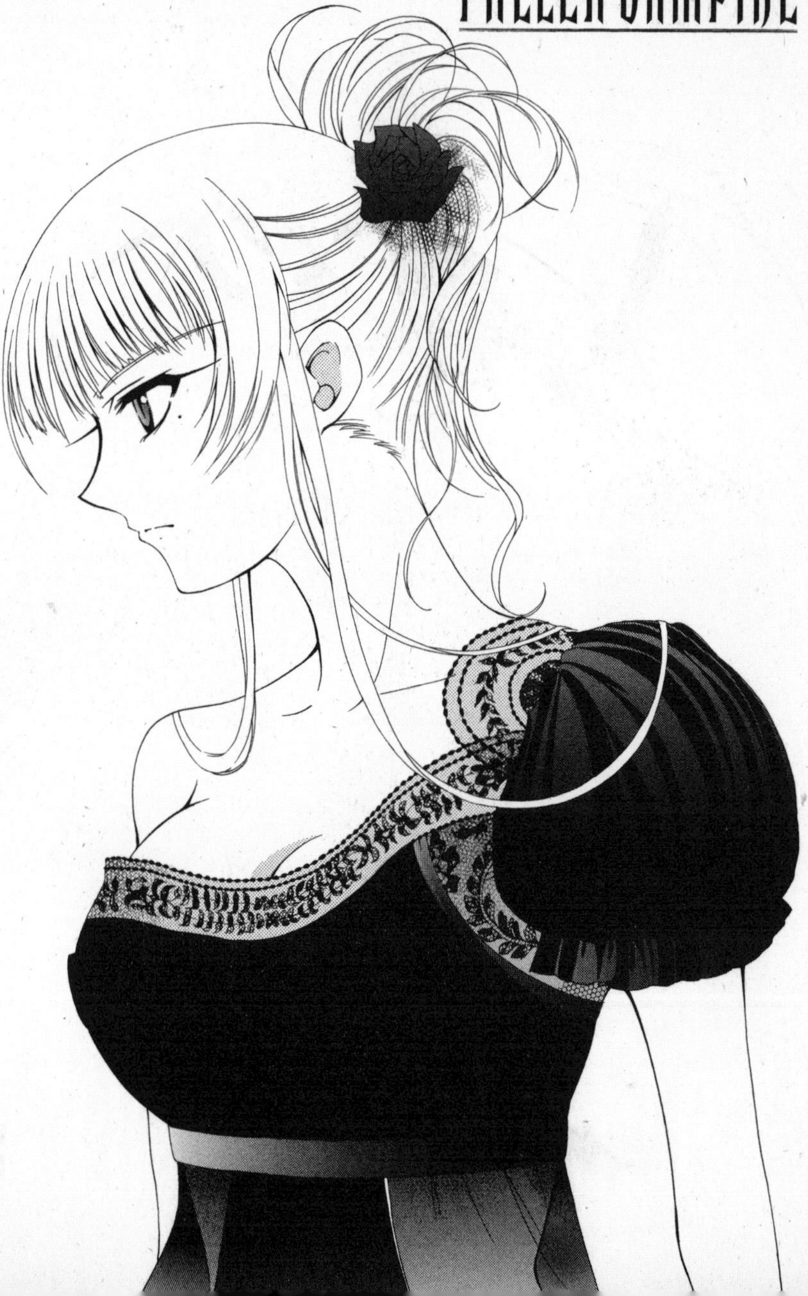

ILLUSTRATION OF

THE RECORD OF A

FALLEN VAMPIRE

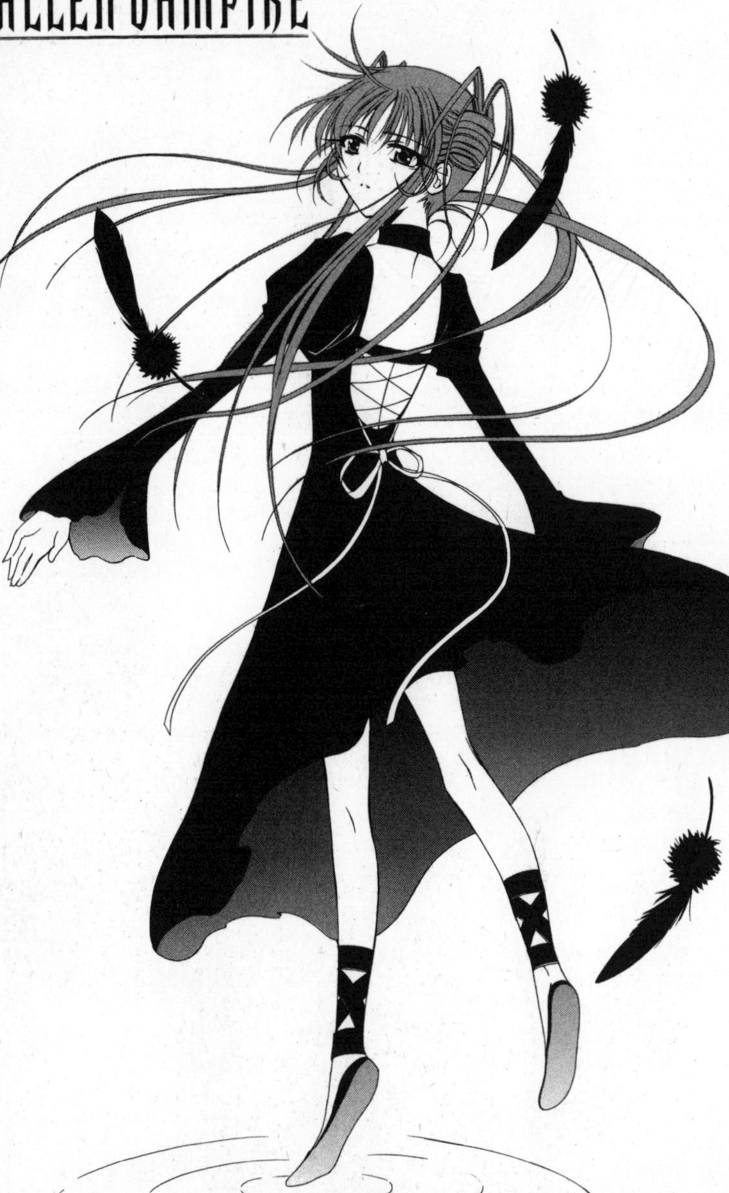

THE RECORD OF A FALLEN VAMPIRE 6!

AT THIS POINT IN THE STORY I OFTEN FIND MYSELF THINKING, "WAIT, I DIDN'T THINK THAT WAS GOING TO HAPPEN..." LIKE STELLA'S NECKLACE. IN CHAPTER ONE, I JUST ASSUMED IT BELONGED TO THE QUEEN, SO I WORKED REALLY HARD TO MAKE IT LOOK ART NOUVEAU. AND NOW WE GET TO SEE A LOT OF IT, AND I REALLY WISH I'D GIVEN IT A MORE AUSTERE DESIGN.

AND BRIDGET, AT FIRST, WAS NOT INTENDED TO HAVE SUCH A WEIGHTY DESTINY. I ORIGINALLY BELIEVED HER TO BE A CHEERFUL VILLAINESS, ONE WITH A VERY CUTE SMILE... MAYBE I WAS WRONG. NOW HER HAPPINESS IS SO INEXTRICABLY TIED TO STRAUSS THAT I DOUBT WE'LL EVER SEE HER SMILE UNLESS HE TAKES ACTION. HIS GREATEST SIN!

I HOPE WE MEET AGAIN IN VOLUME 7.
–YURI KIMURA

THE RECORD OF A
FALLEN VAMPIRE 6

SPECIAL THANKS
MARUKO ASAGAYA
TEPPEI TAKUMI
CHIKA HANAZAWA

•

AKIRA KIMURA
RESEARCH HELP: K AND Y (VERY HELPFUL)
EDITOR: NOBUAKI YUMURA
AND ALL MY READERS

•

REFERENCE MATERIAL
SHIPS OF THE WORLD: UMIBITOSHA
SUBMERSIBLES OF THE WORLD: UMIBITOSHA
MODERN SUBMARINES: GAKUSHU KENKYUSHA

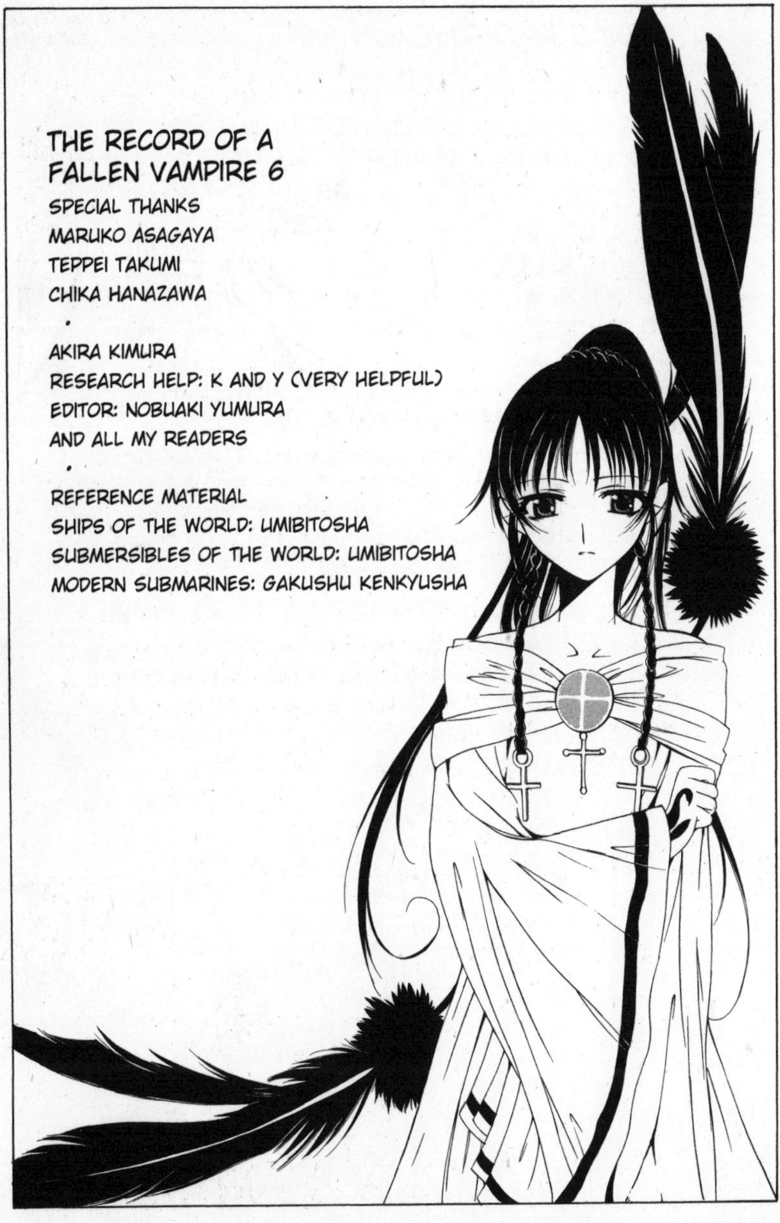

AUTHOR'S AFTERWORD

MAN, *THE RECORD OF A FALLEN VAMPIRE* HAS A REALLY COMPLICATED STORY. AM I NOT CAPABLE OF WRITING STRAIGHTFORWARD, SIMPLE THINGS?

I SEEM TO GET A LOT OF PRAISE FOR FASCINATINGLY COMPLICATED STORIES, BEAUTIFULLY CALCULATED CONCOCTIONS, AND I CERTAINLY PREFER THAT SORT OF THING. AT THE SAME TIME I DEFINITELY CAN APPRECIATE THE BEAUTY OF SIMPLICITY, AND ADMIRE THE PURITY SIMPLICITY CAN BRING. I GUESS YOU COULD SAY I HAVE A COMPLEX ABOUT MY OWN WRITING'S COMPLEXITY.

KICKING OFF WITH A LITTLE SELF-DEPRECATION, I AM KYO SHIRODAIRA, AND THIS IS VOLUME 6.

WRITING COMPLICATED STORIES IS WHAT I LIKE TO DO, AND ALL I APPEAR ABLE TO DO, BUT BECAUSE OF THAT *THE RECORD OF A FALLEN VAMPIRE* HAS BECOME A STORY ALMOST IMPOSSIBLE TO DESCRIBE IN A PITHY ONE-LINER. THIS IS NOT DESIRABLE. IF YOU TRIED SOMETHING LIKE, "IT'S GOT VAMPIRES AND ALIENS AND THE WHOLE WORLD IN A PANIC," I DOUBT MANY PEOPLE WOULD SAY, "SOUNDS AWESOME." WHICH IS BAD. EVEN IF THINGS GET COMPLICATED, IT IS A GOOD IDEA TO HAVE A GREAT HOOK YOU CAN HANG THINGS ON. THIS GREATLY INCREASES THE NUMBER OF PEOPLE WILLING TO GIVE IT A TRY.

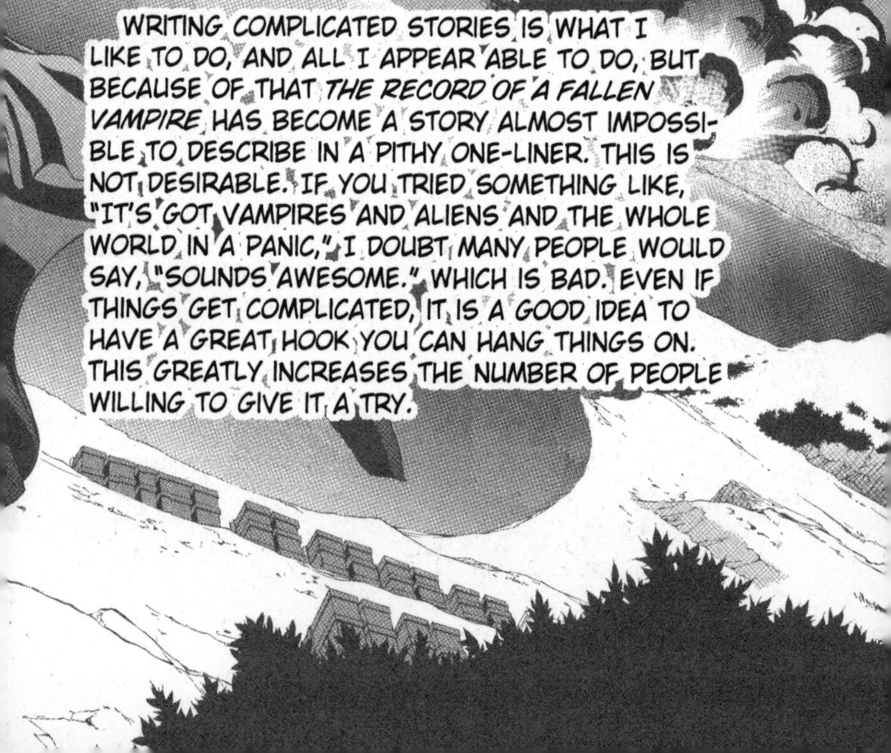

AND THE TITLE IS NOT EXACTLY ATTRACTIVE, EITHER; "RECORD? WHAT?" IT CAN'T POSSIBLY HOLD UP TO A MOVIE TITLE LIKE *THE ONE ARMED KUNG FU MASTER VS THE FLYING GUILLOTINE*, ONE THAT PERFECTLY ENCAPSULATES THE CONTENT. (I REJECT THE NOTION THAT A TITLE LIKE THAT APPEALS TO A TINY MINORITY.)

EVEN IF YOU FOCUS ON THE IDEA OF VAMPIRES FIGHTING ALIEN INVADERS, IT HAS AN UNDENIABLE TENDENCY TO STUN RATHER THAN ATTRACT. (AND I WOULD BE HARD PRESSED TO DEFINE THAT AS THE REAL POINT OF THE STORY.) COMPARED TO THAT, A MOVIE CONCEPT LIKE THE INVISIBLE MAN FIGHTS THE MAN-FLY MAKES THE HEART DANCE—DOZENS OF POSSIBILITIES COME TO MIND, AND THE HEART FILLS WITH ANTICIPATION. (I ALSO REJECT THE NOTION THAT SUCH ANTICIPATION IS ONLY FELT BY A TINY MINORITY.)

HAVE I MANAGED TO OVERCOME THESE FLAWS YET? THE STORY HAS PASSED ITS HALFWAY POINT, SO PERHAPS IT IS A MISTAKE TO EVEN TALK ABOUT SUCH THINGS. BUT EVEN IF IT IS, I HOPE THE STORY REMAINS ENTERTAINING.

NEXT VOLUME, THE QUEEN WILL AWAKEN AT LAST, AND ALL THE MYSTERIES AND DIFFICULTIES LAID OUT IN THIS VOLUME WILL BEGIN TO RESOLVE THEMSELVES. AS WE HEAD TOWARDS THE CLIMAX, THINGS HAD BETTER GET EVEN MORE EXCITING!

I PRAY WE WILL MEET AGAIN IN VOLUME 7.

—KYO SHIRODAIRA

THE RECORD OF A FALLEN VAMPIRE

VOL. 6
VIZ MEDIA EDITION

STORY BY: KYO SHIRODAIRA   ART BY: YURI KIMURA

Translation & Adaptation...**Andrew Cunningham**
Touch-up Art & Lettering...**Susan Daigle-Leach**
Cover Design...**Ronnie Casson**
Interior Design...**Ronnie Casson**
Editor...**Gary Leach**

Editor in Chief, Books...**Alvin Lu**
Editor in Chief, Magazines...**Marc Weidenbaum**
VP, Publishing Licensing...**Rika Inouye**
VP, Sales & Product Marketing...**Gonzalo Ferreyra**
VP, Creative...**Linda Espinosa**
Publisher...**Hyoe Narita**

Printed in the U.S.A.

Published by VIZ Media, LLC
P.O. Box 77010
San Francisco, CA 94107

10 9 8 7 6 5 4 3 2 1
First printing, August 2009

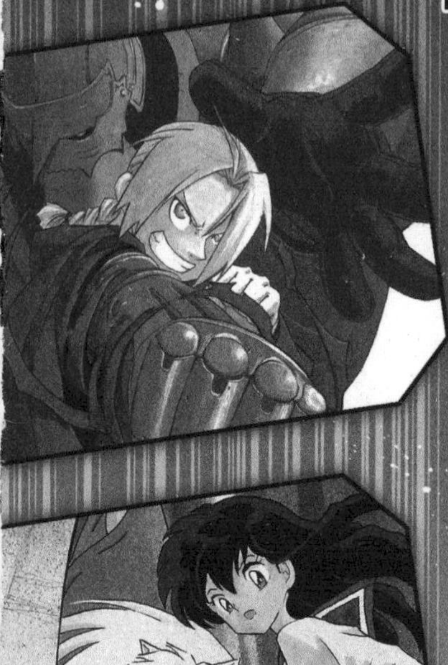

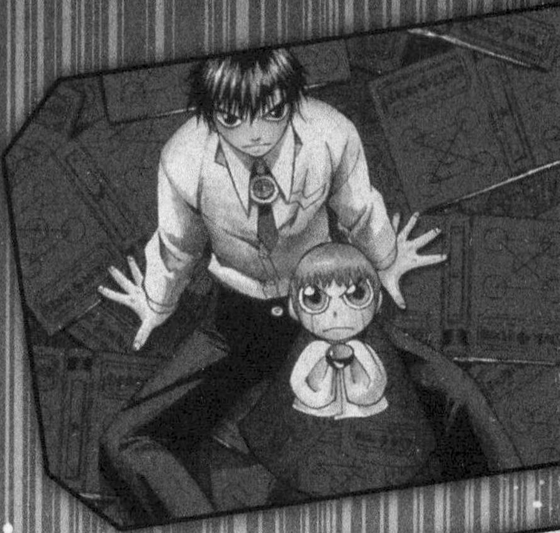

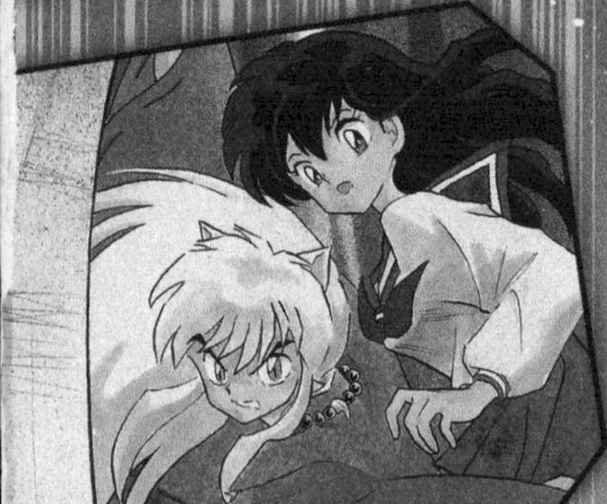

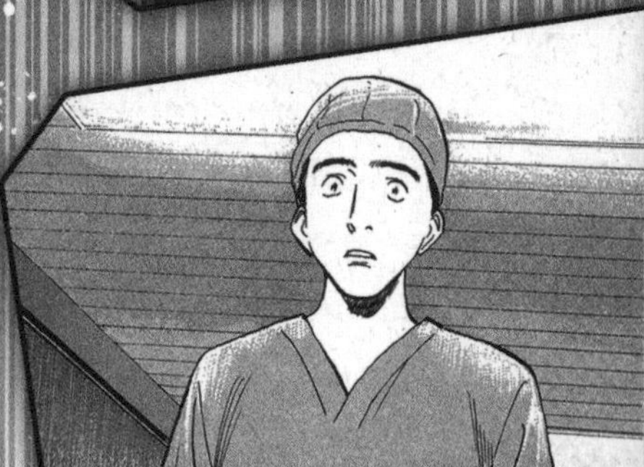